William T Wawn, William Delisle Hay

The South Sea Islanders And the Queensland Labour Trade

William T Wawn, William Delisle Hay

The South Sea Islanders And the Queensland Labour Trade

ISBN/EAN: 9783744725811

Printed in Europe, USA, Canada, Australia, Japan

Cover: Foto ©ninafisch / pixelio.de

More available books at **www.hansebooks.com**

THE SOUTH SEA ISLANDERS

AND THE

QUEENSLAND LABOUR TRADE

A Record of Voyages and Experiences in the
Western Pacific, from 1875 to 1891.

BY

WILLIAM T. WAWN

Master Mariner

WITH NUMEROUS ILLUSTRATIONS BY THE SAME

London
SWAN SONNENSCHEIN & CO.
PATERNOSTER SQUARE
1893

To the
SUGAR-PLANTERS OF QUEENSLAND,
who have spent the Best Years of their Lives and
MILLIONS OF MONEY
in Developing an Industry which represents not less than
NINETY PER CENT.
of the Total Agricultural Value of that Colony ; and
which at one time bade fair to eclipse even the great
PASTORAL AND MINING INDUSTRIES
in Wealth and Importance :

To those
BOLD PIONEERS
who have opened up the Rich Agricultural Districts along
the Coast, and have been the means of settling
THOUSANDS OF EUROPEANS
on the Land ;
and who have done more towards the
PRACTICAL CIVILIZATION
of the
CANNIBAL AND THE SAVAGE
than all the Well-intentioned but Narrow-minded Enthusiasts of the
SOUTHERN PACIFIC:

To those
GOOD MEN AND TRUE
who, after a QUARTER OF A CENTURY of Hard Work and
Doubtful Prosperity, have been Basely Betrayed, and
UNSCRUPULOUSLY SACRIFICED
to the Greed of the Political Place-hunter and the
Howling Ignorance which follows in his train,—
I DEDICATE
THIS WORK WITH MUCH SYMPATHY AND RESPECT.

THE AUTHOR.

INTRODUCTION.

THE Author of this volume being now in Australia, and so not available for immediate reference, it has been deemed desirable to preface his work with a few explanatory remarks. These are more particularly addressed to English readers.

Among political controversies in the Colony of Queensland, the "Kanaka Question" held a prominent place for many years, becoming at length of almost supreme importance. Along the coast, more especially of Northern Queensland, there stretches a belt of country adapted for the cultivation of tropical products, chief among them being the sugar-cane. To develop the resources of this region it was necessary to find a class of labourers better able to endure the climate than Europeans, as well as to work at a cheaper rate. Thus arose the demand for labourers brought from the various island groups of the Western Pacific—Papuans and Polynesians, loosely termed "Kanakas."

Captain Wawn was engaged in recruiting such labourers, from 1875, when they were first introduced, down to 1891, when the Queensland Government legislated against the importation of Kanakas into the Colony, and their employment there. His narrative is that of a practical man, than whom none could be better acquainted with the subject he treats of. He has recorded much that is interesting relative to numerous little-known islands, and the tale he has to tell may well be regarded as a valuable contribution to the history of Queensland and the Western Pacific.

It was while the labour controversy was at its height in Queensland, that Captain Wawn sent his manuscript to England for publication. Forwarded on board the ill-fated s.s. *Quetta*, it was lost in the wreck of that vessel. By the time that the Author had re-written his narrative, bringing it down to a later date, the political situation in the Colony had changed. The Kanaka Question had passed out of the region of debate, and the abolition of "the Labour Trade" had become an accomplished fact.

Under these circumstances it was thought desirable to make some alteration in the original plan of the work. Much controversial matter had been gathered into it for which the occasion had passed. Written as the "log" of a practical seaman, details were also contained in it that were only suitable for inclusion in a Nautical Directory. These features, it was felt, might be dispensed with, and the whole remodelled into a less tedious and more attractive form.

The manuscript was therefore entrusted to Mr. W. Delisle Hay, whose experience of revisionary work has been considerable. At his hands such reduction was made as has been just indicated, and the whole narrative carefully re-shaped. No alteration of the text here given was attempted, except of a purely literary kind; the most scrupulous care having been taken to preserve Captain Wawn's own words and to present his views without material change or any substitution. The illustrations have been reproduced from the Author's own sketches, and the maps, supplied by Messrs W. and A. K. Johnston, have been conformed to Captain Wawn's charts.

SWAN SONNENSCHEIN & CO.

LONDON,
September, 1893.

CONTENTS.

CHAPTER I.
THE FIRST VOYAGE OF THE *STANLEY*, 1875 — PAGE 1

CHAPTER II.
FIRST VOYAGE OF THE *STANLEY*, 1875 (*concluded*) . 40

CHAPTER III.
SECOND VOYAGE OF THE *STANLEY*, 1875 . 54

CHAPTER IV.
THIRD VOYAGE OF THE *STANLEY*, 1875-6 . 66

CHAPTER V.
FOURTH VOYAGE OF THE *STANLEY*, 1876 . 83

CHAPTER VI.
FIFTH VOYAGE OF THE *STANLEY*, 1876 . 100

CHAPTER VII.
SIXTH VOYAGE OF THE *STANLEY*, 1876-7 . 109

CHAPTER VIII.
LAST VOYAGE OF THE *BOBTAIL NAG* . 119

CHAPTER IX.
SHIPWRECKED ON VILA ISLAND, 1878 . . . 138

CHAPTER X.
FIRST VOYAGE OF THE *STORMBIRD*, 1878 . . 155

CHAPTER XI.
SECOND VOYAGE OF THE *STORMBIRD*, 1878-9 . 171

CHAPTER XII.
VOYAGES OF THE *LUCY AND ADELAIDE*, 1879 . 187

CHAPTER XIII.
FIRST VOYAGE OF THE *JABBERWOCK*, 1880 195

CHAPTER XIV.
SEVENTH VOYAGE OF THE *STANLEY*, 1881 . . 215

CHAPTER XV.
EIGHTH VOYAGE OF THE *STANLEY*, 1881 242

CHAPTER XVI.
SECOND VOYAGE OF THE *JABBERWOCK*, 1882 . 251

CHAPTER XVII.
FIRST VOYAGE OF THE *FANNY*, 1882-3 . 264

CHAPTER XVIII.
SECOND VOYAGE OF THE *FANNY*, 1883 . 279

CHAPTER XIX.
FIRST VOYAGE OF THE *LIZZIE*, 1883-4 . . 309

CHAPTER XX.

SECOND VOYAGE OF THE *LIZZIE*, 1884   325

CHAPTER XXI.

VOYAGE OF THE *HEATH*, 1884   339

CHAPTER XXII.

THE CRUISE OF THE *VICTORIA*, 1885   359

CHAPTER XXIII.

THE CRUISE OF THE *VICTORIA* (*continued*)   379

CHAPTER XXIV.

VOYAGE OF THE *ARIEL*, 1888   400

CHAPTER XXV.

VOYAGE OF THE *BOROUGH BELLE*, 1890–91   423

LIST OF ILLUSTRATIONS.

	PAGE
RECRUITING AT MANNO KWOI, MALAYTA I.	*Frontispiece*
RECRUITS' QUARTERS IN A LABOUR SHIP	4
WALPOLE I.	6
RECRUITING BOAT	9
RECRUITING	11
BOLTING	12
RETURNED FROM ABROAD	18
MAN OF THE NEW HEBRIDES	19
HEAD-DRESS OF TANNA MAN	20
BOWS AND ARROWS—PENTECOST I.	22
STONE ADZE	24
ROASTING A BOMBSHELL	26
LANDING RETURNS	29
YAMS, TARO, BREAD-FRUIT	33, 34
ATTACK AT NAROVOROVO	37
A RUNAWAY HUSBAND	39
THE DOCTOR'S INSPECTION	52
DRUMS IN THE "SING-SING" GROUND	59
WEAPONS—NEW HEBRIDES	64
A HOT CORNER	74
A MALLICOLO ISLANDER	77
CARVED POSTS AT ARAMBAGH	80
SHOOTING FISH—ESPIRITU SANTO I.	86
IN A TIGHT PLACE	92
PUCK	117
WRECK OF THE *BOBTAIL NAG*	133
MARY BETARRI	175
A BATHE INTERRUPTED	177
TATTOOED WOMAN OF TANNA	198
SAU AND NINA	202
KING BERRY	219
A COPRA STATION	220

	PAGE
HUSKING AND SCRAPING COCOANUTS	221
COCOANUT-OIL STATION	222
SEPULCHRE—ISABEL I.	228
A STRANGE DERELICT.	230
A LAGOON HARBOUR—MALAYTA I.	233
TOUCHING NOSES.	237
WAR CANOE—SOLOMON IS.	239
WEAPONS—SOLOMON IS.	241
MANDOLIANNA I.	245
"WHAT FOR YOU 'FRAID?"	258
WOMEN BOLTING.	262
SPEARING FISH BY TORCHLIGHT	278
WEAPONS—BLANCHE BAY.	283
HOUSES AND NATIVES—BLANCHE BAY	284
OUTRIGGER CANOE—NEW BRITAIN.	285
A CATAMARAN—NEW IRELAND.	296
FISHING-NETS—LOUISIADE ARCHIPELAGO.	316
NATIVE HOUSES.	318
MT. RATTLESNAKE—SUDEST I.	319
FISHING.	327
FISH-HOOKS—SOLOMON IS.	338
RECRUITS	356
POLYNESIAN WOMEN IN QUEENSLAND	398
WOMAN OF LORD HOWE I.	410
FISHING AT ALITE BAY	413
AN ATTAR BELLE—MALAYTA I.	417
A HEAD-COFFIN	422
MBOLI HARBOUR, FLORIDA IS.	429
VILLAGE AT MARAU SOUND, GUADALCANAR I.	435
MRS. ROBINSON'S PUPILS	437

FINIS.

MAP I.

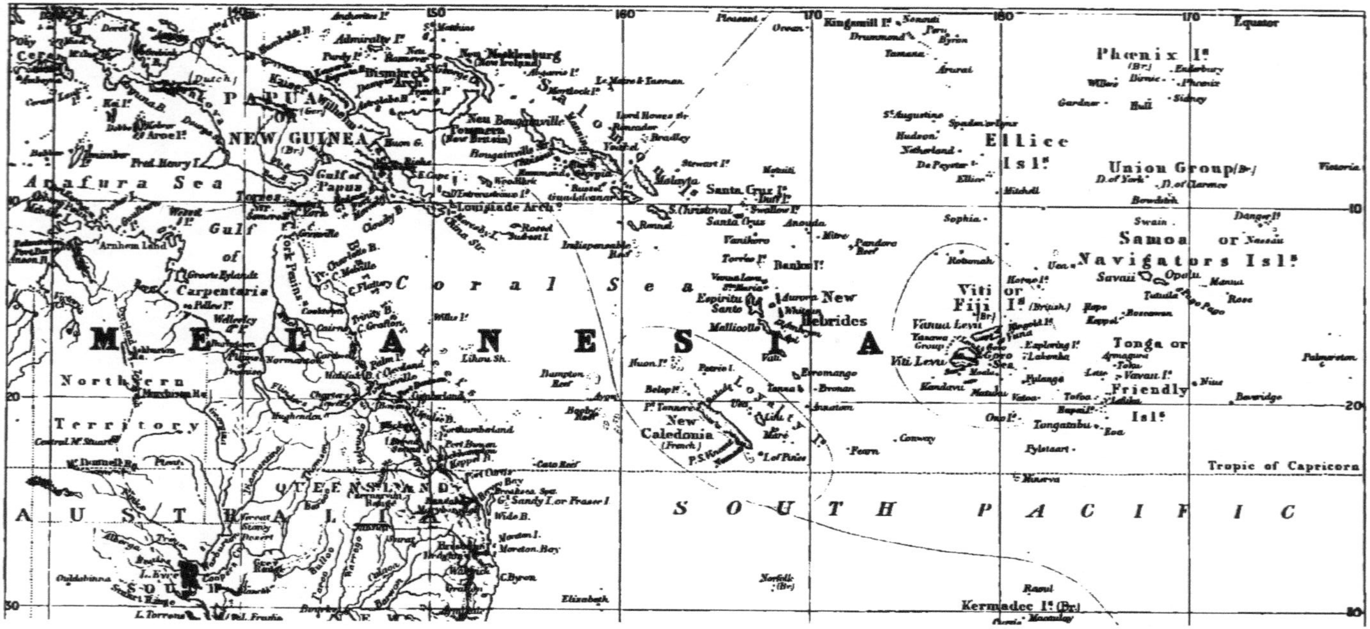
MELANESIA
PAPUA OR NEW GUINEA
Arafura Sea
Gulf of Carpentaria
Gulf of Papua
Coral Sea
Northern Territory
QUEENSLAND
AUSTRALIA
New Hebrides
New Caledonia (French)
Loyalty Is.
Santa Cruz Is.
Louisiade Arch.
Bismarck Arch.
Viti or Fiji Is. (British)
Tonga or Friendly Isls.
Samoa or Navigators Isls.
Ellice Isls.
Union Group (Br.)
Phœnix Is.
Kingsmill Is.
Kermadec Is. (Br.)
SOUTH PACIFIC
Tropic of Capricorn
Equator

THE SOUTH SEA ISLANDERS.

CHAPTER I.

THE FIRST VOYAGE OF THE *STANLEY*, 1875.

I arrive at Sydney—The James Birnie massacre—Appointed to the Stanley—Preparations for a recruiting voyage—Sail from Maryborough, 1875—Fraser I.—Arrival at Maré I.—The Loyalty Group—Races of the South Pacific—Missionary work—To Tanna I.—System of recruiting—Goods for island traffic—Firearms—Customary presents—Buying slaves—Refutation of the slander—Misuse of words " buy," " sell," and " steal"—Reflections on kidnapping—Tanna I.—A storm—Mode of engaging recruits—Exchange and barter—The "guileless" native—Missionaries and recruiters—War between Catholic and Protestant converts—The returned labourer—The New Hebrideans—Languages—Dress—Productions—Curious land sale—Poisoned arrows—British colonization stopped by Exeter Hall—How the French stepped in—Bombardment of Tanna I.—Incident of the shell—Kava, the native intoxicant—Curious superstition—Niu's clothes—Falsely accused by a missionary—Erromanga I.—Massacres—Christianity or smallpox!—Murder of the Gordons—"Devil country"—Api I.—Yams, taro, and breadfruit—A shot from the shore—Paama I.—Ambrym I.—Narovorovo—Attack on a bathing party—Flight of the enemy—Port Sandwich, Mallicolo I.—Volcanoes.

IN the beginning of 1875 I arrived at Sydney, New South Wales, in command of the schooner *Flora*, from Samoa and Fiji, after spending five years among the islands of the South-Western Pacific. During that period I had been some time afloat as master or mate, more often ashore, living amongst the natives as a trader. I had visited New Caledonia, the Loyalty, New Hebrides, Samoa, Fiji, Caroline, Marshall and Gilbert groups. I had also gone through a short but adventurous experience along the shores of New Britain and Duke of York I. The *Flora* was sold to another firm after discharging cargo, and fitted out for the Queensland Polynesian labour trade under the command of Captain Mackay, and I was thrown out of employment.

At this time the second mate of the brig *James Birnie* was in Sydney. This vessel had sailed during the previous year under the command of Captain Fletcher to collect *bêche-de-mer* * amongst the South Sea Islands. Captain Fletcher's idea of savage character appears to have been founded on the mistake that, if you treat a savage kindly, he will therefore behave well to you. At the Mortlock or Lord Howe Is., a huge atoll lying north-east of the Solomon group, the ship was anchored within the lagoon, and several stations for collecting and curing *bêche-de-mer* were formed on the numerous islets scattered along the encircling reef. The chief and his subjects professed the greatest friendliness towards the strangers, and deceived Fletcher so far that the latter forbade his men to carry firearms.

The natural consequence was that the captain and most of the crew were massacred, and the ship was plundered and burnt. The second mate, who had sense enough to carry his revolver concealed about him, and some five or six Polynesians, natives of other islands, escaped in an open boat and made for the Solomon group, whence they got a passage to Sydney.

One of Her Majesty's ships afterwards visited the place, but recovered nothing, though she gave the natives a severe lesson as to their future behaviour towards

---

* *Bêche-de-mer*, also called trepang or tripang, is a large marine slug, inhabiting coral reefs. Its scientific name is *Holothuria edulis*. It is collected, cured, and sent to the Chinese markets, where it fetches a high price, being highly esteemed by Chinese epicures.

white men. The good effects of this action I experienced thirteen years later, when I visited the Mortlocks in the *Ariel*, rescued a white castaway, and recruited some of the inhabitants. Would that all our ships of war acted as promptly in our defence! I am happy to say that no Queensland labour vessel had before this time visited the Mortlock group, so that the cause of the *James Birnie* massacre cannot be laid to our charge. I mention this because, all through my experience of the labour trade, it has been the fashion to lay the blame on us for all South Sea Island outrages.

Through the good offices of the late owner of the *Flora*, and in consequence of my varied experience in the South Pacific, I was not long out of a berth. On Feb. 19 I took charge, as master, of the schooner *Stanley*, 115 tons register. Built at Granton, Scotland, she was a handy, weatherly vessel, admirably suited for South Sea work. Having had her re-caulked, coppered, and fitted with two suitable boats and davits, I took in cargo, and sailed for Maryborough, Queensland. H.M.S. *Alacrity* went to sea at the same time, bound for the islands. She was one of the schooners built or purchased in Australia, employed as cruisers among the islands to suppress kidnapping—a crime very common before Fiji was annexed.

At Maryborough I discharged my cargo, and the *Stanley* was fitted with a lower deck on top of her iron ballast, two long shelves or bunks, six feet wide, extending the whole length of the hold, as sleeping quarters for the expected recruits. A bulkhead of four-inch wooden battens, at a like distance apart, divided the whole space into two unequal parts, the after one, to which there was admission by the outer hatch only, being reserved for females.

On May 12 we were ready for sea. The hull and rigging had been examined by the shipping inspector of the port, who had also measured the hold to determine how many recruits the vessel should be licensed to carry.

The immigration agent had seen that the accommodation was satisfactory, and that there were sufficient provisions, clothing for recruits, and blankets on board. I had signed a bond for £500 as a guarantee against kidnapping. A Government agent (generally styled the "G. A.") was appointed, and a licence to recruit and carry not more than 109 Polynesian labourers was issued to us.

Besides the G. A., I had three passengers, all friends of the owners. One, generally known as "Cades," having had some experience of the islands, was to engage the natives on shore, and sailed as recruiting agent. A

RECRUITS' QUARTERS IN A LABOUR SHIP.

second was the Doctor, while the third, whom we called "Cash," had nothing to do but amuse himself and others. There were also seven natives of Erromanga, labourers returning home after three years' service, £3 per head having been paid by their late employers for their passage. At this time, if a "boy" did not return home when his first service expired, he lost the opportunity of having his passage paid by his late employer. Subsequently, on the arrival of a labourer, his first employer had to pay £5 to the Government to cover a return passage. If a labourer died in Queensland, the Government did not refund that £5.

Cabin stores were liberally provided, especially all sorts of liquors, from champagne down to "square gin" and schnapps. A dinner at the "Royal," given by the owner to the cabin party and other friends, and a "drunk" and free fight "forward" among the hands, took place on the eve of departure, and, before heads were level, the schooner was dropping down the river Mary in charge of Pilot Minnahin.

Opposite the mouth of the Mary, and parallel with the coast line, lies Fraser I., long and low, remarkable only for its sterility. There is abundance of fresh water, however, and the island is used as a reserve for the few aboriginals of the district, whom "rum and civilization" have not yet killed off. This island was named after Captain Fraser, who was wrecked on it and lost his life there. His two children, girls, were rescued from the blacks in the early days of Maryborough.

At Fraser I. we lay off the White Cliffs for three days, taking in water and firewood. As soon as the tanks were filled and the vacant space between the bunks and the lower deck stocked with good split logs of she-oak for firewood, the anchor was hove up for good, and the schooner headed northward in order to reach the open ocean round Breaksea Spit, beyond the northern point of the island.

The first week of the voyage was spent in beating against a strong south-easterly breeze, taking advantage of the steady southerly current which runs along the coast from here to Cape Howe. A little to the southward of Cape Moreton, the breeze died away, and was followed by a fresh westerly wind, which gave us a splendid run to the reefs off the south-east end of New Caledonia, and thence past Walpole I. to North Bay, Maré I., one of the Loyalty group, a dependency of the French colony of New Caledonia. Here we lay two days, engaging as boatmen four strapping natives of the island, whom we agreed to re-land on our way home.

Near our anchorage was the English mission station, in charge of the Rev. Mr. Jones, a gentleman respected and liked by all who came in contact with him. He was one of the few of his calling who attended to his own affairs, and did not, without good cause, interfere with his neighbours.

A native of Maré, whom I had shipped in Maryborough as boatman for the voyage, attempted to desert here, probably influenced by his friends on shore. I had some difficulty in getting him back to the beach and on board, after discovering him concealed in a hut about a mile inland. However, I offered a reward for his appre-

WALPOLE I.

hension, not payable until he was safe on board; so interested parties helped me, and he went the voyage with me until our return.

The Loyalties are of coral formation, almost flat on the top, with deep water all round. Uea I. has a vast extent of shoal water on its northern side. Maré and Lifu, with the intervening islets, have been raised by volcanic agency to the height of 150 feet above the sea. But Uea is much less elevated. These islands are densely wooded, but are not considered fertile, owing to the absence of volcanic soil.

Walpole I., 75 miles south-east, is of the same formation. It is 230 feet high, very precipitous, with deep water all round, and is covered with brushwood. It is the haunt of thousands of sea-birds. The Loyalty Islanders are, I think, mostly of Papuan descent, but with a strain of the true Polynesian.

Touching on this subject, I may explain here that there are three races native to the South Pacific. The Papuan, or Negrito, distinguished by black, or nearly black, skin and "kinky" wool, is found, more or less pure, in New Guinea, the Bismarck Archipelago, the Solomon, Santa Cruz, New Hebrides, and Loyalty groups, New Caledonia, and to a small extent in Fiji. The true Polynesian, having a brown skin and frizzly hair, is found in New Zealand, Tonga, Fiji, Samoa, and elsewhere to the east and north. The Malay race, with brown skin and straight black hair, is spread over the Equatorial islands, namely, the Caroline, Marshall, Gilbert, and Ellice groups. There is, of course, some admixture where these races have come in contact with each other.

At the time I am writing of, I believe all the inhabitants of the Loyalties had adopted the Christian religion, two-thirds, at least, being Protestants. But what they are now I cannot say, both the Revs. Jones and Macfarlane (of Lifu I.) having been forced to leave these islands on account of the machinations of the French priests. An attempt had been previously made, in 1872, to oust these missionaries, but the late Emperor Napoleon prevented it. He would not permit such intolerance in religious matters.

The men, especially those of Maré, make good sailors and boatmen, and are in great request among traders and whalers. As swimmers and divers they stand in the foremost rank, even among South Sea Islanders. The native dress—a span breadth of banana leaf or bark for the man, and a grass petticoat, or fringe, for the woman—is rapidly giving way to European styles. Their food consists of fish, occasionally turtle and pork, yam, taro, and cocoanut.

From Maré to Tanna I., New Hebrides, occupied us a day, and recruiting, or at least, an attempt to recruit, commenced near Black Beach, a well-known anchorage on the lee side of the island. In these latitudes—the region of the south-east trade winds—the "lee side" signifies the north and west coasts. The south and east constitute the weather side.

Up to this time it had not become necessary to employ a covering boat to lie off at a little distance, so as to protect the recruiting boat when along shore. After this voyage I always adopted the plan which, though a most necessary precaution, was not officially enjoined until some years later, and even then it was frequently neglected.

Our boats, two in number, were each pulled by four islanders, having a mast stepped well forward when required, and a standing or "Spanish" lug-sail, the handiest rig with an island crew. The white man in charge used an eighteen-foot steering oar generally, but rudders and tillers were provided in case of running any considerable distance under sail in a sea-way. Each native boatman was armed with a smooth-bore musket, cut short so as to lie fore and aft on the boat's thwarts under the gunwale, to which was nailed a long strip of canvas, painted, and hanging down to protect the arms from the salt spray. The whites—the recruiter in one boat, and the mate and G.A. in the other—had revolvers and Snider carbines. The smooth-bores of the boatmen were, a few years later, changed for Snider carbines, and the whites generally adopted the Winchester. Each boat carried a "trade box," containing about a dozen pounds of twist tobacco, two dozen short clay pipes, half a dozen pounds of gunpowder in quarter, half, and one pound flasks, some boxes of military percussion caps, a bag of small coloured beads, a few fathoms of cheap print calico, a piece (twelve yards) of Turkey red twill, half a dozen large knives, with blades sixteen or eighteen inches long, the same number of smaller knives, half a dozen fantail tomahawks, a few Jews'-harps, mirrors, fish-hooks, and other trifles. Paint was then in frequent demand. For this we provided a tin canister of vermilion powder and some balls of Reckitt's washing blue. On the thwarts amidships, along with the mast and sail, lay three or four Brown Bess muskets in a painted canvas bag ; good serviceable weapons, despite their age. The cheap German fowling-piece, however bright and new, was of no use to us. Tanna men, especially, were very particular about the

RECRUITING BOAT.

guns having "TOWER" on the locks. They knew that these would bear a big charge. I have seen a Tanna man load one with powder enough for three charges, and ball on top, fire it off, and, when the gun kicked him over on his back, jump up again and shout, " Remassan! Remassan!—Good! Good!" He would buy that gun, and think he had the best of the bargain by a long way. But a Tanna man would not look at a smooth-bore now. Nothing, nowadays, will go down with him but a repeating rifle.

Those Brown Besses were intended as presents to the recruits' friends. We were not frequently called upon to give guns then, and one gun would satisfy two or three parties. A knife and a tomahawk, a handful of beads, ten sticks or about half a pound of tobacco, a few pipes, and a fathom of calico, were considered sufficient for man or woman. But the demand for firearms was rapidly increasing, and, two years after this, I had to give a musket, as well as tobacco and pipes, before a man was allowed to leave the beach.

This custom of making presents to recruits' friends has been eagerly seized upon by our opponents as proof that we really bought the recruits—that the latter were simply slaves, probably captured in war; which is simply absurd. New Hebrideans never spare their enemies in battle, or make prisoners of the men. Slavery is unknown to them; they are not yet sufficiently advanced to appreciate it. The theory that recruits are sold by their chiefs might be true to a certain extent, were it not that the power of the chiefs in these islands is extremely limited, far more so than it is among Polynesians, as in Samoa and elsewhere. But here each village constitutes a tribe, possessing its own chief, whose territory is measured by yards, not by miles.

The fighting power of a New Hebridean tribe is rarely more than twenty to eighty men. Consequently, if a warrior elects to go to Queensland, his departure is felt as a serious loss, to make up for which it is only natural that the tribe should require a musket, powder, and ball. Besides, you will get no article or service from a South Sea Islander without paying for it. Your necessity is his opportunity. To take a recruit in the presence of his friends without "paying" for him, however willing to go he might be himself, would be, at any rate, extremely dangerous.

Owing to their limited knowledge of the English language, such terms as "buy," "sell," and "steal," have a wide and comprehensive meaning. "You buy boy?" is often the first question asked of the recruiter when he arrives at a landing-place. This simply means, "Do you wish to engage boys?" "Boys," as elsewhere, signifies men of any age. The term "steal" is also frequently misunderstood. If you take away a recruit from his home without "buying" or "paying" for him,—that is, without making presents to his friends to compensate them for losing him,—they will say you "steal" him.

In 1879 a woman, Betarri, came on board the *Stormbird* on her own account, and was engaged. Owing to subsequent events no present or "pay" was sent on shore. She afterwards told the wife of her employer,

RECRUITING.

Mr. Monckton, of Narada plantation, Maryborough, that "Captain he steal me," which the lady of course interpreted literally.

When it could be done conveniently and with safety, I have generally sent the "pay" ashore to the friends of any recruit who has joined my ship without their consent. Some "boys," who have already served one term of three years in Queensland, are, however, too knowing for their countrymen, and make a bargain for money on arrival in port, varying from 10s. to £2. These have to get away quietly, of course, and they are said to be "stolen." By sending the pay for a runaway recruit on shore, any danger to the next comer will probably be averted.

This free use of the term "steal" amongst the islanders accounts for numbers of unfounded charges of kidnapping made against us. But kidnapping has been occasionally perpetrated in these waters, and was, even at the time I write of.

Previous to the annexation of Fiji, in 1874, recruiters from thence never missed an opportunity of "wooling 'em." Many a canoe was run down, and its occupants saved, to work in Fijian cotton-fields. Australians will

BOLTING.

remember the *Carl* and *Daphne*. In 1872, at Bonape, in the Caroline group, I was, for a few hours, on board the *Carl*, then on her most notorious cruise, and I heard some of the crew boasting of their exploits. Even of late years—in 1884—we had the *Hopeful* case; and I know, from personal experience, that one at least of the prisoners in that affair richly deserved the fate meted out to him. Apart from the immorality of such a proceeding, kidnapping would be extremely impolitic on the part of a recruiter who expected to be engaged for any length of time in the labour trade. One case of kidnapping would spoil the captain's, the recruiter's, and the ship's reputation on the islands, and the friends of the kidnapped man would not fail to kill the offenders at the first opportunity.

I mentioned that, in 1875, kidnapping was still occasionally heard of. I never witnessed it; but, from the reports of natives all over the New Hebrides, I have very good reason to believe that men were often carried off forcibly by French and Samoan vessels, between 1875 and 1883. One could only expect outrages to be committed by the crews of these; for, although the French vessels carried an officer whose duties were similar to those of our Government agents, I never saw one of them accompany his boats to the shore. The French boats were invariably manned and officered by Polynesians only. As for vessels out of Samoa, I may cite the *Mary Anderson* by way of illustration. She flew the British flag, was commanded by a foreigner who held no certificate except a licence to recruit from the British Consul at Samoa, and was employed to collect labourers for German planters. This vessel carried no Government agent, and the master alone had full control over the recruiting.

To return to my own voyage. The first day's attempt at recruiting in Tanna I. resulted in disappointment. Few natives were seen, and these were chiefly very old men or children. The able-bodied of both sexes were all inland attending a "Sing-sing," as their native feasts and dances are termed in South Sea English. During the afternoon I anchored the ship in ten fathoms of water, about two hundred yards from shore, near the northern end of Black Beach. A moderate breeze from the south-east was blowing all day, with fine weather, and I considered we were in perfect safety for the night. But it was not so.

Just before sunset a dense black bank of cloud rose in the south-east, over the land. Still, as the barometer remained tolerably high and steady, I thought little of it, merely anticipating a deluge of rain. I certainly never expected the wind to shift from the south-east quarter with a high glass. Gradually, but swiftly, two-thirds of the sky became overcast with clouds of a dark red hue, the north-west quarter alone remaining bright with the sunset glow. Then came a blinding flash of lightning and a rattle of thunder, and seeing that I must expect something out of the common, I had the mainsail double-reefed and one of the boats hoisted up to the davits. There was no time to hoist the other, which was lying astern, for in a moment a small breeze sprang up from the north-west. Within two minutes from its commencement a hard gale was blowing from the same quarter, accompanied by blinding rain, thunder, and lightning. Luckily, we had good holding ground, for I could not get under way now. The second anchor was let go, and chain paid out on both. The gale lasted for about an hour and a half, and veered to south, gradually dying away at south-west. By midnight we had clear weather and the usual south-east trade wind again. Our boat astern was swamped, but luckily uninjured. The breeze was a small but true cyclone, travelling in a northerly direction, a most unusual phenomenon, the only instance I recollect of a cyclone occurring in the month of June in these waters. The barometer, an aneroid, fell only ·20° during the cyclone.

Black Beach and its neighbourhood proving a failure, the anchor was tripped next day, and the western shores made for in search of recruits. Our mode of working is as follows :—

At daybreak, if the ship is under way, she is taken close into the land, whilst all hands have an early breakfast. Presently the boats are lowered, and pulled or sailed along the coast, stopping wherever natives collect, the ship keeping as near to them as possible. Trading for yams and other native produce, which recruits prefer to rice, is carried on at the same time that recruits are sought for. The recruiter's boat having been backed on to the beach stern first, the keel just touching or resting on the sand, the savages crowd about the boat, scrutinizing the crew, and perhaps recognizing some old island hand amongst them, most likely a returned labourer. Then follows much such a conversation as this :—

Native. " What name ship ?
Recruiter. " Stanley."
N. " What name cappen ? "
R. " Cappen Wawn."
N. " Where you come from ? " *i.e.*, What port do you come from ?
R. " Maryborough."
N. " Mallybulla, very good." Maryborough was a favourite place with the New Hebrideans at this time. " You buy boy ? "
R. " Yes ; you got boy ? He like come ? "
N. " P'raps, by-and-by. You buy yam ? "
R. " Yes ; we buy yam altogether—all you have."

Now commences a noisy chaffering for yams, tobacco, paint, beads, etc. A dozen yams, sometimes bundles of them, are offered ; and in five minutes, if no ship has been along that way lately, the boat is covered with soil, and half full of yams, taro, cocoanuts, sugar-cane, now and then a few fish, a pig or two, and some curios, such as bows and arrows, clubs, sea-shells, and other unconsidered trifles. Sometimes one has to buy a lot of things that are not wanted, to keep the savages in good humour.

In the meantime the recruiter keeps a sharp look-out for possible recruits. When he sees a boy give his weapons to another, quietly slip off all his bead and shell ornaments, and part from them, he knows that there is luck in store for him. The conversation is renewed :—

Native. " Boy he like go."

Recruiter (trying to appear not at all eager for recruits). " Um, very good. Me look him."

The intending recruit comes close to the boat for inspection, a friend carefully guarding him on each side, not so much to prevent kidnapping as to stop him from getting into the boat before he is "paid" for, and thus spoiling the bargain. The amount of "pay" once settled, the recruit gets into the boat, and passes forward into the bows. If the covering boat is on the scene, it is backed in, and the recruit transferred to her and taken off to the ship if convenient. The "pay" is handed over as soon as the recruit gets into the boat. Sometimes a boy pretends he will go, in order to get some "pay," and after it has been handed to his friends quietly slips away into the bush. With the same object, others go on board ship when at anchor and desert by swimming at night.

For a long time we were allowed to apprehend and detain all deserters who had signed the agreement on board ship, but the "cast iron" regulations of the Act of 1884 put a stop to that, allowing a Kanaka to sign the agreement for three years' service, travel about in the ship in receipt of the regular rations, cadge all he could, and leave when he thought fit, so long as he did not extend his pleasure trip to Queensland.

If a vessel happens to return to an island during the same trip, the chances are that she will lose a few of her recruits obtained during the first visit. And as these generally "flit" by night, they take care not to go empty-handed. Guileless persons love to represent the South Sea Islander as a grown-up child; but he is one who would prove a deal of trouble to his parents! Sometimes a "boy," whose friends are unwilling that he should leave home, or who demand too much pay, will make a rush and get into the boat. It is dangerous then to interfere. The best thing to do is to let them fight it out, unless the recruiter lends a hand to get the boy out of the boat. For, of course, the surest way for the savages to prevent a "boy" going away is to tomahawk the recruiter and his crew. The trade box will probably repay them for a little extra risk. There would be more danger of this sort in the work of recruiting were it not that the natives of the New Hebrides and Solomon groups look upon it as a regular institution, and see that it works as much for their own benefit as for ours.

The visit of any ship to their shores is a change in the dull monotony of their lives. They have an opportunity of bartering their surplus food and what are curiosities to us, in exchange for weapons, tools, tobacco, and other desirable articles.

On the other hand, they lose a few warriors out of each village, but an extra musket in the tribe makes up for that deficiency. The proportion of female emigrants is very small; but, since polygamy prevails in these islands, that does not matter so much. Ninety-nine out of every hundred recruits are between the ages of sixteen and twenty. When one returns from his three years' service he is still a young man, in the prime of life, strengthened and set up by his late labour, possessed of knowledge and experience of the world which has raised him above his stay-at-home fellows. It is this last fact which has made some missionaries so bitter against us. The raw, untravelled "nig" is a very pliable article in their hands. He imagines that there must be something supernatural about the "servant of God," and it is only after a long acquaintance that he finds out that he is but a poor weak mortal after all. By that time he has discovered that the missionary is under the protection of the man-of-war, as well as that if he were killed he has nothing worth stealing. His chief succumbs, most probably, through fear and the hope of protection against his bush enemies, and our "nig" follows suit. Sunday-school children's pennies supply him with various knick-knacks, and he leads a lazy, shiftless life. Dread of the man-of-war secures him peace against his enemies, if his house is close to the mission; but in return he is not allowed to thrash his wife, though she is often the worst of the two. But I doubt if his capacity for fighting and blood-thirstiness is lessened.

In 1880, during the civil war which raged on Maré I. between the Protestant and Roman Catholic natives, these qualities came out rather conspicuously. The wounded were invariably massacred by the victors. Infants were swung by the legs, and their brains dashed out against trees and stones. Villages and plantations were destroyed, and every cruelty was perpetrated that the mind of a savage could invent. Yet, in the midst of such scenes, the minds of these "Christian" warriors were capable of reflection; for, during one massacre, the Roman Catholic priest was not molested in his house,

RETURNED FROM ABROAD.

because the Protestant victors knew that they would meet with no mercy from the authorities if they meddled with a Frenchman.

The returned islander, however, is a very different personage for the missionary to operate on. He has seen the world. He does not believe in offerings to the church in the shape of pigs, fowls, yams, or bread-fruit. He knows how clergymen are regarded by the white workmen with whom he has come in contact. His experience and strength, together with his knowledge of the English language, which last enables him always to act as interpreter and middleman when dealing with whites, and most likely the possession of a new rifle, whether brought from Queensland or purchased in the island, combine to give him a prominent position in his tribe. The young, untravelled men listen to his stories of Queensland, and follow his example in many ways. So the missionary finds him a terrible stumbling-block in his path.

The New Hebrides group, which includes the Torres and Banks Is., forms a chain of about a dozen large islands, and double that number of smaller ones, all inhabited and fertile, extending 500 miles, from latitude 20° 15' S to 13° S. With the exception of the Torres Is. at the

MEN OF THE NEW HEBRIDES.

north-west end, and of Aniwa near the south-east, which are of elevated coral formation, they are all volcanic and mountainous, richly fertile, generally covered with dense forests, and unhealthy for Europeans, fever and ague being especially prevalent. The inhabitants are of the Papuan race, intermixed here and there with the true Polynesian, notably in Aoba and the Banks and Torres Is. Their language varies considerably, so much so that a New Hebridean has often a difficulty in making himself understood a dozen miles from his own home, even in the same island.

In Tanna I. three distinct dialects are spoken, and in Pentecost I. there is a marked difference between the languages at either end, only thirty miles apart. In 1875, the people were all cannibals, except in Aneiteum, Fotuna, Aniwa, and Mota, where missionary influence was supreme. Dress does not trouble these savages much. In Tanna and its neighbour islands, in parts where the missionaries have not prevailed upon them to adopt the waist-cloth or a more European style of dress, the men appear simply more disgusting than if they contented themselves with nothing at all. The women wear a kilt or short petticoat of grass or leaves.

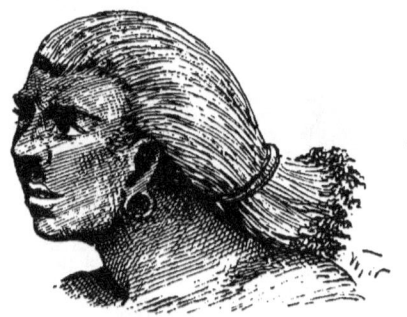

HEAD-DRESS OF TANNA MAN.

On Sandwich I. and the Shepherd Is. a mat round the loins and a loose calico cloth depending from it serves the men, while further north a bunch of leaves or even a single leaf suffices. Sometimes they dispense even with this. The women generally tie a strip of mat or of banana leaf round their waists, occasionally a bunch of leaves only. Tanna men dress their hair in a peculiar manner. Each separate lock of their kinky wool is drawn out to full length, generally about a foot, and served round with very fine strips of white bark, which prevents it from curling up again. On the northern islands the women often, if not generally, shave their heads.

We have always made it a practice to cut off recruits' hair close to the head, invariably finding it tightly matted with earth and lime, and full of certain insects. The "boys" always appeared relieved after the operation, but it was then necessary to provide them with calico turbans to protect their heads from cold or sunstroke. Native dwellings, as a rule, are simply low, miserable hovels of palm leaves and grass. Of vegetable food they have an abundance. Yam and taro form the staple articles, besides which they have the sweet yam or ufelai, sweet potatoes, cocoanut, a great variety of edible nuts, and fruits which I cannot name, bread-fruit of rather a poor description as compared with that of the Carolines, bananas and sugar-cane. Each village possesses a good number of pigs—half head and legs—and fowls. Dogs—miserable curs—abound everywhere, and form an article of food, though, I am told, it is only the women who indulge in that savoury dish.

I encountered rather a curious circumstance in connection with the sale and purchase of land in the island of Tanna, during 1870. A white man named Thomas Davis, resident at Port Resolution, purchased a piece of ground from a native and paid for it. In order to get room to put up a building, he cut down a tree. The seller of the land complained, and Davis discovered that his bargain did not include the trees growing on the land. He had to pay more for them before he was allowed to clear his property.

The New Hebrideans, as a rule, do not travel much by water. Very seldom we met with an ungainly craft, half canoe, half raft, with an unwieldy triangular mat-sail, bowling along before a fair wind.

The villagers on the coasts have plenty of small canoes however, from seven to ten feet long, hollowed out of the solid log, and provided with a light outrigger, in which they venture out a mile or two to sea to visit passing ships. Arms of native manufacture, with the exception of spears, had almost disappeared from Tanna by 1870. Bows and arrows had been superseded by muskets, wooden and stone clubs by "fantail" tomahawks and long sixteen-inch knives. Every Tanna-man owned a musket or two. Further north most of the men carried poisoned spears and arrows, also a tough four-foot bow. One scratch from a poisoned arrow is sufficient to cause death almost invariably. The arrow, or spear-head, is prepared by dipping the bone point into decomposing flesh—human flesh being regarded as the best for the purpose—and allowing it to dry. Two or three coats are necessary. On the islands of Aurora

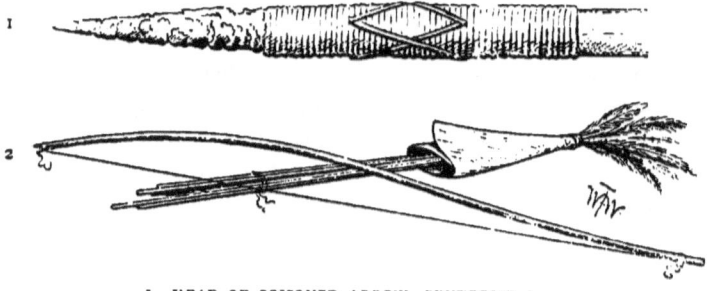

1. HEAD OF POISONED ARROW, PENTECOST I.
2. BOW AND ARROWS, PENTECOST I.

and Pentecost, they point out a small straggling tree, very common on the coasts, which is said to contribute to the deadly qualities of their arrows. A thick, milky, sticky sap exudes from the bark when cut, which they handle very carefully, being especially cautious not to let it get into their eyes or into open wounds. This sap is used in preparing the poisoned arrows, perhaps to assist the decayed animal matter to adhere. The shafts of the arrows are of light cane, and no feathers are attached to the butts. Bows, especially on Pentecost and Aurora Is., exhibit no regular curve when strung for use. The greatest "belly," as sailors would call it, is about two-fifths from the end. The small bone tip is only insecurely fastened to the shaft, so that it may be left inside when the arrow is withdrawn from the wound. The wound may heal up, but even when the bone tip has been extracted, tetanus supervenes within three weeks after the injury.

The island of Tanna is remarkably fertile, rising to a height of over 3,000 feet in the south. Near Port Resolution, on the eastern side, there is an active volcano, the crater of which is about six hundred feet above sea-level. There are two fairly good anchorages, safe enough during the trade-wind season; namely, Waisissa, a few miles north-west from Port Resolution, with nine to twelve fathoms, and Black Beach on the north-west side, with eight to fourteen fathoms of water; but both are open roadsteads. There is a stream of good fresh water at the latter place. In 1870 the beach was banked up throughout its whole length, forming a large lagoon, with about fifty yards intervening between it and the sea. By 1875 the stream had broken through the bank and was rather shallow, but was still convenient for watering. With the wind well to the eastward there is anchorage in eighteen fathoms close in at Sangali. Port Resolution was ruined as a harbour by an earthquake at the end of 1877. Five years before the time of which I write, Tanna was in a fair way to be colonized by British settlers, but missionary jealousy and Exeter Hall influence stepped in and spoiled all.

From Emolau Point, a little south of Sangali, to Black Beach, nearly fifteen miles of coast and a mile or so back from it, the land was purchased by British subjects with the intention of settling on it and growing cotton. Three plantations—those of McLeod at Ibet, of Bell Brothers at Worgus, and of Ross Lewin at Sangali—had land cleared and cotton growing, Lewin having already gathered and shipped one cargo. These men employed labourers from other islands of the group, for it is an established fact that the New Hebridean men object to work, and certainly will not become regular labourers on their own islands. The women do all their own plantation work. But they make good enough labourers when transported among strangers. Then they become dependent on their employer for food, pay, and means of returning home, also acting as a protection against the treachery of the native inhabitants. The Tanna people made no objection to the presence of these labourers, refusing to harbour them when they were inclined to shirk their work and leave their employers; being aware that if the white settlers lost their labourers, then the

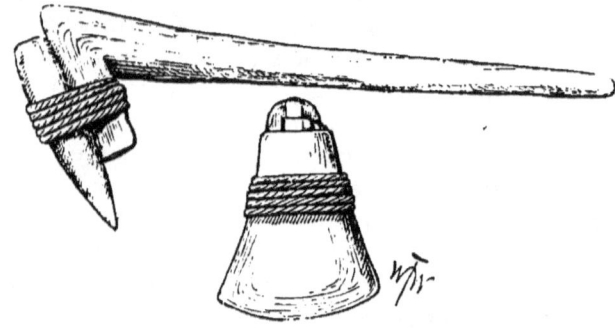

STONE ADZE, BANKS I.

market for the surplus food supply of the island would necessarily fail.

However, the planter's influence might impair that of the missionary; wherefore representations were made to the home government through the captain of one of our ships of war, and all British subjects in these waters were ordered to return labourers to their homes and employ only the natives of the particular island on which they were located. The consequence was that these plantations were all abandoned, though not until one of the Bells and Ross Lewin had been murdered. Of course this influence of Exeter Hall did not extend over the settlers of other nationalities, so many of the British subjects in the New Hebrides transferred their allegiance to

France, and thus the trade of these islands was directed to Noumea, the capital of New Caledonia. In place of the British colonists, who might have settled on these islands, the group is now full of a lot of the sweepings of the French penal colony. A large company—the *Compagnie Caledonienne des Nouvelles Hebrides*—was formed in 1882, and now owns all the most desirable lands in the group. Its stone boundary-marks may be seen at every anchorage and bay, while there is hardly a good bit of water frontage left for any future settler to select.

Of late years the missionaries have several times stirred up the Australian people to agitate for annexation of the New Hebrides to the British Empire: but it is too late now. The French have a joint protectorate over the group with Great Britain. They own all the best land and have all the best trade in their hands. They have the best right to those islands. Once we had it, but we have lost it.

The south-west coast of Tanna gave us a few recruits, and then I steered for Port Resolution, where I anchored in the middle of the harbour. At that time it was a smooth and safe anchorage during the trade-winds, but in 1877 an earthquake occurred, which raised the northwest side of the port, and shoaled it so much that it is now suitable only for the smallest vessels. I anchored there in 1880 in the *Jabberwock*, but I had auxiliary steam-power, or I should not have attempted it.

A Presbyterian mission station, in charge of the Rev. Mr. Neilson, was situated on the south-east side. On the opposite shore is the shelf of rock to which Captain Cook hove down his ship, the *Resolution*. The iron ring he used on that occasion disappeared long ago, for the natives dug the bolt which held it out of the rock, in order to get the cementing lead to make bullets. In 1870 there was a trading station on the north-west side, where Captain Ashmore, of the *Sea Witch* schooner, placed an agent to purchase sulphur, which natives brought down from the volcano. The mission had been established for many years, but there were no converts in my time. H.M.S. *Curaçoa* made it lively for the natives in 1867. For some wrong done to the missionaries—driving them away, I believe—she shelled the native village and landed her marines and blue-jackets. Each side lost only one man, according to the natives. However, after the *Curaçoa* had sailed, the Tanna men, searching about for broken shells, found an unexploded one nearly buried in an earthen bank near the head of the bay. This was their first experience of shells, and they wanted to find out the contents. One of them

ROASTING A BOMBSHELL.

had travelled, and knew that white men rendered iron soft enough to be cut by putting it in fire. The result of their experiment was disastrous. Nine of them derived no benefit from it. An old Tanna man told me this story, and I quite believed it.

The mission schooner *Dayspring* came to an anchor here the day after we arrived. On board were some passengers, natives of Tanna, who had been granted a passage in her to and from the neighbouring island of Fotuna. These men now went on shore, and I was rather surprised to see several large roots of kava accompany them. I should have thought that a missionary vessel would have been forbidden to carry such an article.

The kava is a species of pepper, called *Macropiper methysticum* by botanists. It grows as a straggling bush with jointed, crooked branches, and leaves as large as the palm of my hand. From the root an intoxicating drink is made. The mode of preparing this drink is simply disgusting. The root is washed, chopped into small pieces, and then chewed. In the large groups to the eastward, young girls alone perform this operation, but in the New Hebrides the men do it for themselves. After having been well masticated, the root is mixed with sufficient water in large wooden bowls, and is then fit for use. In the Caroline group alone, the root, well washed and scraped, is pounded upon large flat stones, mixed with water, and filtered through a fine, fibrous bark. So prepared, I have often drunk it. A taste for it is soon acquired, though at first it reminds one of a mixture of soap-suds with a dash of pepper. It has a very different effect from alcohol. It is soothing, and a pint of strong kava, or even half that quantity for a beginner, will apparently have no more effect than to make a man feel desirous of being let alone and allowed to sit quietly and smoke his pipe. It is when he gets up to walk that he feels the effects. When his knees give way, he discovers that kava acts in contrary fashion to alcohol. The latter first affects the head, but kava goes to a man's legs at once. Alcohol excites, kava soothes, and then stupefies.

Tanna women are not allowed to indulge in kava, or even to see men drinking it. When I first visited this island in 1870, I noticed that, just before sundown, the women and children disappeared from the beaches, and their voices were not to be heard anywhere. I was told that the reason for this was because the men prepared and drank kava at that hour; and if any unfortunate woman happened to see a man under its influence, she would be immediately clubbed.

Before leaving Tanna I must mention a peculiar form

of superstition which has often occasioned embarrassment, if no worse, to the unsophisticated white man trading with the natives. They imagine that if an enemy, especially if he is one of their own "bushmen," gets hold of a portion of any article belonging to one of them—say a part of a stick of tobacco, or the peel of a banana—he can work the owner of it some ill, such as causing sickness or even death. Consequently, when buying anything from a Tanna man for tobacco, he will never receive a piece of a stick unless a fellow-tribesman receives the remaining moiety. When eating a yam or banana, he will always bury or secretly make away with the skin, or any portion that he or his friends do not consume.

I weighed anchor and left Port Resolution on a Sunday morning, running down to Aniwa, a small island about twelve miles to the north, where I kept the ship "dodging" under the lee, there being no anchorage, whilst the boats visited the shore. A mission station had been established here two or three years before this, I believe; but the missionary was then absent on board the *Dayspring*, so our party did not visit his residence. A former chief of Port Resolution was living on the island with a few of his followers, one of whom we recruited. Old Maiaki had been a big chief in Port Resolution when I knew him five years before; but his reign was over now, and he was an outlaw.

Another recruit we obtained here was a native of the island. This boy, whose name was Niu, had served the missionary for some time as a house servant. When his employer went away on his present trip, he locked his kitchen door, some of Niu's clothes being left inside. After Niu's departure in the *Stanley*, the boy's relatives, knowing that his clothes were there, broke into the kitchen, abstracted them, and told the missionary, on his return, that the crew of the *Stanley* were the burglars. Before the year was out every man in the group—and the news went further than that—knew that the reverend gentleman accused Captain Wawn of breaking into his house. The kitchen, by the way, was a building detached from the dwelling-house. I suppose it was not worth his while to sift the matter properly, so long as he could get a good story to tell against a "slaver." Many of the stories told by this gentleman about "labour" vessels have just as good a foundation, and no better.

From Aniwa we crossed to Erromanga. We visited Cook's Bay on the east, and afterwards landed our "returns" at their home, Norras, on the south-west coast.

LANDING "RETURNS."

When the boats were seen pulling in towards Norras, a crowd of about a hundred men mustered to meet them, no women or children being visible. This was a bad sign, but the sight of the "returns," with their boxes and bundles, appeared to put most of them in a better temper. No other recruits were forthcoming, so we left and squared away for Sandwich Island.

The mountains in the interior of Erromanga rise to about the same height as those of Tanna, and are of the same description. The coast is almost entirely of coral, elevated on the west to 200 feet. There are three anchorages, of which I have used only one, in Dillon's Bay. There is a mission station here. No less than five missionaries, three of them resident, have been murdered by the natives, who have the reputation of being the most treacherous of all New Hebrideans— though it is merely "blackening the devil" to say so. The Revs. Williams and Harris were killed here in 1839. Gordon and his wife were murdered in 1861; and, subsequently, the brother of the last-named gentleman met his death at the hands of these savages.

There is a story current in these islands about the death of the elder Gordon and his wife, which I give here as I had it from a native of Dillon's Bay. He stated that the reverend gentleman experienced great difficulty in making converts; in fact, that he could not induce a single soul to enter the fold. One day he fell in with some of the chiefs and old men, and straightway delivered to them a powerful harangue on their sinfulness, winding up by telling them that surely, if they did not repent and become Christians, God would inflict some terrible punishment upon them. However, they continued to chance it until, sure enough, a whaling ship anchored in the bay and introduced some disease among them, measles or smallpox, which swept them off wholesale. The Erromanga man told me they died so fast that the living could not bury the dead, but blocked up the doors of the houses and left the corpses to rot in them. The survivors thought, like all savages, that some one must have "made" this sickness, and their suspicion, finally amounting to certainty, fell upon the poor missionary.

He had told them God would send some punishment along, if they did not become "missionary" Christians; consequently they imagined he had prayed to his God to send sickness, which had accordingly been sent. Though it had begun to diminish, it might any day arise again. As long as the missionaries were alive, they had merely the choice of Christianity or smallpox. They did not like either, so they killed Gordon to stop his praying, and his wife also to complete the job.

There is a fine stream of water here. The anchorages at Polenia and Elizabeth Bay are, I believe, very confined. There is none at Cook's Bay, and a heavy swell sets inshore, dangerous in light winds. The shore reefs extend a great distance from the land on the north side of the bay, and were not represented on the charts up to 1890. With the exception of these places, the coast all round is steep. Pango Point, long and low, forms the south-east side of Pango Bay, at the head of which is Port Vila or Sou'-West Harbour, a well-sheltered port, but with limited anchorage. The eastern part is too deep, and the north-west arm is blocked up with coral reef. The only fair anchorage is between Vila Islet, on the starboard as one enters, and Lelika Islet, in the middle of the harbour.

There was a mission station on Lelika I. in charge of the Rev. Mr. Annan, but his labours did not appear to be very successful. About a mile and a half from Vila, and also at the head of the bay, is Mele I., connected with the mainland by a sunken reef. A powerful tribe lives on this islet, having plantations on the mainland. The Mele and the Vila people differ very much from the other Sandwich I. natives in language and customs. They seem to have a strong strain of the true Polynesian in their blood. The north side of Pango Bay is "devil" country; it is unproductive land, and is therefore supposed by the natives to be infested with devils, or spirits hostile to man. I know of several small districts on other islands bearing a similar reputation.

Vila Harbour and Mele I. proving unproductive in the way of recruits, we kept on to the north, passing Havannah Harbour on the north-west coast of Sandwich I., a common port of call for vessels visiting this group. Mai, or "Three Hills" I., was next tried. The anchorage here is in a bay on the north-west side, the wide fringe reef of which extends over half a mile out from the shore along the whole length of the island. The inhabitants of Mai and those of the Shepherd Is. to the eastward, one of which, Tongoa, was in sight from this anchorage, speak the Sandwich I. language, and have the same dress and customs. Api I., with the peak of Lopevi appearing over and beyond it, lay to the north. We did fairly well and spent a couple of days here before running over to the west coast of Api, where I anchored in Ibo Bay, about three miles beyond the south-west point, in nine fathoms. This is a good watering-place, and as there is no village of "salt water" or coast natives here, we had free communication with several inland tribes, "man-o'-bush," as they are termed in South Sea English. Thence we worked the west coast as far as Duane, the north-western point.

This part of Api is thickly populated, and the beaches between the Foreland (a remarkable bluff promontory) and Duane Point have witnessed some bloody scenes. At this period a native of the part, known as "Three-fingered Jack," was a notorious character. He had been concerned in the murder of the mate and the son of the master of the schooner *Zephyr* of Sydney, towards the end of 1874. In Lammen, a low islet on the west side of Point Duane, the natives are also very dangerous; but, previous to this, they had received a good dressing from Captain McLeod, who traded between New Caledonia and the New Hebrides under the French flag, and they were now tolerably quiet and well behaved. Api resembles Tanna and Erromanga in its formation, but its mountains are scarcely so high. At Tassi-wor and Sakari, near the south-eastern extremity, the native dress and language resemble those of the Sandwich and Shepherd Is.; but in the central and western parts the men dispense with any dress beyond a handful of leaves, and their language differs considerably from that of other tribes. There are two or three other anchorages on the west coast, besides Ibo Bay.

In the southern islands of this group the common yam is the principal article of food, though we bought the ufelei or sweet yam largely; further north, taro became commoner than either. Bread-fruit was also to be had more frequently. but I never saw it in this group equal to that which the " Line " islands produce. Yams are the tuberous roots of a long creeping plant, or vine, and sometimes grow to a large size on volcanic soil, as in Tanna, where a yam weighing a hundred-weight is, or was a few years ago, not such a very unusual sight. Five to ten pounds is the average weight.

YAM PLANTS.   YAMS.

In Tanna I. this vegetable is grown on mounds, the vines being trained over to shelter the roots. In the northern islands of this group, and in New Caledonia, each plant is grown separately, and the vines are trained up long sticks.

In Bonape I., one of the Carolines, a piece of cord pegged at one end to the ground and the other fastened to the limb of a tree, often suffices as a support for the vine, without any clearing of grass or shrubs except for a foot or two round the roots. The yam will not grow on the low islands of the coral atolls.

Taro is an arum, the bulb of which is farinaceous, and

not unlike a dumpling when boiled. The best kind is grown in running water, and the natives sometimes go to considerable trouble—for them—in cutting ditches to convey water from neighbouring streams to the taro patches. Another and bigger kind, with a large dark leaf, grows in dry soil. This keeps well, and is used chiefly on journeys and canoe voyages in New Caledonia.

The bread-fruit tree does not attain to such a size in the New Hebrides as in the "Line" islands, neither is the fruit either so large or so good as that I have eaten in Bonape. There the young tree is propagated from suckers springing from the roots of the old one; and the

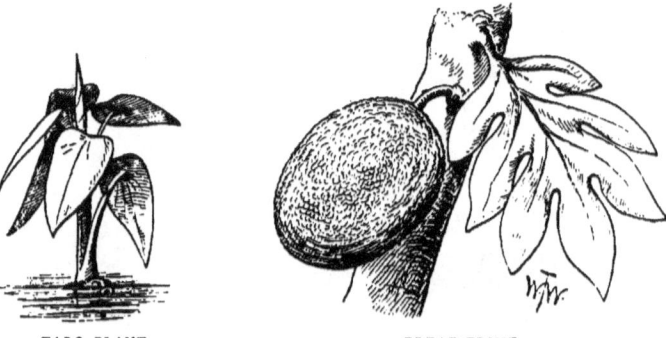

TARO PLANT.   BREAD-FRUIT.

fruit, perhaps on account of this method of cultivation, has no nuts or seeds in it, besides growing to double the size it attains to in the New Hebrides. The fruit of the pandanus tree is largely used by the natives of the coral islands near the Equator as an article of food, for which purpose it is admirably suited. In the New Hebrides it is of a very inferior quality, being regarded as useless. Its leaves form a very durable thatch for houses.

We engaged two or three recruits on this coast, but the fact of the recruiter and the boat's crew being comparative strangers militated against us. Owing to frequent kidnappings by vessels from Fiji, Honolulu, Samoa, and possibly also from Queensland and New

Caledonia, the inhabitants were very chary about venturing near the boats when they saw them manned by strangers. We engaged a man named Sorso to act as boatman and interpreter at Mallicolo, where we intended to proceed shortly. We had now great hopes of making a "good haul" at Paama I., which we visited after leaving Api. The recruiter had had some boys from this island working under him in Queensland. These had since returned home, and he made sure that he would meet some old acquaintances who would either engage again themselves or prevail upon others to accompany us. However, we were grievously disappointed, and we sailed away again without taking a man or woman out of the island. As the boats were being pulled off to the ship, a shot was fired at them from the shore, but fortunately the bullet flew wide of the mark. I mention this as being the first shot, if I recollect aright, fired at my boats in this trade, though afterwards it often occurred. In fact, I never made a voyage either in this or the Solomon groups without most of us experiencing the sensation of a bullet or an arrow whistling past us occasionally. Special cases I shall mention in due course.

Paama is a small, rugged, lofty island, with an anchorage of twelve to sixteen fathoms on its western side, near the Marie Stuart reef. This, which is a dangerous coral reef extending a mile westward of the southwest point, derives its name from a vessel wrecked on it. The Paama natives are an especially filthy lot, and, to me, have always appeared hostile to whites. The island of Lopevi lies about three miles east of Paama. It rises from the ocean in the form of a huge cone, on the top of which is the crater of a volcano. My Admiralty chart gives the height as 5,000 feet, but I think that is rather excessive. A few natives have habitations on the north side. I have never seen this volcano in an active state, but mariners have reported smoke issuing from the summit, and the natives say that they are sometimes alarmed by subterranean disturbances.

From Paama I steered to the south-west coast of Ambrym. In this island there is a very large volcano with two craters, according to native report, which rises to a height of more than 3,000 feet above the sea. The coast is generally rocky and steep, but there are two or three small anchorages. In Champion's Bay, on the south-west, I found from five to twenty fathoms of water, with not much roll from the sea. When these islands are clouded over, as they generally are during the daytime, the prevailing wind is not felt, and in its place an "eddy-wind" almost always sets in the opposite direction.

Under Ambrym I.—probably owing to the huge volume of smoke arising from the craters and intensifying the bank of cloud resting on the summits—this is especially the case.

We engaged three or four boys on the north-west coast, and two men promised to steal away at night with their wives from their village. I stood close in to the coast at night, and sent the boats to a spot appointed as the rendezvous; but we were disappointed. Fresh water was now running short on board; and as there is no convenient watering-place on this side of Ambrym, I squared away and ran down to Narovorovo, on the west of Aurora I. (Maiwo). I might have obtained a fresh supply on Pentecost I. (Aragh), but at this time I was not at all acquainted with that island.

The natives of Aurora I. hardly come up to the standard of Papuans in these waters. A large proportion of the men appeared to me stunted and misshapen. The village nearest to the anchorage at Narovorovo is situated about a mile away northward, and the inhabitants did not make an appearance until we had been at anchor some hours. It was then afternoon, our watering was all completed, but the boats were still at the beach. Our party were enjoying the luxury of a bath in the running stream, a number of the recruits disporting themselves in the sea or on the beach. Fortunately the Maré men and other boatmen had been posted all day within the outskirts of the dense forests overhanging the beach, and were concealed from view.

Suddenly, without warning, a long line of about fifty savages issued from the forest about 200 yards from the boats, making directly for them at a run. Possibly they thought they had the whole party cheap. But they pulled up short, about fifty yards off, when out from the trees and bushes rushed our Maré and Tanna men, outflanking them, each with his gun ready in his hand.

ATTACK AT NAROVOROVO.

They changed their attitude at once; but as no women or children accompanied them, and they were all fully armed with bows and poisoned arrows, spears, clubs, and tomahawks, it was quite plain what their object had been. Besides, they had brought nothing with them for sale.

Some conversation then took place between the two parties, after which the natives began slowly to return to their village. Suddenly one of them turned and let fly an arrow at one of the boatmen. It missed its mark, and in a few moments not one of them was to be seen. Our fellows chased them into the forest without firing a shot. The master of the *La-lia* cutter, of Fiji, had been murdered here during the previous year, together with one or two of his boatmen.

From Aurora I. we went to Port Sandwich in Mallicolo I., speaking H.M. schooner *Alacrity* on the way, at the east end of Aoba or Lepers' I. Port Sandwich is one of the few safe harbours in this group. It is a long, narrow bay, about four miles in extent; but the anchorage is very limited, the outer position being too deep, and two-thirds of the whole port being blocked by coral patches or mud banks. The entrance is contracted by jutting coral reefs. The French "New Hebrides Co." have now a trading station on Sandy Point. The fringe reefs on the south-east side have to be carefully avoided, as near Sandy Point they extend a considerable distance from the shore. There is also a large native village on this side near the entrance, and habitations are scattered about the hills on both sides. Two small rivers flow into the harbour—one, the Erskine, on the west side, and the other, unnamed, into the extreme head; but neither of them affords a suitable watering-place.

The Mallicolo natives differ to no great extent from the others, being just as savage and warlike. During the previous year a native boat's crew from Sandwich I. had been tomahawked and speared to death on the sandy point abreast of where we lay. They were, however, very friendly towards us, and several men soon came off on a tour of inspection, most of them in a canoe, and two or three by swimming. We gleaned three men here, and then stood northward along the coast.

Mallicolo is the largest of the New Hebrides, with the exception of Espiritu Santo I. (commonly called "Santo"). Its mountains attain a height of over 3,000 feet. It has not been ascertained for certain whether there is a volcano on Mallicolo or not. All I know of this matter is derived from an account given me by a native at Ura, an islet on the south-west coast. He said there were two large holes in the ground, a long way back in the interior of the island, each inhabited by a fiery "devil-devil." That these alternately emerged, each for a few days at a time, and that one of them "kai-kaied"—devoured—grass, and the other stones. These are possibly small craters, which are only occasionally active, and then only one at a time, grass growing about the edges of one of them during the periods of quiescence. The shores of Mallicolo are more diversified than those of the islands we had hitherto visited, being varied by islets and dangerous outlying coral reefs and patches. The anchorages are numerous.

A RUNAWAY HUSBAND.

CHAPTER II.

FIRST VOYAGE OF THE *STANLEY*, 1875 (*concluded*).

Down the coast of Mallicolo I.—A volunteer recruited—Interpreters—Mbangon Bay—Natives seize a boat—Ururiki I.—Sorso tempted—Sorso deserts—Islanders scared—A night alarm—Sorso's tale—Port Stanley—St. Bartholomew I.—Marlo "Pass"—Reputation of the women—Lepers' I.—Attack on the recruiting boat—List of casualties—Maiwo I.—Homeward bound—Sakau—A storm—Picking up passengers—Tongoa I.—H.M.S. Pearl—Interview with Commodore Goodenough—My advice to him—His fate—Havannah Harbour — Tragedies enacted there — Settlers in Sandwich I.—How wet weather affects recruiting—Leaving Tanna I.—Measles on board—Rigging up a hospital—Rounding Fraser I.—The pilot—A colonial "official"—Inspection of recruits—The affair at Lepers' I.—Newspaper slanders.

FROM Port Sandwich, Mallicolo I., we ran down the coast for about three miles to Mbangon Bay, which is well sheltered from the trade winds, anchoring there half a mile from the shore. We got four boys very quickly. One youngster, who had been some years among white people, volunteered as interpreter, and made himself very useful. Interpreters seldom join as recruits themselves; however, as the boat was being pushed off from the beach with the four recruits, this youngster quietly said to the recruiter,—

"Now, mate, very good you buy me."

A knife, a tomahawk, etc., were accordingly passed ashore to the friends of the lad, and he filled the office of cabin boy on board for the remainder of the voyage to Maryborough.

In those days it sometimes happened that interpreters

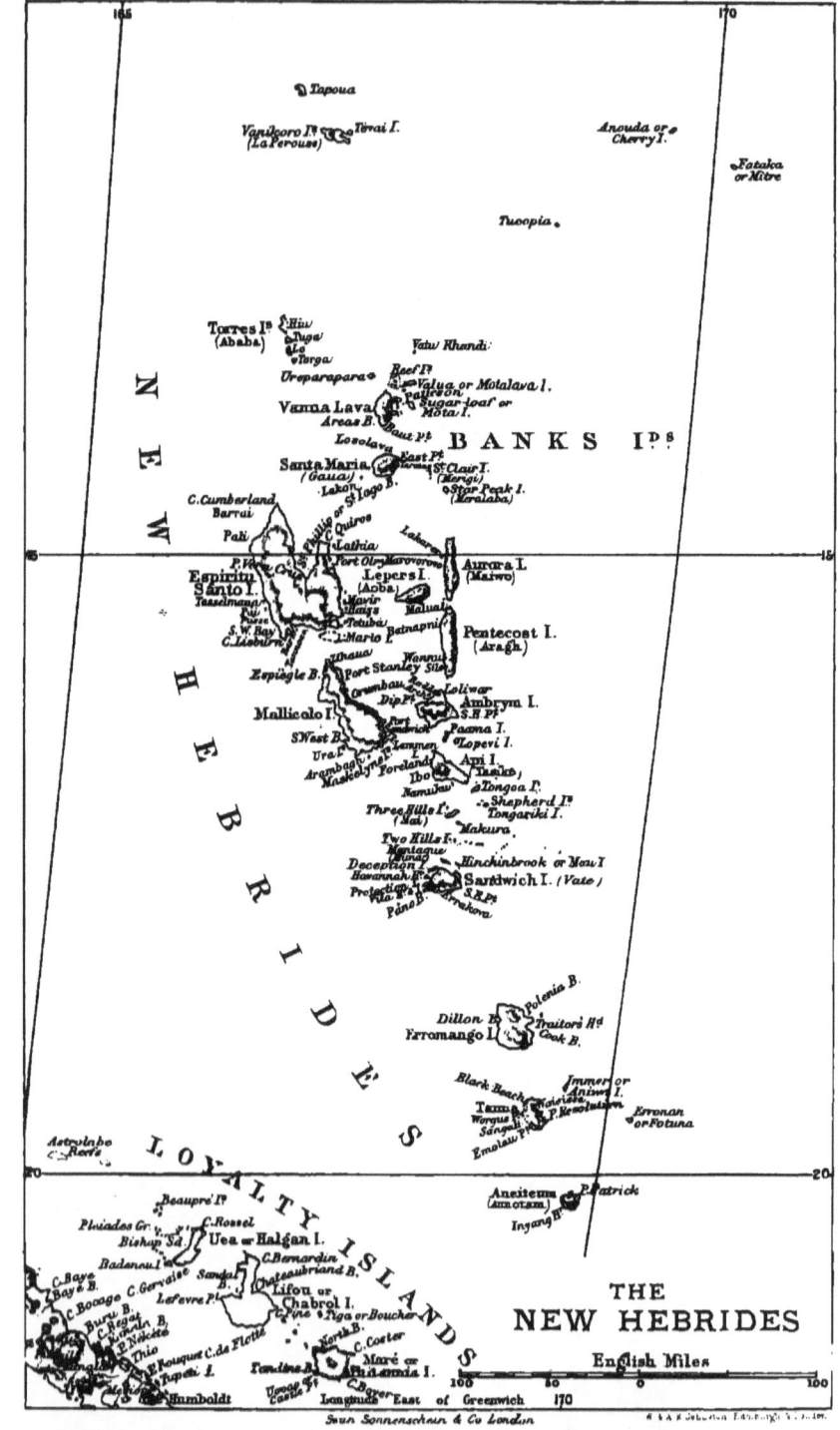

were not forthcoming when required, while now it would be very remarkable if one did not find a single English-speaking native among ten men on any beach in this group. I am of opinion that fully one half of the men belonging to tribes residing within three miles of the coasts have fulfilled a term of service in one or other of our colonies. Even in the far interior of Mallicolo and Espiritu Santo Is., interpreters may be obtained with very little trouble. Children pick up South Sea English very quickly; and I have known boys who came on board my vessel converse fluently, having acquired the language from returned labourers and by visiting trading and labour vessels.

On the north of Mbangon a long point and coral reef extend about four miles out from the coast. In the second bay southward of this point is situated the large and populous village of Merrabwei. Here I hove to, and the recruiter pulled off to the beach under the village. For some reason, I forget what, the second boat did not leave the ship until the recruiter had already got among the natives. A crowd of about two hundred surrounded his boat as soon as she touched the sand, and, seizing her, with all her crew in her, pulled her up almost clear of the water. They evidently meant mischief, and probably the whole boat's crew would have been massacred had they rashly offered resistance. Luckily the ship lay within rifle-shot, and the second boat, with the mate and the G.A. in her, pulled quickly off to assist the first. The natives then retreated, leaving the boat and its occupants unharmed. The latter were glad to get back to the ship, although unsuccessful.

From the "long reef" we ran down the coast to the north-west, until opposite the centre of the island. There extensive fringe reefs were seen, and, northward of the first small islet, a deep bay appeared. This has the mainland on the south-west, and on the opposite side a low, curved promontory of coral formation, thickly wooded. At the extreme end of this is the inhabited islet of Ururiki. In the midst of the bay are some large reefs and islets, on the extreme north of which I anchored in eighteen fathoms. The sun was very low when I arrived, and I was glad to find bottom anywhere; though this was hardly a safe anchorage. The islet of Orambau is situated about a mile northward of Ururiki, a deep channel lying between.

The day after our arrival the boats visited the mainland at various points, but the natives were very shy. Sorso, the interpreter engaged at Lammen I., conversed with them, however, and at one point more than a dozen crowded about the recruiting boat. We never knew what arguments they used to induce Sorso to desert; but after a while he made an excuse to go up the beach into the bush, and on that day we saw him no more. The natives quietly but quickly slipped away, leaving two iron tomahawks, and some bows and arrows, behind them on the sand.

As Sorso did not return, search was made for him in the vicinity of the boats; but no trace of him being found, the recruiter came to the conclusion that he had deserted, though at first fancying he might have been killed. To make up for his loss a small brindled pig was captured and brought off, together with the abandoned weapons.

Not liking the present anchorage, on account of a heavy swell setting in round the point of Ururiki, I shifted our moorings next day to the south end of the islet. As soon as we had anchored again, several canoes left the islet, filled with women and children, apparently clearing out to the main for safety—a needless precaution on their part. Some seven or eight men ventured alongside, however, after our boats had paid a visit to the beach near the village, and then confidence was restored, and by the next morning all the runaways had returned.

The "trades" were now blowing almost a gale of wind; but we lay sheltered in smooth water, the boats meanwhile coasting all round the bay in search of recruits, but without success. On the mainland no natives appeared, probably owing to Sorso's secession.

Just before dawn, the second night we spent here, I was awakened by the anchor watch (one seaman) running aft and calling out to me that a fleet of canoes were coming down on the ship from the head of the harbour. Mindful of Captain McLeod's experience in the Maskelynes a year or two before this, and how a fleet of canoes attacked his vessel, the *Donald McLean*, and were only beaten off after sharp fighting, I immediately roused all hands, and in a minute or two the deck bristled with arms, and every preparation was made for repelling an attack.

The cries became more distinct and drew nearer, making us sure we were in for a fight. However, it turned out at length that the sounds proceeded from one person only; and presently a canoe, with a single occupant, came into view out of the darkness, driving down to the ship before the wind. A rope thrown from the bows was caught and made fast, and then the deserter, Sorso, shivering in his old shirt, and as pale as it is possible for a brown skin to become, climbed on deck.

His story was soon told. The natives had persuaded him to bolt, pretending they had ascertained that we meant to carry him off to Queensland. At first they treated him well, but, during the second night, he had overheard the headmen saying it was their intention to "make meat" of him, so he ran off into the bush and had kept himself concealed there during the previous day. When night fell, he coasted round the bay, stole a canoe, and made for the ship, knowing that a thrashing was the worst he had to expect from us.

Even this he escaped, an unmerciful chaffing being all the punishment dealt out to him. We broke up his stolen canoe for firewood, and then got under way, it being now broad daylight.

A few weeks afterwards I was on board H.M.S. *Pearl*, giving all the information I could about anchorages and so forth to the late Commodore Goodenough. I mentioned this bay to him, calling it "Port Stanley" in memory of our visit, and that name it still retains.

Thence I shaped a northerly course, passing the Nor'-East Is., which Sorso called "Sissi," a word meaning "small."

Having arrived off the north-western coast of St. Bartholomew I., I dropped anchor in twelve fathoms, to the east of a dangerous projecting reef, commonly known as the "Robert Towns" Reef. This was named after a Sydney barque, which had been wrecked on it some two or three years before this. Here we had the good fortune to engage a few recruits, and then beat back in an easterly direction, passing between St. Bartholomew and Mallicolo Is.

St. Bartholomew, or, as the natives call it, Marlo, is entirely of coral formation, I believe, the western end being elevated to 800 feet, the eastern portion being low. The channel between it and the south coast of Espiritu Santo is dangerous, except with a fair and commanding breeze, being much beset with reefs, and the tides running very strongly through it. The eastern end of the channel is generally known as Marlo "Pass" or "Passage," and in it anchorage can be obtained at various depths. On the south-east coast there is a sheltered bay, formed by two low islets connected with the main island by a reef.

The north shore of Marlo Pass is not formed by the "mainland"—Espiritu Santo I.—itself, but by the island of Arore, which another channel divides from the main. These channels are connected on the west. The eastern extremity of the northernmost of them, which is known as Segond Channel, terminates in a bay behind Tetuba, an islet lying off the south-eastern corner of Espiritu Santo I.

The inhabitants of Marlo Pass have acquired an unenviable reputation. Probably nowhere throughout the South Seas are the natives conspicuously careful of the virtue of chastity. Here, in St. Bartholomew and Arore Is., it is still less understood or appreciated, and, in the lack of it, the women of these islands may be fairly said to " bang Banagher."

At daybreak one morning we found ourselves a mile to windward of the western end of Aoba, or Lepers' I. It was then blowing half a gale from the south-west, with dirty weather. Squaring away before the breeze, we soon found smooth water under the lee of the island. Viewed at a distance, either from north or south, it resembles a whale's back, consisting of a huge rounded mountain lying east and west.

The inhabitants of this island are extremely treacherous, and very hostile to white men. This they have proved on a number of occasions, murdering and afterwards eating those who fell into their hands. There seems to be an admixture of Polynesian with Papuan blood among them.

The afternoon of our arrival at Lepers' I. the schooner was lying almost becalmed under the lee of the lofty central portion of the island, about three-quarters of a mile from the shore. The boats were in sight at some distance. The recruiter, with whom were the Doctor and "Cash," had run his boat into a small nook on the rocky coast, under a high bank, above which stood a solitary hut backed by dense forest. The G.A. and mate in the second boat lay about 400 yards to the westward.

Suddenly we heard the sound of firing, followed by yells from the natives on shore, and then we saw the recruiter's boat push out with a seemingly diminished crew. The mate's boat pulled quickly up, took her in tow, and presently brought her alongside, all her own crew being more or less hurt. It seems the natives had called them into the place on pretence of friendship. A crowd gathered about the stern of the boat, and several fellows even got into her. All of a sudden our men were attacked with clubs and tomahawks. The recruiter escaped the first blows aimed at him, making play with his fists until he had an opportunity to draw his revolver. "Tom Sayers," a Maré man, received a tomahawk blow on the head, which laid the scalp open, but did not penetrate his skull, fortunately. Bobby Towns, another Maré boatman, had both his thumbs cut in warding off blows, one of them being so nearly severed from the hand that the doctor had to finish that operation. Lahu, a Lifu boy, the recruiter's special attendant, was cut and pricked in various places, but nowhere seriously. Jack, an unlucky Tanna recruit, who had been engaged to act as boatman, received an arrow through his forearm, the head of which—a piece of bone seven or eight inches long—was still in the limb, protruding from both sides, when the boats returned. The Doctor and "Cash" were both thrown down in the boat at the commencement of the affray, and suffered no hurt. The recruiter would have got off scot-free had not an arrow pinned one of his fingers to the loom of the steering-oar just as they were getting off. The fight had been short, but sharp. Considering the numbers of the Aoba men, and the unexpectedness of the attack, it is a wonder that all our people were not massacred.

The enemy lost two men, at least, both shot dead. None of the arrows that wounded our men proved to have been poisoned, happily. Tom Sayers had received the most serious injury. At first I was afraid he would lose his life, the gash on his head looking bad enough. However, when the doctor overhauled him, it was found that the thickness of his skull had saved him. Had he been a white man, the bone would certainly have given way under the blow he had received.

After dark the clouds cleared off the land, the true "trade wind" filled the sails again, and a course was shaped for the northern end of Aurora, or Maiwo I. Next morning I anchored off Lakareré, or the "Double Waterfall," and lay there two days and nights.

Lakareré was the turning-point of the voyage, for thence we shaped a homeward course, usually working back through the group against the trade wind by night, and in the daytime keeping near the boats as they pulled along the lee shores of the islands, looking for recruits.

The west coasts of Ambrym and Paama Is. were again tried, but proved singularly unproductive. On the western and southern coasts of Api I. the inhabitants complained so much of the ravages of measles, and of its frequent consequence, dysentery, that we did not delay there long.

One day I anchored off Sakau, on the south-east coast of Api I., the wind then blowing lightly from north-east, with rather a dull, cloudy sky. Towards evening the sky became still more overcast, with a threatening aspect towards north-east. About 7 p.m. a vivid flash of lightning showed in the same quarter. I immediately weighed anchor and got both boats out ahead—the northerly wind being exceedingly light—to tow the vessel out of the anchorage. Having gained a mile of offing, I hoisted in my boats, and had hardly done so when a violent squall of wind, accompanied by thunder and lightning and dense rain, burst upon us. Having taken good bearings before it reached us, I was enabled to point the ship's head so as to run for the open sea, passing between Mai I. and the Shepherd Is. I expected this breeze would last through the night, since the barometer was rather low and showed no sign of rising. But I was wrong in my calculations. When we were nearly abreast of the east end of Mai I. the wind lessened for a while, then, hauling round into the south, increased to a gale. This necessitated our beating about under short canvas all night under the lee of the island, only managing to reach our anchorage by daylight next morning.

Here we met four natives of Tongoa I., who had paddled across to Mai on a visit, and were afraid to trust themselves and their canoe in the heavy sea now rolling in between them and their home.

Having received a pig as payment for their passage, I shipped them and their canoe on board, and crossed over to Tongoa, the northernmost of the Shepherd Is., two days later.

Close to the western point of this island, which is mountainous and rugged, I found a stony beach, with a steep bank or cliff rising behind it, above which was the native village of Panita. Here I dropped anchor. While we lay there, an unpleasant roll of the sea set in, coming round the point.

The recruiter landed our passengers close under the lee of this point, as they were afraid to trust themselves among the Panita people. Cades reported on his return that the four hauled up their canoe above high-water mark, quickly disappearing into the bush. He subsequently saw a party of Panita men hastily following them. I only hope my late passengers got safely home, but I have some doubts about it.

Next morning the recruiter was ashore on the beach with his boat's crew, when H.M.S. *Pearl* hove in sight, coming round the western end of the island under sail. Shortly after her lieutenant boarded the *Stanley*, overhauled the ship and my papers. This formality having been satisfactorily concluded, I repaired on board the *Pearl* to report the attack on my boat by the Aoba natives to Commodore Goodenough, who was then in command of the Australian squadron. After the story of the skirmish was ended, I remained more than an hour with the Commodore, giving him such information as I could with regard to harbours, anchorages, etc. In the course of conversation he said it was very probable he would attempt to ascend the volcanoes on Ambrym I.

This I endeavoured to dissuade him from doing, assuring him that he would thereby risk his own and his men's lives, by exposing them to native treachery. This advice, however, he rather pooh-poohed, stating as his firm belief that savages, if kindly treated, would show no hostility.

He did not attempt the ascent of the volcano, after all; but very shortly afterwards he found out the mistake of trusting to the good feelings of natives—only too late, for he was mortally wounded by poisoned arrows on Nitendi I., in the Santa Cruz group.

We obtained three recruits at Tongoa, sailing thence to Havannah Harbour, Sandwich I., where we took on board wood and water.

This spacious harbour lies on the north-western coast of Sandwich I., protected by the smaller Deception I. and Protection I., both of which are elevated and of coral formation. It has a length of five miles by an average width of one mile. At its southern end, between the main island and Protection I., there is a clear and very deep passage, which is the principal entrance to the port. There is another ship's passage between the two islets, much narrower and shallower.

The natives living on the shores of Havannah Harbour are now tolerably quiet and peaceable. I assume that this is due rather to intercourse with traders, and to a wholesome experience of ship's guns, than to the work of the missionary, whose influence hardly extends a quarter of a mile beyond his house. However this may be, it is certain that, in former times, many a white man's blood has stained the shores of Havannah Harbour. In April, 1847, these savages massacred all but two of the crew of the wrecked barque *British Sovereign*, and the crew of another vessel, previously lost near the harbour, had suffered a like fate before them.

The settlement at Semma, with its central position, fine harbour, and other natural advantages, may be looked upon as the nucleus of the future capital of the New Hebrides. For, though progressing very slowly, it is steadily increasing. Messrs. Trueman and Macleod were, I believe, the first whites who settled here with the intention of cultivating land to a considerable extent. Their attempt was abruptly terminated by a mournful tragedy. During a drunken quarrel Macleod shot Trueman dead, though in self-defence as reported; and for a short time afterwards the place was abandoned. This affair occurred in 1870.

At the time of our visit, Mr. Hebblewhite, of Sydney, had taken up his residence there. He had erected a good weather-board dwelling-house, and had also a large store well supplied with goods suitable for the native trade, and for furnishing ships. There were two or three other settlers besides; but the lack of an established government, together with difficulties arising out of the introduction of labourers from other islands of the group, had tended towards preventing any permanent occupation by British subjects for purposes of agriculture.

Sandwich I. possesses a similar formation to its larger neighbours, consisting of a backbone of mountains rising from a flat, low-lying coast of coral. Havannah and Vila Harbours afford the only landlocked anchorages on this coast.

From Havannah Harbour we sailed to Tanna I., leaving Erromanga I. unvisited, as the weather was so wet that the boats would have had small chance of success. Wet weather impedes the recruiter's work. The naked savage prefers the shelter of his hut to the less efficient cover of dripping trees. Even if he does venture out, he will not come down to the open beach, where the wind would have full play upon his wet and shivering carcase.

Only one day was spent at Tanna I., and even

a portion of that on board the Maryborough labour schooner *Sibyl*—Captain Taylor; Mr. Andrews, G.A.

The weather was still too wet for recruiting, no sign of a change being apparent. So, although we had only seventy-two recruits on board, instead of a hundred and eight—the complement we were licensed to carry—our recruiter deemed it better to return to Maryborough at once with those we had engaged, than to run any further risk of measles and dysentery. These diseases were both very prevalent just then in all the islands we had visited.

Accordingly, towards evening, the boats were secured, the yards braced sharp up on the port tack, the ensign thrice dipped "good-bye" to the *Sibyl*, and off we went on our way home, shaping our course so as to weather the southern extremity of New Caledonia.

During the whole cruise among the islands, we had been as careful to avoid infection as was possible consistently with the work of recruiting; and especially had we made it a rule not to enter any of the native huts. However, as it turned out, one of our boatmen had disobeyed orders in this respect, by allowing himself to be beguiled into a hut in the mission village at Havannah Harbour. The consequence was that on the day after our departure from Tanna, he was taken ill, and the doctor pronounced his case to be one of measles. Of course this spread consternation throughout the ship. The boat on the port davits, being on the "weather" side, was selected as a hospital. A tarpaulin was rigged up over it for a roof, and planks were laid across the thwarts for patients to lie on. Happily, we had not much occasion to use our hospital, however, this being the only case of measles we were destined to have on board. It proved to be a slight attack, and did not spread. Another boy even lay in the boat by the side of the first patient without taking the infection. He had only a severe cold, though at first it was feared he was going to develop measles also.

We weathered the extensive reefs off the south-eastern coast of New Caledonia, running thence with a fair wind to Maryborough. The currents set very strongly, as also variably, off the Isle of Pines. Several times we experienced "rips" over what looked like surf breaking upon coral reefs.

As we were nearing Breaksea Spit, Fraser I., the wind fell very light, hauling round to nor'-nor'-west, the current carrying us southward at the same time. I was therefore obliged to make for Wide Bay bar, at the southern end of Fraser I., instead of rounding the northern point of the Spit and reaching Maryborough

THE DOCTOR'S INSPECTION.

by way of Hervey Bay. After some further difficulties of a similar sort, I beat in over the bar with the flood, against a westerly wind, and anchored near the pilot station.

The pilot boarded us off the station, and took the *Stanley* up to her anchorage. Of course he was informed before he came on board that we had had a case of measles, as likewise that the ship was now clear of that disorder. However, no sooner was the anchor down than he left the ship, no doubt deeming discretion the better part of valour. Next day he sent his coxswain to take the *Stanley* on to Maryborough, where we arrived about the end of August.

As soon as the ship was moored alongside the river bank, opposite to the town, the sub-immigration agent came on board. This gentleman was also protector or inspector—I forget which—of Polynesians, sub-collector of customs, shipping master, and various other things. In fact, he "milked the Government cow" to a considerable extent, filling sundry offices in his own person. With him came the Government medical officer. The inspector examined our recruits as to the manner in which they had been induced to venture to Queensland, and as to the length of time they had agreed to serve, and so forth. The medical officer, at the same time, made a reasonably careful survey of them, to ascertain that all were fit, mentally as well as physically, to do labourers' work.

This being over, and all the recruits having been passed satisfactorily, during the next three or four days they were gradually engaged for service, leaving us one after another, until the ship was clear of them.

About a week after our arrival the police magistrate held an inquiry into the skirmish at Lepers' I. (Aoba). This affair had been made to appear much more serious than it really was by the reporter of "The Brisbane Courier." In the interest of the "Anti-Kanaka" party he had dressed up the plain facts, adding to his account of the affray that "the whites retaliated by burning villages." The inquiry over, I heard nothing more about the matter.

CHAPTER III.

SECOND VOYAGE OF THE *STANLEY*, 1875.

Passengers on board—Reasons for taking them—A lengthy passage—Arrival at Port Resolution, Tanna I.—Visit to a native chief—"Washerwoman"—Waisissa and Itoa—Vila and Havannah—Hostilities at Merrabwei—The mate's ruse—Aurora I.—Visit to Lakarere Falls—Croton plants—A "sing-sing" ground—Ambrym, Api, and Tongoa Is.—A re-enlistment—Vila Harbour—Mr. Hebblewhite and slavery—Cabin-boys—Dillon's Bay, Erromanga I.—Drifting ashore—"Down with the boats!"—A struggle for safety—Natives waiting for the wreck—A welcome breeze—Homeward bound—The Great Queensland—*John Renton—Eight years in the Solomon Is.—Rescued at last—Wreck of the* Lyttona.

I SAILED again in command of the *Stanley* in October, on a recruiting trip as before. The Government agent, who had accompanied me during the last voyage, was re-appointed; but our former recruiter, the doctor, and "Cash," as well as the piano, remained on shore. I had two fresh passengers in the cabin in their places—young fellows who wished to see the islands, and who paid handsomely for the privilege of making the round trip in the schooner.

In a general way passengers would be simply a nuisance on a labour vessel; every inch of space, both in the ship and in the boats, being required for stores and for recruits. However, I foresaw that there would be a sensible advantage in taking these gentlemen, apart from the hard cash gained thereby. We were so often dubbed "slavers," and so frequently accused of kidnapping—as though Kanakas could not be induced to come to the colony, except by compulsion—that I, for one, was always glad to show disinterested persons how recruiting was really carried on, hoping that thereby erroneous impressions might be dispelled, in some measure, from the public mind.

After taking in wood and water at the White Cliffs, I got to sea—as on the last voyage—by rounding Breaksea Spit, whence we had a rough and lengthy passage before reaching the Isle of Pines. I had to fight the trade-wind the whole way, failing to find any westerly breeze in my favour.

We passed the Loyalty Is. without paying them a visit, our first call being at Port Resolution, Tanna I., where I obtained boatmen.

The day we anchored, the G.A. and I landed on the western side of the harbour, and walked a mile or more, along a very rough and rocky native track, to the village of a chief, who was known to Europeans as "Washerwoman"—which designation was, I suppose, a perversion of his native name. We found this gentleman at home; but since our object was to obtain recruits, our walk did not profit us. "Washerwoman" could not spare a single man, even if any had wished to leave. It appeared that he had quarrelled with some of his neighbours on the other side of the harbour, and a conflict between the tribes was impending. However, I believe no fighting took place, a hollow truce having been patched up between the contending parties, shortly after which treaty "Washerwoman" was treacherously murdered by some of his enemies.

I was not the only European sorry to hear of his death; for he had always been a good friend to white men.

The G.A. and I undertook another trip, this time by boat, as far as Waisissa, where I met an old acquaintance. This was Yova, the chief of a village overlooking the little bay on the western side of the island. From him I obtained two recruits. Five years before this Yova had been a powerful chief, dividing the sovereignty of the beach with Kauass, another headman. Now he was obliged to live in the bush, having been driven there by misfortune in war. "Spanish Charley," a South American half-breed, had been another resident on the beach during the period of Yova's supremacy there. He likewise was constrained to leave, going to Aoba, where he was murdered by the natives in 1874.

Leaving Port Resolution, I took ship and boats on northward, to a spot about three miles from Waisissa, where I found good anchorage off the "black rocks" of Nimatahin. The natives in the vicinity of this place have the reputation of being the wildest in Tanna I. I was tolerably fortunate there. Proceeding thence I next visited the north coast, dropping anchor beneath a village called Itoa. I was obliged to go so close in shore here to get bottom that I had barely room to swing to the anchor. It would have been an ugly place to have been caught in, if the natives had proved hostile, and had chosen to try the range of their guns from the cliffs.

From Itoa to Blackbeach, and thence to Sangali, completed our work on the coasts of Tanna I. We then directed our attention to Erromanga I., where, however, we drew blank along the whole length of the west coast.

We next touched at Vila, in Sandwich I. There I engaged three men, but, unluckily, left the place too soon. A few hours after we had sailed, six men came down from the bush with the intention of joining. They were quickly picked up by another vessel—the *Lady Darling*, I think—which called at Vila the day after our departure.

I put into Havannah Harbour to take wood and water on board, but obtained no recruits there. Thence we cruised northward, seeking recruits at most of the villages in the islands visited during the previous voyage, and with considerable success.

At Paama I. we met with hostilities again. Our boats

were greeted with a volley, which fortunately hurt no one. The people of Merrabwei also made another attempt to seize the recruiting boat. On this occasion, however, the mate—who was in charge of her along with the G.A.—had not ventured close in to the beach, but kept the boat well away, though in shallow water. As she was thus lying to, a party of natives waded towards her from the beach, others remaining partly hidden among the trees near the shore. There were no women or children to be seen, although the village was not more than a hundred yards distant. It was also apparent that the waders carried no commodities to trade with, but that all of them were fully armed.

As the savages slowly approached, wading through water that rose to their knees, the boatmen gave a short pull every now and then. The waders, following the movements of the boat, were drawn further and further out, until they had got so far from the beach that they were waist-deep in the water, while the boats were beyond the range of any arrows that might be discharged from the forest. At length the attacking party got tired of this game and made a rush on the boat, brandishing their tomahawks, clubs, and spears. However, our people were too wary for them. A vigorous stroke or two sent the boat well away out of their reach, and spears thrown after it missed their mark. A couple of shots from the white men's rifles quickly sent the whole crowd splashing and scuttling back to dry land and the cover of the trees.

This incident made it evident to us that nothing was to be obtained at Merrabwei but hard knocks. I therefore took the ship round to the other side of the point, and anchored her. In the evening two couples—husbands and wives—joined us there. They were Merrabwei people, and their friends would certainly have stopped them from coming to us, had their intention been known. We also engaged two "bush men" at this place. They came from the very centre of the island, so they said.

At Lakarere, Aurora I.—as we happened to have two or three natives of the island on board—a visit was made to the waterfalls, which give the place its English name. There are two of them, and these are not alike in character.

The northern fall, which we came to first, is not visible from the beach or from the bay. The water rushes out from a mountain gorge overhung by dense forest growth. Falling over the edge of a precipice, it descends upon two great projecting rocks, which divide its mass, and lower down, upon a huge rocky shelf. Over this it flows in a thin clear sheet of falling water, till broken again below. The whole contour of the fall suggests a woman's dress—the glistening sheet being the skirt, the dark points of rock and white spray reminding one of ornaments and lace. We named it "The Bridal Robe Fall."

The other fall is at little distance to the right of this one. It consists of a single stream of water, about four feet wide, which rushes down a steep slope of slippery rock. From the appearance of the water-worn rocks edging these falls, I fancy there must be a tremendous rush of water after heavy rains.

Leaving the falls we made a circuit through the forest to a village about a mile northward of our anchorage. There I obtained some slips of different varieties of croton. Planted in boxes, these struck root and throve wonderfully on board. Subsequently they figured in the public gardens at Maryborough, together with numerous other plants which I had brought from the islands, and deposited there, from time to time.

Though situated on the top of a hill, looking down on the sea, the village appeared terribly damp, overhung and surrounded, as it was, by large trees. There were a dozen rude huts, one of them larger than any of the others. They consisted merely of a thatched roof, sloping to an insignificant wall, not more than two feet in height. In an open space at one end of the village, stood half a dozen native drums—hollow logs, having an opening cut in one side—planted on end in the ground. This was the "sing-sing" ground, where dances and festivities were carried on.

Descending a rough and narrow path down the precipitous face of the hill, we waded through a muddy taro patch or cultivation. In the middle of this grew a huge croton bush, planted there to keep off evil spirits from the garden. We thence regained the creek, getting back

DRUMS IN THE "SING-SING" GROUND.

to the boats without having heard any poisoned arrows whistle about our heads—a danger one had often to risk in those days.

Some years later a mission station was established at Lakarere, by the Rev. — Bice.

Sailing on southward I next visited Ambrym and Api Is. without result, and finally anchored, one afternoon, under the lee of Tongoa I. The mate, who now took command of the boats and did the recruiting alongshore, thought that Tongoa would yield no boys to us, judging by the attitude of the natives on the previous voyage. The G.A. held a like opinion, in consequence of which I visited the beach myself. Hardly had my boat touched the sand, when a tall man, holding a gun in his hand, quietly stepped into her, and stood calmly looking at the crowd on shore. Two others quickly followed him.

These men told us they were returned labourers from Queensland. They had been at home for about a month, and were now determined to undertake a second term of service, though in opposition to the wishes of their tribe.

The example set by Bisop—as he styled himself—and his two "mates" was imitated by eight men and a couple of women next morning, making thirteen in all from Tongoa I. "But," remarked the mate when I brought them off, "you never know when you have 'em."

The presents given to the friends of these recruits were more liberal than was customary. Ten fathoms of calico, white or coloured, were allowed for each individual, as well as pipes and tobacco.

Our next call was at Tongariki, an island surmounted by a lofty peak, lying seven or eight miles south-east of Tongoa. There I anchored for one night, recruiting two men and a woman—the wife of one of them.

At Havannah Harbour we took in wood and water. Several other labour vessels lay there at the same time, and H.M.S. *Sappho* came in for a night or two afterwards, following me round to Vila, whither I went next.

A white settler, who was a British subject, had died recently at Vila; and some natives of Espiritu Santo, who had been his labourers, were still there. These now wished to engage with me for Maryborough. Mr. Hebblewhite, to whom the deceased employer had been in debt, heard of this. He immediately put in an objection to my engaging these men, claiming their services as belonging to the estate — which would have been simply treating them as slaves. The matter was referred to the captain of the *Sappho*, who declined to listen to the claim asserted by Mr. Hebblewhite. I therefore engaged the Santo men as recruits, with one exception.

This one, a youngster called Puck—whose native name was Massan—I shipped for service on board the *Stanley* as cabin boy. He was to remain with me until discharged at his home, or till he was old enough to land in Queensland as a recruit, if he desired to do so.

At that time most labour vessels carried a youngster to act as cabin boy. Subsequently, however, the practice was forbidden; the authorities choosing to consider it a breach of the Polynesian Act.

Having shipped over ninety recruits, I now resolved to return to Queensland, and accordingly beat down to the south.

One afternoon we were about two miles distant from the western coast of Erromanga I. As the ship seemed to be in perfect safety—heading southward with a light wind off the land—I laid myself down on the settee in the deck-house to read, and presently dropped off to sleep. I had no sooner closed my eyes than the wind fell off, veered round, and then came up in light puffs from the west. The mate, who was attending too intently to some work on deck, trimmed the yards, and then carelessly allowed the ship to drift close in to the land, a few miles south of Dillon's Bay.

The first intimation of our danger that I received was given by a native, who hailed us from the shore. Opening my eyes and looking out of the cabin door, I saw green trees not two hundred yards from the ship! I jumped right out on deck; and then, for a moment, I thought the *Stanley's* career was ended. Not three ship-lengths away from the port-quarter I saw a line of small breakers beating against the face of a level terrace of coral, eight feet in height. This extended back to the foot of a precipice which rose nearly three hundred feet, and was crowned with dense forest stretching up towards the interior until lost to view. To seaward a smooth glistening sheet of water extended far away, till a dark, quivering line showed where the trade-wind from overhead was rushing down upon the surface. Now and then a "cat's paw" ruffled the glassy expanse, setting inward towards the shore, catching our sails, and gently aiding the ground-swell to drift us, broadside on, into the line of breakers.

"Down with the boats!" I shouted. A rattle of blocks, splashing and commotion, immediately succeeded. Then, with the two boats working ahead, each towing a long line made fast to the jib-boom on either side— which lines were always hung there, coiled up, in readiness for such an emergency—I got the ship's head round to seaward. Meanwhile, on board, we clewed up the square sails and flattened in the sheets of the fore-and-aft canvas.

Now ensued a hard fight for safety. The eight oarsmen pulled their level best, the long steering oars sculling in aid of them; yet not an inch away from the rocks could they haul the vessel, a powerful current drifting her slowly southward along the coast.

For half an hour or more the swell, with the eddying puffs of wind, neutralized all our efforts. At last—oh, welcome sight!—a short spit of sunken reef showed up just under our keel. Against the extreme point of this we dropped our anchor. I say *against* the point; for, in truth, the anchor hung from our bows with a taut, perpendicular cable, resting along the sloping side of the reef rather than upon it. The ship's stern lay in little more than two fathoms of water, while an active man could have jumped from the taffrail into the breakers. Thus we remained for more than two hours, it being impossible to get away until the clouds had cleared from off the land, and till the true trade-wind had reached us.

In the meantime some fifty of the natives, all armed, assembled on the rocks astern and close to us. The talking and shouting we could hear all along the shore and cliffs indicated, too, that these only formed a part of the crowds assembled. They were fully aware there was a very fair chance of a shipwreck, and, no doubt, were well disposed to do all they could to contribute towards such a desirable result. So, when one of them inquired whether we meant to lie there all night, he was promptly informed that we did, as we considered it a good locality in which to buy yams and "boy."

It was possible—even probable—that if they had been told we should leave at the first opportunity, they would have commenced hostilities forthwith to prevent our doing so. And what nice pot-shots at us they might have had, looking right down upon our deck!

At last, just as the sun was setting, when most of the savages had gone home for the night, a puff of wind blew off the land, coming down a small gully not far off on the south, and making a long tongue of dark water across the glassy surface. Our loose sails shook, and filled as fast as they were sheeted home. The boats were again sent ahead with the tow-lines, but were no longer necessary, for the breeze came down in a hurry from the cliffs astern of us. Away we went, out of danger, with the anchor hanging low under the bows. Nor did we heave to until we had gained two miles off shore, when I rounded to and hoisted the boats aboard.

Another day was spent at Tanna I., though without profit. I then sailed for Maryborough, rounding the southern end of New Caledonia, as on my last voyage. I arrived in port about the first of December, passing the *Great Queensland* lying at anchor off the Fairway buoy in Hervey Bay, outward bound. It was the last occasion on which she was destined to sail these waters. She left England, subsequently, for Australia, but was never heard of again.

During my absence on this voyage, the labour schooner, *Bobtail Nag*—Captain Murray, Mr. Slade, G.A.—had arrived at Bowen, in Northern Queensland. She had on board one John Renton, a native of Renfrewshire, Scotland.

Some eight years before, this man had been a seaman on board a whaling ship. Whilst cruising in the vicinity of the Kingsmill Is., he, with several others of the crew, had deserted the ship in one of her boats. After drifting and sailing for several weeks, undergoing horrible privations from hunger and thirst, from which some of them died, the survivors landed on Manoba I., a small appendage of Malayta I. in the Solomon group.

Renton's companions soon died or were killed by the savages. His own life was saved by a chief named Kabbau, who took him away from Manoba to his own village on the mainland, treating him as his adopted son.

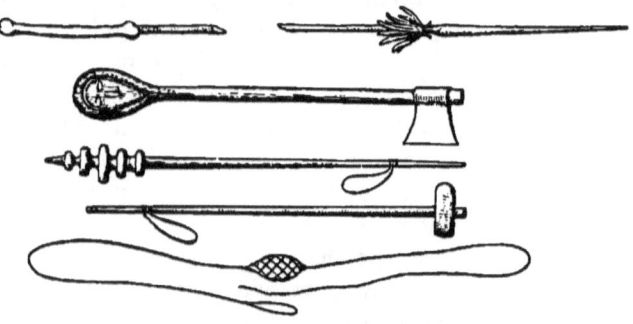

WEAPONS, NEW HEBRIDES.

Renton lived with Kabbau nearly eight years. During that time a vessel was wrecked, or seized, at Manoba I. He heard reports of a white man living on that islet, and subsequently of his rescue by a passing vessel—the crew of which never dreamed that another white man, requiring like assistance, was dwelling only seven or eight miles away.

At last the *Bobtail Nag* hove in sight. However, there was a strong party in the village opposed to Renton's going. So, it was only after considerable delay and difficulty that he was able to send a short message to Captain Murray. This he scrawled with some native pigment on a piece of wood—a fragment of an old canoe.

By means of what seemed to the natives valuable presents, Captain Murray effected his release. The piece of wood with Renton's message on it is still preserved in the Brisbane Museum. He himself entered the Queensland Government service as a G.A. in the labour trade, serving in which capacity he was killed at Aoba I. in 1878.

When I was in Maryborough, waiting for a licence to sail on a third recruiting voyage, news arrived of the wreck of the labour schooner *Lyttona*—Captain Rosengren, Mr. Alliott, G.A., with forty-five recruits—at Hada Bay, on the north-west coast of Christoval I., one of the Solomon group. All hands were saved, arriving at Brisbane in December.

CHAPTER IV.

THIRD VOYAGE OF THE *STANLEY*, 1875-6.

Masters and recruiters—Head-money—I sail from Maryborough—Ashore on a mud-bank—Aneiteum I.—Missionary rule—Consequences of it—Decrease of population—Causes—Boatmen—Tanna I.—We are fired at—The hurricane season — Cyclones—A determined recruit—Calms—Effects of the heat—Women bolting—An ugly crowd—Champion Bay—A skirmish—A coward on board—A hot corner—Mallicolo I.—Assemblage of natives—Young recruits—" Train up the child"—A contrast—Tommy's I.—The chief Aipanpan—Conical heads—How they are shaped—Examining a child—Our G.A. frightens the women—His exterior man—His height measured—Gods or sign-posts?—Discharging boatmen—An angry missionary—Variable currents—The Queensland public and Kanaka labour—Magisterial inquiry—" You did wrong, sir!"—Party politics and native wrongs.

DURING my two previous recruiting voyages I had seldom taken part in the actual work of the boats between the shore and the ship. I did sometimes leave the ship, but only from curiosity, or to supervise the engagement of recruits by the G.A. before I received them on board. During the first voyage I had acted as sailing master only; while on the second, I was the legal recruiter, having, before we sailed, signed a bond for £500, with one surety, under the provisions of the Imperial " Kidnapping Act," 1872. This I did on every succeeding voyage I undertook in the Queensland Polynesian labour trade.

At that period it was customary for the ship-owner to pay the master, in addition to his regular monthly wages, a small sum per head for all recruits brought to Queensland and passed as fit for service by the medical inspector. On my second voyage I had received five shillings for each recruit, which I divided with the mate, as he did the boating work and engaged the recruits on shore.

The practice of paying "head-money" was stopped 10th March, 1884, by the "Act to Amend the Pacific Island Labourers' Act of 1880," and "the prosecution of the duties of 'recruiter' by the master" was prohibited by the "Additional Regulations" of June, 1887.

On the two following voyages, the particulars of which I am about to relate, I had a mate with no previous experience of South Sea Islanders. I engaged him solely because he was a sober man, a rarity then in the labour trade. Consequently, I was obliged "to do my own recruiting," as we termed it, leaving the vessel in his charge during my absences ashore.

I think the Queensland Government need not have legislated against "head-money." No doubt it seemed likely to induce evil practices, such as kidnapping; but, on the other hand, good wages and competition would be just as likely to stimulate enterprise in precisely the same way. When "head-money" was abolished, masters' wages—formerly £15 to £20 per month—at once rose to £28 and £35, whilst recruiters got £4 to £5 per month over and above their ordinary wages.

I sailed from Maryborough on Dec. 20, this time without any cabin passengers. My former G.A. was gone too, and another had been appointed in his place. Christmas Day was spent at anchor at the White Cliffs. The day after that we weighed anchor and stood for Fraser I. Straits and Wide Bay bar. A breeze was blowing fresh from the northward, and it mattered little whether I went out by the northern or the southern channel.

I did not get out without an accident, however. Hardly an hour after the anchor was tripped, I called out "starboard" to the man at the wheel. But he happened to be "suffering a recovery" from a drunken spree over-night, and so put the helm hard-a-port, running the vessel on to a sandbank. There she lay for ten hours, part of which time we spent prowling about in the mud picking up oysters. Then, next morning, before I had been an hour under way, the wind suddenly failed me, and, nearly all that day, we roosted on another bank and ate more oysters.

A newspaper man in Maryborough heard of this, and for more than a week kept reporting "*Stanley* still ashore in Great Sandy Island (Fraser I.) Straits."

I finally got off, crossing Wide Bay bar next day. Nine days later we were at anchor in Inyang Harbour, on the south-west coast of Aneiteum I., the southernmost of the New Hebrides.

Aneiteum I. rises nearly 3,000 feet above sea-level. To judge from its appearance, it is not so fertile as the neighbouring island of Tanna. The inhabitants are all Christians, having been converted many years ago by Presbyterian missionaries, who, in fact, rule the whole island. No traders have ever settled on the main island, though a whaling-station, employing only mission boys, was then located at Annau-unse, a small boat-harbour on the north-western coast.

There used to be another whaling and trading station belonging to Captain Paddon, in the little Inyang I., which lies within the harbour. Paddon, when he removed his establishment to New Caledonia, abandoned this station to a Mr. Underwood, who had been one of his employés. I found the islet deserted, only the ruins of a house remaining on it. A tidal or storm-wave had flooded it a year or two previously, and had swept everything away.

The missionaries have had full and unopposed scope in governing this island; but whether the natives are any happier than they used to be, remains an open question. One thing is certain—they are dying out! The population is not so numerous by two-thirds, at least, as it was when the inhabitants were first converted to Christianity. Yet this decrease has not occurred in consequence of emigration; for the missionaries have not permitted that, except in very rare instances. Fighting has been put a stop to also, and I remember hearing a missionary say that murder had been unknown in the island for more than fifteen years previous to this time.

A similar decrease of population has occurred elsewhere, as in the Hawaiian Is. especially. There, in 1877-8, the native government was inviting Maoris from New Zealand to take up lands in the group, in the hope of thereby resuscitating the native population.

After more than twenty years' experience of South Sea Island people and races, I have come to a certain conclusion, which is, that missionary Christianity has operated to kill them off as surely, perhaps as quickly, as have traders' guns and rum. It has put the wolf into a cage, so to speak, where he has simply pined away, becoming a miserable, sneaking, pitiable wretch. Missionary teachings have also abolished club-law as an element of domestic life; but they have failed to inculcate the virtue of chastity in the minds of Polynesian women, and promiscuous intercourse between the sexes will suffice to destroy any race.

I visited Aneiteum for the purpose of obtaining boatmen, in which I succeeded. The resident missionaries of Inyang Harbour were absent during my stay there. I was therefore able to engage four young men who had learned how to "pull a good oar" in the whaling-boats. But, alas! instead of the plucky savages their fathers used to be, I found these fellows nervous and easily frightened. Luckily for me, on one occasion, their practice enabled them to pull well instinctively when running away. If I had been obliged to fight, they would have been of no use at all.

I anchored here on the northern side of the harbour, opposite the mission station. The harbour is a convenient one when "the trades" are blowing, but lies open to the north-west. Water is obtainable near the mission. When leaving the harbour to go northward, mariners should be careful of a dangerous outlying reef not far from it on the western coast.

There is a boat passage on the eastern side of the harbour, through which the master of a barque—either in ignorance of the proper entrance, or through stress of weather—once ran his vessel without injury, more by good luck than by good management.

From Aneiteum I proceeded to Port Resolution, Tanna I., where the first recruits were engaged. One of these ran away from his friends, shouting and jeering at them when he arrived on board, and found I was getting under way to leave the place. The "pay" was taken ashore by the G.A., who landed a white trader, who resided there, at the same time.

In the dusk, as the G.A. was pulling back to the ship, which was lying to outside, a shot, which just missed the boat, was fired from the missionary's garden, that gentleman being absent from home. The G.A. sent a bullet back in reply, continuing on his way to the ship. The north-eastern coast yielded us a few boys; but, as the hurricane season was now due, and the trade-wind becoming unsteady, I did not delay there long. Thence I made for Sandwich I. whilst I still had a fair wind, passing to the east of Erromanga. Making but a short stay at Vila, and then at Havannah Harbour, I ran down to Api with the last good trade-wind we were to have that season.

The months of January, February, and March are termed, in this part of the world, the "Hurricane Season." Some years later than this, however, I met with a hurricane in December, and they have been known to occur in November and in April. This year I was fortunate, though in place of hurricanes I had calms, or exceedingly light winds. The only hard blow I encountered was on our return, between Tanna and Aneiteum Is., when I think I must have been on the verge of a cyclone. These storms, rotating from north to east, from east to south, and so on round the compass, travel in a south-easterly direction, the centre generally passing westward of the New Hebrides.

On the west coast of Api I. we obtained a few recruits whilst anchored at Ibo. Further north we got another boy. The G.A. and I then judged it expedient to leave that place, thankful to get away safely with even one. The boy had been determined to go, showing fight when his friends attempted to drag him out of the boat; even snatching up a boatman's carbine, and threatening to shoot at them. After that the crowd retreated to the cover of the trees, some of the men waving their hands and shouting to us to go away—a request we quickly complied with, more through regard for our own skins than from any particular wish to please them.

The calms were now frequent and protracted. Sometimes the ship remained at anchor for two or three days for want of wind. Usually there was a light easterly breeze for a few hours in the evening. At other times we were becalmed out in the open sea, miles away from the land, broiling under the "Bengal Tiger" (the sun), and drifting slowly westward. This necessitated a long pull ashore for the boats during the sweltering heat of the forenoon. Towards evening the mate had to work the ship in our direction with the light evening breeze, to pick us up.

One morning, I remember, the G.A. was unable to accompany me—the only occasion on which he missed during the voyage—for the sun had affected his head the day before. I left the ship with the two boats, having a pull of several miles before I reached a long sandy beach, on the south coast of Ambrym. It was about 1 p.m.

when I reached the shore, and the ship was quite out of sight over the horizon. So great was the heat of the sun that a carbine, planted nearly upright in the bows, exploded as we were on our way, simply through the sun's heat upon the barrel. The surface of the ocean was like a sheet of glass, not even a catspaw to be seen.

When we reached the beach, a crowd of men, women, and children came round the boat, the former leaving their spears and other weapons at a distance. The usual noisy chaffering for yams, and so forth, ensued, and about a hundredweight was purchased, principally for beads and tobacco.

A boy then offered to engage, and a long knife, a "fantail" tomahawk, beads, tobacco and pipes having satisfied his friends, he got into my boat, from which he was transferred to the covering boat as it backed in to receive him.

A destitute French sailor, whom I had picked up at Vila Harbour, was this day steering the covering boat.

Two other natives—a man and his wife—also wished to come, but the man was forcibly removed from the beach by his countrymen, his wife following him. Just as I was shoving off, another boy made a rush into the water, grasped the gunwale, and, with my help, got into the boat. Some of the tribe wanted to prevent his leaving. However, after a lot of jabbering and noisy quarreling, they were over-ruled by the majority, and the boy remained where he was, the usual "pay" being given in return. I then pulled westward along the shore.

About a mile further on, we saw a couple of women trying to bolt; but their countrymen were too vigilant, and, after a smart race, they were caught and dragged back into the forest. This happened close to a rocky point crowned with trees, where I noticed a quantity of columnar basalt near the water's edge. Beyond this point a small bay, where there was a stony beach, opened to the north-west. A party of about a dozen men hailed us here, and I backed the boats in to interview them.

These fellows did not bear the friendly appearance of the crowd I had just left. No women or children were present, and nothing was offered for sale.

All had firearms—in a few cases, rifles—tomahawks and clubs. Their bearing was so suspicious that I got away as soon as I decently could, after a short conversation. Some of them, I noticed, were looking at the steersman of the other boat with anything but friendly eyes, and I heard the word " man-o-wee-wee " ("oui, oui," *i.e.* Frenchman) uttered several times. Others, during our stay there, kept within the shade of the trees, and did not come near us.

I then went about a mile further on, to a low point, beyond which was a low black rock, with a crowd of natives on it. They had lit a fire to make a smoke—which is the signal they wish to trade—as soon as they saw us. Pulling round the rock, into what is now called Champion Bay, I backed my boat to the beach, in order to begin trading.

The natives seemed friendly. About a dozen women, with bundles and baskets of yams, and several children, were squatted on the sand, under the thick bushes which overhung the beach, about twelve yards away.

I had been there about half an hour, and had bought all they had to sell, when a boy offered to engage with me, and, getting into the boat, sat down close to me in the stern-sheets.

I had just handed the knife and tomahawk to a man who was standing in the water, near the boat, and was giving him a handful of tobacco, when, suddenly, the rest of the party—both the men near us and the women on the beach—rushed away yelling, while half a dozen muskets exploded close at hand. Two bullets whizzed close to my ears, one on each side, others tearing up the water about the covering boat, splitting the blade of one of the oars. But it was the worst shooting I ever witnessed, for not a man of us was touched.

My first impulse was to shoot the man alongside, who was now cowering down in the water; but remembering the men I had spoken to in the other bay, I surmised it was they who had fired on us, not the party we had been trading with.

A vigorous thrust of the steering-oar sent the boat away from the beach, and my fellows laid back and pulled with a will.

A bit of fringe reef, with a break of the sea on it, here and there, was in the way. Luckily, there was just water

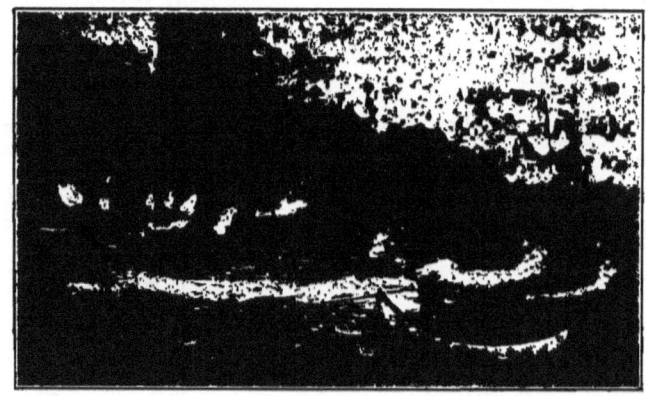

A HOT CORNER.

enough to enable the boat to graze over it. Meanwhile, the scoundrels kept banging away at us; but every shot missed, while I fired back at the puffs of smoke coming out of the bushes. As for my recruit, I had him safe between my legs.

Before we got out of range, I saw the bow oarsman of the other boat pull in his oar, topple over the bows into the water, and hang with his hands to the gunwale, almost stopping the boat, of course. At first I thought he was hit, but presently perceived he was only frightened. I was just putting my last cartridge into the breech of my rifle, and, instead of sending it ashore, it went so near Sam's head, that he was glad to scramble back into the boat and resume his work.

A light breeze from south-east had been blowing for the last hour, and had brought the schooner up within a mile of us. We were soon on board of her, glad to escape with nothing worse than a good scare.

I was afterwards informed by Captain McLeod, a Noumea trader, that these fellows had, for some months back, attacked every boat that came within reach of their bullets.

Next morning I anchored in Port Sandwich, Mallicolo I., and I thought that here also we were likely to get into trouble; for, all that day, bands of natives were seen walking along the beach towards the principal village. They appeared to be assembling there in large numbers, and, as they were all fully armed, painted, and feathered, and especially since no women seemed to accompany them, we surmised that they contemplated hostilities towards us. Perhaps we were mistaken; at any rate, no trouble occurred while we lay there, or during the next two days.

Soon after I had anchored, a canoe full of men and boys came alongside—on a tour of inspection, apparently. One of them, named Jack, a returned labourer from Fiji, who could speak a mixture of English and Fijian, explained that the men of the neighbouring tribes were assembling at a large village to hold a " sing-sing," or feast. This may have been the truth; but if it were, it is rather strange we never heard the drums or choruses whilst we lay there.

There proved to be little need to leave the ship. I made one cruise round the harbour, taking the boats some distance up the little river Erskine. On the second morning of our stay, our acquaintance, Jack, offered himself as a recruit, bringing two others with him. When I sailed I had nine youths on board, two or three of whom, I acknowledge, were legally too young to be recruited, being evidently under the age of sixteen. But, at that time, I knew there would be no difficulty in getting them passed as fit by the immigration agent at Maryborough, although I should not have cared to try it on in later years.

In order to train the Polynesian to work, and to make him of some use in the world, it is necessary to commence at an early age. At sixteen he is a man, with all his savage habits rooted in him. When middle-aged he cannot be altered, except for the worse. Take him away from savagery as a child, and you can make him what you like.

When we got back to port, these young boys were all engaged as house servants—an occupation they were allowed to fill, notwithstanding the outcry against it in Queensland. Three or four years afterwards, I met two of them in Maryborough. Their employer was staying at the Royal Hotel, on a visit, and had brought them to town with him. I failed to recognize them, when one bade me " Good-morning, Captain "—in pure English.

Instead of the dirty, pot-bellied little wretch, who climbed up on to the ship, with drops of water trickling off his greasy hide—for he had swum off to the ship to engage—grinning, yet scared at his own temerity, without a good point about him except his big bright eyes, I now saw a quiet, self-possessed, well-made Kanaka, wearing dark clean clothes. Had it not been for his brown skin, I should have taken him for a white man, and a decent-looking one at that. I am certain no mission-station on the islands ever produced a more trustworthy, civilized specimen of humanity than that lad. Nor was his case an exceptional one.

With a light wind from north-east, I beat out of Port Sandwich, rounded the Maskelyne Is., and worked the south coast of the island, anchoring off Arambagh, or " Tommy's Island." The veritable Tommy himself came on board, acting as interpreter, until I became acquainted with Aipanpan, a "big chief" residing some three miles east of Arambagh, on the main island near the large village of Assagh.

Aipanpan has since gone the way of nearly all flesh in these islands, having been knocked on the head by his neighbours and enemies. At this time he ruled supreme in the bight of the coast between the Maskelynes and Timben, the point of land just beyond Lennurr I. During the four or five days the ship lay here, this chief slept on board and accompanied the G.A. and myself

MALLICOLO ISLANDER

in our boats; Tommy, who had picked up a little English in Fiji, being the interpreter between us.

In Port Sandwich, as well as on this coast, both the G.A. and myself had remarked the extraordinary shape of most of the heads of men and boys. They had very retreating foreheads, the back part of the crown elongated in a conical form, and the eyes protruding. This extraordinary feature is attained by artificial means, adopted in infancy.

One evening we landed on Lennurr I., where there was then a small village of half a dozen mean huts. We were sitting on a log, talking, through our interpreter, with the few men living there, when a woman passed by with an infant. She held it on her hip—not in her arms like our women—supporting the child's head with one hand.

A bandage round the child's head excited my curiosity. I got up and walked towards her to examine it, thinking that the child had met with some injury.

The mother, however, scuttled off to the huts as I approached; and Aipanpan had to put on his "big chief" air, and order her to come back, before she would allow me to examine her child.

It was a male child, not a year old, probably only a few months. Around its head, just above the ears, several bands of plaited bark were tightly wrapped, each of them half an inch wide. These would effectually prevent the skull from enlarging laterally. The top of the head was covered with a black, semi-liquid substance, having the appearance of tar, being also protected by leaves. It was thus rendered so heavy that the child could not hold it up without its mother's assistance. The desired conical shape was already produced, and the child's eyeballs protruded as if a shake of its head would cause them to drop out.

The Mallicolo people consider this curious deformity beautiful; and, after all, how can we blame them? Our own women think a wasp-like waist the height of beauty, although it often carries with it a temper to match, if nothing worse.

The woman seemed to be in a terrible fright while I was examining her dirty offspring. I believe she thought I intended to eat it, and was glad to get it out of my clutches at last.

We visited Timben Point one day, and the village on it, engaging three men there. We landed under the shelter of the point, and were loitering near the boats, when a crowd of men, women, and children suddenly ran out from the bushes on to the beach. They evidently did not expect to come on us so quickly ; for, when they saw the G.A. standing on the beach, within a few yards of them, there was a yell and a general stampede into the bush at the sight of him.

He certainly was, even among white men, a remarkable object. He stood over six feet in height, possessed decidedly red hair, including a rather full beard and moustache, with a face burnt by the sun to the hue of a brick. His under lip had suffered terribly from the heat, and, to protect it, he had stuck a bit of brown paper on it, like a small shelf. He always wore spectacles. His rig consisted of a cloth cap adorned with a bunch of feathers, stuck upright on one side ; a flannel singlet, rather disreputable trousers, at the waist-belt of which were slung a revolver and a sheath-knife ; and, to complete all, a pair of immense blucher boots.

When our G.A. beamed on a mob of niggers with his spectacles, he generally created a sensation.

The natives here were all rather undersized. At Timben they wished to preserve some record of our giant. So they persuaded him to stand upright against a straight-stemmed tree, directing him to show how far he could stretch his arm up the trunk above him. This he complied with, and an active little warrior made a chop with a long-handled tomahawk at the place where the G.A.'s fingers extended to. Had not the latter dropped his hand quickly, he would certainly have been shortened by two or three inches.

At Tommy's Island, on the outskirts of the village, there were numerous carved wooden posts, planted in the ground in various places. They were made from the stem of the fern-tree, which is plentiful in these islands. I think they were intended to serve merely as ornaments, and were not "gods," as we at first supposed, for the natives treated them with little reverence, and were quite willing to part with a few to us, as they did, for tobacco and beads.

From Arambagh, or Tommy's I., it was my intention to have gone further along this coast, to South-west Bay. However, as the light northerly winds that should have prevailed then were wanting, clouds resting on the mountain summits of the island, and calms prevailing under the lee, I crossed over to Ambrym I. Taking good care to avoid the scene of my late skirmish, I worked back to the south, watering at Havannah Harbour as usual. On the south coast of Sandwich I. we picked up three recruits, one of them representing himself to be a mission teacher from Aruntabau village. I had now over ninety recruits on board, and thought it time to return to Queensland. So, with a light northerly

CARVED POSTS—ARAMBAGH I.

wind, I steered for Aneiteum, in order to land my four boatmen there.

There was one care off our minds this time, which had troubled me so much during the former voyages. Measles and dysentery, which had committed such havoc among Kanakas, in their own islands, as well as in Queensland, had apparently quite disappeared. When passing Tanna we ran before a lively gale from northward, with a confused sea and heavy rain squalls. Next day I was almost becalmed, about four miles south-west of Aneiteum, light airs occasionally coming from north-east. My four Aneiteum boatmen received their pay, £2 per month, in "trade," as they preferred to have it that way. Tobacco, pipes, calico, knives and axes were accordingly given to them in lieu of cash. They were landed, after a long pull, by the mate and G.A. The latter, on his return, informed me that the resident white missionary was at home, and that he was very angry because four of his promising flock had accepted service in a "slaver." He need not have been afraid of my visiting his island again, to hire boatmen. Those I got there were certainly good oarsmen, but in a "row" they were not worth their salt.

The passage home was a long and tedious one, as the wind was light and variable the whole way. Off the south-eastern extremity of New Caledonia I found the currents very variable, and, while delayed there for two or three days by calm weather, I always found myself at noon fifteen or twenty miles short of the position my "dead reckoning" placed me in—at one time north, at another south.

At this time the employment of Kanakas in Queensland was looked upon with great disfavour by a large portion of the Queensland public; particularly in the southern portion of the colony. In the north, where the white workmen could see that a cheap and servile labour was absolutely necessary for the cultivation of sugar-cane under a tropical sun, the traffic was viewed with more favour. Shopkeepers, also, in the northern parts, were favourable to it. For the islanders spent all their wages, to the uttermost farthing, before leaving the colony; preferring a chest full of calicoes and beads, tobacco and cutlery, to the hard cash which would be entirely useless to them in their islands. The mining population, however, was dead against it, being afraid that the Polynesian cheap labour might be introduced on the goldfields: a fear that political agitators on the opposition side took good care not to allay—quite the reverse!

By the "Polynesian Act" of 1880, the employment

of Polynesians in Queensland was restricted to certain branches of agriculture only ; so that, with the exception of the very few who had elected to remain in the colony prior to the passing of that Act, as house servants or in the mines, it became practically impossible to engage them for other purposes.

A day or two after our arrival at Maryborough, a preliminary inquiry was held by the police magistrate at his office, concerning the attack on us at Ambrym I. Nothing more came of it, however, although the P.M., who was an avowed Anti-Kanaka-ite, seemed to consider that I had done wrong in firing back at the natives.

"But you fired back, did you not?" asked he.

"Yes, I fired back to flurry them and spoil their shooting. It was done in self-defence."

"You did wrong, sir; you did wrong!" and he would have made trouble for me, I dare say, had he been able to do so.

Yet, apparently nobody had disapproved when "The Brisbane Courier," six weeks before our arrival in port, announced that, while ascending the Fly River, New Guinea, in the s.s. *Ellangowan*, in opposition to the wish of the inhabitants, Mr. Chester, a Queensland police magistrate, and the Rev. Mr. MacFarlane, a missionary, had fired on the natives, defeating and driving them away, and had broken up one of their canoes!

But then, neither of the political parties of the day were much interested in those proceedings :—

There was no money in it!

CHAPTER V.

FOURTH VOYAGE OF THE *STANLEY*, 1876.

I leave Maryborough in April—Tanna and Sandwich Is.—Meet with the Sibyl—Her luck—Pentecost I.—Daly—Beachmen and bushmen—Dragging the anchor—Batnapni—Espiritu Santo I.—Haiss and Mavir Is.—Malvat Bay—A cool customer—Engagement of a sorceress—Native names—A "coo-ee" from the beach—Easy recruiting—Tea and satisfaction—Runaways—The chase—Recaptured—Levatleluldum—Threatened hostilities—"All's well that ends well!"—Lammen I.—The chiefs prevent us from engaging men—Departure and return—A rival recruiter—My success and gratification—The Lady Darling *has no such luck !—Sandwich I.—Homeward—Recruits wonder at the lighthouse—The horse and his rider—Arrival in port—The* Dancing Wave—*The massacre at Gala—Escape of Broad—His rescue —* H.M.S. Barracouta *sent to inflict punishment—Action stopped by missionaries — Effects of a planter's bankruptcy — Polynesian claims and the Act of 1876—Murders elsewhere—A false report—Vessels in the labour trade.*

I SAILED from Maryborough again in the middle of April, having a new G.A. on board. I had a long passage across to the New Hebrides, beating up against head winds. At last, one evening, we sighted Amédée light, on the reefs outside the harbour of Noumea, the capital of New Caledonia. I ran thence with a strong current, setting to windward along and outside of the barrier reefs, which helped me considerably.

At Waisissa and at Itoa, Tanna I., some recruits joined; and then we ran down to Sandwich I., anchoring in Havannah Harbour, to obtain wood and water as well as boatmen. I engaged four men there in that capacity—natives of Protection I.

This port I left by the smaller ship's channel on the north-west. Just outside it I "spoke" and boarded the *Sibyl*, of Maryborough—Captain Taylor, Mr. Kirby G.A. She had "made a haul" at Pentecost I., and being now "full up," was returning home. While cruising off the north side of Ambrym I., the *Sibyl's* jib-boom had been carried away one night by a violent squall, and less than half an hour after that her main-boom had been badly injured. In order to repair damages properly, Captain Taylor had sought for an anchorage on the lee side of Pentecost I., and had had to sail some distance northward before he found one to suit his purpose.

Hitherto we had been in the habit of considering Pentecost I. as rather a poor place for recruiting. It appeared now, from the accounts of Taylor and Kirby, that the natives there were eager to leave home, instead of the contrary. In one anchorage the *Sibyl* had lain for three entire days. During the first, a few natives were spoken to on the beach; during the second, three men were engaged; while, on the third, thirty-six were received on board, making up the full complement the ship was licensed to carry.

Such news was too good to be neglected. So, as no recruiting work was possible that day—the sun then sinking fast—I hauled up to north-east and cleared the group by passing between Muna and Mataso Is. Next morning I lay off "Daly's" beach, on the southern extremity of Pentecost I. looking towards Ambrym I. Having got hold of "Daly" himself—a native who had adopted the name of a Sydney skipper with whom he had formerly sailed—I took him on board as interpreter, and anchored in South-West Bay.

The creek running into the head of the bay, near our anchorage, divided the territory of the beach tribe from that of another living up in the forest, styled by us "bushmen." Daly took care to keep on his own side of the creek when he landed; the twenty or thirty bushmen—who came down from the hills with some of their women about an hour after I anchored—keeping as carefully to theirs. In fact, Daly would not have ventured to have left the boat at all, had not a party of his own tribesmen appeared on the scene.

I obtained a couple of men here, though with difficulty. They were both bushmen, and could not be induced to go on board until Daly and his crowd had gone home, and until they were assured that the ship would sail early next morning.

I worked the southern coasts of Pentecost I. for a week, anchoring at Sile and Wannu, and obtained a fair number of recruits. Still, I did not come in for such luck as the *Sibyl's* people had done.

One afternoon I dropped anchor on a projecting ledge of shore-reef—with four fathoms of water, but barely room to swing—a little south of Batnapni Bluff, near the village of Verramatmat. There I recruited two women. At night the trade-wind came off the high land in heavy gusts; and about 10 p.m. the ship quietly dragged her anchor off the coral shelf, and went to sea of her own accord. Luckily, I chanced to come on deck, and discovered the state of affairs before worse happened. For the anchor watch, a thick-headed German, was whistling up and down the deck, blissfully unconscious of it all.

Next morning I anchored in Batnapni Bay, soon discovering from the natives that this was Taylor's late anchorage. But I had not luck equal to his. Too many men had gone away already, so the chiefs thought. In consequence, I had to content myself with mere gleanings.

I then went over to Espiritu Santo I., seeking an anchorage on the lee side of Tetuba I., but without avail. At last I espied a sunken ledge of the shore-reef jutting out, on which I let go the anchor, keeping the topsail sheeted home, to prevent the ship from swinging shorewards.

I worked this islet, but obtained only two men, and they were runaways. So in the evening I weighed anchor again, and stood out to sea, as it was not a safe place to lie in. The next three weeks were spent on the eastern coast, only half a dozen more boys being recruited there.

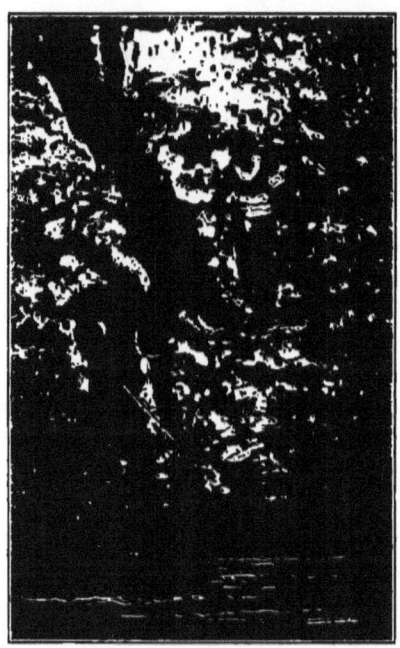

SHOOTING FISH—ESPIRITU SANTO I.

The coast of Espiritu Santo I. is composed entirely of coral and coral rock. This becomes elevated to the north of the point off which lies Tetuba, a small islet, only a few feet above sea-level. The same formation underlies the soil for some miles back into the interior, until it meets the volcanic tufa of the mountains.

From Tetuba I sailed northward, past a low promontory forming a large bay open to the same quarter.

Here there is a native village, called Benkula. The two large islets, Haiss and Mavir, lie parallel to the coast, north of Benkula Point; and another very small one, bearing only a few trees, lies a mile or so beyond Mavir. There appears to be very deep water all round, except between this little islet and Mavir.

I spent three weeks on this coast, and recruited only eight men. So small a number was due, doubtless, to the very wet weather we experienced, which, together with unsteady winds, and a heavy swell setting in on the coast, obliged us to keep the vessel a good distance away from the shore when the boats were at work. The natives have much more confidence in us when the vessel is close at hand, especially if she is anchored.

But I was not done with Pentecost I. yet. Recollections of the thirty-six men recruited in one day by the *Sibyl* still tempted me. So, having tried Lathi I. with no success, I hauled up one evening, on the starboard tack, and made a "long board" all night to north-east. Next forenoon I tacked, as the trade-wind generally veers to east in the daytime, and to south at night, and so fetched the northern coast of Aurora I. I watered at Narovorovo, keeping a bright look-out for the hostile villagers at the far end of the northern beach. Thence working south, I anchored in Malvat Bay for the first time. There I lay for two nights, and was fairly successful.

The first recruit engaged at this place assumed a very independent manner, though he was so young a lad that I much doubt if he was quite as old as the statute required. I had pulled into the bay, chaffered with a mob of natives, taken soundings with the lead, and was pulling out again to bring the ship in to an anchorage, when this youngster paddled up to us. He began by asking a few questions about the ship, her destination, and so forth, and was answered by a native of Pentecost, who was acting as interpreter for me. Then he followed us to the ship, making his cockle-shell of a canoe fast to one of the boats. Coming on board with us, he calmly proceeded to survey the whole ship, examining everything on deck and below. Having concluded these investigations, apparently to his satisfaction, he condescended to signify that it was his intention to accompany me. The interpreter soon explained the agreement he was to enter into, and his name was then put upon the list. His friends made no objection subsequently. They received the "pay" without a word, not even saying good-bye to him, as far as one could see. The boy made friends with Puck, who had no objection to employ him as an assistant, notwithstanding that they could converse only by signs.

This visit to Pentecost I. proved more successful than my former one. I engaged fully thirty recruits there in all. Among them was a woman that the tribe seemed quite anxious to get rid of, but for what reason I was unable to discover at the time. She was thin, certainly, but she was young and in good health. Yet she seemed just as eager to depart as was her tribe to get the "pay" and be well rid of her. I subsequently ascertained that she was supposed to be a witch, and had been suspected of causing the death of a chief of her village. If I had not accepted her, in all probability she would have been killed. She rejoiced in the euphonious name of Mettawamamakan, which made an elegant addition to our recruit list.

On this island, nine out of every ten women's names are prefixed by the word Metta, while nineteen out of twenty men's names begin with Tari or Tabbi.

While we lay at Batnapni, there was an appearance of an approaching shift of wind one afternoon. I therefore deemed it safest to get under way and dodge about all night, as the anchorage was close to the shore, and was so confined that it would have been a difficult matter to have got out of it in the dark, with a foul wind. Accordingly, towards sundown, the chain was hove short.

As the hands were making sail, a "coo-ee" sounded from the shore. This cry, the well-known Australian signal, has been introduced into the islands by returned labourers. Most of the natives who had been on the beach all day, had now gone home to the hills; and, when I backed the boat in, I found only three grown men and two small boys. One of the former wished to engage as a recruit, so the interpreter discovered and informed me.

Preliminaries were quickly adjusted. The new recruit got into the boat, and the "pay," consisting of a knife, a tomahawk, etc., was handed to the others on shore. I then made signs to a second man, inviting him to accompany us also. To my surprise he quietly handed his tomahawk over to the remaining fellow, and stepped into the boat. Another knife, tomahawk, etc., were passed out.

Still the third man lingered at the boat's stern, the boys keeping a few yards off.

"You come too," I said to him, which was duly interpreted.

Very quickly he turned round, dumped the pay received for the first two at the boys' feet, returned to the boat, got in and sat down.

The lads were too young for recruits, even at that time; so I contentedly paid for the last man, and pulled quickly off, fearing lest my recruits should change their minds.

"By Jove!" I said to myself, "this is easy work. If it was all like this, I'd depopulate the group, and then come back and shift the islands themselves!"

Now it appears that these three gentlemen had no real intention of going to Queensland at all. However, they *did* go, as we shall see.

As soon as we got on board they were examined by the G.A., and their names—Kaipan was one of them, I think—were put on the list of recruits.

Sail having been made during my absence, and the anchor having been heaved up and secured, the boat was hoisted in, and the ship allowed to drift off the land with her topsail aback and stay-foresail to windward. Meanwhile we took our evening meal, which consisted of dinner and tea rolled into one. We fared very well in those little "hookers"; far better than in any other sailing ships, big or little, that I have been aboard of.

As for the new recruits, they were all right, apparently. With lighted pipes in their mouths, their blankets over their arms or round their shoulders, they lounged against the rail for awhile, and then disappeared—at any rate, two of them did—down the main hatchway.

The sky was clouded over, and the land, two miles away, appeared black and close to us. As the ship was only drifting broadside on, and making no headway, I fancy they must have thought we were still at anchor, and that we were not three hundred yards from the shore.

We had taken our meal on deck, as we usually did in fair weather, the flat-topped skylight serving for a table. Having finished, we were just filling our pipes for a comfortable smoke, when suddenly, borne on the light wind off the land, there came a sharp yell, followed by other broken cries.

"Runaways swimming off!" sung out some one forward.

Down went the port boat with a rattle and splash, the crew tumbling into her as she descended. After them I went, delighted at the idea of picking up half a dozen recruits, perhaps.

The cries continued, as we pulled lustily in the direction they seemed to come from. Presently we found—not the fugitives from the shore we had expected to see—but a runaway from the ship, one of the three just enlisted, thoroughly spent with his long swim. When I grasped his wool under the boat's counter, the water actually bubbled in his throat as he tried to cry out ; and, so great was the way on the boat, that he nearly dragged me overboard, grabbing at my arm with both hands as energetically as I did at his wool.

I soon had him in the boat, where he laid himself down to recover. The other boat had followed me, and, for a time, we cruised round about, and in towards the land, expecting that his two companions must have bolted likewise. Then we listened awhile, for it was now nearly calm ; but nothing was to be heard. As for *seeing* anything, it was as dark "as the inside of a cow."

When tired of this, we pulled back to the ship, and had the satisfaction of finding the other two worthies stowed away below. They seemed to have expected violence, for one of them was armed with a rusty bayonet which he had found "between decks," while the other had secured a billet of firewood. These weapons I took away from them, and then left them to sleep off their ill humour, placing sentinels over both the fore and the main hatches to prevent any further attempt at evasion.

This little dodge of first getting " trade," and then deserting, was often tried on, too frequently proving successful.

Less than a mile south of Bulhagh Bluff there is a precipitous hill, below which extends a narrow strip of boulder-strewn beach, bearing the name of Levatleluldum. There some of us had a narrow escape from death by poisoned arrows, as I shall now relate.

On this beach, one fine morning, a crowd of thirty or forty men, headed by a grey-headed but active old chief, had assembled near my boat. They were all armed with spears, clubs, and poisoned arrows. Some women stood watching us, at a little distance from the water. I perceived that several boys were inclined to enlist, but were rather frightened about it ; so of course I tried to do my level best to encourage and persuade them.

The boat was lying with her iron-shod keel grating and

grinding on the shingle, while the natives were gathered round me, trading away their yams and curios. The

IN A TIGHT PLACE.

G. A. was sitting in the stern-sheets beside me, and the crew were all in their places.

Suddenly, without a word of warning, every savage

in the group before me drew himself up and stood fixed and motionless, with spear poised or bow stretched, the whole array of points levelled straight at me. My heart seemed to jump up into my throat, and all the hair I had left on the top of my head fairly bristled up.

There was no getting out of it this time, and I must acknowledge I was in a "blue funk."

Involuntarily my hand went up, palm from me, as a sign of peace. I raised a smile on my countenance—a pitiful one, I do not doubt—as I gasped out, " You darned fool! What for you want to fight ? "

The old chief and several of his men could understand a little English.

I became aware, then, that the G.A. was drawing his rifle out of the locker at my feet; so I just put my foot on it to prevent him from exposing it. I also felt that the boat's crew had got hold of their guns. I think I caught sight of the stroke oarsman's barrel. Putting my other hand behind me, I privately motioned to them to lay the guns down. This they did, and presently the menacing spears and arrows were slowly lowered, though still held ready for instant action.

After a little the old chief descended from a boulder on which he had been standing, a few yards off, and, coming close to the boat, shook hands with me and made peace again.

This demonstration on the part of the natives had been occasioned by my men, who had handled their guns in consequence of seeing a native, near me, snatch a small bag of tobacco out of the stern-sheets, and bolt into the bush with it.

The chief was very angry, or, at any rate, pretended he was. He sent after the thief, obliging him to restore the bag. Half of its contents had been abstracted, however; but the reader may be assured I made no further inquiries about it; for we were overmatched, and were decidedly in a tight place.

Hardly had this matter been settled, when three men made a rush into the boat. For a few moments, I thought the threatened attack upon us had really begun. I was tumbled over the G.A., momently expecting to feel a tomahawk or a spear strike me. When I had picked myself up, I found the rush had been made by three would-be recruits, whose friends were unwilling they should go. The old chief, however, consented to permit of their departure; so I handed over the "pay," and thankfully returned to the ship.

Leaving Pentecost I., I next weathered Ambrym I. There I made no call, as the natives along the western coast were disposed to be hostile at that time. I paid a passing visit to Paama I., going on thence to Api I.

Rather late one evening, I pulled in to Lammen islet, which lies off Duane, the north-western corner of Api I. There I engaged three men, and might have got more; but, unfortunately, I had not a sufficient number of muskets in the boat wherewith to "pay" for them. I therefore pulled back to the ship, taking my three recruits on board, and then returned to the islet with the required muskets. It was dark by the time I got there. While I was making the trip to and fro, the elders of the village were informed of the departure of the three men I had enlisted, disapproving of which they determined to spoil my little game.

I pulled over the fringing reef, into a bight on the south-eastern coast of the islet—the tide being well up—and, getting close to the beach, held on to some overhanging branches. While in that position we could hear a mob of natives squabbling on the shore not far off. Presently, one of the boatmen, a Paama man, told me he overheard some of them proposing to fire into the boat, so as to prevent further recruiting. Had they done so, they would have had a fair shot at us out in the open, whilst we could see nothing of them, hidden as they were by the shadow of the trees. So, as quietly as possible, we pulled away, expecting a volley every instant. However, we got back to the ship without that little treat, much to our satisfaction.

Early next morning I took the ship close into the land, and then pulled round the islet again, but without getting a single man. The chiefs and old men walked round the shore, following the course of our boats, driving back all who showed any inclination to join us. At last, after both parties were pretty well tired of this work, it became evident that mischief would result, if I persisted in my attempts. The chiefs called out to me, "Go away!" menacing us with their guns and spears. So I pulled back to the ship, hoisted in the boats, and ran down to windward, making for the Foreland.

An hour later a sail appeared in the south, bearing down upon us. Thinking that the sight of another vessel might deter the natives from attempting actual hostilities, I went about and returned to Lammen, where I hove to close under the lee of the islet.

I suppose that after seeing the *Stanley* depart, the chiefs had relaxed their vigilance. For, when I backed the topsail, three canoes went across from the islet to the mainland. As soon as we were observed, a tremendous yelling and shouting arose on the islet; several warriors, waving spears and tomahawks, rushed out from the trees on to the shallow shore-reefs, splashing about and cutting all sorts of capers in their excitement.

The two foremost canoes were filled with women, probably going to their plantations on the main island; but the third and hindermost was manned solely by nine young fellows, who, as it turned out, desired to join me. It had been their intention to cross to the main island, on pretence of guarding the women, and then to follow us along the coast, hoping that we should see and take them off before they got upon hostile territory.

The chiefs and their partisans on the shores of Lammen shouted and signalled to the canoe people to come back. However, the two foremost canoes—which were already near the Api side of the channel—were paddled on faster to that shore, where the women landed, hauled up the canoes, and disappeared into the forest. The third crew turned about and paddled in our direction.

The other schooner I mentioned as coming up from the south had now drawn near. Down went my boats, therefore, and I had the pleasing satisfaction of securing nine able-bodied recruits, right under the bows of the *Lady Darling*, of Brisbane. Having shipped them, I proceeded to pay a visit to the new-comer. Her boats were already off, drawing the coast of the islet. However, they speedily returned, the *Darling's* recruiter reporting that the natives had threatened to fire at him.

No wonder! He ought to have known that the Lammen chiefs would be furious at my snapping up a lot of their young men, as he had seen me do. I know I should not have cared to have shown myself on that islet for at least a month to come.

I watered the ship, for the last time on this voyage, at Ibo, Sandwich I. I did not go into Havannah Harbour, merely anchoring off the mouth of the North-west Passage, where I landed my Lorss boatmen, also cutting firewood—tough, twisty she-oak. Thence I sailed for Maryborough, passing north of New Caledonia, and south of the Bampton Reefs.

The revolving light on Sandy Cape, the northern extremity of Fraser I., puzzled the recruits a good deal. We were beating into the bay one night, after rounding the point of Breaksea Spit, when I happened to go forward. A dozen of our recruits were standing about, watching the distant light as it blazed out, and then disappeared for a short while, every two minutes. At last one of them—who had a fair knowledge of English, though he had never visited the colonies—turned, and seeing me, remarked, "My word, Cappen, that feller break plenty match!" I suppose he thought the lighthouse keeper extinguished and relit the lamp every time it revolved.

But his astonishment was greater, when, going up the river Mary, we came round a bend, and saw two young colonials at work breaking in a young horse. One was holding the horse's head, the other being in the saddle, as we came in sight. The first let go his hold, and away went the brute, kicking and bucking all across the paddock. Suddenly, girths and surcingle gave way, and off came the rider on to the ground, with the saddle between his legs. "Cappen! Cappen! he broke!" roared out our "new chum." He must have thought horse and man were one animal.

Previous to my arrival at Maryborough, at the end of July, the schooner *Dancing Wave* had come into Sydney harbour in charge of Mr. Davis, formerly mate of the barque *Sydney*. The *Dancing Wave* had sailed from Sydney in June, commanded by Captain Harrison, her mate being James Dare, an old friend of mine, and her crew consisting of four A.B.'s. Her ultimate destination was Torres Straits, to collect pearl-shell. For the work of collecting, a gang of South Sea Islanders was indispensable; and, in order to engage them, Captain Harrison went to the Solomon Is., anchoring off Gala, one of the Florida Is. A native interpreter, named Freeman, had been engaged at Hada Bay, San Christoval I.

While the ship lay at Gala, some seventy natives offered their services, and came on board. Suddenly, without warning, every man, of the ship's company, except one, was struck down and killed. Broad, the seaman who alone escaped death, shot two or three of the savages, and then concealed himself in the cabin. After a while the murderers left the ship, leaving some nine or ten natives of Guadalcanar I. on board. Broad then came on deck, thinking all were gone; but, seeing the Guadalcanar men, and being frenzied with fear, jumped into the sea. Harry, a Guadalcanar man, called him back, and got him on board again. The cable was slipped, Broad and the Guadalcanar men getting the vessel away, with the intention of going to Savo I., where a white trader was then residing. Broad soon discovered that Harry and his companions were just as treacherous as the Florida men. He therefore seized an opportunity of escaping from the schooner in a small boat, during a violent squall. Fortunately, he was rescued by Captain Woodhouse, of the *Sydney* barque, at Savo. The *Sydney* went in search of the *Dancing Wave*, retaking her off Wanderer's Bay, Guadalcanar I. H.M.S. *Barracouta*, Captain Stevens, was subsequently sent to the Florida Is. to apprehend or punish the murderers. Owing to missionary interference, and to Exeter Hall influence, however, she left again without doing anything. Captain Stevens had made an appointment with Ferguson—the well-known and respected trader—to meet him there, but did not wait for him. When Ferguson reached Gala, he was terribly disgusted to find Stevens gone, by whose want of action more harm than good was likely to result, the perpetrators of the massacre getting off scot-free.

I subsequently heard, from natives who were concerned in it, the reason why this massacre occurred. It appears that a number of natives of Gala had been employed on a Queensland plantation, the owner of which was in difficulties. When their term of service had nearly expired, and their wages and passage-money were about to become due, the mortgagees of the estate—a well-known Brisbane firm—took possession of it, and repudiated any liability for the wages, etc. Such was the state of the law respecting South Sea Island labour, at that time, that the boys had no legal claim on the estate; and, although such a proceeding was certain to result in outrage and murder, they were actually sent home by the ministry of that day without receiving a farthing of their hard-earned wages.

I am bound to add, however, on reliable authority, that the bill to amend the Polynesian Act—which, amongst other items, gives the Polynesian a claim on the estate for his wages and passage home—was in print before the news of the *Dancing Wave* massacre arrived.

Also, just before my arrival, news came of the murder of Captain Anderson, of the schooner *Lucy and Adelaide*, in St. Bartholomew I., New Hebrides, on the 25th of June, 1876. I had met Anderson and his G.A., Mr. McGavin, at Havannah Harbour, during my late voyage. The *Lucy and Adelaide* had put in there to repair damages to her foremast.

Close on the heels of this ill news came more of a similar sort. Luckily, it turned out to be a false report this time.

Mr. Layard, consul at Noumea, New Caledonia, sent word to Sydney that the crew of the labour schooner *May Queen*—Captain Kilgour, Mr. Lynde G.A.—had been cut off by the natives at Tanna I.

As soon as this news was received in Brisbane, a well-known tradesman, a rabid opponent of the Polynesian labour trade, exposed to view a portrait of Kilgour as the "captain of the slaver" killed in Tanna. Unfortunately for the shopkeeper, however, the *May Queen*, with Kilgour and Lynde safe on board, arrived at Brisbane a day or two after. Then the skipper made things rather warm for that tradesman, who had paid no attention to the principle—*De mortuis nil nisi bonum*.

At this time, the number of vessels employed in the labour trade amounted to less than a dozen, all rigged as schooners or brigantines, and ranging from 80 to 140 tons register. I remember the names *Stanley, Sibyl, Chance, Lady Darling, May Queen, Isabella, Bobtail Nag, Lucy and Adelaide,* and *Flora*. The *Jason* had been burnt, the *Lyttona* wrecked, and the *Native Lass* condemned, since I had engaged in the trade.

CHAPTER VI.

FIFTH VOYAGE OF THE *STANLEY*, 1876.

I sail in August—Worgus, Tanna I.—Natives tell us a yarn—Recruiting with "liquor"—Muna I.—Story of Naumeta—He engages with me—His treatment by the missionary—The reverend gentleman gives chase—He comes on board—He demands a surrender—" Is the boy your slave?"—I am accused of housebreaking—"Get out of the ship!"—Complaint to the Government—Result—Inspection at Maryborough —Puck's three fingers—The inspector's report—Letter from a member of the committee—Some Government regulations —Comments upon them—Order to discharge cabin-boys—The inspector's revenge.

AFTER lying three weeks in harbour, waiting for the licences, I sailed again in the *Stanley*, towards the middle of August. The same G.A. who was with me before accompanied me again, but I had a different mate, whom I had engaged to fill the office of recruiter, and to do the boating work, as well as his regular duties on board.

The work of recruiting commenced at Tanna I., as on previous occasions; but there was only one circumstance connected with our stay there which is worth recording.

At Worgus Point we were informed by the natives that a schooner had been there two or three weeks previously. Her captain, they said, had landed, gone to the village, and there treated all of them to "plenty grog." By this means he had induced a number of men to go on board his vessel; and, of these, not all had returned to the shore. The names of the captain and of the vessel were told us; but as the first is now dead, and as the latter was afterwards wrecked, and is also no more, I see no use in naming either. Besides which, I have one good reason for doubting this story. It was notorious among us that the captain in question never had any grog on board his vessel, whilst at the islands. Not that he was a teetotaler; quite the contrary. But it was his practice to drink up all the liquor he was allowed to take out of Maryborough, on each voyage, before he even got as far as the New Hebrides. Again, too, I am certain that the G.A. who accompanied him was not the man to have sanctioned such a proceeding as that which was related to us.

I do not like to allude to this report; but as I desire to tell all I know about the trade—against as well as in favour of it—I feel bound to mention the matter. Moreover, I can honestly avouch that this was the only instance of such a practice being resorted to, for the purpose of obtaining recruits, that I ever heard of.

After watering at Havannah Harbour, I went northward. And now I must refer to a circumstance which had occurred on a previous voyage—either my third or fourth—I cannot recollect precisely which. I had then called at the small island of Muna (Three Hills I.). There, a youth named Naumeta had offered himself as a recruit. I declined to take him on that occasion, for two reasons. First, he was not a native of Muna, but of Aneiteum; and, second, he was in the employment of a missionary, at Muna. He told me a pitiful story of the treatment he had received from his employer. Calling at this island again, on the present voyage, the lad once more turned up, with what result I will now go on to relate.

I hove to off the south-eastern coast of Muna I., in what was known to us as "The Sound," on the shore of which was the mission station. The G.A. and mate, having been on shore, brought off this boy with them. The former was of opinion that the Government would make no objection to his being engaged as a recruit, since he was under no agreement now to remain with the missionary, his term of service having expired previous to our former visit.

On my questioning Naumeta, who was able to speak a little English, he told me that sixteen or seventeen months before he had been engaged in Aneiteum, his native island. He was to accompany the missionary to Muna, and act as a house servant. His term of service was not to exceed twelve months; and, at the expiration of that time, he was to be paid—how, I could not ascertain—and to be sent home in the mission schooner, free of charge. He said he had told the missionary he wished to go home; and, latterly, that he would like to engage as a labourer and go to Queensland. Since he had preferred the first request, the mission schooner had been to Muna twice, but he had been refused a passage home in her. He also stated that he could not get any payment for the services he had rendered.

Now, it was my business to obtain recruits as quickly as possible, by lawful means. It was not my business, nor was it my desire, to assist missionaries, or any one else, in deluding natives and keeping them in servitude when they had a right to leave it if they wished. So I explained the nature of our agreement to Naumeta, and put his name on my recruit list. Then, with his pipe, tobacco, and blanket, he dived down the main hatch out of sight. For, just then, we could see the missionary coming off to the ship in his boat, which two of his teachers were rapidly pulling alongside.

Thinking that very few words would settle this matter, as far as the reverend gentleman was concerned, I went to the gangway to receive him. In fact, I wished to have as little conversation with him as was possible under the circumstances, experience having taught me that some of these holy men—of the Presbyterian denomination especially—are rather disposed to exaggerate, to use a mild term, when recounting the details of such incidents as the present one. I told my visitor as much, too, before we parted.

He wasted no words on any preliminary greeting, as he came over the gangway.

"You hae gettin' a boy o' mine aboarrd here," said he, in an accent unmistakably Scottish.

"A boy of *yours!* Is the boy your slave, then?" I retorted.

"No, he's no ma slave, but he's ma sairvant, an' a want him ashore."

Then I said the boy had engaged himself to accompany me to Queensland, his term of service with my visitor having expired some time since. I also recounted the lad's story, which the other acknowledged was correct, even to the non-payment of his wages. For all that, he still stuck to his demand that I should send Naumeta back to the shore, threatening to appeal to the first ship of war which came that way.

Now it so happened that I had just left one of H.M. ships at anchor in Havannah Harbour. Therefore, I at once offered to await her arrival, or that of any of her officers, if he chose to communicate with her. He would have had to traverse only six or seven miles of smooth water in order to have reached her. This proposal, as I anticipated, he declined to accept. Leaving the gangway, he then walked to windward, and, planting himself against the rail on the weather quarter, poured out a string of mild abuse against "labour" seekers in general and myself in particular. He wound up his tirade with a personal accusation; to wit, that I had "bruk into Mr. Paton's hoose in Aniwa I."[1]

Up to this point I had kept my temper, having been particularly careful not to make use of any "cuss" words. Now the cork came right out, and I bubbled over.

"Did Paton tell you I broke into his house?" roared I.

"Yes, he did."

"Then, next time you see him, you can tell him he's a d——d liar!"

[1] See chap. i.

"A didna come on boarrd here to have that language addressed to me," said he.

"No, you didn't, I dare say; and you won't get any more. For if you don't get out of the ship at once, I'll bundle you out quicker than you came."

Whereat my gentleman thought it best to depart, without more ado.

I have omitted one portion of our conversation, however. In the course of it, I taxed him with not having paid the boy his wages. In reply, he said he had not done so because suitable goods—calicoes, etc.—had not been obtainable on board the *Dayspring*—the mission schooner—when she last visited Muna. I offered to sell him calico there and then, on board the *Stanley*, so that he could pay his debt; and, furthermore, to charge him no more than his own price. This proposition he declined.

This missionary afterwards laid a formal complaint before the Queensland Government, alleging that I had taken away *his servant*. Some three years later, I ascertained that a certain police magistrate had received instructions from the Government to examine the boy in regard to the manner of his engagement.

The P.M. accordingly visited the house of Naumeta's employer, near Bundaberg. The gentleman himself happened to be absent from home at the time; but the servant who received the official in his place was no other than Naumeta. Nothing more came of it.

I cannot help thinking, however, that if one of *us* had engaged a Polynesian for twelve months, had kept him sixteen, and even then had never paid him his wages, he might have seen the inside of a prison, and assuredly would have done so, if a missionary had been the prosecutor.

The remainder of this cruise was, I think, uneventful. The islands that supplied me with the greater number of my ninety-odd recruits were Marlo and Pentecost.

We arrived at Maryborough about November 20th.

As soon as the ship had been passed by the medical inspector, the immigration agent of the port set to work to examine each recruit, inquiring into the manner of his engagement, and the number of years he had agreed to serve in Queensland. Of course a good deal of the questioning was effected through interpreters.

In order to ascertain the number of years each recruit contracted to serve, he directed them to hold up their fingers. Now, if indicating numbers, a Kanaka turns *down* his fingers, instead of holding *up* the number he wishes to express. Ignorant of this, the immigration agent fancied he had discovered another "outrage," when my boys turned *down* three fingers, leaving only two upright.

Little Puck was standing by at the time, and thought he must shove *his* oar in. So he perched himself on the end of the winch, amidships, in which position he was hidden from the inspector, who was stationed abaft of the deck-house. There he commenced to instruct the recruits, who were waiting their turn, how to hold their fingers.

About a score had passed, when, suddenly, a long, lanky Pentecost man came round the house, holding up three fingers all ready, without waiting to be questioned. Up jumped the inspector, and there, behind the first man, he saw a string of others, each of them holding up three fingers, as though it was some sort of ceremony. Finally, his eye fell on Puck, amidships, industriously demonstrating to the crowd.

There was a roar of laughter among the ship's company and others present. But the great man did not join in it. He felt insulted. It was a "put up" thing! I had set the boy on to incite the recruits into deceiving him. And so forth. By degrees things were explained, and he condescended to let us appease his wrath. Puck was ordered to desist; and the examination ended satisfactorily.

This gentleman had lately volunteered a report to the Queensland Government on the Polynesian labour-traffic; which afforded then, and for many years after, one of the leading questions among politicians in the colony. The result of this report, which had been deemed of sufficient importance to warrant the appointment of a "Polynesian Labour Select Committee," to inquire into the charges brought against employers of Kanaka labour, may be gathered from the following :—

"The main cause or origin of the committee arose from the report of Mr. ———, sent to the colonial secretary, uninvited by the Government, and containing many serious charges—or at least implied charges—against, not only the employers of, but all connected with Polynesian labour. These charges were not substantiated, and the evidence given by Mr. ——— will clearly show that his report was dealing with (to use his own words) the most extreme possibilities; that it was based, not on facts, but on suspicions, and I feel certain that an impartial perusal of the mass of evidence collected will clearly show this to be the case."—*Extract from a letter in " The Brisbane Courier," Nov. 27th, 1876, signed by one of the members of the Committee.*

In the "Government Gazette," December 23rd, 1876, a notification appeared that the Governor, with the advice of the Executive Council, had formed some new regulations with reference to the Polynesian Act of 1868, which I summarize as follows :—

1. Before a licence to recruit shall be granted, the district in which the labourer is to be employed must be specified.

This regulation was much needed. Maryborough, about this time, was a favourite place with the New Hebrideans; but frequently, after arrival there, they had been drafted off to some other district. In revenge for this, after their return home, some of them had "taken it out" of the first unsuspecting white man who had fallen into their power.

2. Agreements—*i.e.*, the final agreement, when the labourer is transferred to the employer on shore from his agent, the master of the vessel —shall be entered into on board on arrival, only with the person who has applied for and to whom the licence has been issued.

3. No transfer of a labourer from one employer to another shall be allowed until after proper inquiry shall have been made by the inspector, and then only under a bond, and only when the first employer shall have ceased to require the services of the Polynesian.

4. No transfer shall be allowed to any employer in another district until after the lapse of a reasonable time from arrival.

Unfortunately, it was not stated precisely what His Excellency and the Executive Council considered "a reasonable time,"—an omission that made the regulation valueless, in my opinion.

5. The employer shall pay wages to each labourer annually. Such wages shall be paid in current coin, and shall be paid in the presence of a Government inspector, or of a police magistrate.

From the foregoing epitome of the regulations at that date, it will be evident that Queenslanders were doing their best to regulate the Polynesian trade, and to check abuses on shore as well as afloat.

I may also state that, in the transfers of labourers from one employer to another, it was the duty of the inspector to ascertain if the labourer was willing to be so transferred. I know of one instance only in which this was not strictly carried out. In that case the offender was an officer who avowedly belonged to the political party that opposed Polynesian labour altogether. I shall refer to it later on.

The immigration inspector at Maryborough, having had a rap over the knuckles for his report, as I have shown above, took his revenge out of us skippers, since he could not reach any higher. Two of the Polynesian labour vessels—the *Stanley* and the *Sibyl*—had each, for the last year or more, carried a cabin-boy. These lads were engaged in the islands, and their names were borne on the ship's articles. Shortly after arrival in port, the crews were discharged, the cabin-boys included. However, as the Act provided that "no Polynesian shall be introduced into this colony except under the provisions of this Act," new articles for the next voyage were signed by the cabin-boy, immediately after he had received his wages and discharge from the first.

The inspector decided that the discharge from the first articles was an infringement of the Act. He therefore notified us that our cabin-boys were to be landed at their respective homes on our ensuing voyages. That is to say, their engagement was held by him to have been illegal.

I cannot help thinking that this was nothing more than petty revenge. Scores of times I have known of Polynesian boatmen who had never visited Queensland before, being brought to Maryborough, and there discharged and shipped again, precisely in the same manner as our cabin-boys. Yet our inspector never took notice of such cases, apparently reserving "the letter of the law" for those who had offended him.

CHAPTER VII.

SIXTH VOYAGE OF THE *STANLEY*, 1876-7.

Christmas at the White Cliffs—Run to the Banks' Is.—Landing returned labourers—A dirty night—Curious weather—Running for the open—A whirlwind—Racing the swell—Out of the cyclone—The Stanley *wins renown—Meralaba I.—Effects of the hurricane—Remarks on the Banks' Is.—Port Olry—Tanoa I.—Recruits from inland—Adam, the interpreter—Failure to reach Pussé—At Port Sandwich—The W. S. Fox—Sunken coral reefs—Round New Caledonia—Arrival at Maryborough — Quarantine — Red fire—Puck ordered home—Reasons for his reluctance to go—I resign command of the* Stanley*—How Puck evaded the authorities—An abuse—Cottons instead of woollens—A case in court—Change of officials.*

I SAILED again from Maryborough towards the end of December, spending Christmas at anchor off the White Cliffs, Fraser I. On the thirtieth of the month, at night, I rounded Breaksea Spit, and thence stood to the east with a southerly breeze. This, however, soon drew round to south-east, blowing freshly, and bringing thick, dirty weather.

I had a number of Kanaka labourers on board, returning to their homes; and, as the destination of most of them was the Banks' Is., the northernmost of the New Hebrides group, I kept the ship to north-eastward, passing just to leeward of the Bampton reefs, and hauling up again sharp on the starboard tack. In the vicinity of the Torres Is.—which I sighted but did not visit—the wind fell off for a while, then hauling round to north-north-east, carried me to Mota Lava, or Saddle I., one of the Banks' Is., where, one forenoon, I landed several of my passengers. This was on or about January 15th, 1877.

While the boats were at work landing men and women, with their huge heavy chests—the ship meanwhile dodging off and on—the breeze freshened up, with squalls of wind and rain, under a dull cloudy sky. My aneroid was falling, and, as the hurricane season was now due, I hastened the men in the boats, hoping I might be able to anchor in Port Pattison, on the west of Vanua Lava I., before dark. This was not to be, however. It was late in the afternoon before my work at Mota Lava was ended, and night began to fall before I got to the port Being unacquainted with the anchorage, I decided to take my chance in the open sea. So, passing south of Mota I., I stood to eastward under double reefs.

The sea was still running easily, and the wind was no more than·fresh, but the night drew in pitch-dark, while rain fell in torrents. The glass was going down slowly but surely, and there was every prospect of a cyclone. I therefore wore the ship in towards the land again, at about 2 a.m.

About seven we stood in between Saddle I. and Sugar-Loaf I., a hard gale blowing from the north and west. Overhead and astern of us, the sky was bright and cloudless ; but before our course a dense black bank of clouds rose from the horizon almost to the zenith. The sun was shining on us, and the sea was bright and sparkling, just flecked with white driving foam. The schooner laid herself down to it, and, smothered in drift, seemed to do her level best to get to an anchorage before the worst of the hurricane caught her.

But our luck was no better in the morning than it had been overnight. I should have had to have beaten into the port, had I adhered to my original intention ; and, from the outside, this looked an almost impossible feat. So I kept away for the passage between Vanua Lava and the two small islets—Pakea and Nivula—which lie off its south-eastern shore.

When we got into the passage the wind suddenly fell; for we were then under the high land of the main island. Then a whirlwind caught the schooner aback, dashing the booms and the fore-and-aft canvas over to the contrary side, nearly capsizing the starboard boat on the davits—in which I was standing to con the ship—and smothering us in a whirling cloud of salt drift.

This did not last more than half a minute, ceasing as quickly as it begun. Two or three similar whirlwinds passed close to the ship. I was much relieved when the schooner shot out of the passage into the open sea, and the gale once more howled through the rigging.

There was nothing for it now but to run clear away from the land. I headed the ship to the east, before the heavy swell that came rolling round the south coast of the island. The boats were got in on deck and secured, the hatches battened down, the topgallant yard sent on deck, and sail was shortened to a close-reefed topsail and inner jib.

Near the island the swell rose in long and regular rollers; less than two miles off, we suddenly plunged into a raging broken sea, the effect of cross currents. The wind had now hauled round to north-west almost, and the aneroid was down to 29·40. The black cloud-bank appeared to be travelling in a south-easterly direction. To keep away from it as much as possible, I missed no opportunity, when the heavy seas allowed me, of steering with the wind on the port quarter.

I should have heaved to under the storm-main-trysail, if the swell had not been so dangerous. In that raging sea, however, both the mate and myself were afraid to attempt it. We thought it safer to run down east until the swell subsided, or we could haul out of it.

In the afternoon the centre of the cyclone appeared to be abeam of us, bearing S.W. to S.S.W., the wind coming from about N.W. by W. We were then scudding under the topsail, beneath the edge of the cloud-bank. The sky to the north and east was blue and cloudless, the remainder being hidden by a uniform mass of dark cloud. Just overhead of us, the cloud-bank assumed a lumpy and rounded appearance, like a bunch of black grapes, and took a tint of indigo blue.

On one side the horizon came clearly in view whenever the ship rose on the top of the swell; on the other our prospect was bounded by a wall of driving rain, falling at a few hundred yards distance. Now and then this falling sheet drew near and enveloped the ship, pouring down upon us with pitiless force; while the tempest of wind shrieked through the rigging, and the huge seas roared alongside as they raced past us. As we rose on the wave-tops we could breathe; each time we sank into the trough between them we were half suffocated and smothered in salt drift and foam. The *Stanley* seemed to be simply running a race with a hurricane; while, on board, we were praying that she might not win!

The aneroid had now fallen to 29·10, remaining steady at that point; so—barring accidents—we knew we were safe; since the centre of the cyclone was not likely to approach any nearer. This state of things lasted until nearly sundown, when the wind began to veer towards the west and slacken in force. Very early next morning I hove the ship to, under the storm-main-trysail and such other canvas as she had been running under. After that the cyclone had the race to itself, dying away towards south-east. At 8 a.m. the *Stanley* lay on the port tack, under all ordinary sail, breasting the seas with a light south-west breeze and fine clear weather, beating back to the Banks' Is.

The manner in which she had behaved in this gale won a great name for the *Stanley* throughout the islands. My "returns" had been down below all through the gale, the only ventilation they had being through the scuttle of the after-hatch and the battened bulkhead of the women's quarters; so they must have had a very rough time of it. They probably thought that the ship had been in much greater danger than was the case. When they came on deck next morning, and found she had sustained no damage, they were loud in their praises. For Kanakas dread nothing so much as the "big wind."

Meralaba, or Starpeak I., was the first land I made, and there I obtained three recruits. This island is of a conical shape,—the old crater of an extinct volcano forming its summit,—having an elevation of nearly 3,000 feet above sea level. Its shores are abrupt, and there is no anchorage off them. From Meralaba I went to Santa Maria I., thence working southward through the group as far as Havannah Harbour, whence I sailed for home with ninety-eight recruits.

The hurricane we had encountered passed throughout the whole group of the New Hebrides. The beaches and forests of every island we visited bore witness to its violence. The inhabitants were fearful that a famine would result, so much damage had it done to their plantations; frequently refusing, in consequence, to sell yams, taro, and other provisions.

Banks' Is., the northernmost division of the New Hebrides, are five or six in number. They are of volcanic formation, and are mountainous. Mota I., included with them, is, however, coralline in structure for the most part.

Santa Maria, or Gaua I., and Vanua Lava, have the only anchorages worth mentioning; those at Lakon, fourteen fathoms, and at Losolava, twelve fathoms, both off Santa Maria I., being the best. The Admiralty plans of these, and of Port Pattison, Vanua Lava I., are excellent and reliable.

I had intended to go to the west coast of Espiritu Santo I. after leaving the Banks' Is.; but the weather looked so threatening, when we sailed, that I ran to Port Olry, on the east coast, for shelter. After an improvement had shown itself, I found it more convenient to work round to the south, trusting to get an opportunity to visit Pussé, on the western coast, for which place I had two returns. Pussé was Puck's native place, also, and I had been ordered to land him there.

North-west of Bartholomew I., and near the south coast of Espiritu Santo, there are four islets. Of these, the nearest to the main is Tanoa, divided from it only by a narrow channel. Inside this channel there are good anchorages, in eight to twelve fathoms of water. I lay there for several days, while it blew hard from the north-west.

I obtained several recruits while lying at this place, not from the islet but from the main. Some of them came down from the interior of the island. A returned labourer from Queensland, named Adam, who lived on the mainland coast near our anchorage, acted as my messenger to the inland tribes on this occasion, as well as subsequently. Some of the men who came to engage said it had taken them two days to travel down to the coast from their villages.

I hung about the south coast of Espiritu Santo for more than a fortnight, hoping that an opportunity of getting to Pussé would occur. The wind hung to the northward, sometimes light and baffling, sometimes blowing a gale of wind, regular monsoon weather. I got within three or four miles of the place once, when it fell almost calm, and a current carried me back to Cape Lisburne, the south-western extremity of the island. At last I gave it up, since I could not afford to waste more time over such a job. Then I squared away for Pentecost, giving that island a trial, with excellent results.

At Port Sandwich, Mallicolo, I lay for two days. There I was told by the natives that a French schooner had left the port just before the recent hurricane had broken over the island. They supposed she had been lost, for some inquiries had since been made for her by white men. The vessel they spoke of may have been the *Tanna*, as she disappeared about that time. A small ketch, the *W. S. Fox*, was lying at Port Sandwich near us, but left before we did.

With a few more boys on board I sailed from Port Sandwich, getting a moderate breeze from the southward for a wonder. Off the Maskelyne islets I found the *W. S. Fox* again lying at anchor inside the reefs. Her master came off to me, and piloted the *Stanley* to an anchorage off Olunduva islet. This was a delightful as well as protected berth. It was surrounded by picturesque islets, the mountainous coast of Mallicolo, and a vast extent of coral reefs. The last prevented the heaviest sea from disturbing the surface of its waters.

Here, and on the south coast, I recruited a sufficient number of boys to make up my list to over ninety. I then sailed to Tongoa, working the west coast of Api on the way. I lay there no more than an hour or two one morning, getting under way again speedily because the barometer was falling very fast. A few hours' run took me to Havannah Harbour, where I found the settlers preparing for a hurricane—an example I thought it wise to follow. However, it blew only a hard gale, beginning in the north, as usual, and veering round to west, where it died down. In the midst of it the little *W. S. Fox* bowled in through the north-west passage, and very glad was her "Geordie" skipper to get to an anchor.

I beat out of the southern passage with the last of this breeze. Off Tukatuka, the western point of Sandwich I., the wind fell light, suddenly chopping round to the east. While standing off the land on the port tack, we unexpectedly ran by two patches of sunken coral, which were not marked on the Admiralty chart. Hat I. (off the west coast of Sandwich I.) lay north-east from this spot, being fourteen or sixteen miles distant, perhaps even less. There was a moderate sea running at the time, but no breakers were visible.

I made for home by the southern route, round New Caledonia. Notwithstanding light winds and several calms, we made a quick voyage, on the whole. We arrived at Maryborough on the morning of March 23rd, but the immigration agent considered 2 p.m. much too late an hour for him to visit the ship. So we were not released from quarantine until the following morning.

However, the quarantine laws could not prevent our host of the Melbourne Hotel from sending off to us a little "refreshment." So we had some merriment in the evening, ending by illuminating the ship with all the blue lights and red fire we had left. We made such a blaze that half the town was scared; especially as the powder magazine was hardly fifty yards from where we lay.

Touching this "red fire"—most labour vessels carried a small gun to announce their presence to the natives living in the forests, when they came to an anchor under any of the islands. I was unprovided with any such weapon, and therefore used to explode dynamite; or at night I sometimes flared off a preparation I got from a chemist in Maryborough. This burned with a brilliant red light, and was altogether more effective and not so ghostly as the ordinary blue light, besides being cheaper.

Of course I had some trouble with the immigration agent, as soon as he discovered that Puck was still on board. It ended in smoke, however, though he insinuated that I had purposely refrained from landing the boy, which was untrue.

The *Sibyl* was then lying at the wharves nearly ready for sea, and it was decreed that Puck should be taken home in her.

Now Puck, about a year before I engaged him, had run away from his home in Espiritu Santo I. in company with another youngster, the son of his chief. The latter fell ill and died soon after, in Sandwich I. Puck, who was the eldest, was afraid that, if he made his appearance at Pussé without his late companion, he would be

PUCK EVADES THE AUTHORITIES.

accused of having beguiled him away, and be himself killed for doing so. Wherefore poor Puck had no desire to go home.

In the meantime, whilst Puck's affairs were being arranged for him, I had resigned my command of the *Stanley*. This was because a slight disagreement had arisen between the owner and myself. About a week after that Puck disappeared.

He was to have gone home, as I said before, in the *Sibyl*. A few hours before she sailed the two Govern-

PUCK.

ment agents and the two skippers—Captain Kilgour having been appointed to the *Stanley* in my place—met on board the latter vessel. The *Sibyl* was lying at a wharf at some distance. The party, having started to walk from one vessel to the other, ordered Puck to follow them.

Now, across the road along the river-bank which connected the two wharves, there was a fence with a gap in it. The two skippers passed through this gap, and walked on arm-in-arm; the two G.A.'s. followed them. Lastly poor Puck, weeping bitterly, came to the gap in his turn. But he did not pass through it. An idea suddenly occurred to him. He turned to the left, ran along the fence, and disappeared. Puck did not go home in the *Sibyl*. I met him in Sydney about eight years after this.

About a month previous to my arrival, another abuse had been ferretted out and exposed by our friend the immigration agent. I venture to say that, if he and other officers holding a similar position elsewhere had but kept their eyes open, they might have discovered it long ago. For the fact was obvious to everybody else connected with labour vessels then. This abuse lay in the fact that recruits were supplied with the cheapest and worst clothing that could be obtained in the market. Thin cottons were generally given to them, in lieu of the strong woollen stuffs prescribed by the Act.

The *Sibyl* had arrived in Hervey Bay about February 26th, and, as was the custom in those days, clothing was served out to the recruits just before the vessel entered the river. As soon as she had arrived at her moorings, the immigration agent summoned the owner before the court, for not supplying a "flannel" shirt to one of the recruits.

The *Sibyl* had ninety-seven recruits on board, but only one case was tried as a test-case, the other ninety-six being withdrawn. The owner was fined five shillings and costs (£25). He ought to have been thankful to the immigration agent for withdrawing the other cases. He does not appear, however, to have been in that desirable state of mind, since he applied, by his counsel, for "prohibition."

Shortly after my arrival, the immigration agent referred to was relieved of a portion of his onerous duties by the appointment of an assistant-immigration agent and Polynesian inspector. A little later, another shipping master was appointed to the post. Our "friend," therefore, of the multifarious offices, retained only that of sub-collector of customs. No one in Maryborough was sorry for this re-division of the executive powers—unless it were the officer aforesaid!

CHAPTER VIII.

LAST VOYAGE OF THE *BOBTAIL NAG*.

I meet with an accident—I take command of the Bobtail Nag *—Death of Bully Hayes, the freebooter—Sail to Fiji—At Levuka—Fijian labour system—Regulations and pay—Fitting ship—An abuse—Queensland and Fijian labourers—Paying off—In a Fijian store—Diddling the boys—I sail from Levuka—My boatmen—Hostilities at Tanna I.—Boys unwilling to land—Returns unwelcome—Scarcity of food—Beachmen plunder bushmen—I escape death—Lose my galvanic belt—Effects of the drought—Aurora and Pentecost Is.—The* Charybdis *ashore—I leave Havannah Harbour—Bad weather—Put back to Vila—I go ashore—Visit Roddin—The cyclone upon us—Hasty preparations—A roaring hurricane—Driven on the reef—The wreck—Cutting away the masts—The centre of the cyclone—" All hands ashore ! "—Saving provisions—Encamped on the islet—Expedition to the village—Fire—The night of the wreck.*

In August, 1878, I was offered the command of the *Lady Darling*, which vessel was then lying at Brisbane. I had accepted the proposal, when an accident occurred which obliged me to withdraw from it—a fall, when out riding one evening, having laid me up for three weeks. By September, though still suffering from the effects of the accident, I was able to get to work again, and took command of the *Bobtail Nag*, a brigantine chartered by the Government of Fiji for recruiting work. I sailed in her for Levuka on the twenty-first of that month.

Just before we left Brisbane, news had been received there that " Bully " Hayes, the notorious South Sea freebooter, had been killed. This man was a native of Cleveland, Ohio, U.S. His exploits had consisted chiefly of ship robberies and occasional abductions of women, accompanied by more or less violence. I had met him once at Kusaie, Caroline Is., in 1871. He was killed by one of his piratical crew, a Norwegian named Janssen or Johnson, during a quarrel on board the *Lotus*, a vessel he had stolen. Johnson afterwards took the *Lotus* to Jaluit, Marshall Is., and gave her up to a German trader resident there.

The *Bobtail Nag* was a very indifferent vessel compared with my late command, the *Stanley*. Let it blow high or low, the latter shipped no more water than enough to keep her bilges sweet, while the poor old "*Bob*" leaked like a sieve in heavy weather, and even in fine she gave the watch a fifteen minutes' spell at the pumps every evening. We had to keep her "wee-gee" always rigged.

Off Norfolk I. we came in for a gale, during which one of the boats was carried away. This I had to replace at Levuka. After three weeks out we sighted Matuku I., one of the Fiji group, and, next morning, the rugged peaks of Ovalau I. lay right ahead of us, the white houses of Levuka—then the capital—nestling at their base. By noon the *Bobtail Nag* lay at anchor off the town, inside the barrier reef that forms the harbour. Here we remained for nearly a month, repairing and outfitting.

The system of recruiting labourers at the islands for Fiji was similar to that under Queensland regulations, but the manner of dealing with them on arrival was different. At Levuka, recruits were inspected on board by the immigration agent and the medical officer, were then landed and housed at the Polynesian depôt at Vagadace, and thence distributed by the Government to such employers as required their services.

The boys' passage money, both to and from Levuka, was paid by the Government; the former within twenty-four hours after inspection, and the latter forty-eight hours after sailing from Levuka. Ship-owners and agents were thus relieved from all responsibility in respect of the disposal of the recruits after their arrival in Fiji.

The owner of the *Bobtail Nag* received £8 per head for all recruits over sixteen years of age. Of such as were younger, two were paid for as one. For returns, £3 per head was allowed. Recruits were engaged for three years, at £3 per annum. Clothing on board ship consisted only of two "sulus"—loose linen waistcloths—one supplied to each man on engagement, the other on arrival in port. Sleeping mats were provided instead of blankets.

The *Bobtail Nag* was fitted with the usual fore-and-aft shelves or "bunks," two on each side of her hold, in compliance with the Queensland Government regulations. Fijian labour vessels usually dispensed with bunks, however, the recruits sleeping on mats ranged along the deck. By this plan less sleeping room was obtained than by the other; but, on the other hand, greater cleanliness could be enforced.

On board Fijian vessels the food consisted solely of yams and other native vegetables. Pipes and tobacco were supplied in addition. The full complement of passengers was fixed at the rate of three for each two tons of the vessel's registered measurement, two youngsters being reckoned and paid for as one adult.

So far, good. But in the payment of the labourers at the expiration of their term of service—three years at this time, previously five—there was abuse. This I affirm to have been the case, because I saw that the boys I took back to their homes in the *Bobtail Nag* had not received anything like the value of the money they had earned in Fiji.

Now the Queensland labourer had frequent opportunities for learning the value of money. He had his holiday on Saturday, as well as Sunday. On the former day he could visit the neighbouring town and its stores, and thus pick up some knowledge of the money value of things, besides picking up a little English.

The Fijian labourer, on the other hand, was generally employed on some island of the group far removed from either town or store. He acquired but little English, though he quickly learnt the native Fijian. When paid off, he knew little more of the value of what he had earned than he did when he arrived.

To prevent his being cheated by the store-keeper, I suppose, his money was retained by the Government until he had completed his purchases, and a clerk from the Immigration Office accompanied him to the stores to assist him in getting what he wanted—or, as it would seem, what the storekeeper thought he ought to want.

One day, I happened to be in a general store at Levuka, when a clerk from the Immigration Office entered, followed by a score or so of boys who were being paid off. These had been at work for either three or five years on some distant island. They mostly looked as wild and scared as if they had just been imported. One only, who had been a house servant in Levuka, could talk English, and he accordingly acted as spokesman for the rest.

The storekeeper had expected their arrival, and was prepared for them. Indeed, it seemed to me that he had brought to the front all the damaged articles he was possessed of.

Conspicuously displayed was a number of three-legged iron pots, without covers, chipped round the edges, and all thickly coated with rust.

"Very good belong boil yam," remarked the clerk to the English-speaking boy, touching one of these pots with his foot.

"Very good belonga yam," assented the boy, as to a mere passing remark.

"Give each boy a pot," said the clerk to the storekeeper, pretending to take the boy's words as an expression of the general desire to buy these wares.

Accordingly, each member of the party was forthwith saddled with a rusty iron pot to take home and boil his yams in; cooking the vegetable in such a way being a method never employed—nor considered desirable by the islanders.

"You like calico?" asked the clerk, fingering a "bolt" of it all stained and damaged.

"Yes, me like calico," mumbled the lad, looking with evident disfavour upon the sample before him. But this was considered a purchase by the clerk and the storekeeper, and the stuff was served out, the wishes of each individual being not even inquired into.

Then the clerk noticed me observing his proceedings, and the rest of the conversation was cautiously carried on in Fijian, with which language I was unacquainted.

I took these boys home in the *Bobtail Nag*, and saw what they—or the clerk for them, rather—had bought. The goods each of them had, if they had been good and new, would have cost, at the usual prices in that store, no more than six pounds, if as much. This estimate included the clothes in wear, as well as the box.

A Queensland "return's" box measured, on an average, 3 feet × 1 foot 6 inches, and would be chock-full and weighty. A Fijian labourer, if he possessed a box at all, had one scarcely two-thirds of that size, with, possibly, a cheap German shot-gun, almost as dangerous to fire as to stand in front of. The "Brown-Besses" sold to Queensland labourers were very superior weapons by comparison. Besides his chest and gun, the Queensland labourer often had a huge bundle or two.

I noticed a great difference between these Fiji "returns" and the majority of labourers from Queensland. The latter were vastly superior in manners, personal appearance, and intelligence. The Fijian boys, after their experience of hard work under a just and reasonable employer, no doubt presented signs of improvement on the original savage. These were noticeable, however, to a far greater extent in the Queensland "returns," who had mingled with white labourers on comparatively familiar terms.

I have often said—and I say it still—that if I was placed on a New Hebrides beach with a hundred of the inhabitants, one half of whom had served their three years in Queensland, and returned, say, within the last twelve months, I could pick out forty-five of the fifty solely by their personal appearance. They would present a healthier aspect, possess more muscular frames, and be devoid of the furtive, "wild dog" expression which the genuine savage usually wears.

I sailed from Levuka in the beginning of November, with over a hundred and sixty "returns." I had also a Government agent on board as a passenger. I think it was on the morning of November 3rd when I took a departure from Mount Washington, Kandavu I. The first land I made after that was Fotuna I., where I landed several "returns," and obtained two fresh recruits. These came on board unsolicited, having got into the boat without a word, simply making signs that they wished to go away in the ship. They were aware of her destination, the "returns" having told them. They knew no language except their own; but, before we reached Levuka, they could converse freely in Fijian, having acquired it from my four Fijian boatmen.

These boatmen were big lusty fellows of the true Polynesian type. They were nominally Christians, and, sooth to say, as consummate rascals as one could wish to meet. They said their prayers every morning and evening. Not infrequently also, they indulged in what they believed to be hymn-singing—but cats are musical in comparison to them! Whenever recruiting was slack they were constantly advising the mate to kidnap boys, pointing out various opportunities when it might have been done.

The chief of the four, Jeremiah, told me he had been

a servant of the British Consul at Levuka, before the annexation of the Fijis by the British Government. Surely he could not have picked up his rascality in that service!

From Fotuna I went to Tanna I. There, about three miles north-west of Waisissa, the mate met with a warm reception as he approached the shore. A volley from at least a dozen muskets saluted him ; the enemy lying concealed behind rocks and bushes, not twenty yards distant. Fortunately not a man was hurt, though both the boats were struck by some of the bullets. A short quick pull carried them out of range.

Tanna was generally unfavourable to us. I therefore landed some "returns" I had on board, who belonged to the island, and then sailed northwards.

There were three Tanna men that I did not put ashore, however. These had been taken, along with their goods, to a point on the north-east coast, near to which they had been engaged some years before. On reaching the shore, however, they saw a party of men belonging to a hostile tribe awaiting them, and were consequently afraid to leave the boat. The mate pulled away along the coast to another part of the beach. There they got scared again, and so, finally, begged to be taken back on board ship.

It appears they belonged to a village up among the hills inland, which they could not reach without passing through a hostile district. So they preferred to remain on board, trusting that peace would have been made by the time I should return to the island on my way back to Fiji. If not, they would rather go back to the colony, and engage for another term of service there, than risk their lives in attempting to get home.

At Erromanga I. some more "returns" were landed in Cook's Bay and in Polenia Bay. Thence I sailed to Sandwich I., where I put another batch ashore at Fareire, on the north-eastern coast. At this place the poor "returns," instead of being welcomed home, were coolly told that they had better have remained in Fiji. It would seem that, owing to a prolonged and most unusual drought, the food supply of the district was running short.

I waited two or three hours at Fareire, dodging off and on, in hopes that this scarcity of food might stimulate some of the natives to leave home. None offered to recruit, however, so I squared away for Hinchinbrook I., where I anchored.

Next morning, having a fresh fair wind, I ran through the narrow but deep passage between Pele I. and the little islet of Kakula, near the Sandwich coast, and so into "the Sound." It was a short cut to Havannah Harbour, where I watered the ship.

At various islands north of Sandwich I. the work of landing "returns" and engaging recruits went on briskly. We secured many boys in consequence, I think, of the scarcity of food on the islands. The drought had not affected the yam plantations to any great extent apparently. The taro plants, however, on which root the northern islanders depend as their staple article of food, had failed miserably. The attenuated bodies of many of my recruits too plainly evidenced the extent and consequences of the drought.

I recruited two young women at Mai I., who subsequently deserted at Vila. About them I shall have more to say presently.

Touching at a part of the south coast of Espiritu Santo I., we landed three "returns," with their goods. They belonged to a "bush" tribe, and, unluckily for them, there was a village of a "beach" tribe not a mile off where they landed. A party of natives belonging to this village assembled on the beach as soon as they saw us. They received the "returns" with seeming friendliness; but, no sooner were our boats well on their way back to the ship, than they seized the boxes and bundles and made off with them. We could see the unfortunate "returns" standing disconsolately where we had landed them. All they had left to represent their three years' labour was their guns. Probably the possession of these had alone saved their lives.

At Narovorovo our old enemies of the village near by planned another attack on us, and were again frustrated in their pleasant little game.

I was bathing in the stream, from which we had just filled our water-tanks, when the second mate chanced to observe some natives dodging behind the bushes close at hand. He gave the alarm at once. Our boys immediately charged into the scrub and drove out the lurkers—about a dozen fellows, armed with bows and arrows. They had sneaked down to try and get a shot at me, but were thus disappointed. Another five minutes, however, and my last voyage would have been concluded in a way I had not bargained for.

At this time I was in the habit of wearing one of Pulvermacher's Galvanic Belts. I had found it useful as a preventive of rheumatism, though it failed to cure me of that affliction altogether. In my hurry to get dressed, when the alarm was given, I forgot to put it on, and left it lying on the beach when we returned to the ship. Subsequently an old native woman found it, picked it up, and, the next time I returned to the place, restored it to me, to my great relief. I gave her a butcher's knife, which she appreciated as much as I did the belt.

The night after this incident I crossed over to Mallicolo I., and, next day, anchored among the Maskelyne Is. There I was obliged to lie for four days, rheumatism keeping me on my back, unable to move without acute pain. This did not stop recruiting, however, which went on merrily meanwhile.

As soon as I was able to move about I got under way, and, issuing by the south-western passage, worked along the south coast as far as Lennurr I., between which and the mainland I came to an anchor. Here we spent Christmas Day.

The effects of the drought were very manifest at this place. Each of the inhabitants looked as if a good square meal was a thing he had not enjoyed for a long time. Of course it was impossible to purchase any native food, and the supply I had brought from Fiji was already beginning to run short. Luckily, I had brought two tons of rice with me from Brisbane, as well as a quantity of biscuit. I had also shipped five tons of yams in Fiji. But for these provisions, I must have cut my cruise short long before this.

A large crowd of natives constantly assembled on the beach of the mainland, during the three days I stayed at Lennurr. The recruit list soon rose to 135. That, however, seemed to be the limit, so I sailed on eastward, with a light southerly breeze, and tried Aurora I.

At Pentecost I. we were again successful. The provisioning of the ship now became a serious question; so the G.A. and I held council, coming to the conclusion that we must return to Fiji forthwith. So he delivered to me an official letter, notifying me to the effect that I should, if unable to obtain more provisions, return to Fiji at once. Whereupon, the boats were hoisted up and secured, and we began beating back to Havannah Harbour.

There I purchased all the provisions suitable for natives that I could find in the place. These were little enough: a few bags of small white beans, the sort grown in Fiji for Polynesian labourers, and some maize. With these additions to such rice and biscuits as I had left, we reckoned we could last out for three weeks.

When all was done, I had one hundred and forty-four recruits on board, to which number must be added the three Tanna boys I still hoped to land at their home.

There were two vessels lying in Havannah Harbour

during our visit. The cutter *New York*, last from Fiji, and the labour schooner *Charybdis*. The last-named had proved too leaky to return to Fiji. Her master had shipped the labourers she had collected—about forty in number—on board the schooner *Samoa*, and had gone with them to Fiji in that vessel, leaving the *Charybdis* at Havannah Harbour. Her crew, in order to save themselves the trouble of pumping, laid the *Charybdis* on the mud near Semma, and there the relics of her are probably still lying.

I left Havannah Harbour on the evening of January 7, 1878. Taking advantage of the smooth water under the lee of the land outside, I there pumped the ship out dry—and a long spell of work it was, too. Had there been plenty of provisions on board, I think I should not have gone to sea that day, for the weather looked dull and threatening, and the glass was falling. The last might have been only an indication that the wind was about to shift into the north-west, which would have given me a quick run across. Regarding it as such, I stood off southward on the port tack, the wind freshening up from E. by S. with a dull cloudy sky.

At four next morning I tacked to northward, heading for the coast of Sandwich I. The breeze now began to freshen, becoming squally, with almost continual rain. During the forenoon we kept an anxious look-out for the land, for it was now evident that the ship was on the verge of a cyclone, the centre of which was bearing northward of her. Plainly, the sooner we could get into a safe anchorage the better; for both pumps had to be kept going continually to free the ship from water. The sea was now running strongly, and the old craft was plunging and straining through it under her lower canvas and double topsail.

A very heavy squall of wind and dense rain compelled me to let go the topsail and throat halyards, and to haul the jib down. After this, about eleven, the rain

K

cleared away, and the south-east point of Sandwich I. became visible to us on the weather bow, about eight miles distant. This gave me our position. Sail was made again, the yards were checked and the sheets eased off; and then the ship's head was pointed for South-West Bay.

I anchored in Vila Harbour at 5 p.m., between the islets of Vila and Lelika. There I stowed sails, and pumped three feet of water out of the hold. We were just in time. That night it blew a hard gale, with very heavy squalls and thick rain. Had we been outside in it, I verily believe the old *Nag* would have foundered under us.

At daylight, on the 9th, when I turned out of my bunk, I found the aneroid had fallen very little during the night, and was then at 29·65. Going on deck, I thought at first the weather had improved. Just then the rain had ceased, and the wind abated considerably. This might have been due to our position under the lee of the land. Overhead the sky was dark, a thin scud now and then flying across it from the east.

I had a sick man in the forecastle—one of my white crew—for whom I wished to obtain some eggs, or a fowl or two. Our stock of poultry, purchased in the islands, had been exhausted. With this in view, therefore, I went ashore in the north-west arm of the harbour to visit John Roddin, a settler there. Him I found at home, engaged in planting maize, along with his native wife and four or five labourers from some other island.

This was his third crop that season; two previous plantings having been ruined by the drought. He scouted the idea of a hurricane, because the wind was not coming from north or north-west, but blew steadily from the east. He thought this would prove no more than a gale—not a cyclone.

No eggs were procurable, but Roddin's wife caught a couple of fowls for me, while he and I were breakfasting. Just as we finished our meal the gale rose again, a terrific squall bursting over the harbour. It shook the house we were in, until I thought it would come down about our ears. Outside, the air was filled with flying leaves and twigs from the forest; while sheets of blinding rain descended, completely hiding everything more than twenty yards off.

This lasted about half an hour, when a lull allowed the air to clear sufficiently for us to see the flat top of Pango Hill, at the other end of the harbour. Seizing my fowls, I bade Roddin and his wife a hasty good-bye. Then, slipping and stumbling down the "greasy" hill, I got into my boat, and pulled energetically back to the ship. Hardly were we alongside, when another howling squall enveloped us, catching the ship nearly abeam as she swung at anchor, and heeling her over to her scuppers nearly.

One glance at the aneroid in my cabin was enough to show me that the fullest force of the cyclone was at hand. The indicator had sunk two-tenths during my absence, while the steadiness of the wind, blowing from the east, and its increasing violence, proved to me that the cyclone was moving directly towards us, and that the calm centre, round which the hurricane revolved, would pass over our anchorage.

There was but little time left us in which to make preparations. Half an hour sufficed to complete all. The maintopmast was housed, and all the bent sails were marled down to the yards, masts, or booms, with spare running gear, by the white crew. Meanwhile, the boatmen and recruits hove in some of the chain the ship was riding by, during a lull between the squalls. As soon as this chain was short enough, I let go the second anchor in twelve fathoms, the other lying in nineteen. Next, I paid out both cables, until I had only five fathoms on one side and about twenty on the other, to veer and haul upon in case of a shift of wind.

As soon as the next squall brought up the cables taut, I dropped the lead over the vessel's stern in eight fathoms, about fifty yards from the fringing reef of Vila islet. Then I got the port boat on deck, lashing the starboard one to the davits, so as to leave one side of the deck clear, as well as to have a boat ready for lowering in case it should be required.

Now, I thought, the ship would be safe if only the anchors would hold securely in the coral bottom, for the water was as smooth as the top of a table. When the starboard braces were hauled in until the yards were braced sharp up, there was as little surface as possible for the wind to take hold of.

At noon the glass had run down to 29 inches, and was still falling fast. The lulls between the squalls were of less duration. At one o'clock the wind blew steadily, but as fiercely as any squall, gradually increasing in force until it became a roaring hurricane, enveloping the ship in a thick mist of driving rain, which half choked us as we crouched under the lee of the bulwarks and the deck-house. Still the anchors held fast, and the ship kept her position pretty well.

Once I went below, and found that the aneroid had fallen to 28·40. Shortly after I had crawled back to my shelter under the deck-house, the roar of the wind suddenly rose to a perfect scream, apparently shifting a couple of points or so southward.

For a moment or two the ship lay trembling, but without leaving her position. Then her head fell off to port. A chain had parted, or an anchor had dragged. A moment she hung steady, then fell off still more, sweeping round broadside to the wind, being then instantly borne down by the force of the wind until her spars and port rail were under water.

As I held on to the weather rail aft, looking down upon the water becalmed under our lee, I saw its dull grey colour change to a light green. Then I felt a grating and grinding sensation under my feet, and I knew that all was over with the old *Nag*.

Almost on her beam ends as she was, the vessel caught the coral first with the upper part of her port bilge. Then, as the hurricane pressed her on up the reef, she righted. So suddenly did she heel over to windward, that a dozen of us who were hanging on to the weather rail, were fairly flung on deck by the pressure of wind. The canvas cover of the deck-house, just above my head, was ripped off and carried away, my sou'wester going with it. The last was discovered some

WRECK OF THE "BOBTAIL NAG."

days after on the other side of Vila islet, impaled on the broken branch of a tree.

The rocks on shore were now dimly visible through the driving mist. That we could see them, in conjunction with the grinding and jerking we felt beneath us, too plainly intimated that the ship was being slowly driven over the reef towards the harbour mouth. Should she get into deep water, I knew she must now go down at once. What was more, we should all be drowned in that case, for no one could swim amid the churning foam.

However, she was still partly held by the anchor, and two hundred fathoms of chain hanging from the bows.

The wind had most hold upon the foremast, so our axes went to work without delay. A few cuts divided the lanyards of the weather rigging, and then, the wind helping the axe, the mast with all its yards and gear was sent into the water under the lee bow. About the same time the ship's nose stuck fast in a hollow of the reef, and her further progress was thus arrested.

The water had now risen to within two feet of the upper deck forward, while abaft it was three feet above the keelson. The recruits presently tumbled up from below in hot haste, crouching down on deck, under cover of the weather bulwark.

Two of the Fijians jumped over the lee quarter with a life buoy, taking the end of a thin line with them. Their intention was to swim ashore, and then, by means of the line, to land a warp from the ship. However, they were swept away, and, for a time, I thought they were drowned. Fortunately, I was mistaken; they got ashore all right under the lee of the island, and joined us again within half an hour.

We then lifted the boat that had been lashed on deck and launched her over the lee taffrail; the infernal roaring and shrieking of the hurricane continuing all the while with unabated vigour. Talking—even shouting—was of no use. You might have discharged a musket within a yard of a man's ear without his hearing it!

Just as the boat slipped over the rail into the water, there came a sudden change. The uproar seemed to cease all at once, and there fell a dead calm. The shore became faintly visible through the thin mist of drizzling rain. Jumping down into the cabin, I found the aneroid had fallen to 28·32. This was not very low for a hurricane, but the instrument was an old one. The time was twenty minutes past three in the afternoon.

I judged we were now within the calm centre of the cyclone. As soon as that should have passed over us, a renewal of the hurricane was to be expected, probably from an opposite quarter. Now, therefore, was the best time for seizing a chance of getting ashore.

The second boat was accordingly lowered into the water, and got round on the shoreward side of the ship. The women, over a dozen in number, were first landed, most of the men swimming. Their woolly heads, bobbing about in the water, looked like a raft of cocoa-nuts. Some of the "bushmen" were unable to swim. These were supported by others who could. All reached the land safely, at about eighty yards distance from the ship.

Our revolvers, which we kept always loaded, were buckled on; the second boat taking ashore all our guns and ammunition. There was a large village on the islet of Vila, and I knew that the inhabitants would take every advantage they could of our necessities. The ship's papers and chronometer were also put into the boat, together with all the provisions we could collect from above or below water. Amongst other things, we saved a ten-gallon keg about half full of good Ageston rum—a Queensland brand. This got put on one side, however, and was not landed till the next day.

The calm lasted fifty minutes, and then a light puff came up from the south-west. There was not a moment to lose.

"All hands ashore!" I shouted, tumbling into a boat, followed quickly by the G.A. and the Fijians. Hardly had we got half way to the shore when the hurricane once more burst upon us—right in our teeth, too. Fortunately, the trees and rocks of the islet somewhat broke its force. By leaping into the water up to our waists, we were just able to bring the boat to the beach and haul her up above high-water mark.

The vessel was now completely hidden from sight by the rain and spray. Three of the sailors and two Tanna islanders were still on board of her, the second boat remaining alongside.

We had landed near the northern end of the beach fringing the east coast of Vila. Extending back from this beach there was level ground for some thirty yards, beyond which the land rose abruptly to a height of seventy or eighty feet. The whole of the little island was covered with dense brushwood and forest, under the lee of which we were completely sheltered.

Our first thought was bestowed on our firearms; our second concern was for our provisions. We piled up the last in a heap, placing our loaded rifles on the top, and covering the whole with a main-hatch tarpaulin.

Materials for a fire were then collected, but the only box of matches brought on shore turned out to be wet and useless. I therefore proposed to the G.A. that he and I should go to the native village and get a "fire-stick." To this he agreed, so off we set, taking a bee-line through the "bush" in the direction I thought would bring us to the village.

It was a rough journey. We had to force our way through thick underwood, matted together with vines and creepers; while, overhead, the hurricane tore and roared through the tree-tops, rending off huge branches, and occasionally prostrating trees.

At last, breathless and not without bruises, we reached the village. The first house we came to—or what remained of it rather—lay flat on the ground. The next was being blown away piecemeal, for the open "sing-sing" ground lying to windward of it gave free access to the wind. An old Kanaka was the only inhabitant to be seen. He was dancing wildly about the ruin, yelling and gesticulating.

Close by was another house, which had caught fire, and was blazing furiously. Here was what we wanted. I seized a blazing brand, part of a rafter, and made off back on our tracks with the G.A. close to my heels.

Getting into an open path leading to the beach, the wind bowled the two of us along at a great rate, till a fallen tree across the track brought us both up breathless.

After all, we had taken our trouble for nothing. My fire-stick had gone out by the time we gained the beach. Happily, during our absence, the mate had found a bottle of brandy and a box of dry matches amongst the stores. So we freshened ourselves up with a nip, turned the boat keel uppermost, lit our pipes, and laid down under it just as night fell.

As for the miserable naked recruits, they stowed themselves away in holes and corners of the rocks, or behind trees, no doubt cursing the white men for having persuaded them to leave home. Notwithstanding wet clothes and the rough stony ground, I managed to get a few hours' sleep. Waking up about midnight, I found that the hurricane was over, and only a light breeze blowing from south-west. The weather had become fair, though the sky was still overcast.

CHAPTER IX.

SHIPWRECKED ON VILA ISLAND, 1878.

After the hurricane—Changes in the landscape—The wreck—The keg of rum—Erecting a camp—How I disposed it—Our supply of provisions—I set off for Havannah Harbour—Effects of the cyclone there—The New York *and the* Charybdis *wrecked—Return to Vila—Inspection of the wreck—The* Sibyl *and the* Stanley*—Arrangement with Captain Kilgour—The natives upon us—A Kanaka "man-o'-wee-wee"—A parley—They try to bounce me—I resort to strategy—With excellent results—Visited by a missionary—We ought to thank Providence!—My simple little plan—The missionary saves us—Hospitalities—The islanders relieve me—Discipline—Mele islanders visit us—Our women elope—Details—Vessels visit us—The islanders have no more food to spare—I meditate a raid—Return of my "boys"—The* Stanley *to the rescue—We sail for Fiji—I go into hospital—My certificate—Return to Queensland—Government regulations—The question of firearms—How the French and Germans step in—Affair of the* Chance*—Politics—Obnoxious regulations—The Premier and the Polynesians—"Big fella chief no plenty good!"—Return passage money—An unfounded accusation—"Big Massa Johnny Douglas!"*

THE morning after the wreck was a bright and clear one. The harbour wore an aspect that was quite novel to us. The day before, the hills and shores around us had been sumptuously clothed with rich tropical verdure—greens of many tints and varying degrees of brilliancy, relieved by scattered patches of bright yellow, red, brown, purple or crimson.

Now, alas! a blight seemed to have passed over the landscape, leaving it as dead and forlorn as though it had just endured a northern winter. Not a leaf was left on the trees: they stood naked, stripped bare of their foliage, bruised, gashed, and torn by their recent struggle with the hurricane. The whole land had been desolated, and now wore a dull grey aspect, streaked here and there with patches of white, where the coral rock showed out on the hill-sides.

The strips of yellow sand along the shores were strewn with broken boughs. In some places, great trees lay prone across them, their once lofty crowns half buried in the lapping waves. Alone the water smiled and sparkled in the morning sun, as though laughing at the ruin which had swept over the land.

The *Nag* lay where we had left her, though her position was somewhat altered. The main-mast had now disappeared as well as the fore, which we had cut away. The second boat was still alongside, but full of water.

Our first consideration was breakfast. A tin of meat, with some of the few dry biscuits we had saved, sufficed us, and then the G.A. and I went off to the wreck. We found the vessel lying listed over to starboard.

The hands who had been left on board, being afraid that she might be blown off the reef again, had cut away the main-mast, which was floating in the water under the quarter. Then they had got hold of the rum keg, and, after that, I suppose, the hurricane did not much trouble most of them. The boatswain was sober, but all the rest were helplessly drunk. The seamen were noisy and quarrelsome, the Kanakas almost insensible.

We set to work to fish up out of the hold everything in the shape of provisions that was worth saving. The biscuit was found to be irretrievably ruined. The sails were sent ashore and spread out to dry on the beach. Some of them were used for building tents; upon others such rice, maize, and beans, as we could save were laid out to dry in the sun. By nightfall our temporary camp had been fixed up, and we had got our ammunition and stores under cover.

I triced up the main-boom between two large trees, lashing it to them. Over this I spread the main-sail, extending it out on either side, tent-fashion, and securing the flaps to the nearest trees and stumps. Under the boom I fixed the topgallant-mast, spreading another sail over it and underneath the mainsail, so as to form a tent-and-fly— and a capacious one at that. This served me for headquarters.

Of course the rum keg was carefully stowed there, since it appeared to possess a strong attraction for at least two of my four seamen. I gave them the foresail, with such spars as they wanted, and marked out a spot some fifty yards away from my tent. There they erected one for themselves. The four Fijian boatmen put up a small tent close to headquarters. The recruits stripped the bunks and lower deck out of the wreck, and with the planks and scantling constructed rude huts along the beach, on either side of my tent.

All the culinary gear had been brought ashore, and the recruits' cooking pots were set up. However, when I came to overhaul the stock of provisions, I found I could afford them only one meal a day; even then there would be no more than enough to last ten days.

There was an ample supply of fishing-lines and hooks, however, as well as three or four pounds of dynamite, and some detonators. Fish of many kinds abounded in the harbour, and might be had for the trouble of getting them. Wood suitable for bows, fishing-arrows, and spears was also plentiful enough. So the boys easily managed to obtain further provision than their allowance of "crowdy"—as we termed a mixture of damaged maize, beans, and rice, all boiled together.

I left Vila on January 11th in one of the boats, with the Fijians, making for Havannah Harbour, in order to obtain news, as well as give notice of my disaster. In passing Tukatuka, I observed that the houses belonging to Ford—a settler who resided there—had suffered severely. I could not afford time to visit him then, however.

When I arrived at Havannah Harbour, I found Mr. Young, the proprietor of Rahni plantation, taking luncheon with a visitor. They were seated under Young's roof-tree, certainly, but the walls of his house had been blown down, and the roof itself was on the ground! The mission house half-way up the harbour had been completely gutted—doors, window-frames, and most of the roof, had been carried away bodily.

At Semma, the house formerly inhabited by the late Mr. Hebblewhite, which was now occupied by Captain Brown, had escaped uninjured, though the large store at the back of it had been levelled to the ground. "Black Harry" Palmer's houses had disappeared altogether, and so had Salisbury's new iron store. The little cutter *New York* had sunk while at anchor, and the *Charybdis* had lost her masts and was a total wreck.

There being no other vessel in the port, it was useless for me to remain there. So, next day, I started on my way back to Vila, taking with me Messrs. Brown and Salisbury, also the skipper and owner of the *New York*. These gentlemen came, at my suggestion, to survey the wreck of the *Bobtail Nag*. We stayed overnight with Ford, at Tukatuka, reaching my camp at Vila on the following day.

During my absence the Rev. Mr. Mackenzie, of Errakova—a mission on the south coast about two miles distant—had paid a visit to Vila. He had left word for me that he would come over again when I returned.

Our survey of the old *Nag* was a brief one, for it was too plainly evident that she could never float again. Her "back" was broken and hogged up; the stump of the main-mast had risen through the deck, tearing its "coat" adrift; while the main-beam was in two pieces, and several butts had started above water. In the hold some of the floor-planks were protruding through the stone ballast, and her bottom had completely given way to the weight of the ship. She was a complete wreck, and a report was drawn up accordingly.

A day or two after this I was informed that the *Stanley* and the *Sibyl* were at anchor in Havannah Harbour, so off I went again to seek assistance from one or other of them. The *Sibyl* was homeward bound with recruits. Her master, Captain Turner, offered to call at Vila and take my white crew on board, giving them a passage to Maryborough.

The *Stanley* had "returns" on board, whom she was taking to their homes. Not without a great deal of bargaining I induced Captain Kilgour to come to an agreement. He was to take my recruits to Fiji for the sum of £4 10s. per adult head. The boatmen, my three Tanna "returns," the G.A. and myself were to have free passages granted to us in addition. Finally, he was to have three weeks' grace in order to land the returns he then had on board.

This agreement was formally drawn up in duplicate, and I then went on board the *Sibyl*. That vessel presently got under way, and in due course we arrived at Vila. Captain Turner then took on board my white seamen, six in number, and sailed with them. I must say I was glad to get rid of these fellows. One or two of them were only a source of trouble to me, quarrelling and squabbling continually, and, I was afraid, might occasion trouble with the natives of the island.

As I had expected, it was not long before the islanders sought to make profit out of our mishap. Fortunately, my knowledge of one of their superstitions enabled me to choke them off easily enough.

But I must go back in my narrative to relate this. During the afternoon of the day after the wreck, when we were all at work fixing up our camp, one of the

Fijians—who seemed to keep their eyes all round them—said to me :—

"Cappen! man Vila, he come!"

About a score of the natives of the islet presently hove in sight, coming towards us in single file along the beach. Each man of them carried some weapon or another, and all were more or less painted and feathered. The leader was a great swell. He sported a bunch of cock's tail-feathers stuck in his wool; he had red paint daubed on his face; and his waist-mat and ample body-cloth were stained a bright turmeric-yellow. As I soon discovered, this genius had served a term in New Caledonia. He presented, consequently, a burlesque imitation of his former employers. In particular, he had learned how to jabber and gesticulate as well as any Frenchman.

Now, I had rather a large quantity of tobacco, beads, and other "trade" wares, lying about loose in my tent. As it was decidedly inadvisable, under our circumstances, to let these gentlemen see what I was possessed of, I advanced to meet them.

"What do you want?" asked I.

"Me want to speak you," replied the imitation "man-o'-wee-wee." And he tried to walk past me to the tent. I brought him quickly to a halt by seizing his arm.

"What you want?" I again asked.

"Very good you go look chief belonga me; he like speak you."

"Suppose chief he want to speak me, very good he come here." But this did not suit our swell. Every cock fights best on his own dunghill!

"Chief, he old man. No savey walk good."

This was a lie, and I knew it.

"Me Cappen," I objected, with an assumption of dignity.

"Suppose chief he want speak me, very good he come here. What he want?"

Seeing that there was little chance of persuading me to accompany him to the village, the "noble savage" folded his arms, struck an attitude, and said:—

"Chief, he speak—how much you pay belong stop along Vila."

I had expected this, knowing their cheerful little ways, and was ready for him.

"Me no pay chief belong stop along Vila."

At this my lord stamped his foot and frowned. I continued:—

"You been broke ship belonga me!"

The frown now gave way to a look of surprise.

"By-an-by, man-o'-war come; me speak Cappen belong man-o'-war—Man Sandwich make big wind, big wind broke ship belonga me!"

Consternation and surprise appeared in his face at this, a total abandonment of the defiant attitude showing how it had impressed him.

"Man Sandwich no make big wind," he blurted out.

"Yes, man Sandwich make him. All atime, big wind he come along here," said I, pointing to north-west.

"This fellow no all the same; he come along here,"—pointing easterly towards the mainland of Sandwich; "that fellow big wind, man Sandwich make him; he broke ship alonga island belonga you. Me speak Cappen belong man-o'-war, suppose you no look out."

It was such an absurd idea to me that I was rather surprised at the effect of my words.

There was a little muttering, after which the whole party turned round and walked away; and that was the last I heard of the matter.

On the first Sunday after the wreck, Mr. Mackenzie visited me for the second time. I was in camp, but he only stayed long enough to hold service. In his discourse he endeavoured to impress upon our minds that we ought to be thankful to Providence for our preservation. By the same rule, I suppose, we ought to have thanked Providence for the loss of the ship! I was more disposed to attribute our escape from drowning to the fact that I had put back into Vila Harbour, than to consider it due to a special interposition in our favour. Next day Mr. Mackenzie appeared again, and this time inquired into my resources. I told him briefly what they were, specifying the number of days for which I had rations, and what "trade" I had to barter for more; finally hinting that we were well armed, and that food must be procured somehow.

"But surely you would not fight to obtain it?" he inquired, if I remember aright.

My answer was short, but very much to the point. I fancy it rather fluttered the reverend gentleman. I merely intimated that, if the natives possessed any store of food at all, I meant to have some of it, by whatever means I could, when my own supplies gave out.

"I will speak to the chiefs of my villages of 'worshippers'—I call them *worshippers*, for I cannot say they are Christians. I shall endeavour to make some arrangement for your people;" and away he went back to his home.

He was as good as his word, and better. I am glad I have it in my power to express my sense of gratitude to this good man and to his "worshippers."

On the morrow he appeared again, accompanied by the chief men of three villages—Pango, Errakova, and Erratapa. After very little parleying, these chiefs walked off with ninety of my recruits, promising to keep them as long as they had any food to spare, till the *Stanley* should arrive to take us away. The boys were divided into three parties, numbering respectively thirty-five, thirty, and twenty-five. One party was told off to each village; the one comprising thirty men going to Errakova, I remember.

At the same time another contingent, six in number, went to stay with Roddin, on similar terms. All Jack's

L

houses and fences had been blown down. He had begun to rebuild, and was sowing corn, so he was glad to have some assistance.

A day or two later a bush chief who lived a few miles distant from Roddin's place, took away ten more. This potentate had a neighbour who was likewise smitten with the desire to do a charitable action. Perhaps he was not unwilling to seize the chance of entertaining strangers who could teach his tribe dances and songs new to them, and relate stories. He visited my camp accordingly, and walked off with another batch of ten boys.

I had now only twenty-eight recruits, the three Tanna "returns," and the four Fijians to feed. The G.A. and I had plenty for ourselves, the cabin stores having been saved almost uninjured.

The recruits left in camp included all the women, the married men, and those who were accustomed to the use of firearms. Yet even this small complement gave me trouble occasionally. They were still on a short allowance of food, and sometimes, when they had not been fortunate in catching fish, they were apt to steal from the Vila people whenever a chance offered. Trouble naturally arose in consequence. Whenever an offence of the kind was proved, I always made restitution; then I triced the offender up to a tree, and gave him a sound thrashing.

One day a native of Mai I., who was then residing in the islet of Mele, in Pango Bay, two miles from us, visited the camp along with several Mele men. They got into conversation with the two women I had recruited at Mai, and about whom I mentioned I should have something to relate. The night after these women deserted us, stealing a Vila canoe, and crossing over in it to the other side of the harbour-mouth.

They were missed next morning, and the canoe could be seen lying on the opposite beach. The boys who went over to fetch it back reported that the women's footmarks were plainly discernible on the sand, pointing in the direction of Mele. In the afternoon I visited the islet, but was unable to recover the fair deserters. They were subsequently removed from Mele and taken back to their own island in one of Her Majesty's schooners.

Once or twice a week two of the Fijian boatmen and half a dozen of the boys got a Vila man to guide them, and went inland to the bush villages. There they would pass the night and come back next day. The Fijians took tobacco and pipes along with them, and the whole party would return laden with food, chiefly consisting of bananas. While on these visits they would be sure to have enjoyed two or three good meals to boot.

Another cyclone passed over about three weeks after the wreck. We felt only the north-eastern quadrant of it. The camp was so well sheltered that we suffered no injury. An earthquake of short duration also occurred about the same time. The G.A. happened to be bathing, and his head was under water when the first shock came. It gave him a good scare, as may be supposed. He said he thought the bottom of the harbour was giving way under him.

Three vessels visited the harbour before the *Stanley* arrived to take us away. These were the *Daphne*, Captain Mackay, from Fiji; the *Chance*, Captain Satini, from Maryborough; and the *Aurora*, a French schooner, from Noumea. Each of the British masters visited us, and offered me all the assistance that lay in their power, Captain Satini purchasing one of my boats. The French skipper, on the contrary, never came near us.

Nearly a month slowly elapsed after the departure of the *Stanley* from Havannah Harbour. I looked out anxiously for her day after day. The natives who had befriended us were finding it a serious drain on their resources to support my recruits, and at last matters came to a climax.

One day some Errakova men came down to our camp, and told me they had no more food to spare for my recruits. So, the next day, the whole ninety were to be returned on my hands.

Here was a pretty go! I had no more than sufficient damaged rice to furnish five or six meals all round. The question arose, therefore, what was to be done when that small supply had been exhausted? The only solution of the problem that I could see, lay in this:—The Mele men had taken advantage of my situation, and evinced some hostility. They had persuaded the two Mai women to desert, and were keeping them from me. The plantations belonging to these Mele people were upon the main island. I could certainly obtain food by blockading the islet of Mele, and so prevent the inhabitants from crossing over to the main, while I took their yams. I should afterwards have paid them in "trade," of course. It would have been rather a rough way of driving a bargain, no doubt; but, had it been necessary to obtain a further supply of provisions for my people, I believe I must have adopted such an expedient.

But where was the *Stanley* all this time?

In order to get news of her, I started off in the boat next morning, taking the Fijian crew, intending to run for Havannah Harbour. Just after leaving the shore, I saw a long string of half-starved boys, carrying their bundles of sleeping mats, slowly crawling along the beach towards the camp. They comprised the first batch of recruits returned on my hands. Long before I got back to Vila, the whole ninety had come in.

With a fresh fair wind I ran the boat across the bay, and past the "devil" country. When we were nearing Tukatuka Point, a boatman sang out, "Sail ho!" and, right ahead of us, there appeared a schooner, standing towards us close-hauled. It proved to be the *Stanley* at last.

On boarding her, I found that all the settlers of

Havannah Harbour had come in her. I had given out that, before leaving Vila, I intended to sell the wreck, with all the remaining stores. So these gentlemen had come along to attend the sale. Captain Kilgour had some of his "returns" on board still, which was contrary to our agreement. However, I could sooner put up with that than that he should have delayed any longer, in order to land them.

The *Stanley* anchored in Vila Harbour during the afternoon, and my recruits were shipped at once, together with such provisions as remained. For Captain Kilgour had not a great stock on board, so he said, though he had contracted to feed my boys on the passage to Fiji.

Next day the wreck and gear were sold, as also some of the "trade." A considerable quantity of this, however, I gave away to the chiefs who had entertained my men at their villages, not forgetting the two "bush" chiefs, to whom I sent off messengers as soon as the *Stanley* had anchored.

Captain Kilgour purchased the wreck, leaving a man in charge of her when we sailed for Fiji. The hull was afterwards burned, for the sake of obtaining the copper fastenings ; the anchors and chains were recovered also.

Our passage to Levuka in the *Stanley* occupied about ten days. Lucky it was that it took no longer ; for, when we anchored, we had only one day's food and two days' water remaining on board.

The medical inspector passed all the boys as fit for service—after a little good feeding. Four of them were pronounced to be under age, however; so I received payment for a hundred and forty adults only.

While I remained at Levuka, a huge ulcer developed on the inside of my right thigh. It was a result of the accident that had befallen me at Maryborough, previous to this voyage, no doubt accelerated by chronic rheumatism. I was obliged to become an inmate of the hospital, where I lay for three weeks under the care of Dr.—now Sir William—MacGregor, subsequently Administrator of British New Guinea.

On my arrival, I had made out a report of the wreck for the collector of customs, and had enclosed with it my master's certificate, pending an inquiry. No inquiry was held, however, but my certificate was not returned. As the time drew nigh when the monthly steamer was due to leave for Sydney, in which I wished to return, I was obliged to threaten the collector with legal proceedings if he retained my certificate any longer. Then I got it back. No inquiry was made by the Fijian authorities; but I believe the evidence of my crew was taken at Maryborough, when the *Sibyl* arrived there.

I left Fiji in the beginning of May, taking passage in the Australian Steam Navigation Company's s.s. *Wentworth*, Captain Saunders. On reaching Sydney I remained there about a week, when, in consequence of a telegram from Maryborough, I went on thither in the s.s. *Balclutha*, Captain Beel.

We arrived at Maryborough in the evening of May 24. Next day I accepted the command of the brigantine *Stormbird*, 160 tons register, which was then lying in the river. She was owned by a Maryborough firm.

During my absence from Queensland, a *Regulation* had been passed forbidding the export of firearms from the colony to the South Sea Islands. Another *Regulation*, passed about the same time, forbade the giving of "trade" to the friends of recruits.

These two *Regulations* were passed as "party" measures, I think, not from merely humane motives. If, however, they *were* so intended, then the ministry of that day must have been extremely short-sighted.

Luckily for us, they were not enforced for some time after. When they were, the immediate and only result was to transfer the firearms trade from British Colonial hands into those of German and French traders.

At the present time the principal article of trade in the New Hebrides and Solomon Is., with the French and German traders, consists of British-made Snider carbines. A large proportion of these bear the " TOWER " mark upon the locks—whether forged or not, I cannot say. Had the Queensland ministries which enacted these *Regulations* been wide awake, or, perhaps, not wilfully blind, they might have foreseen this.

It has materially conduced to transfer the South Sea Island trade out of British and into German hands.

Since the date of these *Regulations*, Polynesians, when leaving Queensland, have acquired the habit of taking home with them small sums of money—say two to five pounds—in order to purchase firearms and ammunition from French and German traders. Previously, they had always spent every farthing of their wages before leaving the colony.

The iron schooner *Chance* was one of the first labour vessels which sailed after the *Firearms Regulation* became law. In the beginning of January she was cleared at the custom house, at Maryborough, for a recruiting voyage. She had a long list of "returns" on board, with their baggage, which latter, as usual, included a number of muskets.

In the afternoon of the day she was cleared, the harbour-master made a raid on her, and confiscated all the firearms and ammunition to be found on board, except such as was provided for the vessel's protection. Most of the confiscated firearms owned by the " boys " had been purchased by them prior to the publication of the new *Regulation*. The vessel's owner, or agent, at once wired to Brisbane, complaining of this most unjust proceeding. Eventually, the arms were returned to the boys ; but the minister of the day added, as a rider to his licence, that the restitution was "not to be taken as a precedent."

On January 21, a deputation of gentlemen, interested in the Polynesian labour trade, waited upon the Hon.

John Douglas, who was then the Premier, to make representations against the new *Regulations*. The Premier refused to sanction the giving of "trade," but said he would consult with his colleagues respecting firearms. When I sailed in the *Stormbird*, in June, the G.A. who accompanied me was instructed not to enforce these obnoxious *Regulations*.

The Premier was afterwards obliged to receive another deputation on this subject. In March, when at Maryborough, he paid a visit to the Magnolia sugar plantation. The Kanaka labourers there, hearing that the "big fella chief," who would not allow them to take their firearms to the islands, was then in the manager's house, rolled up and demanded an audience. The manager, Mr. Boughey, refused to allow his guest to be troubled by them. However, the boys forced their way in, and spoke their minds to the Premier pretty freely. They felt they had been deceived by the Government, which, when they arrived in the colony, allowed them to purchase firearms, but now prohibited them from taking their property home with them.

They got no satisfactory answer, and, in a very bad humour, they left the "big fella chief," whom they characterized as being "no plenty good."

Of course, Boughey did his best to pacify them. When they were leaving, he happened to propose that they should give three cheers for the Queen. This, however, they flatly refused to do.

On March 11, a meeting of employers of Polynesian labour was held at Mackay, to consider a recent demand that had been made by the Government, through the sub-immigration agent of the port, for the quarterly payment of fifteen shillings on account of each Polynesian labourer, as a provision for his return passage. This, at the end of a boy's three years' service, would amount to nine pounds, whereas three to five pounds was the ruling rate for a "return's" passage money.

Hitherto it had been left to the option of an employer to make these payments, or else to provide two sureties in ten pounds apiece, to guarantee the cost of each Polynesian's return passage. Planters usually preferred the latter alternative.

The minister now demanded both payments and bonds as well. In one of his speeches or reports, he gave as his reason for this that three employers had become insolvent, and, the bonds and sureties having been neglected, their labourers' return home had not been provided for.

That this accusation was an unfounded one, was shown by Mr. Paxton, of Mackay, in a letter published in "The Brisbane Courier" of April 3. He showed that the labourers on the estates of the three insolvents referred to, had been paid their wages, and had been provided with their passages home by the mortgagees, in each instance.

But then, politicians are apt to "embroider" a little, when election times draw nigh; which puts me in mind of some verses that appeared about this time in a Mackay newspaper, and, I think, in a Maryborough one also. We often roared them out over our evening grog, on board the *Stormbird.*

Some stories of alleged ill-treatment of Polynesian labourers, in the Mackay district, having been circulated by interested parties, the recently appointed immigration agent at Maryborough was instructed by the Government to proceed to Mackay, and to investigate these charges. This he did, and made his report with the usual result—none at all!

Here are the verses, with which I shall close this chapter.

(Air — *The fine old English Gentleman.*)
Severe and grave of aspect, from Maryborough town
He came, with book and pencil, and with dark official frown.
He shuddered as he dwelt upon the horrors of Mackay,
And when he met a coloured gent, in dulcet tones would say —

(Air—*Up in a Balloon.*)

" Have you got your ki-ki ? Do you like him tea ?
Suppose him overseer fight, just talk alonga me.
Do you like him hard work, or plenty walk about ;
Big Massa Johnny Douglas, he plenty good, look out."

He wandered through plantations, and he fossicked through the cane,
With tales of dread atrocities still flitting through his brain.
At last he met a sable youth from Tongoa's sunny isle,
Who greeted the inspector with a mild fraternal smile—

" Yes, me got me ki-ki. What for you no can see ?
Overseer bery good ; no fight alonga me.
But wine, blancmange, and oyster sauce me nebber yet enjoy ;
Big Massa Johnny Douglas, plenty gammon, longa boy."

That stern official closed his book and shed a silent tear,
And thought of rosy billets with six hundred pounds a year.
Then, rolling up his humble swag, he quickly sped away,
And standing on the steamer's deck he warbled forth this lay—

"Yes, they've got their ki-ki, as I can plainly see ;
Election times are drawing nigh—the game is up with me.
From the Logan to the Pioneer the cry is still the same—
Big Massa Johnny Douglas must try some other game ! "

CHAPTER X.

FIRST VOYAGE OF THE *STORMBIRD*, 1878.

I sail for the New Hebrides—Tom Tamoan—His story—Black Beach, Tanna I.—Battle between Ibet and Worgus tribes—Fugitive women recruited—Dinah—The conquerors demand the runaways—I decline to surrender them—Boat swamped at Verigo—The mate chases a thief—Fotuna I.—" The Baby "—Aniwa I.—I visit Mr. Paton—Explanations and promises—A lunatic recruited—At Batnapni Bay—Story of Tabbiseisei—Murders committed by him—Mota I.—Ureparapara I.—Towing the ship out of the lagoon—At Valua I.—Recovering an anchor with dynamite—How another skipper tried the dodge—Espiritu Santo I.—Pentecost I.—How Tabbiseisei murdered Mr. Brown—Tabbisangwul's tale—Commander De Houghton takes vengeance—Trivial punishment occasions more murders—Respective action of British and French naval officers—Why British subjects naturalize as French citizens—Ford's runaways—How I adjusted matters—A squall off Cato Reef—Nearly lost—Arrival at Maryborough—Bankruptcy of owner—Reappointment—The Rev. George Brown—His expedition—Chastisement of the savages—Reflections upon this incident.

I SAILED from Maryborough in command of the *Stormbird*, on June 12, 1878, bound first for the New Hebrides with " returns."

Among the Kanaka boatmen I had shipped for the voyage was one ordinarily called Tom—an abbreviation of his real name—Tamoan. He had been a long time in Queensland, ever since he was a child, and could neither remember the name of the vessel that had brought him there nor that of her master. Soon after his arrival, he had run off from his employer with some others, stolen a boat with them, and gone north along the coast. They came to grief on Wide Bay bar, and all were drowned except Tom. He was found by some lumberers in a half-crazy state, and had been taken to Maryborough by them, where he had worked for various employers during ten or twelve years.

I had known this youth for a couple of years, and he constantly asked me to find his island and take him home. All he knew about it was that its native name was Mungigi, and that it was near other islands, of which one was called Mungava. I had searched all my charts and "directories" in vain—I could not locate his home. At last he had fastened himself upon me, persuading me to engage him as a boatman; in the hope that, while cruising with me, he might some day come to his native island.

After a rather long passage, the *Stormbird* reached Tanna I., where I anchored off Black Beach one morning. The boats were soon down, and off looking for recruits, but without success. Towards evening the sound of firing was heard in the direction of Ibet, a bay and islet about half a mile away from our anchorage. It speedily became evident that a battle was going on. As we learned eventually, the Worgus people had attacked the Ibet tribe, and defeated them. Ere long the various sounds of conflict died away, while thick smoke rising above the trees proclaimed that the victors had set fire to the houses of the village.

Shortly afterwards a faint "coo-ee" was heard from the shore. Away went the boats in the direction of the hail, presently returning with five Ibet women. The eldest of these, a woman of about thirty-five, gave her name as Nuswoiu or Dinah, the latter name having been bestowed upon her in Queensland, where she had been in service. Speaking good English, she told us that the village had been destroyed, many of its people killed, and the survivors driven into the forest. She and her companions desired to ship as recruits, and had swum off to the boats with that object. She also stated that she had been a widow for years, and that the Ibet chief who had been killed in the recent action was her brother. The youngest of the fugitives—a slip of a girl—just old enough to be recruited, was the chief's daughter, and consequently Dinah's niece. The husbands of the other women had also been killed in the battle. This story seeming probable enough, I accepted the party as recruits.

Just before sunset, the boats went off to Black Beach again, in response to another "coo-ee." They brought back one more Ibet runaway, a man this time. These were the only individuals of the Ibet tribe we came in contact with.

Before I left Black Beach, which I did the following morning, a party of the Worgus invaders hailed the boats near Ibet. They had witnessed the escape of the women the previous evening, and now demanded that we should give them up. They claimed the poor things as their property, acquired by the fortune of war. As an alternative, they insisted on being paid an exorbitant price in " trade."

It seemed likely that, if their demands were not complied with, they would fire on the boats; so the mate who was in charge of them, and the G.A., were wise enough to temporize. Pretending they must consult me, and promising to return to the shore with either the women or the goods, they were allowed to depart without hostilities.

If these Worgus men had been content to ask no more than the usual amount of trade, I should have sent it to them. As it was, however, they got nothing, and the women went to Queensland with me. But the reader may rest assured that my boats did not go near Worgus again on that voyage.

The day after this we landed some "returns" at Verigo, on the south-western coast. This proved a difficult job, and came very near being a disastrous one to boot.

Tanna men's boxes were almost always exceedingly heavy, on account of the quantity of bullets, and lead for slugs, that they collected to take home with them. The coast was rocky and broken; a considerable swell rolling in to make matters worse.

One boat had discharged her load, not without difficulty, and had shoved off a little way whilst the other backed in. As they were lugging the last chest over the stern, a small line from the shore being attached to it, the boat's keel grounded on a sunken boulder between two seas. She immediately canted over; the top of the succeeding wave rolled right upon her, filling her up to the gunwale, luckily without capsizing or injuring her. The chest was saved, I believe, but everything in it and in the boat was swamped.

A native who was standing in the water, close to the boat, seized the opportunity and grabbed the mate's Snider rifle, with which he incontinently bolted up the rocks and made for the bush. The mate was after him instantly, although he was barefooted, and his feet were terribly cut by the sharp stones. The chase extended over a quarter of a mile or so, till the Tanna man, close pressed and covered by the mate's revolver, came to a halt and delivered up his prize. Had he been aware that the rifle was loaded, he might have turned on his pursuer and made it rough for him. Happily, he did *not* know it.

Next day I visited Fotuna I., landing a boy there, who had been house servant to the manager of Magnolia plantation, near Maryborough. He had been a great favourite with his late employer, and, in consequence thereof, had been nicknamed " Baby."

It was generally supposed that the " Baby" would persuade half the inhabitants of the little island to engage; and that after a few hours' visit to his relatives he would accompany us back to Maryborough. But though I kept the vessel dodging about under the lee of the island, from daylight until late in the afternoon, we saw nothing more of him. Moreover, other natives informed us that "missionary no let man go away!"

Tired of waiting, I hoisted in the boats, and squared away for Tanna I., where I proposed to anchor for the night. However, the wind fell light, and by sunset I had got no further than Aniwa or Niua I. This was the scene of the burglary I had been accused of committing on the missionary's house, in 1875, when I was here with the *Stanley*.

I had often wished for an opportunity of paying the author of this calumny a visit, so that I might demand an explanation from him. So I now proposed to the G.A. that we should go on shore, late as it was, and interview the gentleman. To this he at once assented.

Leaving the ship hove to, about a quarter of a mile distant from the rocky coast of the island, we pulled ashore in the gloaming. There was some difficulty in finding a convenient landing-place. Guided by the voice of a native, who could see us though we could not discern him, I steered into a nook among the rocks which afforded the only fair landing-place on the island, and which was directly opposite to the mission house. Here we landed, and a little further back, under the shadow of the trees, found the missionary, Mr. Paton, waiting to receive us.

The customary greetings having been got over, the reverend gentleman invited us to walk up to his house. This I at first declined to do, and then entered into the subject which had brought me there. I told him that I wished to hear his explanation of the report—emanating from himself—that I had broken into his house on a certain occasion three years previous to this.

Of course he had his excuse ready. He also said he had done and would do all that lay in his power to contradict the report and dispel the false impression it had created. His excuse was satisfactory enough. As to his promise, I feel bound to say that I take quite a different view. Since this interview, I many times made careful inquiry; and though at least a dozen men informed me that this "gentleman" had accused me of robbing his house, not one ever said he had heard him contradict it.

Mr. Paton explained that the Aniwa boy I had recruited at the time of the alleged burglary, had left some clothes locked up in his kitchen, a building detached from the dwelling-house. Immediately after the *Stanley* sailed, certain natives, friends of my recruit, had broken into the kitchen and abstracted the boy's clothes, afterwards laying the blame on me. He said he had been misled by the statements made to him by these natives; he furthermore tendered an apology, and renewed his invitation to us to enter his house and spend an hour with him and his wife.

We did spend an hour—perhaps two—in his house; and very sorry I was, subsequently, that I ever went near it. Out of the occasion there arose another scandal, one that was just as false as the first, and which might have proved much more injurious to me.

In the course of conversation, the incident at Black Beach was mentioned. I described the tribal fight we had heard going on, and how we recruited the five fugitive women. The reverend gentleman then expressed his satisfaction that we had saved the women from being enslaved or murdered by the conquerors of their tribe.

I shall have to refer to this unpleasant topic later in my narrative. It will be enough to record now that sometime after our visit to him, this gentleman actually reported to the Government—either the Imperial or the Queensland Government—that I had *kidnapped* certain women, and that in his house, in his own presence and in that of his wife, I had "boasted of my exploits!"

Now, I think that if I *had* boasted of any kidnapping in his presence that evening, he would scarcely have accompanied us down to the boat as he did, with a boy in front carrying a lantern, and have almost affectionately shaken hands with us and bidden us a hearty "good-night and good-bye."

I think I visited nearly every one of the islands of the New Hebrides this voyage, not even omitting the Torres Is., a small cluster north-west of the Banks' Is., though I obtained no recruits there.

On the south-western coast of Api I., the recruiter and the G.A. brought off a dirty, hairy, wild-looking specimen of humanity. He was a native of Ambrym I., had been a labourer in Fiji, and on his return had been persuaded by some Api men to land with them. Of course their tribe reaped the benefit of his stock of "trade," and then very likely ill-treated him. He had run away from them into the bush, and now offered himself once more as a recruit. He seemed rather scared at first, but we did not suppose he was deranged, as it turned out that he was.

Soon after this man's engagement, he was missed one morning, and was supposed to have gone overboard. By-and-by, however, he was discovered in concealment under the bunks, amongst the firewood. A day or two later I had anchored among the Maskelyne Is. There, some Mallicolo men came on board in the evening, making their canoe fast alongside, and being allowed to sleep on board at their own request. This was a frequent incident; intending recruits often liking to ascertain a vessel's character in that way. In the night our "cranky" recruit disappeared with the canoe, and so I saw the last of him, though the canoe was found on one of the adjacent islets.

At Batnapni, Pentecost I., the natives were friendly for the most part. One party, however, headed by a chief called Tabbiseisei (or Tarisisi), appeared to be rather sulky. Judging by what afterwards happened here, this chief was no doubt looking out for a chance to murder some white man.

A short time before, the French schooner *Aurora* had had a "difficulty" with the natives here. Her people had burnt a small hut, which belonged to Tabbiseisei, serving him as a temporary shelter when he came down to the beach from his village, Manbon. No other mischief was done besides the destruction of this hut—a trumpery roof of leaf-thatch set on bare poles—yet Tabbiseisei wanted the life of a white man to pay for it. Eventually, he succeeded in taking one. Then H.M.S. *Beagle* came, and her crew burnt his village. For that he took another white man's life.

A native of another village warned us against the chief, so my people kept on their guard, giving him no favourable opportunity for attacking them. The G.A. even had a long conversation with him on the beach.

Proceeding northward, I next visited Aoba and Aurora Is., whence I went on to Banks' Is. At Sugar-loaf I. (Mota) some "returns" were landed one morning. While the ship was lying off shore there, drifting along close in to the western coast, several youngsters—apparently belonging to the Rev. Mr. Selwyn's flock—paddled their little canoes under our stern. There they laid awhile, spelling out the ship's name and port of registry. Probably they had been sent off for that purpose. The name *Stormbird* they made out easily, as also *Mary*. The pronunciation of *borough* was too much for them, though I dare say they would be able to report the letters composing it accurately enough.

Arrived at Ureparapara I., I attempted to enter the bay, round which the island extends in a horseshoe form. Hardly were we within the "Heads," when the wind dropped, and I saw the landlocked waters lying calm and still, scarcely creased by occasional catspaws of wind.

The ship was rounded to immediately, the boats lowered and got ahead to tow her out again. However, the swell rolled in so heavily that we had nearly two hours' towing before we could get the ship far enough out to feel the trade-wind, and so beat to sea again.

This island is about three miles across at its widest point, and rises 2,000 feet above sea level. The bay I had intended to anchor in appears to have once been the crater of an immense volcano, the eastern wall of which has given way and admitted the sea.

Here I landed the last returns I had on board; thence going on and visiting the Torres Is., but without any success.

At Motolava, or Valua I., I lay for one night recruiting. The day following, the wind dropped, the glass falling steadily; so I loosened the sails and hove up the anchor, letting the ship swing stern on to the kedge, which I had also down, hauling in the warp as she drifted off the land. I expected the kedge to trip easily, but, to my dismay, it held firmly and refused to come home. Several times the warp was slackened and then hauled upon, yet still the kedge held firmly. I began to think I was going to lose it, along with thirty fathoms of warp; for, when I sounded, I got bottom at thirty-three fathoms.

In this dilemma I got a wrinkle from the G.A. We rove an iron hoop—taken off a beef cask—along the warp from its inboard end, until it came to the taffrail. Then we attached to the hoop a package containing four charges of dynamite, with a detonator and fuse in the middle of it.

The warp holding taut perpendicularly, we lit the fuse, and let the hoop and package slip down over it right on top of the kedge. Less than a minute after the dynamite exploded. We felt it as though a sledge-hammer had struck the vessel's bottom. A mound-like wave of discoloured water rose up at about two fathoms distance from the stern, and numerous dead fish, with other curious objects, presently floated on the surface.

The warp was slackened a little, and then hauled on. Then, much to my relief, up came the kedge, neither it nor the warp proving to be any the worse for the unusual treatment accorded them.

Since then, I have several times tried this plan of freeing an anchor which has hooked fast in the coral, and with a like result.

Not everybody has had the same luck as mine, though. There was a skipper, I remember, who tried it, and got results he did not desire. While lying at Mau I., his anchor got jammed in the coral. He slackened away the cable until his vessel was well clear of the spot. Then he went in his boat and dropped down a tremendous charge of dynamite, in five fathoms of water. His boys got confused at the critical moment, some pulling away, others backing their oars. The charge exploded before they had made a fathom, smashing the stern of the boat, and swamping it. He got his anchor, however.

Sailing southward from Ureparapara, I worked the western coast of Espiritu Santo I. There I anchored first in Barrai Inlet; a nook so small that I had to moor with both anchors. At this place the natives kept us "on a string" for three days, promising recruits and then disappearing, which did not tend to the improvement of our tempers. Thence we worked leisurely along south with fair success, anchoring off Pali, opposite the village, at Tasselmana, and at Pai.

I then paid another visit to Pentecost I., anchoring as before in Batnapni Bay. The broad, sandy beach, on which a crowd of natives had loitered during my last visit, was now deserted. Only two or three men appeared on the other side of the watering-place, coming from Verramatmat. One of them came off to the ship with the G.A.

This man, whose name was Tabbisangwul, had a sad

story to relate. He told us that the Queensland labour schooner, *May Queen*, had anchored here since our last visit. Tabbiseisei, the chief of Manbon village, came down to the beach with a number of his men, still bent on having a white man's blood, to avenge the burning of his hut by the crew of the *Aurora*.

Brown, the mate of the *May Queen*, had gone to the beach in one of the boats, with a crew of four Kanakas. He was standing in the stern of the boat, talking to the Manbon men, when the chief got his opportunity. Coming stealthily behind Brown, he struck him on the back of the neck with his tomahawk, killing him instantly. Two of the boat's crew were simultaneously slain by Tabbiseisei's men, and then the whole party made for the bush and got off scot-free.

Tabbisangwul had witnessed the whole affair from a little distance. He was a returned labourer, and spoke very fair English. I entered his story in my official log, making two copies of it. One of these I left with him, to hand to the commander of the first British ship of war that should call at the island. The second copy I took to Havannah Harbour on my return homeward, leaving it there with similar instructions.

Some time after this, H.M.S. *Beagle*, Commander De Houghton, arrived in Batnapni Bay. The *Sibyl*—Captain Satini, Mr. Lynde G.A.—was then lying at anchor there. A party of blue-jackets was landed, and, reinforced by the crew of the labour vessel, they made a raid upon Tabbiseisei's village in the interior. They destroyed the village, but, I think, did little harm to the inhabitants beyond that.

The boatswain of the *Sibyl* was the only member of the force who was hurt. While they were on the march, a native suddenly sprang out from behind some bushes and struck him on the head with a tomahawk, inflicting a severe wound. This plucky fellow got away, though he left a thick trail of blood behind him.

I am aware that Commander De Houghton was acting under instructions, and that he could do neither more nor less than his orders permitted. Still, I maintain that it would have been much better if he had never come near the island under the circumstances.

The very trivial punishment inflicted only served to exasperate Tabbiseisei, instead of deterring him from further outrages. Before three months had passed after the destruction of his village, he took his revenge for that by killing another white man—the mate of a Fijian vessel, which had visited Batnapni Bay.

I could cite a dozen instances in which the insufficient punishment meted out by our ships of war, has but led to reprisals, instead of cowing the savages into good behaviour. In nine cases out of ten, owing to the way the home authorities have hampered their action, the commanders of British warships have done more harm than good for the interests they have been supposed to protect.

Commanders of French ships of war enjoy much more freedom of action in these waters. This is the reason why so many British-born traders, in the New Hebrides and elsewhere, have transferred their allegiance from Great Britain to France.

Calling next at Api I., I there boarded the *Onward*, of Sydney, a whaling barque, which was soon after wrecked off New Caledonia. Thence I proceeded to Havannah Harbour, Sandwich I., where I took in wood and water. There I heard that the natives of South-West Bay, Mallicolo I., had fired on the boats of the *Janet Stewart*, of Maryborough, and the *Daphne*, of Fiji. One white man had been killed, and some Kanakas wounded.

The evening before I left Havannah Harbour, a canoe came alongside bringing off a dozen men, natives of islands further north. They had run away from their employer—Ford, of Tukatuka—and now wished to go to Queensland with me.

Though I had a good shipload of recruits already, my full complement was not yet made up. Still, it would not do for me to sail away with another man's labourers, as these boys proposed. On the other hand, if I refused to engage them, they would most likely make off into the bush, and remain there until some more compliant recruiter should happen along. So, in the meanwhile, I sent them down below with a pipe and plug of tobacco apiece.

Next day I anchored off Tukatuka, and went on shore to have a talk with Ford. I got him to promise that he would not punish the boys for their escapade, and then, returning on board, I sent them on shore to him.

I returned to Queensland by the north of New Caledonia. The wind being due east, I entered Balade Pass early in the day, getting through the reefs before dark, and coming out by Iande Pass. The wind then went round to north a little, the glass falling, and I was carried into the vicinity of Cato Reef and Islet, about 160 miles from Breaksea Spit.

It was a dull, cloudy morning, when the breeze hauled into the north, soon becoming squally, so that I had to take in the light sails. As the men were doing this, a heavy squall came up from windward, travelling rapidly down on the ship. Then a vivid flash of lightning seemed to split the dense rain-clouds right across.

"Hard up!" I shouted to the man at the wheel, but, unluckily, without waiting to see that he executed the order.

The topgallant-sail was clewed up smartly, and then, just as the wind caught the ship down came the topsail, whilst I let go the main throat halyards myself.

But the helm was only half up! Whether the man at the wheel had been frightened by the appearance of the lightning, or what, I cannot say. The tremendous force of the wind, as it struck the ship, caused her to broach to, though I seized the wheel myself, letting the main sheet rip out to the clinch. Over went the ship, until her lee side, fore and aft, was buried in the water, the boat and davits in the waist being submerged, and the seas pouring over the lee-combings of the main hatch into the hold below. For a moment, I thought the *Stormbird* must founder under us.

Happily, the squall passed off as quickly as it came, and the ship righted herself. We had just begun cutting at the weather rigging, hoping the foremast would go over the side and relieve her.

We encountered other squalls during that day; then the wind gradually hauled round to west-south-west, freshening into a steady fine-weather gale, which, in three days, carried the *Stormbird* about a hundred miles; for she was like a bladder on the water, being very lightly ballasted. The first land I made was the Australian coast, about twenty miles south of Wide Bay.

I crossed the bar and anchored off the pilot station at the southern end of Fraser I. Strait, on September 24. There I received news that the owner of the *Stormbird* had become insolvent. However, as the vessel was safe under our feet, with a shipload of recruits on board, this did not affect me much. The late owner still continued to act as agent for the vessel.

Owing to the northerly wind, which still continued blowing stiffly, a week elapsed after my arrival before I could get the vessel up to town. During this week one of the Australian Steam Navigation Co.'s steamers, the *Tinonee*, made an attempt to tow us up the river alongside of her, but had to abandon it.

On the third day after our arrival at Maryborough, I was legally bound to pay my crew off. I had considerable difficulty in procuring the necessary sum for this purpose. In fact, I had to go to the lawyers. Seeing, I suppose, that I "knew the ropes," the Bank of New South Wales, which held the mortgages upon the ship, advanced the money required, paid my lawyer, and then took possession of her, retaining my services as master and agent. This was a very nice billet for me, for a month, at the end of which time the *Stormbird* was sold. The late owner was re-appointed agent for her, while I was again installed as master.

About this time news had arrived in Queensland of some stirring scenes on the island of New Britain, now called Neu Pommern. I took especial interest in this because one John Nash and I had been the first two white men who had ventured to form trading stations on that island, namely, in 1873. We were both then employed by the South Sea trading firm of J. C. Godeffroy & Sons, of Hamburg.

A missionary, the Rev. George Brown, had since located himself on Duke of York I., now called Neu Lauenburg, the largest of a group situated in St. George's Channel, between New Britain and New Ireland. Thence he had sent Polynesian teachers and their wives into the two great islands.

Some of these had been murdered by the natives of New Britain, the news reaching Mr. Brown at Duke of York I. about April 8. To prevent further murders, he had immediately organized an expedition, by which some fifty of the natives had been killed, and several villages and plantations destroyed.

No doubt, as Commander De Houghton remarked to me, Brown's promptitude had punished the natives and checked further outrages. I feel certain, however, that if such reprisals had been undertaken by a layman, a howl of indignation would have arisen from Exeter Hall. Likely enough, too, the leader of the expedition would have been hanged when he got home. At any rate, he would have been sharply informed that, instead of taking the law into his own hands, he should have withdrawn his remaining followers out of danger, and have waited for the arrival of a man-of-war. When one came, her commander would make believe to punish the murderers by promiscuous firing away of powder and shell, cutting down cocoanut trees, and killing pigs. This, too, after having first warned the murderers to get clear away out of danger!

Mr. Brown evidently failed to appreciate the quality of the public feeling which extricated him from this scrape. When speaking in his own defence, at a public meeting, held in Albert Street Church, Brisbane, in aid of the Australian Wesleyan Foreign Mission, May 19, 1879, he said :—

"I claim to be a man first, and then to be a missionary —above all an Englishman!" He ought rather to have said :—

"I claim to be a missionary first, a man next, and last of all an Englishman!" It would have fitted the facts more accurately, perhaps.

CHAPTER XI.

SECOND VOYAGE OF THE *STORMBIRD*, 1878–9.

I sail for the New Hebrides—Fresh instructions—News at Havannah Harbour—Renton and Muir murdered—A cannibal feast—Christmas at Tongoa I.—Bad weather—The hurricane season—Port Sandwich—Dodging the weather—Tannoa islet.—A visit in the night—" Me go Mallybulla "—Betarri—Matrimonial customs—Inquiries—A warning—The attack—A bath interrupted—Dangerous quarters—Shokki declines an amnesty—I capture the island fleet—A battle in the dark—A lucky mistake—Getting to sea—How a story grows—Tabbisangwul and Tabbiseisei—Sam's mishap—Ship surgery—Visit of a missionary—Altercation and argument—My Bible—The missionary retreats—The Astrolabe Reef—Arrive at Maryborough—Allotment of recruits—Official blundering—A few hard words—Slavery !—I lose my command—Murders at Brooker I.—Mr. McFarlane's report—My opinion of the savage nature.

I LEFT Maryborough about November 18, and, having taken in wood and water at the White Cliffs, as usual, I ran through Fraser I. Strait with a northerly wind, across Wide Bay bar, bound for the New Hebrides.

I had a large number of "returns" on board; also a passenger in the cabin. This was a young gentleman who was taking the trip with us for the sake of his health. The G.A. who had accompanied me on my last voyage had been reappointed. A fresh proviso had been added to his instructions this time, however. He was ordered to act in conjunction with the master, and to assign the recruits to the various employers they were to serve, before the ship should have arrived in port on her return.

Moderate weather prevailed until I had rounded the

reefs off the southern end of New Caledonia. A stiff breeze then came up from south-west, bringing with it heavy squalls of wind and rain. The sky, when visible between the squalls, showed a dull leaden tint, streaked and spotted with small white clouds. Its general appearance was far from pleasant, a low barometer also seeming to indicate the proximity of a cyclone. As I ran north-eastward, however, the weather gradually improved.

I had nothing to delay me at the southern islands of the New Hebrides, so I pressed on at once to Sandwich I. There I anchored off Semma, in Havannah Harbour, where I received rather startling news.

On November 9, the natives of Aoba, or Lepers' I., had captured a recruiting boat belonging to the *Mystery* labour schooner. They had killed her crew — four native boatmen, and two white men, Thomas Muir, mate, and John Renton, G.A. The last was the man Captain Murray had rescued from Malayta I., as I have previously mentioned.

The motive for these murders was not revenge, but simply cannibalism. A great feast had been arranged to take place, to which all the surrounding tribes were invited. The chief of the tribe that gave it desired to show hospitality on a grand scale, and accordingly provided the rare dainty of white man's flesh, to do honour to his guests on the occasion. So I was told, at any rate, by a man who said he had been present at the feast.

The captured boat was hauled up far above high-water mark, and lay there some time, exposed to view from the sea. It was eventually recovered by Captain Kilgour, during the next voyage of the *Mystery*.

The area of my recruiting work during this voyage was almost entirely limited to Sandwich I. and Espiritu Santo I., with the smaller islands near them. The hurricane season had begun, and it was therefore advisable to keep such a light-ballasted craft as mine was within safe anchorage.

We ate our Christmas pudding at Tongoa I. This dainty we had brought from Maryborough, it being the gift of a kind lady friend of mine. Then, working a northerly course from one anchorage to another, we were off the western coast of Ambrym I. by New Year's Day.

The weather was now generally fine, though very hot, with light northerly winds, and, occasionally, a dead calm of short duration. While these lasted, circular masses of cloud-bank were sometimes seen moving slowly eastward. Such as passed over the ship precipitated a tremendous downpour of rain, with sometimes a flash or two of lightning, and a crackle of thunder. Five minutes after the cloud had passed over, the ship would be out in the blazing sun again, her canvas soaked with rain, and her decks steaming. In weather like this, the smell from the hold was always very powerful, and anything but pleasant; though it was not so pungent, perhaps, as it would have been if we had had negroes on board instead of Kanakas.

On January 1, as it looked like a hurricane, and the glass was down to 29·7 and falling, I struck the royals, top-gallant-yards and mast, and rove a heel rope to the main-top-mast. The indications being still more threatening next day, I brought the ship to an anchor in Port Sandwich, Mallicolo I. I was just in time, for the cloud-bank rose rapidly. By next morning, early, a hard gale was blowing from the north-west, coming over the land in heavy squalls, accompanied by dense blinding rain.

Three days I lay here. Then, as the wind fell light again, though still blowing from the west, I towed and sailed out of the harbour. Before morning it came on to blow again, and I was glad to get back into Port Sandwich and safety once more. Next day, I left the harbour a second time, getting as far as Merrabwei, where I anchored for one night. Much the same game went on next day, and the next after that. In fact, I spent a whole week dodging the weather, before I could get well away. At length the sky cleared, and a light southerly breeze enabled us to get to work, recruiting along the coast northward.

One Saturday evening I trailed into the bay on the eastern extremity of Tannoa islet, off Espiritu Santo I., anchoring there for the night. One or two canoes had met the ship as she entered the bay, and, returning to the islet, spread the news of our arrival. About nine o'clock, I was walking my half-poop, enjoying a pipe, when I heard a splash in the water below, followed by a sound like something rubbing against the side. Looking over, I was just able to make out a small canoe, such as we generally called a one-horse gig, alongside ; while a figure was standing on the lowest step of the side ladder, hanging on by the man-ropes, and in the act of shoving the canoe away, which quickly vanished into the night.

The figure then climbed on deck, coming into the light shining from the cabin sky-light and the deckhouse amidships. It proved to be that of a rather small young woman, plump and good-looking. A glance at her open countenance was sufficient to assure me that this was certainly not her first experience of civilization.

She had brought off all her "plunder" with her, apparently. She had donned two if not three dresses, and wore about a couple of pounds of beads strung as necklaces and bracelets. She carried in her arms a bundle nearly as big as herself, consisting of shawls and other clothes.

"Me want to go Mallybulla," said this young lady, not a whit abashed at the crowd that quickly gathered round her.

"You gimme pipe ; me want to smoke," was her next demand, which was quickly complied with by one of my crew.

This girl proved to be a native of Marlo, or St.

Bartholomew I. She had been to Fiji, in service; returning whence she had been landed on Tannoa I. with some "boys" who belonged to it; and now she wanted to go to Queensland. Her name was Mary Betarri, which was put on the recruit list accordingly. Then, having received her blanket, pipe, and tobacco, she was consigned to the women's quarters for the night.

It was afterwards said that the trouble we presently experienced here arose out of our having abducted a married woman. There is no doubt Betarri had been living with a man since she came to the islet, though

MARY BETARRI.

not before. No matrimonial ceremony is observed, however, on these islands. When a man takes a wife unto himself, he makes some present or payment to her father, or nearest male relative, and that is all. If no such payment has been made, the woman is free to leave her "husband" whenever she may think fit to do so—if his club should not be at hand !

The next day being Sunday, we lay quiet, doing no work besides landing three men. Several canoes came off from the shore, and about a dozen natives visited the ship. Some of them came on deck and prowled about, one or two asking if Betarri was on board—for she kept close down below. The inquirers were told she was in the ship, and they went away without making any further remarks.

Early next morning, I sent the boats ashore to fill the casks with water at a small stream on the main island, and by breakfast-time our tanks had all been replenished. As they were coming off for the last time, I noticed Tannoa canoes going over to the main from the islet.

Now, it is a daily custom among these people to visit their plantations on the mainland, for the purpose of getting thence such food as they require. The women generally perform this task, guarded by a few of the men. The canoes I saw this time held no women, being full of men only. I therefore warned the mate and the G.A. to be careful, and to keep well on their guard when they landed to cut firewood.

After breakfast the boats went ashore again. Notwithstanding my warning, the G.A. thought it would be a good opportunity to treat himself to a fresh-water bath. About half an hour after they were gone, a couple of shots rang out near the boats. Looking in their direction, I saw our boatmen, guns in hand, searching the edge of the forest for the concealed enemy; and I could also see the G.A., lightly attired in a pair of blucher boots, and nothing else, with his Snider rifle in readiness, standing near the water-hole, out of which he had just emerged. Two or three more shots presently came from the point, aimed at the ship; the bullets falling near us, or passing over our heads. I need hardly say no more firewood was cut, the boats returning to the ship without delay.

Just before the firing began, the G.A. had taken a plunge into the water-hole—a pool banked up by the sea across the mouth of the little stream. One bullet struck the water close in front of him, as he rose up from a dip; another splintered a log the mate was chopping, right under his foot.

Fighting was not our business, so I thought the best

thing to be done was to clear out of that, and go to a friendlier spot. The windlass was manned accordingly, and the anchor got up, while the sails were set. With the light air we had, the quickest way of getting out to sea was to run through the channel between the main island and Tannoa. This I attempted, therefore. Unluckily the wind dropped, and I was obliged to anchor again, at not much more than a hundred yards distance from the western end of the islet.

Most of the fighting men of Tannoa seem to have been on the mainland. They gave us a few shots from the point, but the range was too great for their

A BATH INTERRUPTED.

bullets to reach us. They did not dare to show themselves, our Snider bullets going unpleasantly close to them. Had they been on the islet, though, they might have given us a nice peppering, taking cover under the trees and rocks during the daytime. One canoe attempted to cross from the main island to the islet, but a bullet from the ship sent it back in a hurry.

The weather remained calm and dull all day, so I had to lie quietly at anchor, trusting a land breeze would spring up after nightfall and help us out to sea. Towards evening the G.A. and I took the two boats in towards the point, as the enemy had ceased firing. We did not venture very close, however, not knowing whether our foes might not be lurking in ambush still.

Opening communications, we did our best to bring Shokki, the chief, to a parley, but without success. Neither he nor his men would venture near us. They knew they could get back to Tannoa as soon as night fell; and then, when morning came, they would have us cheap—if I was fool enough to stay there.

Since Shokki seemed indisposed to come to terms, we rowed to Tannoa, where twenty or thirty canoes of various sizes lay drawn up on the beach. A nice little fleet indeed, to beat off, if the enemy should try to board us ! One of these canoes—a very large one—I damaged, so that it could not be made use of without considerable repairing. Most of the remainder I towed off to the ship, thus lessening the possible naval force we might have to deal with. I had no immediate intention of destroying the canoes, however.

Night fell without any further disturbance, while we took care not to expose ourselves to chance shots. About midnight a light air came off the land, but as it would have been hardly enough to help us out, I did not then weigh anchor. Besides, I remembered that men generally sleep soundest just before daylight. I waited until four o'clock, therefore, and then called all hands on deck, without noise, to man the windlass.

When this was done, there was noise enough to waken up the entire islet, of course. The clanking of the pauls, and the rattle of the chain cable, rang out clear through the morning air. For some ten or fifteen minutes my fellows worked with a will, undisturbed. Then, suddenly, "bang!" "bang!" "bang!" came from the islet. Not a bullet touched the ship, apparently, though we could hear the "ping" as they flew overhead. The G. A. and I went aft with our Sniders, and lying down on the half-poop, watched for the next shots through the quarter-rails.

A few minutes passed quietly. Then we saw the flash and heard the report of guns again, the bullets whistling high above our heads. This time we replied to them, though the only mark we had to aim at in the darkness was the flash of the enemy's guns.

This amusement was kept up on both sides for heaven only knows how long. Men do not take much account of time under such circumstances. The enemy had a better mark to shoot at than we had, but all their shots flew high, some striking the mast-heads. The sound indicated that they were using rifles; while the long intervals elapsing between the shots proved there could hardly be more than three of them at work. We surmised, therefore, and correctly as it turned out, that the weapons they were using were the muzzle-loading Enfields our three "returns" had taken on shore with them on Sunday.

Subsequently, we heard that the firing party were under the impression that the "long sights" on the Enfields were designed to make the rifles shoot *harder*. Hence they elevated the sights, and their bullets flew too high in consequence. It was a lucky mistake for us!

The sails had remained loose all night, so there was no necessity to expose any of the hands by sending them aloft. When the chain had been hove short, the boats were sent ahead with tow-lines, and as soon as the anchor was up, they fetched the ship round with the assistance of the jibs. Then the square canvas was set, and, amid a din of yelling and firing on both sides, we slowly crept away from the anchorage, and were soon out of range. Not a moment too soon, either, for the last bullet dropped near our stern just as daylight dawned!

I still had the canoes alongside. But, since the owners of them had prevented us from collecting firewood, I chopped our captures up to serve as such; and very poor material for the purpose did they yield. Shokki and his men must have fancied they had us cheap, both ashore and afloat, since they resorted to open hostilities. Had the chief simply spoken to me on the subject, he would have received the usual "pay" for Betarri, and would have saved his canoes into the bargain.

Now for an illustration of how a story will grow as it flies.

About three weeks later I anchored off St. Bartholomew I. There the natives informed us that a schooner's crew had recently attacked Tannoa I. That, having landed, they had destroyed all the canoes, burnt the village, killed a score of men, and had driven the remainder of the inhabitants away from the islet.

Luckily for us there was no missionary in the neighbourhood of Tannoa, to exaggerate the story, and make another blood-curdling atrocity out of it.

At Batnapni, Pentecost I., very few natives appeared. Those who did venture near the boats, came from the village of Verramatmat, on the bluff. They told us that Tabbisangwul—the man to whom I had given a statement of Brown's murder for the next "man-of-war" that touched there—had been obliged to leave home and go to Queensland as a "recruit." Tabbiseisei, the murderer, had sworn vengeance against him for giving information to the captain of the *Beagle*, and acting as interpreter.

A sad mishap overtook one of my boatmen on the south coast of Mallicolo I. While he and others were cleaning their guns, one of them, being loaded, went off accidentally. The ball seriously wounded poor Sam—a native of Errakova, Sandwich I.—severing the great tendon of his heel; that which is called the *tendo Achilles*. No artery seemed to be damaged, as far as I could tell, but the wound had an ugly look. A large flap of skin and flesh hung down from the heel. This was replaced, and the limb was bound up by the G.A., who acted as surgeon. He relied principally on cold water and carbolic acid to keep the wound sweet while it healed; but of course the severed tendon would never unite again.

A swing cot was slung "between decks" near the fore hatch, and there our patient did fairly well. I wished to take him on to Maryborough for proper surgical treatment; but, as he begged to be landed at Vila, before my final departure for Queensland, I left him there.

Having watered at Semma, in Havannah Harbour, I got under way one fine morning, with a very light air from south-east. While the ship was moving slowly down the harbour, I saw a boat from the mission settlement coming off to meet her. As this approached us, I discerned the missionary who resided in Muna, or Montague I., sitting in the stern. This was the gentleman who had opposed my recruiting the boy Naumeta, when I commanded the *Stanley*, as I have related in a previous chapter. It was just as well for him, perhaps, that I was not then aware he had communicated with the Queensland Government on the subject.

His present object in visiting the vessel was to see Sam, the wounded boatman, and he went down below forward for that purpose. Meanwhile I walked the deck aft, as I had no desire for his society. He came on deck again in a few minutes, and walked aft, where he was decidedly not wanted.

"Now, Captain," he commenced, "ye've been a lang time in this trade, can ye conscientiously say ye consider it consistent wi' the Christian releegion?"

I knew what he would be at, before he even opened his mouth. There were only two subjects on which he could, or would, converse—Christianity and the "Labour Trade." As my views on both of these topics did not coincide with his, I "smelt fire."

"Not being a Christian, Mr. ——, I cannot say," was my reply.

"No! ye're no' a Christian, but ye're nominally a Christian, are ye no'?"

I told him what my opinion was about religious matters in general. Then, at it we went, hammer and tongs. I flatter myself he found me a tougher nut to crack than the ignorant, superstitious savages he lived among. Not that he had effected much satisfactory result even amongst them, according to his own showing. For, on a former occasion, he told me that he had lived two years in Muna I., and had not converted a single soul.

At last, just as the vessel arrived close off the mission station, he made an assertion with regard to the two genealogies in the Gospels of Matthew and Luke, that I was uncertain whether to take with contempt or with anger. For it appeared to me that he was either telling a lie, supposing me not to have read the Bible, or that he must be grossly ignorant of the subject himself.

Now, I *had* read the Bible. Some years before, I had been a trader in one of the Caroline Is. There I lived for six months without seeing a white man's face or a ship's sail. Only one man on the island could speak a little broken English, and I was ignorant of the native language. Falling short of reading matter, I set to work on the Bible, and read it through from Genesis to Revelation. A considerable part of it I perused carefully three times. When I began, I was an orthodox Christian; when I left off, a Deist.

"Wait till I get my Bible," said I, diving down into the cabin. But the book required a little searching for; and, when I got on deck again with it in my hand, as red hot for argument as any Cromwellian Independent, my gentleman had gone, his boat being already half-way to the shore.

Having called at Vila and landed my wounded boatman, Sam, I stood to the south-west, intending to round the northern promontory of New Caledonia. But this time I was not favoured with the trade-wind. Light and variable breezes from north-east prevailed, varied with occasional calms or thunderstorms. As we slowly approached the Astrolabe Reefs, a good look-out was kept from the mast-head. In fact, I spent two hours there myself about midnight. At last I saw the breakers on the weather bow. By daybreak we were some ten miles off Tuo.

It took me nearly a week to get clear of this island, owing to frequent calms and light winds. The nights we passed lying at anchor inside the barrier reefs. One day was spent at anchor off Mr. Morgan's station on Paaba I., at the extreme north of the reef. There I got a supply of rather muddy fresh water, from a water-hole near the station. Then, issuing by Yande Pass, I sailed once more for Queensland. On March 23, I anchored in Hewey Bay, off Woody I., reaching Maryborough two days later.

In compliance with the instructions given to the G.A. before we sailed, respecting the allotment of recruits to employers, we had divided the boys into batches proportioned to the numbers specified on the several licences. I had 105 men and 6 women on board, not quite my full complement, which was 125. Consequently, each of the employers would get one or two boys less than he was entitled to.

There was a good deal of swapping and changing from one employer's name to another among the recruits. For the old hands were well acquainted with the characters of the different Maryborough planters. At length all were satisfied with the arrangement made for them by the G.A. and myself. Of course, they naturally expected to be assigned to the several employers according to our list.

The day after our arrival at Maryborough, the immigration agent of the port came on board with the owner's agent, and made out a fresh allotment of the recruits to the licensed employers. By their plan some of the boys were consigned to plantations they decidedly objected to serve upon.

I was on deck, and the first information I had of this was brought me by a boy who came up crying, and complained to me that he had been assigned to an employer whom he objected to serve. Then another and another followed, each of them grieving or wrathful at a like indignity.

Such an arbitrary proceeding as this could only lead to trouble, of course, and that not merely to the employers in Queensland. After these men returned home to their islands, they would hardly fail of having their revenge for the deceit, as they would deem it, that the Government was responsible for.

One "boy," a native of Api I., actually refused to go to the employer he was now assigned to—Mr. Cran, of Mengarie—under whom he had formerly served. We had allotted him to Mr. McPherson. Ultimately, a compromise was effected in his case, and he was employed on Magnolia plantation, to which he made no objection.

The G.A. and I interfered when we saw how the boys were being treated. We were told, in response, to mind our own business, as the Kanakas had now been taken out of our hands. All we could then do was to express our opinion regarding this high-handed proceeding, which we did without fear or favour. I began:—

"Well, sir, I have seen some rough things, and have heard a good deal about slavery in the South Seas; but the nearest attempt at slavery I have ever witnessed has been enacted on board here to-day. You are the biggest slaver in Queensland!"

To which the G.A. added hotly,—

"I quite agree with you, Captain Wawn."

"You, sir, have nothing to do with it," said the immigration agent.

"I beg your pardon," retorted the G.A. "These men, while on board, are in my care, although, when on shore, they will be in yours."

As might be expected, I had a powerful enemy henceforth among the Government officers connected with the labour trade. Twenty-four hours after this, I was informed that my services as master of the *Stormbird* were no longer required.*

During the short subsequent period when recruiting vessels visited the neighbourhood of New Guinea, native attacks on white men occurred. It was often said, then, that these had resulted from actions ascribed to the crews of such vessels. The public was carefully kept in entire ignorance of the fact that the grossest of such incidents transpired long before any labour vessel tried to recruit along those shores!

During 1878, Captain Redlich was murdered by the natives of Brooker I., in the Louisiade Archipelago. Mr. Ingham went in his steamer, the *Voura*, to investigate the affair, and to try and recover some of Redlich's property. The natives, to dispel any suspicion, received Ingham in a friendly manner, giving up to him some of Redlich's arms and other property; thus managing to throw him off his guard. About November 23, the second day after they had arrived at Brooker I., Ingham, with seven others, was killed by the natives. Billy, a native of Torres Strait, was the ringleader in this affair.

According to a report from the Rev. Mr. McFarlane, a missionary, which was published in "The Brisbane Courier" of December 23, 1879, Ingham and his men constituted the sixth party of shipwrecked sailors or *bêche-de-mer* fishers who had been massacred in these islands. The last outrage, however, might have been averted, had not the leader of the victims allowed himself to be deluded by the apparent friendliness of the natives, and so failed to guard against treachery. An acquaintance of his, in a letter published in a later issue of the same paper, said:—

"His one great failing was an unvarying trust that savages would not harm one unless in retaliation for injuries or insults received."

* The registers of the Polynesian Immigration Office have been found to be incomplete as regards the details relating to this voyage!!

It was belief in this theory, so often preached by men who have had no practical experience of savage character —especially of the Papuan—that led to the assassination of Mr. Obbard G.A., in 1874. The murders of Captain Ferguson and of Commodore Goodenough, as well as of scores of less noted white men, were attributable to the same cause.

My own opinion is that these Papuan savages will slay any stranger, white or coloured, if they think they can do so safely, and with profit to themselves.

Later this year, 1879, two other men, Irons and Willis, were murdered at Cloudy Bay, New Guinea.

CHAPTER XII

VOYAGES OF THE *LUCY AND ADELAIDE*, 1879.

Arrival of the Mystery—*Captain Kilgour at Lepers' I.*—*Recovering a stolen boat*—*Affray with the natives*—*Captain Kilgour brought to trial*—*My work at Mallicolo I.*—*My boats menaced*—*The* Mary Anderson—*German recruiting work*—*Facts in my experience*—*The "weather side" of Pentecost I.*—*The Aoba*—*A trial of seamanship*—*A gale*—*Heavy seas off Breaksea Spit*—*Arrival at Bundaberg*—*Second voyage*—*My illness*—*I resign command*—*Captain Satini wrecked*—*The Chevert.*

THE schooner *Mystery* arrived at Mackay from the New Hebrides in May. Her master, Captain Kilgour, had visited Lannawut, Aoba I., the scene of the murder of Renton and Muir. The boat captured by the natives on that occasion was plainly visible from the sea, lying hauled up above high-water mark at the edge of the forest.

As Captain Kilgour approached the beach in his own boat, a crowd of natives collected. Being interrogated, they denied that the boat on the beach was the stolen one, pretending it had been given to the chief by Mr. Bice, a missionary who lived on the other side of the island. Captain Kilgour then returned to the *Mystery* and fetched Buckley, a seaman who had been in the ship during her last voyage. This man at once identified the boat.

Next, some of the natives hauled the boat down to the water's edge, but refused to shove her off, telling Captain Kilgour to come in and take her, if he dared.

Nothing daunted, he mustered all hands he could bring from the ship in his two boats, and pulled in.

Before his boat had touched the shore, however, the natives opened on him with muskets and arrows. He told me that he had two arrows sticking in his legs when he landed. The boat was then shoved off and brought away, without further injuries being received. Apparently no natives were slain, though a few of their huts were set on fire, and three or four pigs were slaughtered by the boatmen.

Now this boat was the property of Mr. Hewitt, the owner of the *Mystery*, who had given strict orders to Captain Kilgour to recover it. The latter had endeavoured to get it back by peaceable means, after the natives had told him to come on shore and take it. It was the natives who began the affray, Kilgour's party fighting only in self-defence. The boat had been lying there for months, and no ship of war had offered to recover it. I am sure no fair-thinking Englishman would blame Captain Kilgour for his plucky deed.

However, many of those good people who had commended the Rev. George Brown for his slaughtering raid into New Britain, now blamed Captain Kilgour for simply recovering his owner's property, merely fighting in self-defence, and that without occasioning any loss of life! The missionary at Lepers' I. was one such, apparently. He took upon himself to send a garbled account of the affair to the Governor of Fiji, who was also High Commissioner for the Western Pacific.

Captain Kilgour sailed on another voyage in the *Mystery*. While in the New Hebrides, he met one of Her Majesty's ships which had come to look for him. Her captain offered him the alternative of going to Fiji as a prisoner on board the man-of-war, or of proceeding there in his own vessel. Captain Kilgour decided to take the latter course.

When he arrived in Fiji, he was tried before Judge

Gorry for his offence (!), and, having been found guilty, was fined £100. His "owner" paid the fine, besides having to bear the expense occasioned by the delay of the *Mystery* on her voyage. Judge Gorry wound up his closing speech with these words :—

"If I had proof of your having killed a native, I would have hanged you, sir—hanged you!"

My next command was the *Lucy and Adelaide*, a schooner of less tonnage than any of my former vessels, but smart and handy to work. I sailed from Brisbane on May 28, bound to the New Hebrides to recruit "boys" for the Bundaberg district. I worked all the islands from Tanna I. to the Banks' Is., with varying success.

On the north-eastern coast of Mallicolo I., particularly at Port Stanley and north of it, the inhabitants showed some hostility, and our recruiting work grew very slack in consequence.

One afternoon I had allowed the boats to get ahead of the ship. I followed them into a narrow channel between the mainland and two long narrow islets, a few miles north-west of Port Stanley. As luck would have it, I brought the vessel round Tararno islet just in time to avert a catastrophe. I could see about a hundred natives lurking among the trees, and they were already poising their spears and drawing their bows for an attack on the boats, which were lying to at a narrow little strip of beach, about fifty yards further along the shores of the islet.

The appearance of the ship checked the intended discharge of weapons. Then, hauling down the jibs, I shot the vessel's nose through the calm water right in towards the steep beach, backing the topsail and letting go the anchor on the very edge of the narrow fringe-reef, so close in shore that the jib-boom nearly touched the branches of the trees. The anchor, together with the light wind coming over the tree-tops, brought her up. The threatening mob of natives cleared out instantly, without discharging a single spear or arrow; but the recruiter had had a narrow escape from being riddled. I weighed again almost immediately and stood on.

There was another schooner a mile or two astern of us at the time. This was the *Mary Anderson*, Captain Schultze. She followed us, and, though no one appeared on the first islet as she passed it, her boat had a narrow escape off the second, a shower of arrows falling around it.

I anchored that evening between the main island and one of the islets off its northern point. Shortly after I had done so, the *Mary Anderson* brought up in company.

This proved to be a British vessel, commanded by a master of German nationality. He held a recruiting licence from the British Consul in Samoa, and carried no Government agent. He was recruiting labourers for German employers in the Samoa Is.

A partnership of nationalities, such as this, applied to the system of recruiting, *may* be to the advantage of the Polynesian, as some have said, though *how* it is I cannot say. It rather suggests to me a concealed system of slavery. I also call to mind the free and easy way in which skippers of German vessels were wont to treat savages, when I was in Godeffroy's employment during previous years, as I have mentioned. Very, very small is the number of islanders I have met, who have *returned* from Samoa, in spite of the many taken there. Frequent, too, have been the reports of kidnapping by Samoan vessels that I have heard from natives, not only then, but through all the years I have been in the trade!

From these islets I sailed to Aoba, or Lepers' I. There I purchased, chiefly with tobacco, a considerable stock of water-taro. This consisted of the largest and finest specimens of the root that I have ever seen in the Pacific

When I was off the northern coast of Mallicolo I. one morning, the weather and the barometer alike indicated wind from the west, which soon freshened into a fine gale from that quarter. I had often wished for an opportunity of visiting the "weather side," that is, the southern and eastern coasts, of Pentecost and Aurora Is., and now the opportunity had come.

Squaring away before the breeze, I ran to the southern point of Pentecost I., and, after dodging about off it for a night, I got a whole day's work on the eastern coast of that island.

It is not often that the natives on this side have a chance of communicating with a vessel, or even of seeing one. They came down in great numbers, therefore, to the few strips of beach scattered along the mostly precipitous coast. A wild-looking lot they were, feathered and painted for the most part, and fully armed with clubs, spears, bows, and poisoned arrows. We saw no guns in their possession, and very few iron tomahawks or knives. On the western coasts nearly every man would be possessed of either one or the other.

The French schooner *Aoba*, Captain Peter Tamsen, was in company with us, recruiting labourers for Noumea. During the forenoon she obtained three or four boys—children, in fact—far too young to be engaged by me for Queensland. We had no good luck at all.

About noon, near the middle of the island, we came to a small indentation in the coast line—hardly to be termed a bay—overhung by steep cliffs and precipitous hills. Here there were some boys who evidently wished to leave home, but were doubtful which boat they should trust themselves to.

To encourage them, Tamsen and I both stood in to the rocks as close as we dared. Then we tacked, lying so as to head off shore, until, drifting to leeward, each of us had to make a tack to windward again to get near our respective boats. This was done two or three times, each schooner trying to cut in closer than the other, while the recruits on board shouted and yelled to the natives on shore.

At last I spied a patch of sunken coral, distant two or three ship-lengths from the rocks, on which the sea was breaking. Standing closer in, I let go my anchor on it. So near to the shore were we then that I had to get my kedge out ahead, with a warp, to stop the ship's sternway.

I did not remain there long, more especially as the wind, now very moderate, had hauled round into the south, and gave tokens of veering easterly. I stayed only long enough to get seven good recruits, and then got under way. This was the only occasion on which I found a chance of working that coast.

As I came round the south-eastern point of the island that morning, I saw the bottom at about eight fathoms depth, for some distance, a quarter of a mile from the shore. It appeared to be of coral.

The homeward passage was a quick one, though rough, before a strong trade-wind. As we were nearing the Queensland coast, this increased to a gale.

It was a bright, sunshiny day when I drew near Breaksea Spit. The schooner was tearing along before the heaviest sea I have ever witnessed in these latitudes. She was under her lower topsail, fore trysail, inner jib and stay foresail, with the wind a little on the port quarter. Every now and then she rolled heavily as her stern rose to the seas, the port boat skimming the "comber," and once nearly filling. The horizon was all mist and drift; it was only from the main rigging that I could get a "sight," and that only now and then, to give me an approximate position as to latitude.

About three p.m. I sighted the sand hills on Sandy Cape, Fraser I., a little forward of the port beam. At the same moment, I saw a huge breaker bearing down on us, about three points on the port bow.

The schooner was then close on to the end of the Spit. Suddenly a huge sea, with a roaring broken crest, swept past and ahead of her, followed by another and yet another.

"Five fathoms!" sung out the boatswain, who was handing in the lead amidships.

The next sea was a "boomer." A long, swiftly moving mountain of undulating blue water swept on. Its crest towered up like a ridge, threatening to break, but as yet only showing a sputter of foam here and there. For a few seconds I thought it would come right over us, but gradually the schooner's stern rose to it, then toppled down again behind the crest, which broke under the bows into a driving cloud of foam and mist.

The sea had taken hold of the schooner, however. In those few minutes I think the little craft travelled faster than she ever did before since she was launched. She beat the wind. Her topsail was for a few seconds flat-aback, and her fore-and-aft canvas swung amidships.

But that sea had evidently taken her over the tail of the Spit. The next one broke astern of her, and gradually I got into smoother water and hauled up for the head of Hervey Bay. There I passed the following night, not liking to make for the Burnett River, on which Bundaberg is situated, in such weather.

Next morning I entered the river, the breeze having dropped, getting up to the town the same day. This was, I think, the twentieth of August, 1879.

I lay at Bundaberg nearly a month, waiting for stores and licences from Brisbane. I then sailed again for the New Hebrides. This second voyage in the *Lucy and Adelaide* was the most uneventful one I made while engaged in the labour trade, and also the shortest.

I recruited for the Brisbane district this time. My northernmost point in the group—the New Hebrides—was Dip Point, Ambrym I.

Unfortunately, when off Tanna I., I was seized with a

bad attack of fever and ague, together with a determination of blood to the head. The last symptom affected my eyesight. My illness, in conjunction with the frequent wet weather, obliged me to keep below, except when it was absolutely necessary for me to go on deck.

Notwithstanding this, recruiting work went on quickly and without accident. After a smart passage home, I arrived at Brisbane on November 18, having been only two months out. I brought with me eighty-eight recruits —the full number my vessel was licensed to carry.

The fever had now left me, and I had recovered from my other ailment. Still, I was weak, and therefore disinclined to risk another attack by going to the islands in the coming hurricane season. So I resigned command of the *Lucy and Adelaide*, and Captain Satini took charge of her in my place. She was wrecked in a cyclone, in Havannah Harbour, on January 23, during her next voyage. She was subsequently got off, was repaired, and is still afloat.

The barque *Chevert*, which had been formerly a French transport, then employed in Macleay's exploring expedition to New Guinea, and finally fitted out as an island trader, was dismasted in the New Hebrides about the same time. Her people managed to bring her to Havannah Harbour, where she was purchased by Captain McLeod, the Noumea trader. He made use of her as a hulk at Semma.

CHAPTER XIII.

FIRST VOYAGE OF THE *JABBERWOCK*, 1880.

The Jabberwock, *auxiliary screw steamer—Great anticipations—
An inexperienced G.A.—Port Resolution—Steamers—A
Fijian kidnapper—The black brigantine—Distrust—A run-
away mother—Reed, the trader—A storm—Peril of the
Lady Darling—Port Olry—Failure of firewood—Sau and
Nina—An instance of missionary rancour—French recruiters
—Their system and its results—Coasting Ambrym and
Paama Is.—I fall in with the* Dayspring—*The* Dauntless
*—Attack on her recruiting boats—Her mate and G.A. killed
—Wreck of the* Mystery—*Visit from a French skipper—I
stand on my dignity—Vila—A walk overland—My wounded
boatman, Sam—A rough scramble—Captain Kilgour's camp
—Its drawbacks—I return to Mackay—My disgust and re-
signation—Attack on the* s.s. Ripple,—*Chinamen killed in
New Guinea—Views of missionaries regarding the massacre
—Murder of Lieut. Bowers—Mandolianna I.—The* Borealis
massacre—A series of outrages—The Esperanza—*The*
Zephyr—*The* Borough Belle—*H.M.S.* Emerald *sent to
chastise the perpetrators—Her proceedings a farce—The
natives enjoy the "fireworks"—Massacres go on—Missionaries, traders, and "Exeter Hall"—Why naval officers dare
not act—Traders' lives of no account.*

AFTER spending some months ashore, I was offered the command of the *Jabberwock*, and I took charge of her at Brisbane, in May, 1880. This vessel was an auxiliary screw steamer rigged as a barquentine, but carrying only a "stump" foretopmast. Great hopes were entertained by her owners that she would prove a success in the labour trade. Others, perhaps the more experienced in such matters, felt grave doubts of her, even predicting that she would prove a dead failure.

It was expected that the *Jabberwock's* steam power would enable her to go into bays and inlets under the lee of the islands, at times when sailing ships could only lie motionless outside. These anticipations were no doubt realized on one or two occasions. When there was a fresh head breeze, however, the auxiliary screw was not powerful enough to propel her against the wind. Again, when it fell calm under an island, the boats could tow her two or three miles before steam could be got up, by which time, probably, it would no longer be required. She carried sufficient coals and coke to last her about thirty days.

The G.A. appointed to her was new to the work. He had been previously a schoolmaster somewhere in "the bush," in Queensland. I think, on the whole, that a more unfit person could scarcely have been selected to fill such a responsible situation. He had a vast idea of his importance as a Government officer, combined with gross ignorance of the duties and want of tact. He had had no previous experience of savages, and possessed little capacity for dealing with them.

I afterwards had another G.A. with me who was new to the work. Both times I failed to make the trip a remunerative one, returning with far less than my proper complement of recruits.

The *Jabberwock* left Brisbane on May 22, bound for the New Hebrides. Steaming down the river, as there was no wind, I found that the greatest speed she could make was barely six knots an hour.

The passage to the New Hebrides was made under sail alone. When close to Tanna I., I got up steam to take the vessel into Port Resolution. The anchorage there had been much contracted by the effect of an earthquake, towards the end of 1877.

The impression made upon the natives by their first sight of the *Jabberwock*, moving along with bare poles, with smoke issuing from her funnel, was that she was a ship of war. They were shy of coming near my boats in consequence. When they were told that we were seeking for recruits, the effect was worse still. For the steam and the vessel's green paint combined caused them to set her down as a Samoan.

Only two other steamers had previously visited these islands to recruit labourers. One of these hailed from Fiji, the other from Samoa. Both had left a very bad record behind them. The stories told of the Fijian's doings were now seven or eight years old, and had been well-nigh forgotten. The cruise of the Samoan was only of recent date, however. Further north, the natives frequently refused to believe that we were recruiting for Queensland, expressing their belief that, if they were engaged by us, they would be taken to Samoa.

At Tanna I., luckily, in the neighbourhood of Port Resolution and Waisissa, the inhabitants of the coast were acquainted with me; so we obtained some recruits in those localities. Between these two places some natives complained bitterly of the conduct of a certain black-painted vessel from Fiji, which, from their description, appeared to have been a brigantine. She had sent a boat to their beach, and had engaged several men, but gave a very small amount of "pay" to the recruits' friends. Her recruiter told them he had very little "trade" then in his boat, but that he would fetch more from the ship; with which he took the men away. Three muskets, with some other articles, had been promised. However, the boat never returned to the shore —in *that* neighbourhood, at any rate. My informants were very indignant about this. Little more would have been needed to induce them to take their revenge out of the next whites who came along that way.

It may have been the same vessel that I heard of a little later at Merrabwei, Mallicolo I., where I passed a night at anchor. There, a man who was commonly known as " Brisbane "—a returned labourer, whom I had landed during a former voyage—came off to the *Jabberwock*. He told us that a black "schooner" (they apply the name to any sailing vessel, no matter what may be her rig), hailing from Fiji, rigged "all the same, *Stormbird*" (a brigantine), had appeared off his village. A canoe, with five men and boys in her, had gone off with bananas and yams to trade. About half an hour

TATTOOED WOMAN—TANNA I.

after they got alongside the brigantine, the canoe drifted away empty, and the boys were taken away to Fiji.

Though this man averred that his friends had been kidnapped, we must recollect that islanders who wish to go away contrary to the wishes of their friends, often adopt some such plan of escaping. Certain Lammen islanders did so during my fourth voyage in the *Stanley*, as I have related. Moreover, such a party, visiting a vessel to trade, would be sure to include one or two "old hands." who could speak English or Fijian. These would certainly make the fact of their having been kidnapped known to the authorities, on their arrival in the colony.

At Port Stanley the inhabitants declined to come near the boats, and one man called out from a little distance, "You go away! You no belong Brisbane! You no good! Me savez you!"

One woman only was engaged here. She had "made a bolt," and came alongside at night in a small canoe. Next morning another canoe came off to the ship, containing a man and—a baby!

The inhuman mother had deserted her child. She was packed off ashore again to rear it, or to be clubbed, as her friends might decide.

Here and there we picked up a few recruits, but it was slow work. At last, one morning, when it was almost calm, I steamed round to the west end of Motalava, one of the Banks' Is. Seeing the smoke rising from the funnel, the natives at first supposed the ship to be a man-of-war. Her small size, perceptible as she got nearer, next led them to think she was a missionary packet—the *Southern Cross*. Finally, when they could make out the green-painted hull, they concluded she was from Samoa, and were excited accordingly.

This false impression was soon dissipated, however. Charlie Reed, a white trader who was an old acquaintance of mine, came on board. When he went ashore again, he vouched for us, satisfying the natives that our destination was Brisbane. The same afternoon I steamed over to Ureparapara. Entering the bay, I found an anchorage close to the head of it.

At this place, too, the natives were very doubtful about us and our destination, notwithstanding that Reed had come over with us, and that he asserted we were bound for Queensland. Another schooner, said to be the *Lady Darling*, may have caused this impression.

Some of the natives said her recruiter, who had been visiting the outer coast of the island, had told them we were from Samoa.

I drew a blank altogether at Ureparapara. So, after spending two nights there, I steamed out of the bay and beat back to Motalava under sail alone. There I anchored, as before, on the north-western coast of the island. I obtained a few recruits there, though not without difficulty. Many of the natives put no faith in us, but believed we were deceiving their friend Charlie. Those who wished to engage were mostly restrained by force from doing so.

I worked southward after leaving Motalava. While we were at anchor off Lakon, the *Lady Darling* arrived and brought up about a mile from us. That evening my glass began to fall, and there were signs of a coming change in the weather. I therefore gave orders to the anchor watch to call me, should there be any alteration during the night. At daylight, when I came on deck, I saw that the sooner I got away out of that anchorage the better. In fact, I ought to have been called up before. The sky was overcast, a heavy black cloud-bank rising in the west.

All hands were summoned on deck, and then, while the recruits hove in the cable, the crew made sail. Just as the anchor was tripped, the squall caught us, and, throwing her head off to port, canted the ship over to her covering board. But the anchor came up cheerily, while the yards were trimmed, and the vessel stood along the land—which was barely visible through the thick rain, close as it was—until we had cleared the south-western point of the island, and had got sea-room to leeward.

The *Lady Darling* was caught at her anchor, and had to ride out the squall, having no room to get under way. Her stern was all the time in unpleasant proximity to the rocks. Luckily for her, the wind only lasted an hour or two, so that the sea did not rise much. Had it been otherwise, little more would have been seen of the *Lady Darling!*

From this island I went to the northern coast of Espiritu Santo I., anchoring in Port Olry. There the *Jabberwock* lay for three days, while she was given a fresh coating of paint to hide her unfortunate green. This time I painted her black, with a narrow red ribbon. After that she was no more mistaken for a Samoan.

While we lay at Port Olry, we were informed by the natives that, shortly before, a black "schooner" had put in there. They said her people had "stolen" two men and three women, who had been engaged cutting a path through the scrub between the village and the shore.

I paid a visit to this village, accompanied by the G.A., the recruiter, and a boat's crew. We found it deserted by all but one man, who was asleep in a hut. How astonished he looked when he woke up to find us gazing in at him! His terror was so great, that, as we blocked up the doorway, he just rushed at the thatched wall of the hut, burst through it, and went off like the wind. No doubt he spread the news of our visit, for we heard some yelling after this, though we saw no more natives on our return to the boats.

Frequent steaming had now reduced my stock of coal to a very low ebb. By way of experiment, therefore, I collected several boatloads of good firewood for the engine furnace. It proved of little use, however, when we came to try it. One fine, calm evening, when the fresh paint had dried, the engineer made up his fire with this wood. It took just four hours to raise sufficient steam with it to propel the vessel out of the harbour and so to sea, at the slow rate of one and a half miles an hour.

Next morning, when we were well away from the land, the fires were drawn, and then all the wood we did not want for the galley was "dumped" overboard.

As soon as steam had been got up again with coal, I stood over to Lepers' I., passing the *Chance* becalmed on the way. There I anchored westward of Walurigi mission station, on the north coast.

At this place I received a visit from two old acquaintances—Sau, and his wife, Nina. When I had last seen them, they were employed at the house of an old friend

SAU AND NINA.

of mine—Mr. Rawson, of Kirkgubbin plantation, near Maryborough. Sau was just as quiet, even dull, as he always had been, while Nina was correspondingly lively. But now, no " Dolly Varden " cap surmounted Nina's woolly head. The neat short dress she had worn in Queensland had made way for a not too decent waist-cloth, and, altogether, the pair looked as if their stock of soap had been long exhausted.

They inquired about the welfare of their old employers, especially about the children. Then Mrs. Nina indulged in a dance round the decks, kissed two or three of the crew who took her fancy, and finally passed some very uncomplimentary remarks upon our G.A.

I tried to persuade them to re-engage and return with me to Queensland. But Nina, who still "bossed" her husband, as she always had done, was not yet tired of her liberty. Having obtained a pipe and some tobacco, she volunteered to act as interpreter in the recruiting boat, in which capacity she actually brought back four boys to the ship, as recruits.

A teacher from the mission station came on board here, and requested me to take him and some others over to Lakarere, Aurora I. He told me that the Rev. Mr. Bice had gone thither from Walurigi, in order to form another mission station there. I declined to take them on board, however, not being then certain as to my next movements.

The following day a light wind from south-east took me to Lakarere, after all. There the natives told us that they were ordered by the missionary to have no communication with any labour vessel, not even to sell food to one. I therefore sailed again, working the western coasts of Aurora I. and Pentecost I., and making southward.

Near the southern extremity of Aurora I., a fore-and-aft schooner passed us one evening, going northward. Next day we were close to the village of Melsisi, Pentecost I. When the boats came back from the shore, my recruiter reported that the natives were in a dangerous state of mind. One who could speak English had told him that the French schooner *Aurora* had been there the day before, and that her boat, manned exclusively by coloured men, had visited their beach.

A few natives had gone to meet them, one man offering a bunch of bananas for sale. The steersman of the boat, finding no boys disposed to go to New Caledonia, attempted to kidnap one of them; but his intended prisoner got away. Then, as all the natives ran off, the steersman, a Lifu man, known as "Black Tom," fired his revolver after them, mortally wounding the unfortunate vendor of bananas. This poor fellow lay at the point of death when my boat left the beach.

So much I gathered from my recruiter. When I spoke to the G.A. about it, he said that *he* had paid no attention to the native's story, as it did not concern him. It is hardly surprising that such outrages should have been committed, when it is remembered that the French Government officers were not in the habit of going ashore with the boats. They were, therefore, not at hand to superintend the actual engagement of recruits. Their boats were usually manned and officered by uncivilized Polynesians.

Off Malvat I fell in with a black-painted brigantine. The *Jabberwock* was under steam at the time, and at a distance might have been mistaken for a man-of-war. As soon as we were sighted, the brigantine—which had been lying off Malvat, with a crowd of canoes round her—squared away, and did not communicate with us. The Malvat people said she was the *Au Revoir*, of Fiji.

About this time, the wind enabled me to get to the southward without using any more coal. The boats meanwhile coasted along the shores of Ambrym and Paama Is., looking for recruits and keeping in company with the vessel. Then the wind shifted into the west, began to freshen, and at last settled down into a stiff south-west breeze, which lasted about two days. During this I lay at anchor off Tautari, on the extreme north of Api I.

At the same time, the mission-packet *Dayspring*, Captain Braithwaite, experienced a rough time of it. She was on the north side of the Foreland, exposed to the full force of wind and sea, and was too close to the land to venture to get under way.

At Tautari we heard that two white men had been lately killed near the Foreland. We supposed that they must have belonged to the *Dayspring*.

As soon as the breeze had blown itself out, the wind chopped round to south-east. I then got under way and " spoke " the mission vessel, which was still at anchor. She was landing building material for a new mission station, a mile or two south of the Foreland. I found all well on board of her; but the report we had heard was not without foundation.

It appeared that on July 20th, the fore-and-aft schooner *Dauntless*, of Fiji, Captain Jones, had sent her boat ashore a little distance north of the Foreland. As the boat approached the beach, some natives, who were ambushed in the scrub which fringed the shore, fired a volley into her. Fraser, the second mate, was shot dead. Nicholl, the G.A., was struck by no less than seven bullets, and mortally wounded. He afterwards died in Levuka hospital. One boatman was shot through the loins, while another, a Fijian, was wounded, but managed to scull the boat off towards the vessel. The other boatmen jumped overboard and swam off.

The natives of the adjoining villages attempted to excuse the perpetrators of these murders. They stated that the deed was done in retaliation for an outrage committed by the boatmen belonging to the French schooner *Aurora*. These had taken away a chief's son, and had shot his father, who had attempted to prevent the boy from going away.

At Mau, where I got two or three recruits, a report was in circulation that a vessel had lately been wrecked on the east coast of Sandwich I. We were unable to obtain particulars, even as to her name. At Havannah Harbour this report was verified. The unlucky vessel proved to have been the *Mystery*, Captain Kilgour, from Mackay, Mr. A. Macdonald G.A. All hands had been saved, and were now camped near the wreck. While I lay at Havannah, the *Aurora*, the French schooner just mentioned, came to an anchor near us.

Having "swung" the *Jabberwock*, in order to adjust my compasses, I sailed next day for Vila, intending to anchor there, and then to travel overland and ascertain if I could be of any assistance to the crew of the *Mystery*. Meanwhile, the recruiter could be doing his best to obtain some more recruits, pending our return home.

The weather was now too boisterous for me to attempt communication with the shipwrecked party on the weather coast.

When off Tukatuka Point, the wind blew so strongly that I was unable to beat up to Vila, so I brought up under the lee of the Point, off Ford's plantation. The *Aurora* came in just behind me, and anchored near. Her skipper said she had sustained some damage in one of the heavy puffs of wind, while passing through the main entrance of Havannah Harbour.

The French captain and his Government officer paid us a visit. Having been told by my G.A. of the reports we had heard about them, they were profuse in their explanations and denials. They left us in a bad humour, for I declined to dine on board the *Aurora* that evening. I knew enough French to understand what the skipper meant, when I overheard him remarking to his companion that my refusal was *diplomatique*. I think he apprehended mischief from me.

Next day I got round to Vila, and anchored there. The day after, with a couple of boatmen and a Vila guide, I landed and walked to Pango village. There another guide was procured, with a canoe, to take me to Errakova. I found Mr. Mackenzie and his family absent from the mission station.

Then I met Sam, the boatman who was accidentally wounded while with me in the *Stormbird*. His wound had never healed properly, very likely the consequence of neglect. There was now a running sore in his foot. It would have been better for him if he had accepted my offer and gone on in the *Stormbird* to Maryborough. He would have been properly treated in hospital there, and would have had a fair chance of recovery.

We canoed some little distance from Errakova, which is an islet, situated in a large and deep lagoon, between the main island and the barrier reef. The rest of the way we walked. It was hard travelling along that native track. In some places it was rough and stony, in others we were over our ankles in wet bog. We had to traverse loose sandy beaches, to wade through creeks, and to climb up the steep faces of lofty coral plateaux, only to tumble and slide down again a few hundred yards further on.

At length, when the sun was getting low, and I was thoroughly fagged out, and hungry as well, we arrived on the bank of a creek, beyond which was a village. A canoe took us across. Then, with two or three sticks of tobacco, I purchased a meal of yam and banana. This we washed down with the *water* of young cocoanuts, not the *milk*, which is a preparation.

Just beyond the village there was a long and deep inlet of the sea. On the further shore of this lay Kilgour's second camp, some miles away from the wreck. The spot we were at was somewhere near the middle of the southern coast of Sandwich I.

The only canoes available here were small and frail. The owners were indisposed to lend them; for a strong swell was running into the inlet from the ocean. Fortunately, the *Mystery's* boat chanced to come within hail. In her my boatmen and I crossed over to the camp, leaving my guides where they were.

A sail converted into a tent, with a "humpy" or two of boughs, constituted this camp. It was situated on a low stony strip of beach facing the inlet, and was backed by thick forest and jungle. The place was swarming with mosquitos and sandflies, an occasional scorpion or centipede creating an unwelcome diversion.

The camp was in charge of two of the white crew of the *Mystery*, with three or four Polynesians, Kilgour and Macdonald being then absent. About sundown they appeared, coming from the wreck, with a train of boatmen and "returns," all laden with provisions, stores, trade, and so forth, part of their salvage.

I did not fancy passing a night here, for the mosquitos and sandflies were terrible. So I was glad when Kilgour announced his attention of starting immediately for Vila in his boat, whence he would afterwards go on to Havannah Harbour. He seemed to think that he and his G.A. could pull through their difficulties all right. He did not care to send his white crew home with me, being unable to spare them then. Some other vessel would be sure to take them later on, and one would be found eventually to take his "returns" home. All I could do for him was to execute some commissions in Mackay, whither I was now bound.

We issued out of the inlet into the open sea, just as the last red glow of sunset was fading from the western sky. Running before a fresh breeze, with a regular sea, we reached Vila, getting on board the *Jabberwock* about midnight.

Next day, I sailed for Mackay with sixty-four recruits. I arrived there on August 31, having just enough coal left on board to take the ship into the Pioneer River the day after, and thence up to the town. There she was moored, alongside the river bank, and her recruits were landed.

Disgusted with the result of the late voyage, my number of recruits being far short of the ship's full complement, as well as with the vessel herself, her "jury" rig and trumpery steam power, I threw up my command—foolishly, I acknowledge.

The vessel soon after went to Brisbane, where her

engine was taken out of her. Though she still continued in the labour trade, it was as a sailing vessel only. Her rig remained unaltered, until, when sold to another owner, I again commanded her in 1882.

In August of this year (1880) the s.s. *Ripple* was nearly captured by natives in Bougainville Strait, Solomon Is. On board of her were Captain Ferguson, a crew of three whites and sixteen Kanakas, and two passengers—a German and an island woman. The captain, two Kanakas, and the woman were killed; Mr. Spence, a passenger, and thirteen Kanakas were wounded, the first seriously. About fifty of the savages were killed before they were beaten off.

The inhabitants of the Louisiade Archipelago, and those of the mainland of New Guinea, still continued to make things lively for strangers who visited them.

A letter in "The Brisbane Courier," October 6, 1880, written by the Revs. J. Chalmers and T. Beswick, and dated from New Guinea, related how at Aroma village, on the mainland, seven heads of Chinamen had then recently been paraded in triumph by the natives. These unfortunates had formed part, or the whole, of the crew of a Chinese junk, and had been engaged in collecting and curing *bêche-de-mer*. On account of their "acting in an excessively free and indecent manner towards the native women," they were desired by the natives to leave that neighbourhood. The Chinamen refused to comply with this demand, and then other troubles arose, until, at last, the natives assembled—most probably—to attack the intruders.

The Chinese took the initiative, and fired first on the natives. In the end they were worsted.

Had this happened at any considerable distance from where the missionaries were residing, even had the victims been Europeans, so long as they were merely traders or recruiters, we might have expected that little notice would have been taken of it. Possibly in such a case, it

P

would have been said that the massacre was only the natural result of the usual conduct of "brutal scoundrels." But Aroma was too near home. Messieurs Chalmers and Beswick acknowledged the justice of the natives' action, but suggested that this slaughter of Chinese, who had abused women and fired first on their relatives and friends, would afford a good opportunity—"excuse" would have been a better word—for the infliction of a salutary and exemplary punishment, and thus, in the long run, be the means of saving the lives of both foreigners and natives. Surely this was an adoption of the Jesuitical doctrine that the end justifies the means!

About September 8, Captain Foreman and his crew, consisting of seven Europeans and as many Chinese, of the schooner *Annie Brookes*, were murdered by natives of Brooker I., in the Louisiade Archipelago.

A month or two later, Captain Frier, of the *Vibilia*, which had been wrecked in that group, brought to Cooktown intelligence of the murder of a party of French naturalists, at James Bay, Moresby I., off the southeastern point of New Guinea.

During the latter part of this year H.M.S. *Sandfly* was cruising among the Solomon Is., and anchored at Mboli, on the north-east coast of one of the Florida Is. Her commander, Lieutenant Bowers, deluded by the friendly attitude of the natives, and probably imagining that the fact of his vessel being a "man-of-war" was sufficient to command respect, left the *Sandfly* at anchor, and started on a boat-cruise round the southernmost of these islands.

Not suspecting that any savages were watching for a good opportunity to attack him, he landed on the little uninhabited islet of Mandolianna, and strolled away from his boat, unarmed. His men, equally off their guard, were bathing, when a party of natives, who had landed on the other side of the islet, rushed on them and slaughtered all but one. The exception was a man named Savage, who escaped by swimming to the main island. There he was protected by the chief of Baranago village until rescued.

The bodies of Lieutenant Bowers, and of the four men murdered with him, were found on the islet a few days after, by a party sent to look for them, and were buried there. So also was the body of another seaman, named Buckley, one of the search party, who was shot dead in the boat, which was also attacked.

On December 7, the schooner *Chance* arrived at Brisbane, bringing news of the capture of the *Borealis*, brigantine, in the Solomon group, and the massacre of most of her crew. This vessel had been on a recruiting voyage from Fiji, and was owned and commanded by Captain Mackenzie, whose son accompanied him as mate. She had anchored off the islet of Kwai, on the north-eastern coast of Malayta I. Mackenzie and his G.A. had left the vessel there, while they went in the boats along the coast to recruit labourers. The mate and the rest of the crew were engaged on board, setting up the rigging.

The natives, being allowed to come on board unrestrainedly, attacked the crew, killing all hands except the cook.

The captain and the G.A., on their return, were obliged to abandon the vessel and coast round the north of the island, where they found the labour schooners *Stanley*, *Flirt*, and *Dauntless*, at anchor.

These vessels immediately weighed anchor and beat round to Kwai. They recaptured the *Borealis*, taking summary vengeance on such of the natives as they caught in the act of plundering her.

The *Borealis* was then taken back to Fiji by the mate of the *Stanley*, with a volunteer crew from her and the other vessels.

Other outrages committed by Kanakas during the same year were the murder of the crew of the *Esperanza*, Captain McIntosh, at Kulambangra I., of part of the crew of the *Zephyr*, at Choiseul I., both in the Solomon group, and of boatmen of the *Borough Belle*, at Gaua, Banks' Is.

In consequence of these affairs, and especially on account of the murder of Lieutenant Bowers, H.M.S. *Emerald*—Captain Maxwell—was sent to the islands; but, as usual, she did little or nothing. She returned to Sydney at the end of January, 1881, her cruise having been a mere farce.

It would seem that she visited Bougainville I., where Captain Ferguson and others had been murdered. There she burned some villages and canoes, and destroyed cocoanut trees, but no natives were hurt.

At Choiseul I., where the crew of the *Zephyr* had been slaughtered, property was destroyed, and one woman was wounded, but no one was killed. At Kulambangra I., where the crew of the *Esperanza* had been killed, nobody was hurt, merely the usual destruction of property. At the Florida Is. much the same programme was carried out, and " one small nigger " captured.

What may have been done at Kwai, Malayta I., where the *Borealis* had been seized, I cannot say. I heard that a man-of-war had anchored there, and that her captain sent word ashore that he intended to bombard the islet. Thus warned, the natives transported all their valuables to the mainland, a quarter of a mile off. Then they sat down on the beach there, and enjoyed the " fireworks ! "

At Brooker I., in the Louisiade Archipelago, one prisoner was made, and two witnesses were brought away. At Mewstone I. one man was taken prisoner, but afterwards released, and a woman was hurt. I think one man was killed, somewhere in the Archipelago, at a place where they captured a canoe with a white man's skull in it.

The paper that reported the events of this cruise also stated that the French war steamer, *D'Estrèes*, had recently visited Brooker I., where her people killed nine of the natives.

So little did their punishment (?) affect the natives of Kwai, that, scarcely a year later, they cut off the brig *Janet Stewart*, massacring all hands on board, save one who managed to conceal himself.

In February, 1881, Captain Schwartz, of the *Leslie*, a Sydney schooner, was murdered near Cape Marsh. This was the same place where Captain Murray, of the *Lælia*, had been killed some little time previously.

The *Lady Darling*, labour schooner, Captain McDougall, was wrecked near Port Sandwich, New Hebrides, in March. Fortunately, three vessels were close at hand at the time—the schooners *Io*, and *Stanley*, and the *Lady Belmore*, brig. The crew of the *Lady Darling* escaped on board the *Io*.

Outrages still continued on the coasts of New Guinea and on neighbouring islands, in districts never yet visited by the trader.

Two teachers, with their wives and children, were murdered at Kalo, New Guinea.

The Rev. Mr. Beswick, and an anonymous writer, addressed letters to the colonial papers, in which they demanded that the murderers should be punished. It was stated that within the last two and a half years, eight massacres had taken place on the south-eastern coast of New Guinea; that hitherto, ships of the British navy had done no good there; and that the natives freely expressed such opinions as, " Man-o'-war like one big woman ! " I may add that I have often heard much the same contempt expressed in the Solomon group.

The influence in Great Britain, and, in a lesser degree, in the Southern Australian colonies, of " *Exeter Hall* " philanthropy,—of men, who, although well meaning, have never travelled outside of civilized countries ; who have lived all their lives in a state of comparative security ; who cannot possibly conceive the feelings of others who live, day by day, with their lives in their hands,—is to be blamed for the majority of these murders in the South

Sea Islands. Were sufficient punishment meted out to the natives for a first offence, it would effectually prevent the commission of others.

Our naval officers know that, were they to shed a " poor savage's " blood, a howl of indignation would be raised, and then "good-bye" to their chance of advancement in the service.

As we have seen, missionaries are not backward in demanding, and even in *taking* vengeance, when their own interests or lives are threatened. But traders' lives are of small account to them; and some are not so good but what they will poison the minds of natives against the traders, through jealous envy of their influence.

Traders may be good or bad, as in civilized countries; but it ought not to be forgotten that it is to the trader's interest to be friendly with, and to behave fairly towards, the islanders.

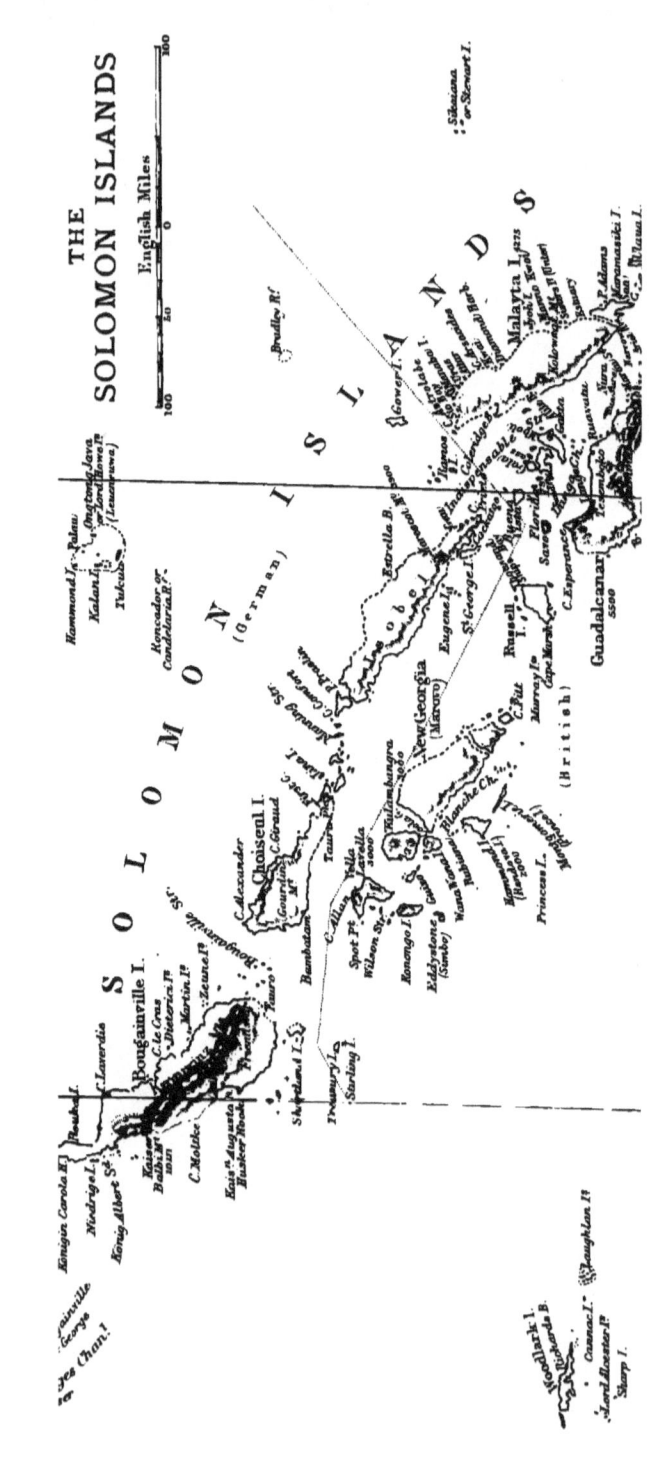

CHAPTER XIV.

SEVENTH VOYAGE OF THE *STANLEY*, 1881.

I take charge of the Stanley—*Sail for the Solomon Is.—Tom Tamoan—The Santa Cruz Is.—No interpreters—Santa Anna I.—San Christoval I.—Massacre of bush natives by a coast tribe—A cannibal feast—Drifting ashore—Maramasiki I.—Aio I.—I meet King Berry—Mode of preparing copra—Cocoanut oil—Collecting and curing bêche-de-mer—The north-eastern coast of Isabel I.—No inhabitants—King Berry's raids—Burning coral for lime—Exploring—A broken anchor—Searching for Port Praslin—Invaders from Choiseul I.—A native sepulchre—Its contents—Relics—The missing boats—Return of the wanderers—Finding a strange derelict—Blockade of the Floridas by British cruisers—Results of their action—The coast of Malayta I.—Desertion of a recruit—Back to the Floridas—Tom Tamoan recognized—His island discovered—The coast of Guadalcanar—Story of Wanderer Bay—Bellona I.—Poor Tom landed—His reception by his people—Their gratitude to me—Touching noses with a chief—Tom prevents recruits from joining—An inquisitive native and a loaded rifle—Kanaka ideas of justice—Remarks on the Solomon Islanders—The Papuan character—Massacre of French priests—I return to Maryborough.*

IN April, 1881, I was once more appointed master of the *Stanley*. I took charge of her at Maryborough, and sailed with the intention of going direct to the Solomon Is.

Tom Tamoan, the islander who had accompanied me in the *Stormbird*, and who, in South Sea vernacular, " had been lose him island," went with me again as a boatman.

Tom still had hopes that I would find out what island he belonged to, so he brought all his property with him. For he was to be landed if our search should prove successful.

I left Hervey Bay with a nice fair wind and stood to northward through the Coral Sea, until I had reached the vicinity of Indispensable Reef, in 13° south latitude. There the wind drew rapidly round from south-east to north, freshening up into a gale. Three days of this drove me back about seventy miles. Then the breeze moderated a little, and I stood eastward on an easy bowline, under the lower canvas, until Santo Espiritu I. was sighted ahead; soon after which the wind died away to a dead calm.

After that came three weeks' "doldrums"—horrible weather—calms under a blazing sun, alternating with variable puffs of wind, generally from north-west, and deluges of rain. I managed to get as far as Nitendi I. and the Duff Is. in the Santa Cruz group, but was unable to secure a single recruit.

At the Reef islets, in the northern part of the group, I think I might have recruited some men. Several came alongside in canoes and boarded us, making signs that they would go in the ship. But, as luck would have it, I was without an interpreter, and not one of the islanders knew a word of English.

One day, while a light breeze was blowing, I found myself to windward of a canoe, which was crossing from the Reef islets to Nitendi. The half-dozen men in her were awfully scared when we ran down to her, hove to, and lowered a boat, in which I went alongside her. She was a well-built craft, but her huge mat sail was a very clumsy affair.

I traded for some taro, which they were willing to part with, and so left them to continue their voyage.

At last, early one morning, a breeze sprang up from south-eastward. I was then off the south-east coast of Nitendi I. It was in a bay on the northern coast of this island that Bishop Patteson was killed, in 1871. The breeze freshened up into a steady "trade," which carried me to the small island of Santa Anna, at the south-eastern extremity of the Solomon group. There I anchored in a small bay, named Port Mary, where the anchorage is protected on the west by a long spit of coral reef. It is a good harbour for small vessels.

Captain McDonald's chief trading station was situated at Port Mary, near a large native village. My stay there was a short one, there being no prospect of recruits. Having shipped such water as was necessary to fill up my tanks, I commenced recruiting at Cape Keibeck, on the northern coast of San Christoval I. I succeeded in getting three recruits from a village named Makira.

The same evening I stood into a bay with a broad sandy beach, a few miles west of the cape; but, finding the water too deep to anchor in, I was obliged to stand out to sea again for the night.

Only a year before this, a party of bushmen, some forty in number, had come down to this bay, intending to ship on board the *Borealis* for service in Fiji. They arrived in the evening, and camped for the night on the beach, meaning to engage next morning.

A mile or two away, there is a large village belonging to a tribe of " beach " men, the hereditary enemies of the " bushmen," or natives of the interior. After it was dark, these beach natives mustered all their strength, and attacked the bush party unawares. They massacred all of them, and, for the rest of the night, fires blazed all along the beach. The crew of the *Borealis* could hear the cannibals shouting and laughing, as they danced and feasted around them.

On the south-east side of Ugi I., the *Stanley* had a narrow escape from shipwreck. It was about one o'clock in the morning, the sky being dark and gloomy and the sea dead calm, when the mate roused me up. He told me that the ship appeared to be drifting on shore, and there was no wind to help her off. When I got on deck, the breakers seemed by the sound to be not more than a hundred yards away, while the swell, rolling in from south-east, was lifting the ship further and further in towards them. This coast of the island is "steep to," so that to let go an anchor would have simply been to lose it, as our cables would not have reached bottom a hundred yards away from the breakers.

Both boats were accordingly sent ahead to tow the ship off; but with no avail. The swell prevented her from gathering headway; so there she hung for a good hour or more, with her stern sometimes not more than ten yards from the breakers. The boatmen were becoming thoroughly tired out, when a light puff came over the island and filled the upper sails. Then, a smart squall struck the ship and ran her out of danger, the boats hanging on alongside while it lasted.

The next day was dull and cloudy, with a strong breeze from the west, which carried the ship to Port Adams, on the eastern coast of Maramasiki I.

This island was formerly represented on the charts as merely a part of its greater neighbour, Malayta I. They are really separated by a narrow channel, about twenty-five miles in length, and, in some places, not more than two cables (400 yards) in width. The southern mouth of it lies about fifteen miles north-west of Cape Zélée, the south-easternmost point of Maramasiki I.

I worked this side of Maramasiki and Malayta Is. as far as Iyoh or Aio I., and obtained a few recruits. One of these, who was engaged on the Malayta side of the north or "estuary" end of the channel, afterwards deserted at Alite Bay.

I anchored on the south-west side of Aio I., in a shallow bay, on the shore of which were some huts, a spit of reef projecting from its southern point. At the end of the spit and close to it, there is a dangerous smooth rock, just under the surface.

Our recruiting was not successful here, for the natives were very shy of approaching the boats. They probably expected reprisals on our part; for my recruiter—an "old hand" here—recognized several Kwai men in the neighbourhood. These had probably fled hither to escape the consequences of participation in the *Borealis* massacre.

It was evening when I left Aio. That night I ran down to the north end of Malayta I., and there tried the coast about Sio Bay, but without much luck. I then crossed over to Isabel I., anchoring at first in Cockatoo Harbour, east of the entrance to Thousand Ships Bay.

There I found the brigantine *Venture*, Captain Walsche, at anchor. On board of her I made the acquaintance of an Isabel I. potentate, known as King

KING BERRY.

Berry. His capital, a collection of huts built upon piles, which crowns the summit of a small rocky peninsula, is situated not far from Cape Prieto.

King Berry was then much dreaded by the inhabitants of Isabel I., along half the length of the south-western coast, and on the opposite side as far as Mt. Marescot. Many a ruined village attested the devastating energy of his forays. When I met him, Captain Walsche was sorting out a large quantity of "trade," to barter with him for copra, bêche-de-mer, tortoise-shell, and other island produce.

As I have occasionally mentioned these articles—copra and bêche-de-mer—a short description of them may not come amiss.

When I first visited the South Sea Islands, in 1868, the cocoanut was chiefly used for the manufacture of cocoanut oil. Owing to the rude appliances used, there was a great waste of the oil during its preparation. The German firms, whose headquarters were in the Navigator's or Samoa Is., then conceived the idea of drying the nuts, and so sending them to Europe. There, powerful machinery could be employed to express the oil, thus effecting a saving of about one-third of it. The refuse, I have heard, is made into a cake as food for cattle.

A COPRA STATION.

The drying process is now all that the nut undergoes in the islands.

The mode of preparing copra is a simple one. The nut is first split into halves with an axe, after which it is exposed to the sun. The heat soon loosens the kernel, which is then picked out, broken into fragments, and yet further dried. Sun-drying affords the best results. The islanders seldom take so much trouble with it. They hang it up over their fires instead, where it soon loses all moisture and becomes hard and brown.

Occasionally, the oil itself is required in the islands, and then this is the plan I have seen adopted in the New

Hebrides for its extraction. The nut is first husked, by driving it down upon a sharp-pointed stake, or bar of iron, set firmly upright in the ground. This penetrates the tough husk—care being taken not to break the shell within it—and a strong wrench or two with both hands suffices to tear it off. Next, a deft blow on the side splits the shell and its contents into two cup-shaped halves. The white "meat," or kernel, is then scraped out.

The scraper employed is generally a piece of stout hoop iron, about nine inches long, fixed on and projecting from the end of a plank or bench, which the

HUSKING AND SCRAPING COCOANUTS.

operator sits upon to steady it. He holds the split nut with both hands, and works the hollow inner side over the end of the scraper, the shredded kernel falling into a basket below.

Formerly, on the Tanna oil-stations, a practised islander would husk, break, and scrape from 200 to 250 nuts per diem.

The scraped kernel is kept for a day or two in the "rotting" cask, a little salt water being sprinkled through it to assist decomposition. It is then mixed and pounded into a pulp—generally by the feet of the "boys"—and placed in the upper part of canoes or hollowed logs, which are tilted up at one end. The heat of the sun acting on the pulp, causes the oil to exude from it and flow down to the lower end of the canoes. It is finally collected, strained, and then run into casks.

Sometimes, instead of this "sweating" process, the shredded kernel is boiled in water in large iron pots, the oil being skimmed off the surface. This is considered the most cleanly and saving process; but pots are not always available on these islands.

Bèche-de-mer—the Malayan "tripang"—is a marine slug found on coal reefs. Imagine a tough flexible mass, not unlike india-rubber, from eight to twelve inches long, and three to five inches thick, the ends rounded, some-

COCOANUT-OIL STATION.

times rather pointed, with a hole in each; colour black, dull red, or yellow. Within this there is a stomach, which seems to hold nothing but sand, with a little soft yellow fat. The creature possesses neither eyes, nose, nor means of locomotion, so far as I can judge. It is simply gathered by hand off the tops of the reefs, or out of the shallows at low water.

This "fish" must be boiled very soon after it has been gathered, then cleaned and dried. So prepared, it is ready for market. It requires to be stored with great care, as the slightest damp will cause it to rot. The boiling must be carefully attended to, since either too long or too short a period would be equally detrimental. The average time allowed is between fifteen and twenty minutes.

When I was "fishing" bèche-de-mer on the coast of Queensland, in 1867, we used to ascertain whether the fish was properly cooked by taking one out of the boiling-pot and throwing it up in the air. If it rebounded sharply when it fell—"stotted," as we called it—then it was not cooked enough. If it fell "squash," it was spoiled by too much cooking. But when it fell pretty dead, hard, without rebounding, the pot was emptied immediately; as that indicated it was just done enough.

The next process is to cut open the "fish" lengthwise, and to take out the entrails and sand contained in it. The more valuable, large, thick fish are then distended by small pieces of wood, to promote drying. The final operation of curing is performed in a smoke-house. Sometimes, chiefly in equatorial latitudes, the Chinese complete the curing by sun-drying only.

In the smoke-houses the fish are arranged on raised floors of cane-work, sometimes of wire netting; a fire of green wood burning on the ground beneath the frames. Smoking takes from ten to sixteen hours; after which the "fish" ought to be thoroughly cured and fit for market.

I was unable to obtain any recruits from Isabel I. King Berry would not allow any of his people to leave home. I dare say Captain Walsche's influence may have been unfavourable to me also. Copra traders are generally opposed to the labour trade. The more men there are on the islands, to make copra and buy tobacco with it, the better for them. Besides—like the missionaries—they cannot bamboozle the "returned" labourers so easily as they do the unsophisticated savage.

Having filled up my water-tanks, the boats made the circuit of Thousand Ships Bay. They obtained nothing more valuable, however, than half a boat-load of huge oysters, which the men gathered off the roots of the mangrove trees at the head of the bay.

Leaving Cockatoo Harbour, I beat round Cape Prieto to the eastern coast of the island. There I got a few recruits at a large village about a couple of miles beyond Ortega or Mahiji islet. The natives told me a vessel had been wrecked there some two years before this. A little further north are three islets—not marked on the chart. Between the largest of these and the main island, I anchored in eighteen fathoms, much to the bewilderment of a huge alligator, which paid us a visit of inspection, quickly disappearing when my boatmen made a target of it.

This coast is very imperfectly laid down on the Admiralty charts. I was much surprised to find a large land-locked harbour, eastward of a remarkable hill called the Mahagga Saddle. This harbour is some miles in extent, and has two entrances. The southernmost of these is narrow but deep, while the northern one is apparently a good channel for any ship. The navigation inside is, I think, rather intricate; extensive reefs projecting from the shore and occupying half the enclosed space. I noticed no villages along the shores, but numerous fishing stages had been erected on the reefs, in different places.

The absence of any village is easily accounted for. The natives of this group are pre-eminently treacherous and bloodthirsty, and they dread their nearest neighbours quite as much as they do strangers. Two or three villages could be made out in the distance, perched, like crows' nests, on peaks high up among the mountains.

The trade-wind had now become very unsteady and fitful; not nice weather for this coast, where the anchorages were few and small, while reefs and islets constantly appeared when least expected. At Gau, a village some miles beyond the harbour above-mentioned, I engaged a man, who informed me that there were no inhabitants for a great distance along the coast, and, in fact, very few at all on that side of Isabel I. However, I placed little reliance at the time on what he said. Now that I know that coast, which I did not then, I may safely assert that, for a hundred miles, from Gau to Port Praslin, there are not as many natives living near it. Just a few small families reside at Estrella Bay, and that is all.

East of Mt. Marescot I passed a bay, or lagoon, with a barrier reef and two islets on its seaward side. I should have sent my boats in, but my Gau man said it would be of no use. He said that King Berry had lately made a foray there, during which that truculent savage had destroyed the villages on the islets, slaughtered the whole of the inhabitants, and wound up his victory with a great cannibal feast.

That evening I stood close in shore, seeking for an anchorage. Finding none, I was obliged to put to sea again. During the night I drifted to leeward, past Estrella Bay, and next day coasted slowly along, with a light south-easterly air. By evening again, I was in an unpleasant position. The wind, light and puffy, was coming from north-east, while a heavy roll was drifting the ship in towards the land. About two miles to leeward, there was a long sandy beach, and, between the ship and it, were several patches of coral, over which the sea was breaking. The beach swept round ahead of our course, forming a large bay, protected on its northerly side by a cluster of islets.

It being absolutely necessary to find an anchorage before dark, I sent the mate ahead in the boat to take soundings. There was a narrow but straight channel between two of the islets, about a mile off on the lee bow. To this we directed our attention, and, just as the sun disappeared, succeeded in getting the ship safely anchored there.

One important article of our outfit had been forgotten,

when we left Maryborough. This was a bag of lime for whitewashing the hold of the ship. So, as wind and weather continued unaltered, and as the place appeared to be devoid of inhabitants to disturb our peace, I allowed the ship to remain where she was for the next two days. During this time, the recruits and some of the crew were sent ashore to collect loose coral blocks and burn them in rough kilns. By this means sufficient lime was collected to answer the purpose of whitewashing.

Meanwhile, the G.A. and I penetrated through the channel in a north-westerly direction, until we came to a long low wooded point on the main island. Between it and the principal islet there was a narrow channel, with four fathoms of water, opening into a large bay facing north-west, with more islets and reefs on the seaward side. On the south-eastern side of this was a point, close to an islet, enclosing a snug little harbour with good anchorage.

We examined the beach in several places, but were unable to discover any signs of man or beast, with the exception of the ashes of an old camp fire, probably made by some party of travellers or castaways.

At sunrise, on the third morning, the windlass was manned, the cable hove short, and sail made. For some time, the anchor refused to come home, being hooked in the coral. At last, after a hearty strain at the windlass, the vessel paid off under the weight of her head canvas, while the pawls rattled cheerily. However, when the anchor had been got up to the hawse-pipe, we found that one of the flukes was gone, having been broken short off at the crown.

Instead of beating out the same way I came in, I now ran through the narrow channel, between the islets and the point on the main, coasting along all the forenoon without seeing a sign of any inhabitants. A barrier reef was now discerned running along the coast. It lay at a gradually increasing distance from the shore, as that extended northward.

In the afternoon I ran the ship inside this reef, through a channel between two small islets. I then stood in towards the main, distant about a mile from the reef at this point. I anchored in a deep inlet that was well sheltered from wind and sea. Less than a mile beyond, the lagoon within the reef was studded with islets and surface-coral.

I anchored here, because I concluded we must have got into the vicinity of Port Praslin, where there was a native village. I was afraid I might run by without observing it, the entrance being reported to be a rather narrow one. Besides, I could see bananas and palm-trees, certain indications of inhabitants.

Shortly after we had anchored, two canoes, containing eight men, came alongside. One of these natives could speak a little English. He told me that their village lay not far off, on the main island; and that it was the only one then existing on this part of the coast.

In former years this end of Isabel I. was fairly populous. Then the people of Choiseul I., a larger and much more powerful race than the Isabel tribes, made frequent raids, killing and eating, or driving away nearly all the inhabitants. Such as survived these onslaughts sought refuge on the south-western coast, or in the interior.

The following morning, after breakfast, the mate and G.A. went off in the boats. Shortly after their departure, I got under way, and, passing through the barrier again, ran down the coast, to look for Port Praslin. I failed to find the entrance to it, as described on the chart, and, towards evening, found myself off the extremity of the island. I then worked back to pick up my boats, but could not see them; so, being unable to make an anchorage, I passed the night at sea.

Next morning I re-entered the lagoon, anchoring about two miles north-west of my last anchorage. I then made "smokes" on the neighbouring islets, and fired guns as signals, to apprise the boat party of our whereabouts.

On one of the islets in the outer reef, whereon I had made a large fire on the ocean side, in case the missing men should have gone out to look for the ship, the recruits, who paddled my boat, found a native sepulchre. Before I knew what they were about, two or three "old hands"— whose superstitions had been civilized away —violated it, in order to obtain the shell and stone armlets, and such other native treasures as it contained.

This erection was a receptacle for the bones of the dead, after the flesh had disappeared from them in ordinary graves. It was a square enclosure on the surface of the ground, surrounded by a wall of loose coral

NATIVE SEPULCHRE—ISABEL I.

blocks. It measured about eight feet in length and breadth, by five feet in height. It was completely filled with human bones, above which a layer of stones had been piled. Apparently it had not been disturbed for years. Within it the number of skulls seemed to be proportionate to the other bones; while outside, on the ground at the base of the wall, there were thirty or forty more skulls, each of which had been broken or fissured, as though from the blow of a club.

I made my boys rebuild the small portion of the wall they had pulled down, leaving it pretty much as we found it. I must admit, though, that several stone and shell armlets found their way on board the ship. Some other relics were also carried off. Among these there was a piece of thick inferior glass, measuring about five inches by four inches. It had probably been, at one time, part of a mirror. There was also the large bowl of a tobacco pipe, apparently of a Dutch kind.

During the past night, and all that day, I had felt very uneasy on account of the absence of the mate and G.A. When the sun set, and no sign of their return was yet evident, I began to be afraid they had fallen into the hands of the savages. A lantern was lit and hung high up in the rigging; while every now and then, a rifle was discharged. I had no larger gun, or I should have used it. Not until eight in the evening were our minds relieved. Then, a gun-shot was heard, in under the land, and ten minutes later the wanderers were alongside, tired and hungry.

They had not understood that it was my intention to remove the ship to a fresh anchorage, but had expected me to return to the old place, if I failed to discover Port Praslin. Not finding us there, they had camped on a small islet for the night. Then they had returned to the village and bought some yams and other food. After that they pulled outside the barrier-reef to sea, just too late to sight us before we got inside again, and also to see my signal fires. There was a canoe with them containing four or five natives, who slept on board the *Stanley* that night, and sold us a few yams and other things.

Next morning the anchor was weighed, and, with three recruits I had obtained here, I stood out from the land, purposing to work back against the "trade" to Malayta I. About a mile to windward of the opening in the barrier reef, through which I issued from the lagoon, a peculiar object was seen, floating, as if moored, just outside the breakers. What this was, we could not make out. So, to solve the mystery, I made a tack to windward, stood in close, and then, leaving the ship hove to, went off in the boat to it.

On coming up to it, we found the object consisted of a couple of square wooden tanks, fastened together by two twenty-inch baulks of timber, one on top, the other below. These baulks were bound to the tanks and to each other by iron bars, with nuts and screws. Each tank was ten or eleven feet square, and about eight feet deep. They had been constructed of four-inch pine, caulked and pitched, but not metalled. There was a two-foot hatch in each of them, fitted with a lid nailed down securely over it. In the space between them, a huge chain cable, composed of stud links branded WOOD, hung down from

A STRANGE DERELICT.

the upper baulk, to which one end of it was shackled, the other end being held merely by a " round turn." The bight of the chain, as it hung down far below, had caught the coral, and held this strange derelict anchored about twenty yards from the breakers. At one end of the upper baulk were a few composition nails, with one of copper, holding some remnants of cotton canvas. One tank was dry and empty, the other contained only about eight inches of water, which had apparently leaked into it.

The crew of this craft consisted of an old booby, which refused to budge, even when I climbed on to the tanks, disputing possession vigorously with his sharp bill when disturbed. I could never ascertain what this affair had been designed for. It may have been part of a pontoon, employed to support the outer end of a wharf over deep water, and have floated from one of the guano islands near the equator.

After beating back to the south-east for a few days, I dropped anchor in North Alite Bay, on the lee side of Malayta I. There, one morning, I fell in with the schooner *Sea Breeze*, Captain Williams, from Fiji.

At this time, H.M.SS. *Cormorant* and *Renard* were blockading the Florida Is., and hunting after the murderers of Lieutenant Bowers and his men. Captain Williams, being unaware of their presence and intentions, hove to there on the previous evening. After dark a man-of-war's boat paid him a visit. The officer in command of her gave him orders to leave the Floridas, all communication with the natives being forbidden until the murderers should have been secured.

The result of this blockade was, that, after a lot of time and trouble, one man was captured and hanged. Another of the culprits was pardoned, on the intercession of Bishop Selwyn, who considered he was too young to comprehend the enormity of his crime, though old enough to wield a tomahawk, and be considered a warrior among his own people. As though the death of only one of them was sufficient atonement for the slaughter of six unoffending white men, or would deter the savages from committing fresh outrages in the future! Little wonder, that, immediately after the execution, the natives at Saaranna village should have said to my mate —" Man-o'-war all the same old woman!"

There was one bit of Captain Williams' news, however, that I deemed worthy of consideration. This was, that, in ten days' time, it was the intention of the naval force to go to Ugi I., in order to take in a supply of coal that was awaiting them there.

From Alite Bay I worked down the coast of Malayta I., but with little success. About half-way between Alite and Maramasiki Passage, I found a safe land-locked harbour called Fulafau. There, a chain of low, narrow coral islets runs parallel to the coast. They are the elevated top of a barrier-reef, which encloses a lagoon some miles in extent, comprehending several bays on the main island, and a few inner islets. I lost one of my recruits by desertion there.

I left the ship one day with the G.A. and some of the recruits, taking one of the boats. As the "boys" had not yet learned how to use oars, they *paddled* us to the southern end of the lagoon, where I visited another vessel that was lying there. On our return we landed on a low point of the main, to obtain young cocoanuts from some trees there, to quench our thirst. As there were no habitations near, and no natives were visible, we helped ourselves. To get the young nuts, some of the boys climbed up the trees and dropped the fruit down.

When all were mustered for the resumption of our cruise, one boy was missing—he whom I had recruited on the Malayta side of the estuary, a month or so previously. I did not see him again until I visited the other side of the island, on my next voyage. His dodge had been a very simple one. He had climbed a tree whilst no one was taking notice of him, and hidden amongst the branches. When searching for him, we never thought of looking upward, or probably somebody would have discovered him. He quietly watched our movements until we had departed. Then he descended, going back to his native village, next day, across the island, a distance of twelve miles on a bee-line.

I went but little further down the coast, after leaving Fulafau. I then crossed over to Guadalcanar I., where I watered the ship at a stream about eight miles west of Marau Sound, whence I proceeded to Langa.

Ten days had now elapsed since I spoke the *Sea Breeze*, and the time mentioned by Captain Williams,

A LAGOON HARBOUR—MALAYTA I.

when the *Cormorant* was to go to Ugi I., had now arrived. So, with a fair wind, I ran over to the Floridas next morning, where I found a snug anchorage near the south-western point of the southern island, not far from the village of Saaranna.

There I lay undisturbed for two or three days, to the advantage of my owner. I then spent a night in Port Purvis, the western end of the narrow channel which separates the southern and middle islands of the Florida group. Recruiting now went on gaily, probably owing to the visit of the ships of war. My list soon began to grow satisfactorily long.

Sandfly Passage was my next anchorage, between the middle and northern of the Florida Is. There, poor Tom Tamoan, who had almost given up all hopes of ever seeing his long-lost home again, at last discovered where his native island lay, although he was still some distance from it.

The boats were at the beach on the northern island, Gala, when a native, who had been gazing at Tom for some time, suddenly accosted him in English, " Hullo, Tom."

Tom stared, but failed to recognize him. Then the Gala man told the recruiter how, years ago—probably ten or twelve—the barque *Woodlark*, of Sydney, had come to Gala; how her captain had engaged and taken away "plenty boy" to work on plantations in Queensland; how, on her return to that colony, she passed close to Bellona, the smallest of the two Rennell Is., and how a canoe came off to her with two men and a boy. The men returned to the island, but the boy, Tamoan, elected to remain on board, and went to Queensland in the *Woodlark*.

At last, then, Tom knew the white man's name for his island. Nothing less would serve him than my getting under way at once, to take him there. For the Gala man had described the island as being close at hand.

I was not disinclined to go there, either. During the first morning of our stay at Gala, the three masts of a ship of war, and the smoke from her funnel, had been descried on the eastern horizon, going southward. It was therefore possible that, at any moment, one of the cruisers might arrive, to make trouble touching my infraction of the blockade. So, having my recruit list more than two-thirds filled up, I weighed anchor and left the Floridas. I made for Savo I., proceeding thence to the coast of Guadalcanar I., on the west of Cape Esperance, where I got three men.

Coasting along the western shores of Guadalcanar I., we spent a day at Boyd Creek, Wanderer Bay, taking in water and firewood. This bay derives its name from the yacht *Wanderer*, in which vessel the well-known old Australian colonist, Benjamin Boyd, visited the place in 1851. Boyd was murdered by the natives there, while on shore pigeon-shooting.

From Wanderer Bay, one "board" on the port tack took the *Stanley* over to Bellona I., which Tom recognized at once as his long-lost home. The native name of this island, as given me by its inhabitants at the time of my visit, was Muighi, though Tom pronounced it Mungigi. The largest of the Rennell group is called Muava.

Standing close in under the lee of the island, which is hardly more than a mile in length, and about two hundred feet in height, I sought for an anchorage without success, the shores all round being "steep to." Off the eastern end I neared the rocks in the boat, but the sea would not allow us to land. Tom, however, was impatient, and, seeing a party of his countrymen at hand watching us, he stripped off his clothing and swam ashore through the breakers. He landed on the rocks at the cost of a bruise or two, then slowly climbed up to the outskirts of the dense forest which covers the island. There a dozen natives had gathered together, watching his every movement.

The noise of the waves breaking on the rocks prevented our hearing any of the conversation, which, it was evident, was passing between them. Presently one man walked cautiously up to Tom, and felt him all over, as though to ascertain if he was really flesh and blood, and not a ghost. This examination having proved satisfactory, the whole party clustered round Tom with loud cries and laughter, and began handling him, jabbering and gesticulating like a lot of excited monkeys.

Next, a small light canoe was lugged down from amongst the trees, and launched clean over the breakers, off the top of a huge boulder. Two fellows took a

TOUCHING NOSES.

header, and so scrambled into her. They then came alongside our boat, stripping off their rude beads and other ornaments, and forcing them upon me, jabbering away all the while like a couple of maniacs.

I then pulled back to the lee end of the island, in search of a safe landing-place. There I managed to get on shore dryshod, with the G.A. Then, accompanied by about a score of the islanders, men and women, we walked to a scattered village near the centre of the island. Arrived there, we touched noses with the old chief, a ceremony which is peculiar to islanders of the true Polynesian race.

These people are apparently pure Polynesians. They are large-framed, fleshy, with brown skins and frizzly hair. Some of the women were very light in colour. They practise tattooing to some extent. Their houses are of the same pattern as those of the Equatorial islands—a roof supported by posts, the sides being left open.

I remained on shore a few hours, but could do nothing in the way of recruiting. Tom seemed half-dazed—he was always a little "daft"—and was either unwilling or too stupid to interpret. Towards evening, however, he let me know that no recruits were to be obtained at present. By-and-by, in the course of weeks, some might be induced to engage.

I was much disappointed. Tom had assured me that he would do all he could to assist me in return for my taking him home. Now, I saw that, having got all he wanted, he was indisposed to fulfil his promises. On a subsequent visit, I discovered that Tom had really acted in opposition to me, dissuading those of his countrymen who wished to engage.

I remained near Muighi I. until late on the second day, when I returned to the Solomons, weathering Guadalcanar, and then steering for the east of the Floridas, hoping that by this time the blockade would have been raised.

It proved to be so. Off the south-eastern point of these islands, I met a barque-rigged ship of war, steaming southward. I supposed her to be the *Cormorant* on her way back to Australia. Mightily pleased I was when I saw her pass by without troubling me. I was as fortunate on the eastern coast of the Floridas as I had been on the western, rapidly filling up my recruit list.

Two miles from the eastern end of Sandfly Passage, I found an extensive patch of sunken coral, in six to eight fathoms of water. There I anchored, while the boats worked the neighbouring coasts.

One forenoon the boats were at the beach near Ravu

village, Gala I. An inquisitive native, who had paddled his canoe alongside the recruiting boat, took up one of the boatmen's rifles, and accidentally discharged it. The ball wounded two natives—one of them being a recruit just engaged—though, fortunately, not seriously. The wounded men were brought off to the ship, where I washed and bound up their hurts, giving them some spare bandages and ointment to take home with them.

When I visited this place again on my next voyage, my patients' wounds were thoroughly healed. The chief told us, however, that, had either of them died, he would have taken some white man's life in revenge; this because the injury was inflicted by a white man's weapon, although

WAR CANOE—SOLOMON IS.

it had been fired by a native. This is a curious example of the South Sea Islander's sense of justice.

When I left the Florida Is., there still wanted four boys to make up my complement. These I succeeded in getting at Fiu, on the lee side of Malayta I., where I also took in fresh water. I then sailed for Queensland with eighty-eight recruits.

Such of the Solomon Is. as I visited on this voyage seemed to be of similar formation to the New Hebrides. They are mountainous and rugged, generally clothed with dense forest and jungle from their highest peaks to the water's edge. Here and there may be found patches of country almost devoid of trees, covered with long coarse grass. The natives are of purer Papuan blood than many of the New Hebrideans; excelling them in bloodthirstiness, treachery, and cannibalism, as much as they do in the construction and ornamentation of their canoes, dwellings, and weapons.

Their canoes are gracefully shaped, and have no outriggers. They are built of planks, hewn with the tomahawk, " seized " together with cocoanut-fibre twine. The seams are "payed" with a black cement, made from a certain nut, dried and ground up very fine. The larger canoes are generally much ornamented with shells and mother-o'-pearl. They are often large enough to carry sixty or eighty men.

Of dress they wear little, in some places none at all, either men, women, or children.

Their supply of food is but little in excess of what they absolutely require for themselves. This is not due to the soil, which is luxuriantly fertile, but to their carelessness, as well as to the destruction resulting from their constant intertribal wars.

I knew of only two Protestant mission-stations in these islands at that time, in Savo I. and in the Floridas, though there may have been some others. In 1847, French missionaries (Roman Catholic) attempted to settle in the group, but were forced to leave, as much on account of the unhealthiness of the climate as of the hostility of the savages. That year, 1881, three priests were murdered at Makira Harbour, San Christoval I., and Bishop Epallé was also killed in Isabel I.

Leaving Malayta behind me, I passed close to the west end of San Christoval, and, making one tack to the southward, brought the *Stanley* off Makira Harbour. Thence, close-hauled, I weathered the Rennell Is. and Indispensable Reef. Then, without touching a brace, I made one long "board" to Hervey Bay, and anchored off Woody I. on the twenty-third of July. I reached Maryborough two days later.

A few weeks previously the *May Queen* had arrived

at Brisbane, bringing labourers from the New Hebrides. She reported that her boats had been attacked by the natives at Walwuki, Lepers' I. Her recruiter, Richard McDonald, with eight boatmen, had been killed. Two others, though wounded, swam off and escaped to the vessel.

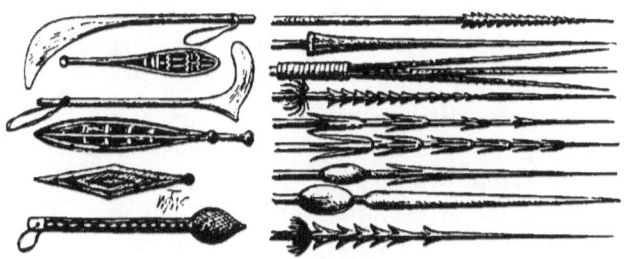

WEAPONS—SOLOMON IS.

CHAPTER XV.

EIGHTH VOYAGE OF THE *STANLEY*, 1881.

*I sail from Hervey Bay—My G.A.—His hostility towards me—
The New Hebrides—Bellona I.—Tom Tamoan again—He
tries to prevent recruiting—But fails—My deserter comes on
board—He is let off—The* Janet Stewart—*Her subsequent
capture by natives—Missionary influence prejudicial to recruiting — Saaranna — Natives attack the boats — Steering-oar
stolen and recovered—Mandolianna I.—More missionary
intolerance—Native agent killed at Gala I.—How a copra-
trader indemnified himself—The G.A. orders me home—
Hada Bay—Chief "Johnson"—A cyclone—Weathering the
storm—Arrival at Maryborough—I go to Brisbane—Interview with the head of a department—A wigging and refreshments!—Survivors of the* Isabella—*Fate of her people.*

I LEFT Hervey Bay on my last voyage in the *Stanley*, on the eighth of September, 1881. I was bound for the New Hebrides and the Solomon Is. with a considerable batch of "returns" on board. The G.A. who had accompanied me on my previous voyage had been re-appointed. During the former trip he had shown himself a careful officer, and at the same time had been a fairly pleasant companion. Now, his manner towards me was changed from the very beginning. Towards the termination of the trip, he appeared to seize every opportunity of impeding the work of recruiting and of otherwise annoying me.

The cause of our trouble at the outset was, possibly, drink. As soon as we were clear of the land, however, he got no more of that than a very moderate allowance. The real reason for his determined hostility towards me afterwards was best known to himself. He had paid a visit to Brisbane, and to the chief Immigration Office there, between our voyages. This somehow seemed to have worked a great change in his disposition. The upshot of it all will appear in due course.

I did not delay long in the New Hebrides, running through the group as quickly as possible, landing my returns. I then pushed on to the Solomons, for the trade-wind season was now far advanced, and that of the hurricanes was approaching.

At Bellona, or Muighi I., we found Tom Tamoan apparently satisfied with his home, and unwilling to leave it again. He came off to the ship with a crowd of his people, in the recruiting boat and canoes ; but none of them, he said, wished to be engaged. Somehow, when Tom told me this, I fancied he was not telling me the truth. The party had not been on board many minutes before I became sure that such was the case.

Some of the younger men appeared to be much excited, and presently a lot of squabbling went on between them and Tom, who was evidently backed up by two or three old fellows. Suddenly one of the boys made a rush towards me, though Tom tried to stop him, threw himself down on his knees, and clasped his arms round my legs, jabbering away at a fine rate. Then I saw what all the fuss was about.

" Tom, this boy wants to go with me ! "

Tom mumbled out something about the man being cranky ; but that was only an excuse to get him back on shore. Finally, he was obliged to give in, and to acknowledge that some of them *did* want to go with me.

I engaged five. Two were youths, but the other three were big, strapping men, and, to look at, splendid fellows for work. Nevertheless, they turned out " soft," proving of little use to their employers. One Papuan would have been worth the lot of them.

At the Rennell Is., none of the natives could be

induced to leave home. At the estuary on the north-eastern coast of Malayta I. a canoe came alongside the ship, having two men in her, one of whom came up on deck. He proved to be the same man who had deserted me near Fulafau, on my preceding voyage. His dismay may be imagined when he found himself among men who, as he would think, would treat him as an enemy. He had failed, for a wonder, to recognize the ship, or, I suppose, he would hardly have ventured near us.

At that time it had not been made illegal to retake a deserter. At first I was disposed to make this fellow go with me, willy-nilly. However, the G.A. objected to that, so my gentleman got nothing worse than a hearty cursing, as he tumbled over the side into his canoe and made off to the shore as fast as his paddle would take him.

Off Sio Bay, on the north of the island, I spoke and boarded the Maryborough brig, *Janet Stewart*, Captain Thomas, Mr. William Lochhead G.A. It was the last time I saw the brig. In the following year she was captured by the natives in the vicinity of Uru and Kwai, being burnt while lying at anchor off Leili I., opposite Kwai. Captain Thomas, with Lowry, the second mate, was absent in the boats when the ship was taken. One man, a seaman named Gustave Germanie, escaped by concealing himself in the chain locker. A fire forward was extinguished when the boats returned, but another soon burst out aft, and destroyed the ship. Lochhead's body was found in his easy-chair on deck, where he had been killed, probably when asleep.

At the Floridas I did not have such good fortune as on the last voyage. Missionary influence was too much for me. At Saaranna a party of old men and chiefs threatened to attack the boats if they did not leave the beach. Several of the younger men were watching for an opportunity to escape from home. Once, when a recruit had been obtained and passed into the covering boat, which lay off in deep water, where his friends could not reach him, a rush was made at the recruiter. He only escaped by quickly shoving his boat off, abandoning his steering-oar, which had been seized by the natives, in the effort to haul the boat up on the beach. A quantity of calico and other "trade" was carried off by the natives at the same time.

Having got the boy who had been recruited safely on board the *Stanley*, the recruiter went back to the village and succeeded in recovering his steering-oar without payment. The stolen calico and other articles were

MANDOLIANNA I.

never seen again by us. When the recruiter threatened to inform "the man-o'-war," if they were not returned, the natives simply laughed and jeered at him.

"Man-o'-war all same old woman!" said they.

I visited the island of Mandolianna next. There a few runaways joined us, paddling over from the main island to the islet during the night, their canoes having been left on the beach for their friends to remove at their leisure. The chiefs soon put a stop to this game.

Near our anchorage we saw a white-painted wooden slab, inscribed with the names of Lieutenant Bowers and his five men, who lay buried beneath it.

On the north-eastern coast, especially at Mboli, the native teachers, trained by the missionaries, made themselves very active in attendance on the boats. They forcibly prevented men from leaving the island. Such proceedings, when viewed by a tolerant mind, must appear very like slavery.

At Rarvu, luckily for us, we found that the two men who had been wounded during my last voyage, were now quite well again. However, the natives there were much excited by another cause. They stated that about a year before, a Sydney schooner, name unknown, had left a native of Guadalcanar, provided with a quantity of "trade," at the principal village on the northern coast of Gala I., the scene of the *Dancing Wave* massacre in 1876. He was left there to purchase copra from the natives, while the schooner returned to Sydney with the cargo she then had on board. Some disturbance occurring, the Guadalcanar man was slain, the "trade" in his charge being appropriated by the Gala people as a matter of course. It being utterly useless to seek redress at the hands of those who are styled by officialism "the proper authorities," the skipper, when he returned from Sydney, determined to pay the natives off in their own coin as far as he could.

Anchoring off the village, he kept on friendly terms with the natives, pretending he was not annoyed in the least by their transactions during his absence, and that he did not want any equivalent for the "trade" they had stolen. He persuaded the chief to fill up his vessel's hold with copra, which was to be paid for in the lump when the cargo had been completed. He got his cargo, and then sailed away without paying for it! They were quits.

At the end of November I anchored off the Two

Sisters Is., native name Untur, on the coast of Malayta I. While there, the G.A. served me with an official letter, ordering me to take the ship home. The reason assigned was that provisions were running short, and little or no further supplies could be obtained from the natives. The weather had become wet and squally, which was unfavourable for recruiting work. There seemed little prospect of its improvement, so I cannot say I was sorry when I received the document, though I was still in want of about a score of recruits to make up my complement.

I had a northerly wind at the time, which carried me to the western limit of San Christoval I., then backing to south-east, a bad sign. Standing southward, I made one tack, but a north-westerly current brought the vessel nearly back to Point Achard. I bore up, therefore, and ran to Hada Bay, where I anchored. There I filled up my water-tanks, and, as I was running short of beef, I purchased some pigs from the chief of a large village a mile or two south of the bay. This chief, who had been named "Johnson" by his white visitors, was hanged, a few years subsequently, for the murder of a white trader.

Putting to sea again, I stood southward with a light, unsteady breeze from the east. By the sixth of December I had made the south-eastern end of Indispensable Reef. The wind was easterly that day, varying a point or two southward occasionally. The sky was dull and grey, a sputter of rain falling now and then; while the barometer, though not alarmingly low, was unsteady.

My mate, an old hand in these latitudes, predicted a hurricane or cyclone; but I scouted the idea, for I considered the season was not yet sufficiently advanced for these tempests. He was right, though.

Late in the afternoon a thick shower passed over. In the middle of it, a whirlwind caught the ship forward, starting the bowsprit, the gammoning of which gave way. I secured it with the chain cables, which were unshackled from the anchors for the purpose.

At nightfall the weather was wet and gloomy, the wind coming from east-south-east, and freshening up. The ship lay on the port tack, under her lower canvas. The barometer stood at 29·75, and I considered we were in for a "straight" gale only.

By eight o'clock I was undeceived. The glass fell two-tenths in less than half an hour, and the wind flew round to north, increasing fast. The mainsail was immediately lowered, the helm being put up to wear the ship round on the starboard tack. As this was being done, while the ship was tearing away before the breeze, there came a blinding flash of lightning. Then a terrific squall caught the ship, ripping the topsail out of the bolt-ropes.

The hurricane was now upon us, and bitterly did I regret my mistake. Down came the head sails, but only to be lost. As the ship lay to, still on the port tack, everything forward was buried when she dipped to the head sea, and it was impossible to stow the canvas.

Fortunately the fore-trysail was new and good. It was immediately reefed, and set "balanced," and so lasted through the night. Under it alone the vessel lay to, lifting to the seas like a duck, with her starboard rail under water, and her deck smothered in flying drift and spray. The wind roared through the rigging meanwhile, ripping off every bit of spread canvas except the trysail, which stood like a board.

The boats on the davits suffered, of course. The lee one went clean away very early. The port boat had her gripes and tackles broken, but was held up by the cranes and jammed against the davits all night. She was secured when the hurricane was over, by which time the raised ends of the cranes had chafed two great holes in her bilge, rendering her unserviceable for some days, until she was patched up.

The barometer fell very quickly after eight o'clock, till it was down to 29·10. Then the indicator got jammed, some water having oozed in and swollen the dial plate, which was composed of some wretched paper-like substance. After that it did not move again until about three o'clock in the morning, rising when the wind had hauled round to W.N.W.

By daylight the gale had moderated; about seven there was a final heavy squall, after which the wind lulled rapidly. At nine, we were rolling about with a light south-west breeze, the weather being fine and sunshiny. The remainder of the passage was long and tedious. It was not until the 24th that we came to our moorings at Maryborough.

A few days after I resigned my command. I then betook myself to Brisbane, there to try conclusions with my G.A. He had made a report to the Government about the voyage, and his official log contained matter that demanded my attention. Of course, I was ignorant of the precise contents of these documents; but I was not without friends, some of whom gave me warning of what I had to expect. It was fortunate for me that I took the course I did.

The only interview I had with the head of a department with respect to the subject ended satisfactorily, though at its commencement I found myself in "stormy weather." Indeed, there appeared a great probability I should be debarred from sailing again in the same capacity.

Long extracts from the G.A.'s official log were read out to me. Some of these recorded details of private conversations which had passed between us, at times when I had supposed we were on friendly terms together. I had indulged in comments on different members of the Government, especially in regard to those connected with the Immigration Department. To judge by the extracts read, I had certainly hit some of them pretty hard. Besides this, I was accused of sundry petty offences against the G.A.'s "Instructions," though, luckily, of none against the Polynesian Act.

After this recital, I got a long lecture on the enormity of my offences, winding up with—"What you have done, sir, was quite in accordance with the Act, but it don't suit the Office, sir!"

So, now, I found I was expected to obey, not merely the Act, with its cartload of "Orders in Council," "Regulations," etc., etc., but also to pay heed to the fads and fancies of heads of departments.

At last the lecture was over, and then *I* chipped in. I did not say much, but what I did say was very much to the point, I think. It seemed to be satisfactory, too, for the big man became mollified. His official frown faded away; he smiled; he took up his hat, and ten minutes later we were in the "Sovereign" Hotel, washing down any bitter feeling that might have arisen, with the usual "Here's luck!" That was the end of the matter, but I fancy I had a narrow escape from being "debarred."

On December 13, the *May Queen*, Captain Dickson, Mr. Hoare G.A., arrived at Brisbane from the islands, *via* Mackay. Her master reported that he had picked up two wounded Fijians, a few miles north of Cape Lisburne, Espiritu Santo I. They were the survivors of a boat's crew belonging to the *Isabella*, of Fiji. The *Mavis*, of Fiji, happened to be at hand, so the crews of the two vessels searched the coast in the vicinity of the spot where the natives had attacked the *Isabella's* boat. The head of Mr. Mayer, her G.A., was found, but no trace of the body of Hampshire, the mate. Where the *Isabella* was at this time, I cannot say.

The master of the *Chance* reported at Mackay on January 9. He mentioned having encountered a hurricane off Lepers' I., New Hebrides, on December 8. This was most probably the same hurricane I had fallen in with on the night of the sixth.

CHAPTER XVI.

SECOND VOYAGE OF THE *JABBERWOCK*, 1882.

The Jabberwock *as a barquentine—We sail from Brisbane—The* Borough Belle *in company—Arrival at Tanna I.—The* Chance*—Loss of her boat and its crew—Their subsequent fate—I part with my consort—Rodd's anchorage—A French recruiting ship—Complaints of the natives—Kidnapping and shooting—A chief's wife carried off—I follow the French boat—And warn the natives—Recrimination—Visit to the French skipper—" Pistols and coffee!"—Mutual threats—Trial at Noumea—Kidnapping dodges—The* Borough Belle *has luck—Santa Maria I.—Natives in ambush—Our boats fired at—The Torres Is.—More firing—Lo I.—Fugitives rescued—Murder of M. Classen—Wounded with poisoned arrows—Remedies tried—Death—French injustice to me—Hayter Bay, Torga I.—The G.A.'s bag—Runaway women—The G.A. jumped upon—Hiu I.—Lakon—Homeward.*

THE *Jabberwock* had continued in the labour trade as a sailing vessel only—since I resigned the command of her in 1880—but her rig had remained unaltered. In January, 1882, she was sold by her Brisbane owners to a Mackay firm, Messrs. Paxton & Co., by whom I was again given the command of her.

She was lying at Peter's Slip, Brisbane, undergoing a thorough overhauling, as well as an alteration of her masts and cabins, which had not been quite completed when I took charge of her, towards the end of February. She was now masted forward in the usual manner, with top-gallant and royal, while her mizzen-mast had also been lengthened.

I sailed early in March, clearing Cape Moreton in company with the *Borough Belle*, which was also owned by Messrs. Paxton & Co., both of us bound for the New Hebrides. While she was an auxiliary screw steamer, the *Jabberwock* had enjoyed a reputation for speed, which she certainly did not act up to now. For the *Borough Belle*, which was considered anything but a clipper, gradually drew ahead, slightly weathering on us as we stood eastward, close-hauled, with a southerly breeze. On the morning of the tenth I went aloft and looked in vain for my consort; she was quite out of sight.

Notwithstanding the disparity in sailing qualities of the two vessels, Captain Belbin reached the New Hebrides only a few hours before me. On the sixteenth we were together again, off Emolau Point, Tanna I., where we also fell in with the brigantine *Helena*, Captain McQuaker, at anchor off Sangali, and the iron schooner *Chance*, Captain McPhie, both from Queensland, recruiting. I boarded the *Borough Belle*, meeting Captain McPhie and his G.A., Mr. Stiddulph, who were in great tribulation about one of the boats of the *Chance*, which, with its crew, was missing.

On the morning of the previous day the two boats had left the *Chance*, pulling along the southern coast of Tanna to try for recruits. They expected the schooner would follow them, as the wind was then very light. When near the land, and at a considerable distance apart, thick weather came on. From that time, Stiddulph, who was in one of the boats, had not seen the other again. He had only just rejoined the *Chance*, having passed the night on board the *Helena*, at Sangali.

As there was every probability that the missing boat and its crew would be found, either at Gomara, on the south-eastern coast, or in Port Resolution—at each of which places there was a mission station—we advised Captain McPhie to beat round the southern coast and visit them. If he had done so, he would have recovered his boat, as it turned out; for Wilson, the mate who was in charge of her, had made for Port Resolution. He was found there by the French ketch, the *Port Vila*, and was taken in her to Noumea; whence he found his way back to Queensland.

As neither Captain Belbin nor myself found anything particular to delay us, there being already too many vessels to work Tanna without interfering with each other, we both pushed on. We had a neck-and-neck race as far as Havannah Harbour. There the *Chance* rejoined us next day, not having visited either Gomara or Port Resolution, and so being still minus a boat and its crew. How McPhie got on without them, I cannot say, for I sailed again shortly. I then parted company with the *Borough Belle*, which went due north, whilst I delayed to work the Shepherd Is.

The "trades" had now set in steadily. Throughout the whole of this cruise in the New Hebrides, we daily enjoyed a moderate or fresh breeze from about east by south, with fine weather generally, and only an occasional shower. I worked the Shepherd Is., Api I., and Ambrym I., without anything special occurring, until I brought up one evening in Rodd's anchorage, on the western side of the northern point of Ambrym I.

The following morning there was a cry of "sail ho!" and we discerned the masts of a brigantine or schooner off the coast of Pentecost. She remained in sight for an hour or two, and then disappeared to northward. My boats were then away alongshore. When they returned, some natives came off with them on a visit to the ship —a common practice—to satisfy themselves as to our destination.

These visitors complained loudly of the conduct of a schooner, that they said was either French or Fijian, which had been there a day or two before our visit. A canoe had gone off to this ship, but had been fired at, one man being killed. Two other boys had been taken away, as well as some pigs that were in the canoe. They gave me the names of these kidnapped men, which I do not now remember. The next occasion on which I visited Pentecost I., I met some natives who had recognized them on board a French schooner—the same one we saw that morning.

After this I crossed over to Pentecost I., working down the lee coast of it. There, the inhabitants of South-West Bay had also a story to tell about the vessel we had seen.

She was a French schooner, the *Havannah*, of Noumea, and had been formerly named the *John S. Lane*, when owned in Sydney. She was commanded by Captain Petersen, and was recruiting labourers for the French colony of New Caledonia.

Petersen appears to have followed the usual practice of French recruiters—sending his boats to the shore in charge of Kanakas only. The consequences of such a system may be imagined.

I anchored in Chaffin's Bay, on the northern coast of Lepers' I., a few days later. There I fell in with the *Havannah*, which was lying at anchor. She remained only two or three hours after the arrival of the *Jabberwock*.

The natives received my recruiter in a friendly manner; though they had mustered at the landing in force, armed, and bent on a fight if the *Havannah's* boats came near. That morning, before our arrival, the young wife of a chief had been beguiled on board the Frenchman, on some pretence or other, and was still there. Some men had gone off to the vessel in a canoe, three of them venturing aboard of her, bearing an offer from the bereaved chief of two male recruits, if Petersen would send his wife back to him. This the French skipper refused to do; and, moreover, he detained the unfortunate ambassadors as well, letting their canoe drift back to the shore empty!

Shortly before sundown, I saw these three men jump overboard, and swim to the land. Immediately after that the *Havannah* got under way, and left. She was still in sight next morning, however, when I moved the *Jabberwock* a short distance westward, and again anchored.

The day following, as I noticed the *Havannah* was still close at hand, her boat being at the shore, I took charge of my own boats in place of the recruiter, and, accompanied by the G.A., pulled ashore to the spot where the French boat was lying. The coast was a rocky and precipitous one, so the *Havannah's* boat had pulled into a small nook among the rocks. We backed in upon her until my boat's stern nearly touched her bows. Then we lay on our oars and " took stock."

The French boat's crew consisted of four Kanakas, the steersman in charge being a big Tanna man. All were armed with guns, the Tanna man carrying a revolver in his belt. There was no white man in the boat, or near it. Three young women were sitting or standing on the rocks, close at hand. The Tanna man was making signs to them, and, with the assistance of an Aoba boy, one of his crew, seemed to be trying to persuade them to get into his boat.

As it happened, I had an Aoba man with me also, whom I had brought with me to interpret. He told me that his countryman was endeavouring to persuade the women to "come and see ship"—merely to visit her. Of course, if they went on board, they would land in New Caledonia before they reached home again! Moreover, if they were once in the ship, they might serve as a bait for some of the men.

This is, or used to be, a common trick practised by the French recruiters. "Get the women on board, and the men will follow!" was their motto. The Frenchman who told me of it expressed himself in coarser terms than I have used.

A few words from my interpreter sent the women flying up the rocks to a safe distance. From that point of advantage they poured out a torrent of chaff upon the French boatmen, accompanied by several expressive gestures, one of which was certainly an imported one, being what is commonly known among sailors as "taking a lunar." Just then the *Havannah* displayed a red flag, and her boat pulled away to her. The Tanna man swore he would have his revenge upon me, if ever he got a fair chance, which I responded to by threatening I would let him feel the weight of my boat's tiller, if ever I caught him at any of his kidnapping tricks again.

As the *Havannah* lay near our course, when we were returning to the *Jabberwock*, we went alongside and boarded her. Our visit was a short one, however. Petersen said I had interfered unwarrantably with his boat, and threatened to lay a complaint before the British Government, through Mr. Layard, our consul at Noumea. In return, I promised to write to the consul and give him *my* version of the matter, as well as to inform him of all I had heard from the natives about the proceedings of the *Havannah*. As for our G.A. and the French Government officer, they got to high words—in French,—and I heard threats pass between them relating to "pistols and coffee." My G.A. had a temper as hot as my own, although we got along together well enough on the whole.

Captain Petersen fulfilled his promises, and so did I. He made his complaint, though I heard nothing further about it; and I wrote to Mr. Layard. My letter arrived in Noumea at a time when there was some stir there, touching the trial of the well-known skipper of a French recruiting vessel, who was accused of kidnapping. I have heard that it occasioned a serious quarrel between the governor of the colony and our consul,—but that is hearsay.

About the trial, I may as well mention that two of the

charges were—one of having run down a canoe in the New Hebrides, some of the crew of which were drowned, whilst others were picked up and kidnapped; and the other of entrapping men in the Maskelyne Is. In the latter case, the skipper had pretended he wanted to move a large and heavy tank in the hold of his vessel—the said tank being, all the while, securely fastened to the lower deck. It was too dark down in the hold for strangers to perceive this. Having made a long stout rope fast round the tank, he got a lot of natives from the shore to pull on it; and, while they were thus engaged, he clapped his hatches on and left the island. I got this from a Noumea trader, who was present at the trial, and I see no reason for disbelieving the story.

Shortly after my meeting with the *Havannah*, I fell in with the *Borough Belle*. She was full up, and homeward bound, while I had only sixty-two recruits as yet. Captain Belbin had made a good haul at the Torres Is., which we generally considered hardly worth visiting. He strongly advised me to go there; but, when I came to consider the number he had taken away, I was afraid there would not be many left for me to recruit. However, I went in that direction, working the east coasts of Espiritu Santo and Santa Maria Is.

One morning I was off the south side of Santa Maria, and sent the boats away. Among my hands forward there was one gentleman who was new to the trade. He had constantly expressed a supreme contempt for all "niggers," as well as for their firearms, spears, and arrows. On this occasion he volunteered to steer the covering boat.

I watched them pulling in to the land, until I saw them enter a bay and disappear behind one of the points. The ship was then standing eastward, along the coast, under easy canvas. Suddenly I heard the faint pop! pop! of firearms. Then wreaths of white smoke rose above the point. A minute later the boats came

s

in sight, the crews lying back with a will; for the bullets continued to fly round them pretty thickly, until they were out of range. They were soon alongside, without a man hurt.

"My word! We got it hot!" said the mate, laughing, as he jumped off the rail on to the deck. "There were a hundred of them, if there was a man." But the steersman of the covering boat said not a word. His "baptism of fire" had caused all the blood to desert his cheeks. He went into the forecastle quietly; and from that time, henceforth, he neither volunteered to steer a boat, nor "gassed" about "niggers."

"WHAT FOR YOU 'FRAID?"

An ambuscade had been regularly planned. When the mate drew near the shore at the head of the little bay, he felt suspicious of a trap; for he could see a few men lurking behind the rocks, as though waiting for him. One fellow, who wore a white shirt, showed himself openly. Waving a green bough in pretence of amity, this fellow sung out to the mate, who was hesitating about going close in—"What for you 'fraid?"

Still the mate declined to go in. The boats were being slewed about, so as to pull to a safer place, when, bang! went a whole volley, the bullets tearing up the water, hissing and pinging all round them.

"Pull! you devils!" was the cry; and back they went

in a hurry, whilst the natives kept popping at them from both sides of the bay, luckily without hitting either boat or man.

Both before and after this attack the boats of several other vessels were fired on by the same fellows. In some cases there was actual loss of life on the side of the boats, whilst the natives came off scot-free.

After watering at Lakon, I went to the Torres Is., as Captain Belbin had advised me, anchoring at first in the bay on the western side of the southern island.

Our arrival caused considerable excitement; for, as we afterwards ascertained, a number of the younger inhabitants—men and women—had been prevented from joining the *Borough Belle* by their elders and chiefs. These were now determined to get away. Several of them managed to elude the vigilance of their friends, and got on board. Some of them came off in our boats, others in canoes, a few by swimming off to the ship. This, naturally, made the stay-at-home folks very wrathy. On the second morning, when I was getting under way, we received a volley from the cliffs. The bullets fell short, luckily, but sufficiently near the ship to send my recruits running from the windlass down below.

There was no harm done, however, and, with a considerably increased recruit list, I ran over to Lo, the next island. There I anchored in a well-sheltered bay on the western side, in ten fathoms.

While we were crossing the channel between these two islands, a sail was sighted to eastward. It was apparently a boat, or some other very small vessel. Shortly after we anchored, a cutter-rigged boat, flying the French tricolour, appeared entering the bay, making for the *Jabberwock*.

A party of natives, who were engaged in cutting firewood for the *Southern Cross* mission steamer—so they had told me—caught sight of the tricolour, and forthwith let fly a couple of shots at the boat, but without hitting her.

Three men were in this boat. They ran her alongside the *Jabberwock*, and, having made her fast, climbed up the side with a little assistance; for they seemed to be terribly weak from exposure and thirst, and one of them from wounds. Their leader and spokesman was an East Indian from Pondicherry. He was able to make himself understood in both English and French. The others were natives of New Caledonia. This was their story.

A naturalized French subject, Classen by name, had landed in the Santa Cruz Is. from a French schooner, a month or two before this. His intention had been to form a station principally for collecting and curing bèche-de-mer. These three men, together with a native of Sandwich I., had accompanied Classen.

Their houses had soon been built, with the help of the natives. Their work was in full swing when, one day, about a week before this, Classen and the Sandwich Islander were beguiled from the station to the top of a hill at some little distance from it, on pretence of looking at a distant sail. There they were tomahawked to death.

The station was then attacked by the natives. Our refugees, however, had managed to escape in Classen's boat, with sufficient food to last them for a fortnight, but without any water. As they were getting off, one of the New Caledonians was wounded with poisoned arrows.

I examined the wounds of this poor fellow, who was now very weak and depressed. I found two small circular wounds in his ribs on the right side, in a line with the heart. The Indian told me he was certain that, when the arrows were withdrawn, the heads had been got out entirely. Still, it was evident that the poison was working in the man's system, for every now and then his limbs gave a spasmodic jerk. The next day his entire body was affected, not being still for five minutes at a time.

Our treatment consisted of poultices, applied to the wounds to draw out any foreign matter that might have remained in them. We injected ammonia, and also gave him doses of it. Beyond these measures we could do nothing. He died during the second night after their arrival.

I took the two survivors to Maryborough, along with their boat. There I communicated with the French Consul in Brisbane about them. He sold the boat, and sent the East Indian back to Noumea. The New Caledonian went into service, and remained in Queensland, I believe. All I got for my trouble was a blackguarding from the New Caledonian paper, in which it was asserted that attempts had been made to "enslave" these men in Queensland.

Having mustered up a few more recruits at Lo I., I next anchored in Hayter Bay, on the western coast of Torga, or Middle I. There, as at the southern island, we found that a number of the younger people had either been prevented from joining the *Borough Belle*, or had changed their minds since. So recruiting went on merrily.

Some of the recruits who had gone in the *Borough Belle* were married men, and they had left their wives behind them. Certain of these women now entertained the idea of going away after their husbands, knowing that we were bound for the same destination.

One forenoon, the boats were alongside the ship, awaiting the arrival of some recruits who had promised to come down from the village inland.

Now, the mate in one boat, and the G.A. in the other, were wont to make a race of it when pulling to or from the ship, the boats' crews being just as eager to beat each other as their officers, and betting sticks of tobacco on the results.

"Smoke oh!" sung out some one, perceiving a thin white cloud rising up from the rocks at the head of the bay. Over the side went the boys at once, the mate with them. But the G.A. delayed, calling to one boy to put his rifle in the boat, to another for a pannikin, and to a third for his wallet. The last article he was seldom seen without. In it he carried a miscellaneous collection of articles: pipes, tobacco, pocket-handkerchief, note-book, and so forth. In Brisbane he had been nicknamed Judas Iscariot, because he always "carried the bag."

The mate had got a hundred yards away before the G.A. started; so the latter lost *this* race. But, though beaten so far, he did not mean to be behindhand in obtain-

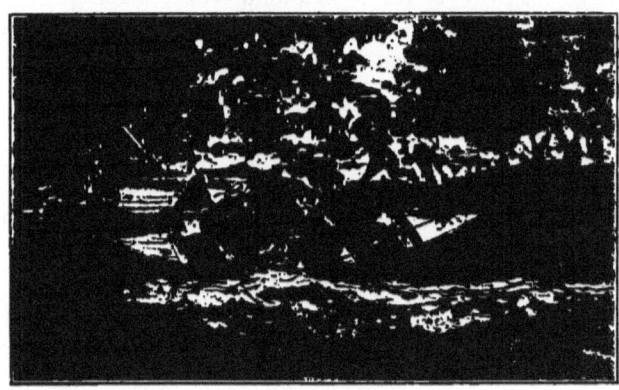

WOMEN BOLTING.

ing recruits. No sooner was he off, than he caught a glimpse of five figures, waving branches in their hands, and rushing out from the bushes and trees on to the open terrace of upraised coral rock which fringes this part of the bay. A sweep or two of the steering-oar turned his boat's head in their direction, and quickly brought him close to the feet of five young women. They were "bolters," whose husbands had gone away in the *Borough Belle*. They waited for no preliminary conversation, but just sprang headlong off the rock into the boat, alighting in a heap on top of the G.A., who was crushed down under them into the bottom of the boat, with nearly all the breath knocked out of his body. He had scarcely recovered his equanimity when he arrived on board, five minutes later, the fair dames who had robbed him of it laughing and dancing with glee at having outwitted their chiefs. For, it seems that these had appropriated the deserted wives, after the departure of their respective husbands.

At Hiu, the northernmost of the Torres Is., I filled up my complement—a total of one hundred and one men and thirty-two women. I might have obtained more easily enough, if my licence had allowed me to carry them.

Two or three tacks from thence brought the *Jabberwock* back to Lakon. There I filled up my water-tanks, and then started for home. I passed to leeward of the Bond and d'Entrecasteaux Reefs, on the north of New Caledonia, then the Bampton Reefs, and so through the Coral Sea, encountering a heavy gale and thick weather on the way. Inside the Great Barrier Reef I met the *Borough Belle*, outward bound again. I arrived off the mouth of the Pioneer River, on which stands Mackay, on the night of June 26.

CHAPTER XVII.

FIRST VOYAGE OF THE *FANNY*, 1882-3.

I resign command of the Jabberwock—*And go to Melbourne—The* Fanny—*The Queensland recruiting fleet—List of casualties—Murders—Accusations of missionaries—Mr. Paton's charges — H.M.S.* Espiègle *sent to investigate — Captain Bridge's report — Article in " The Brisbane Courier" — A reverend misleader—The* Roderick Dhu *case—The missionary view and that of the labour-recruiter—Freedom or slavery ?—Unfounded accusations—The Rev. Shirley Baker—" Sweating" in the South Seas—Mis-statements as to depopulation—Good result of the labour trade—My experience of missionaries—My new G.A.—I solicit another appointment—Brisbane to Mackay—Sail for New Hebrides—Hervey Bay—At Mallicolo I.—An earthquake—The island flooded—Effects on shore—Upheaval of coral—Subsidence—Shock after shock—Position of the ship—Return of the boats—Stranded fish—Homeward—The French New Hebrides Company—Scheme of the French Government—Result of Exeter Hall shortsightedness—Cingalese labourers.*

A FEW days after my arrival at Mackay, I resigned the command of the *Jabberwock*, in accordance with a promise, given long before, to some very old friends of mine. I then went to Melbourne, where I took charge of the *Fanny*, a brigantine which had been purchased by Messrs. Rawson and Co., of Mackay. In this vessel I sailed for Brisbane in August. On arriving there, I laid her up at D. L. Brown's wharf, to be fitted out for the Polynesian labour trade.

During the seven years in which I had now been connected with this trade, the fleet of vessels employed in it which were sailing out of Queensland ports, had gradually increased to the number of thirty or thereabouts. Just previous to the time I sailed in the *Fanny*, this recruiting fleet had sustained some diminution in consequence of wrecks. The *Lady Belmore*, brig, Captain White, had been driven ashore at Mackay by an easterly gale, on March 8, and had afterwards broken up. The schooner, *Leslie*, Captain Turner, had been wrecked at Aneiteum I. on April 26. The *Magnet*, schooner, was lost at Tanna I., having drifted ashore during a calm, on May 17. The *Io*, schooner, Captain McPhie, had struck on a coral reef, one night, just outside the Great Barrier, and had foundered in about ten minutes. The iron schooner *Chance*, formerly a yacht, and the smallest vessel in the trade, had been wrecked in August at Tongoa I. in the New Hebrides.

The crew of the last-mentioned vessel, having narrowly escaped massacre by the natives, were brought to Queensland by the *Stanley*. This vessel also had a prisoner on board, named George Lewis, who had been a seaman in the *Jabberwock*. Attempting to desert his ship in the New Hebrides, this man had shot dead the second mate, Henry Shaw. The murder had been committed on the eighteenth of August. About the same time more bloodshed occurred on the coast of Espiritu Santo, where three Frenchmen, belonging to the *Port Vila*, ketch, of New Caledonia, were killed on shore by the natives; the master and two others only escaping by swimming off to their vessel.

Several masters of vessels that had lately arrived in port, gave notice of attacks on their boats at different islands. But murder and shipwreck were not the only dangers we had to contend against. Some of the missionaries located in the New Hebrides seemed to think that imprisonment, or even hanging, would be hardly sufficient punishment for the "slave traffickers," as they were accustomed to term us. One man in particular, my old acquaintance of Aniwa I., apparently made it his especial business to trump up all sorts of false charges against the labour trade, as well as to exaggerate any petty misdemeanours that came under his notice.

While fitting out the *Fanny*, I received a message one day requesting my attendance at the Immigration Office. There I had read to me portions of a letter written by this person, addressed either to the Government of Queensland generally, or to the leader of the Opposition. In this document I was accused of having forcibly kidnapped women from the island of Tanna. The writer of it wound up his thrilling narrative by saying that the captain and Government agent afterwards came to his house, and there, in the presence of his wife and himself, boasted of their exploits.

The reader already knows what had really occurred on those occasions. In the official letter I was required to write to the Government, I stated the real facts of the case.

In consequence of this, and of other accusations made by this "preacher of the truth," in a letter to "The Melbourne Argus" for December, 1881, Captain Bridge, commanding H.M.S. *Espiègle*, was instructed to investigate the matter. The result of his inquiries was incorporated in an article which appeared in the leading paper in Brisbane—" The Courier "—after Captain Bridge had made his report.

The article says :—

"The Rev. Mr. Paton is a gentleman whose name is well known in this colony as one of the chief accusers of those engaged in the Polynesian trade. His connection with the South Sea missions has given weight to his false and reckless assertions, and there are many who have been led by him to believe that open and violent man-stealing is still practised by labour vessels, sailing from Queensland and elsewhere. Fortunately, Mr. Paton has been thoroughly exposed in the course of a controversy, in which he was foolish enough to engage in the columns of 'The Melbourne Argus,' a journal which for many years has printed his statements and relied on their accuracy. That journal, having found their reverend mis-leader out, has recently called attention to the proof that exists of his want of veracity. In December, 1881, Mr. Paton published a long letter in the 'Argus,' which contained charges so grave, that Captain Bridge, of H.M.S. *Espiègle*, was instructed by Sir Arthur Gordon to investigate them. Three of the principal charges, together with the official report on them, are printed in the 'Argus,' and we reproduce them here.

" The first refers to the island of Erromanga :—

" Mr. Paton's charge :—

' ' That a Queensland vessel, with a Government agent on board, sent two boats on shore ; that the men called out to a little boy to come to them ; that the boy's father held the lad's arm and prevented him ; and that the crews then opened fire and killed the natives."

This is the official report of Captain Bridge :—

" That these men wished to join a labour vessel, but were prevented by the other natives; that on one of them attempting to reach a boat, the natives opened fire and struck the inner boat, whereupon the covering boat fired on the natives."

Mr. Paton's second charge was :—

" A labour vessel decoyed a Christian native teacher on board. Word was sent to the young men and boys of the school that their teacher wanted to see them. So soon as 100 were collected, the vessel sailed away."

This is the official report :—

" A native teacher left by a labour vessel, but he went voluntarily. He was not decoyed. Word was *not* sent to collect the scholars. None were entrapped. There was no such kidnapping incident."

The third incident Mr. Paton said occurred at Tanna I. :—

" Two tribes that were fighting placed their women and children on a reef. A labour vessel stole in, got the women *and children* into the boats and sailed away, despite the firing of the men and the pleading of the women."

The official report says :—

" 'The Revs. Watt and Neilson have been long on Tanna I., and both say that they never heard of any such thing occurring on that island."

The article goes on to say :—

"These charges and their refutation are published in the '.Argus' now, because the reverend gentleman is again on the war path, and claiming, by virtue of his sacred office, belief in his statements. One Melbourne contemporary says of him that he ' appears to combine enthusiasm in a good cause with a perfect genius for scandal-mongering and the imputation of bad motives.' To most of our readers this will appear rather mild censure on an individual who, though a minister of the gospel, persists in spreading calumnies of which the falsehood has been demonstrated."

Here we have samples of the frequent missionary reports of so-called outrages by whites on natives of the South Seas, with the usual result when the Government takes the trouble of investigating them.

But sometimes the writer confined himself to the truth —a trifle coloured. Some years after this, Mr. Paton addressed a letter to Sir Samuel Griffiths, then leader of the Opposition in the Queensland Legislative Assembly, a portion of which I may quote here. It was dated, at Tanna, 10th July, 1889 :—

"On Sabbath, the 30th June, two boats of a vessel, which the agent said was the *Roderick Dhu*, from Brisbane, called here about 2 p.m., on returning from spending the forenoon trading farther round the island. When the men in the boat were talking to the natives, the agent (an old man) came and informed the Rev. Wm. Watt, the resident missionary at Kwamera, that 'The boats were not come in to recruit labour, but to let one of the crew see his sister, a Tanna woman.' He returned to the boats, and we saw both boats leaving without any additional labourers. We were then about to enter the church to observe the Lord's Supper. The agent's voluntary statement that they were not come for recruits, threw the natives off their guard, and after the communion, as we left the church, all were in sorrow, as four lads had been got to go round a point beyond the rocks, where they could not be seen by their friends, and to swim off to the boats in which that agent was, and took them away. The friends of the lads were angry, and the missionary was indeed grieved to have his scholars so taken away, and his work frustrated, as it has often been by the deceiving traffickers."

Now this statement is certainly "somewhat coloured" —some persons would say it contained a lie—in the words "were got to go." I happen to know the facts of this case. The four boys wished to go away in some ship—the *Roderick Dhu* or any other—to Queensland, but knew that, if they made their wish public, their friends— and the missionary through them—would prevent them leaving. So they stole away quietly, apart from the crowd, and, as soon as their friends had gone back from the beach, swam off after the boats, which were then pulling away. The recruiter, seeing them following, put back and picked them up.

These boys were free agents—not the slaves or servants—of the missionary and the chief. They had as much right to emigrate from their home as a European labourer has to leave his. They knew equally well—perhaps better—what sort of a life they were about to experience. They were not even asked to go, but they had heard of Queensland from their returned countrymen; the justice and better treatment of labourers there than that they received from missionaries and chiefs; the better payment for services rendered; the security of life there. To gain these advantages they took the chances of sharks and drowning, and forsook sloth, dirt, and a religion their intellectual faculties are not yet sufficiently developed to entertain, for wealth, comparative freedom, and civilization.

Nor were they forsaking religion either, when they "took a header" off the rocks. The Kanaka schools in Queensland are as numerous, in proportion to numbers, as are the mission schools in the islands. They do quite as much good for the boys, and, along with "the three R's," impart quite as much religion as Kanakas can understand.

In the same letter, a little further on, Mr. Paton wrote:—

> "Were such boats from such vessels seen returning to Brisbane to try by hook and crook to get away your few remaining sons and daughters, surely every man possessing paternal, fraternal, and human feelings would unite and drive the destroyers of your children from your shores, and the world would praise you for it."

This is high colouring with a vengeance! Why "few remaining"? The phrase creates a false impression, which a truthful man would avoid. One would imagine that labour vessels had been in the habit of visiting this place, Gomara, or "Kwamera," as he called it, and sailing away with "sons and daughters" wholesale. Such a statement *could* not be true, for mission stations are generally avoided by the recruiter, owing to the difficulty there is in getting boys away, however willing to go they may be.

The colony of Queensland sends agents to England to lecture about it, and to dilate on the advantages to be derived by Englishmen who will emigrate to the other side of the world, where the conditions of life are easier, and where even wealth may be attained to. Do *they* hesitate to separate even a "few remaining" sons and daughters from their parents? Do *they* take into account the grief of the latter when they lose their children? Do *they* care when they select the healthy and strong, depriving the parents of their support in old age, and leaving only the weak and sickly behind?

We must look to the benefit of the masses, notwithstanding that individuals may undergo hardship to some extent. There can be no doubt that the South Sea Islanders derive benefit, both morally and physically, from being transported into the midst of a civilized community, where they are taught to labour steadily. And do they not appreciate the change? How is it that so many return to Queensland for a second and often for a third term of service? How is it that so many remained in the colony, prior to the passing of that Polynesian Act which compelled them to return home, either at the termination of their first engagement, or of a second, if they chose to serve it.

Nevertheless, missionaries and their friends continued to agitate, crying out about the horrors of "slavery"—of the deceptions, outrages, and bloodshed committed by those they were pleased to stigmatize "labour traffickers." Yet whenever the circumstances detailed in their reckless accusations have been inquired into, they have been found to rest on little or no foundation of fact.

That abuses *have* occurred, I do not deny; but what line of life is exempt from abuses? Are missionaries themselves immaculate? The Rev. Shirley Baker, late prime minister of Tonga, who was deported from that group only the other day, for abusing the power he had acquired over the weak and superstitious king, is an example. Was he the only man in the Pacific who commenced life preaching the gospel of love, charity, and humility with an empty pocket, and who ended with a good banking account? I fancy not. Nor is "sweating" confined to the large cities of Europe. There is plenty of it to be found in the South Sea Islands, by those who choose to open their eyes and look for it—in the New Hebrides as elsewhere.

Accompanying Mr. Paton's letter there was published a " copy of minute of New Hebrides Mission Synod on the labour traffic." In this it was said : " The Kanaka labour traffic has, to a large extent, depopulated the New Hebrides and adjoining islands." This was a gross exaggeration, to say the least of it. The population of Aneiteum I. has decreased much more sensibly than that of any other island in the New Hebrides, *although it has been under the sole control of the Presbyterian mission for about thirty years, and has been almost unvisited by traders or labour vessels !*

Tanna I. comes next. Further north there is very little difference in the number of inhabitants, only the surplus population having been removed. One good result has been apparent : intertribal wars are not nearly so frequent, and cannibalism has been checked. Consequently, the tribes recover much more quickly from any loss of numbers entailed by the labour trade.

I do not wish to create an impression that I "have a down" on missionaries. During my travels I have only become personally acquainted, more or less, with eight. Four of these were Presbyterians, the others belonged to English Church missions. The latter were, I believe, good earnest men, though not angels. They were men willing to give and take ; not devoid of some weaknesses, or even faults, for which we laymen could make allowance, since they did the same for our frailties. The

Presbyterian missionaries, as far as I could judge, were, with one exception, narrow-minded, bigoted, and intolerant. They were men who looked only to one side of a disputed question, which was invariably that side which suited their own interests; while to gain their own ends they would rush into exaggeration, sometimes even to the extent of downright untruth.

A day or two before the outfit of the *Fanny* was completed, a young gentleman, freshly appointed a Government agent, appeared on board, announcing himself to be the officer who was to accompany the vessel to the South Seas. Apparently he was not aware that his visit was premature. As yet the ship was not in the labour trade, since I had not applied for a licence. So, in fact, he had no business there. Like all "new chum" G.A.'s, he was filled with an amazing sense of his own dignity, and treated us with little courtesy. Before he had been a minute on board the ship, he took upon himself, without permission, to order my steward about. So aggressive was his conduct that I was obliged to tell him, at last, that I thought it would be better for both of us that some one else should be appointed to the ship.

Leaving my gentleman to digest this pill at his leisure, I paid a visit to the temporary head of the Immigration Department. This happened to be the person who had been sub-immigration agent at Maryborough, the same with whom I had quarrelled about the allotment of labourers to employers on board the *Stormbird*. I now requested him to appoint some other G.A. to the *Fanny*. It appeared, however, that there was no other available in Brisbane. So, finally, I foolishly allowed myself to be talked over, and consented not to oppose the appointment.

I sailed from Brisbane on September 14, bound to Mackay, in order to ship some "returns" who were awaiting me there. Application had been made in Brisbane for licences to recruit, and the ship had been

surveyed satisfactorily. But I was informed that it was
not until I should be ready to depart from Mackay that
the licences would be granted, when the G.A. would also
come on board. To save any possible delay, however,
the latter joined the *Fanny* in Brisbane, going to Mackay
in her as a passenger only.

I left Mackay on September 27, having ninety
"returns" on board, all for the New Hebrides. I was
licensed to recruit one hundred and forty labourers. I
returned to port again on February 2, 1883, with only
seventy-one, after having been away five months and
seven days. Perhaps I ought to have considered myself
lucky in having obtained so many; for I had never had
the misfortune before of sailing with such an unpleasant
shipmate as my G.A., nor had I ever met with an official
who was so fond of throwing obstacles in the way of the
successful and lawful accomplishment of the object of
our voyage.

After leaving Mackay, I directed my course to Hervey
Bay, where, near Triangular Cliff, I watered the ship at
a small stream. I thence started afresh for the islands
on October 3. During this passage, which was a protracted one, in consequence of light and variable winds,
two of the "returns" died. They had been sent on
board under a doctor's certificate, as having disease of
the lungs—a common complaint amongst these islanders
—on the chance of their lives being prolonged if they
reached their homes.

I worked all the islands of the New Hebrides, from
Tanna to Espiritu Santo inclusive. During the whole
voyage only one incident occurred worth mentioning. It
happened at Mallicolo I.

I was at anchor in the channel between Ura islet and
the south-western coast, lying in smooth water, with a
bright blue sky overhead, and a light easterly wind. The
boats had gone away in the morning, northward, taking
the boatswain, who was also recruiter, and the G.A. The

mate was laid up at the time, as indeed he was during the greater part of the voyage. It was luncheon time, and I was sitting at the cabin table, when, suddenly, we felt the unmistakable vibration of an earthquake.

Although earthquakes are of common occurrence in these islands, this one made me jump. The ship shook and quivered as though she were galvanized. Had all her fastenings been loosened by the shock, I should scarcely have been surprised.

"She's away!" shouted one of the crew. Rushing out of the cabin, I found the ship whirling round eastward, the chain cable grinding and jerking on the windlass, as the anchor turned, dragged a few fathoms, and then caught in the bottom again.

On shore the sight was terrible, though magnificent.

"Oh, my poor boats!" I groaned.

At either side, on the shallow reefs, and high over the low bushes and smaller trees that lined the shores, a huge wave was breaking with a dull roaring sound, sweeping steadily along from the westward, until it disappeared beyond a long, low point of land. It was the swell of this wave, unbroken in the deeper water, which had caught the ship aft, and had slewed her round to her anchor.

On the islet we could hear the yells and cries of the natives, as they fled from an adjacent village, making for higher ground. On the main island, clouds of dust could be seen rising for miles away, showing where landslips had occurred on the sides of the steep hills and mountains.

For miles the whole surface of the earth had subsided, sinking eight feet or so, which had caused the great wave to rush into the deepened channel.

The tremors of the earthquake still continued, at short intervals. Then, slowly and gradually, came an upheaval. The waters poured out from the flooded forest, bearing with them portions of the huts of the savages, canoes, trees and branches, and even two or three squeaking pigs, cascading over the face of the flat shore-reefs. These now rose as high above their normal position as they had before sunk below it, forming flat terraces along the coasts, which were elevated to six feet above the surface of the sea. Masses of "live" coral showed along the face of the raised shore-reefs, displaying brilliant hues, blue, green, yellow, purple, and red, all shining and glistening in the sun.

This was the first act. A pause of a minute followed. Then, gradually and majestically, the upraised coral sank again, and the bright colours disappeared.

Then came another subsidence, and a second vast billow rolled in from westward, making our chain rip and tear at the bows as if it meant to pull the windlass out of the ship. Breaking into clouds of foam, the wave ran roaring along the shores, while every here and there some huge tree came toppling over, with torn roots or broken trunk.

The second upheaval was not equal to the first; the reefs did not rise more than about three feet above the water. Though a third wave rolled in, it was only a "piccaninny" when compared with those that had preceded it.

When the earthquake was over, I could perceive no difference in the height of the shore, from the level of the sea. The only effects remaining visible were the branches and broken trees floating about, or lying strewn along the beaches, with here and there a bare yellow-brown patch on the side of a hill.

The ship, however, had shifted her position, and was now dangerously near the Ura shore-reef. So, taking advantage of a light but favourable wind, I hove up the anchor and moved her further out, nearer to the middle of the channel.

The next consideration was—Where were the boats? Leaving the ship in the third boat—for the *Fanny* carried three—I pulled away in search of them, and met them returning, about a mile from the ship. One boat was half full of fish. During the earthquake, they had been off shore, fortunately, crossing a bay in deep water. When it was over, they had landed, and the boatmen had picked up some of the fish on the beach, while the remainder had been purchased from natives, who had gathered them up in the forest as they came down from the higher land.

Next day I took the ship to South-West Bay, where I anchored in five fathoms of water, on a coral patch near the western side of the bay.

The morning after, we had another scare when getting under way. Just as the chain was " short," while the crew were making sail, there came another smart shock. Luckily no subsidence or wave followed it. I was glad enough when I saw the coral disappear from under the ship, as she slipped into deep water.

Christmas Day was spent among the Maskelyne Is. There we once more heard from the natives the story I have related about the Frenchman's iron tank, and the kidnapping.

On January 19, the G.A. gave me notice to return home, as our provisions were running short. I was nothing loth, since I should be rid of him all the sooner. After an uneventful run, we arrived at Flat-top I., off the mouth of the Pioneer River, on the night of January 2, 1883, with sixty-three men and nine women, recruits, on board.

It was in the early part of October, 1882, that we Queenslanders had received the first news of the formation of the *Compagnie Caledonienne des Nouvelles Hebrides*, at Noumea. This undertaking was headed by Mr. John Higginson, a naturalized French subject. Its capital was equivalent to £20,000, and it had been started with the avowed object of " colonizing the New Hebrides group, and inaugurating a reliable and unobjectionable system for procuring labourers for the Colony of New Caledonia."

The *Compagnie* was supposed to be entirely a private venture, but, in reality, it was due to a scheme on the part of the French Government for getting possession of the New Hebrides. Once started, the *Compagnie* lost no time in acquiring a strong hold upon the islands. A small steamer, having on board an officer of the French navy to supervise all agreements of sale or otherwise, as well as an agent of the *Compagnie*, visited every portion of the group. They bought up all the best land on the shores of the islands, from the native or European owners, including some that had been sold two or three times by the former. These properties were all carefully surveyed, marked out with large hewn stones at the angles, and registered at Noumea. The former European owners, small traders, mostly remained where they were, as employés of the *Compagnie*.

So now, the New Hebrides may be said to practically belong to the French. This has resulted from the short-sighted policy of Exeter Hall, which discouraged or drove away British settlers; thus making room for those who will eventually drive away its missionaries, as they have already done in the Loyalties.

At that time, notwithstanding the large and still increasing fleet of vessels sailing from Queensland to the South Sea Islands, the demand for a cheap and reliable class of labourers was far in excess of the supply. Fresh sugar lands were constantly being taken up and cleared in the northern parts of the colony.

One scheme for supplying the required labour was the introduction of Cingalese from Ceylon. A number of these people had been landed at Mackay in November, 1882, but they had proved a failure. Perhaps they were tampered with; at any rate, they refused point-blank to work on the plantations. While the *Fanny* was lying at Mackay, waiting for licences for another voyage, dozens of them were loafing about the town, whilst a few got employment as house servants, and about the stores. Another batch was subsequently landed at Bundaberg, with a similar result.

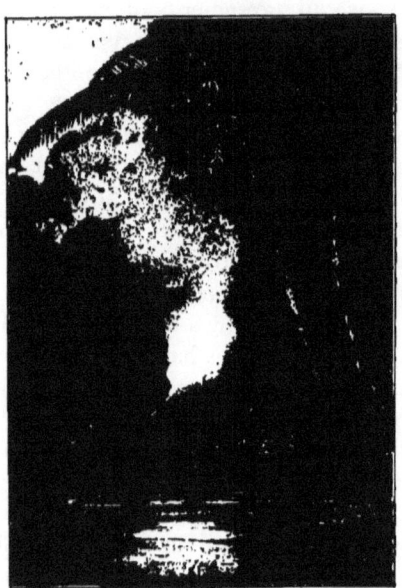

SPEARING FISH BY TORCHLIGHT.

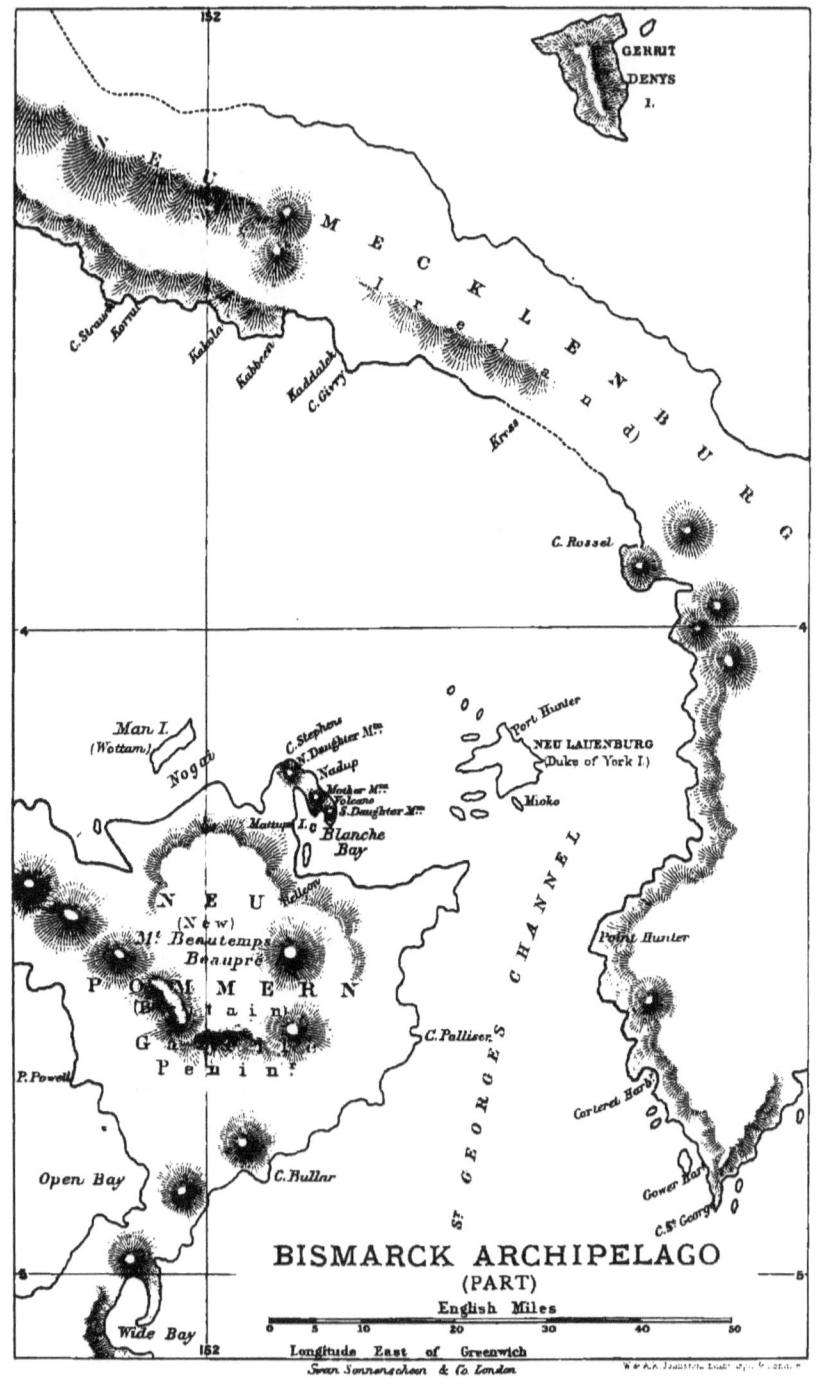

CHAPTER XVIII.

SECOND VOYAGE OF THE *FANNY*, 1883.

Increasing demand for labourers—Father Lanuuzel—I sail for the Bismarck Archipelago—Arrive at New Ireland—The Marquis de Rhys' expedition—The Black Corner—Blanche Bay, New Britain—The Mother and Daughters Mountains—Volcanic eruptions—Character of the natives—King Johnny's views about cannibalism—Weapons and houses—Mountains and forests—Fever and ague—Hernsheim's station—A retrospect—Besieged at Nogai—Nash and I escape—Torloug, the "fighting" chief—Corruption of native names—A visit to Mr. Hernsheim—"One Snider cartridge"—The "Tower mark"—Torlogga appears—Recognition—Making friends—Exchange of presents—Remains of Nash's house—The Hopeful—A mission-teacher checks recruiting—A case of kidnapping—I make inquiries—And threaten to report it—Duke of York I.—The end of King Johnny—His consort in service—A Port Hunter recruit—Natives of New Ireland eager to enlist—A rush to the ship—The decks stormed—" Look out! Cap!"—Slipping away—My recruit list—After-thoughts—Down St. George's Channel—" Man overboard!"—Recovering deserters—Fourteen escape—Nadup again—Tokkolula engaged as interpreter—Wottam I.—Murder of Tokkolula—The native slings—The boats attacked—Bringing off the body—Bearers of bad news—Trouble anticipated—Awaiting events—Taken by surprise—A fight for life—A race for the boats — Escape — " I'm done, boys!" — Counting the casualties—Progress of the wounded—A painful voyage—Kindness of missionaries—In the "doldrums"—The Carola—German offers of assistance—Working homeward—Arrival at Townsville — The G.A. and I go into hospital — My wound—I go to Brisbane—And undergo operation—Recovery.

THE increasing demand for Polynesian labour, and the large number of vessels employed in recruiting, combined to render it necessary that ship-masters should extend their operations beyond the area of the Solomon and New Hebrides groups. I had previously had some experience in the islands of New Britain and New Ireland—Neu Pommern and Neu Mecklenburgh, as they have been respectively re-named since their annexation by Germany. Moreover, one vessel—the *Hopeful*, of Townsville—had already undertaken a recruiting voyage thither, and had met with success. I therefore determined to try my fortune there also.

It happened that a Roman Catholic missionary— Father Lannuzel—who had already resided for some time in New Britain, was then in Queensland, and was desirous of returning to the island.

A bargain was soon struck between us; and, with the permission of the Immigration Office, I received him on board the *Fanny*, as a passenger to Blanche Bay, New Britain. I also shipped some stock belonging to him, for the same destination. This consisted of three head of cattle, half a dozen goats, and a number of fowls. These were berthed in the "'tween decks," which were only occupied as yet by my four boatmen. For, as these islands had not been recruited from for Queensland prior to the visit of the *Hopeful*, I had no "returns" to take back there.

I sailed on March 12, 1883, but was delayed at the outset of the voyage by a violent south-easterly gale, with thick rainy weather. This obliged me to lie at anchor under the Percy Is. for several days, until the wind had abated.

About twelve days after leaving Mackay, I rounded the southern end of the Great Barrier Reef. Then, with the wind abeam, I stood northward through the Coral Sea, and so between the Louisiade Archipelago and the Solomon group.

By the first of April I was close to the Laughlan Is. Some canoes came off to the ship there; but, as none of the men in them could speak English, and since I had not any one who could interpret, no recruiting could be done.

The trade-wind had so far proved a fresh and steady one. Then it dropped, the weather becoming cloudy, wet, and muggy. Every now and then it freshened up, though variably, from south to east, with squalls and showers. Our progress was slow; forty miles a day being the average we made after leaving the Laughlans. When the ship had arrived off Gower Harbour, near Cape St. George, the southern point of New Ireland, the wind died away to a dead calm, leaving her at the mercy of a strong current, which was running through St. George's Channel from the north.

There seems to be always a current in this channel, running either north or south, apparently changing with the prevailing wind. It sets from northward during the monsoon season, and from the opposite direction when the "trades" are blowing.

After drifting back for a couple of miles in a like number of hours, a breeze sprang up from northward, and, for three days, the *Fanny* tacked to and fro between Cape St. George and Cape Buller. We vainly strove to reach either Gower Harbour or Carteret Harbour, in both of which places there is good shelter for shipping, although the anchorage ground is limited, the water being mostly very deep.

At a short distance northward of these harbours lies the spot where the colonizing expedition of the Marquis de Rhys landed in 1880, and attempted to form a settlement. The leaders could not possibly have chosen a worse locality on the whole coast of New Ireland, unless, indeed, it was their object to kill off the victims of their greed, ignorance, and imbecility. Shut off from the influence of the trade-wind as the place is, by high mountains at the back, with a luxuriant and dense tropical vegetation, and a damp volcanic soil, it fairly reeks with fever and ague. Even the natives of the island themselves call it the "Black Corner." The poor immigrants to this place died off by the score, and, in February of the succeeding year, the place was abandoned altogether.

The head-wind we encountered in St. George's Channel nearly proved disastrous to Father Lannuzel's live-stock. Fodder became exhausted, as well as our patience. Had the wind continued a day or two longer, we should have been obliged to make beef of the cattle. Luckily it did not last long enough to drive us to such an extremity. The trade-wind was now working further and further north, as the year advanced. Late one evening, after a short calm, the breeze came up again from southward, fresh and clear, and gave the old *Fanny* as much as she could do to carry her whole topsail, as she ran before it. When we had made Cape Palliser, it moderated, hauling round to east-south-east.

On April 14, I dropped my anchor in eighteen fathoms of water, on the eastern side of Mattupi Islet, in Blanche Bay, on the north-eastern coast of New Britain.

Blanche Bay is a large indentation of the land, running in about seven miles, by four in width, and is open to the east. The western shores are backed by high, steep hills, the ridges of which are clothed in long, coarse grass. To the north and north-east, overshadowing the two inner harbours, there are three lofty peaks, which are known as the "Mother and Daughters Mountains." Between the "Mother" and her southern "Daughter," on the south-western side of the connecting ridge, there is the crater of a volcano.

A few years previous to this an eruption had occurred here, accompanied by an earthquake. Beyond alarming the natives, however, it caused little damage, except in the immediate vicinity of the crater. A new islet arose in the south-western part of the bay.

Eruptions of this volcano seem to have occurred only at long intervals. This was the first that had happened since 1873; in which year I had visited New Britain as a trader, employed by the firm of Godeffroy and Sons, of Hamburg. At that time the elder natives informed me that there had been no disturbance within their recollection. Dampier, however, states that when he passed in 1699, he noticed the smoke of a volcano in this neighbourhood.

The water of Blanche Bay is very deep, and anchorage can only be found close in to the shores at Mattupi Islet. I have been told that, at the extreme head of the bay, it is not so deep.

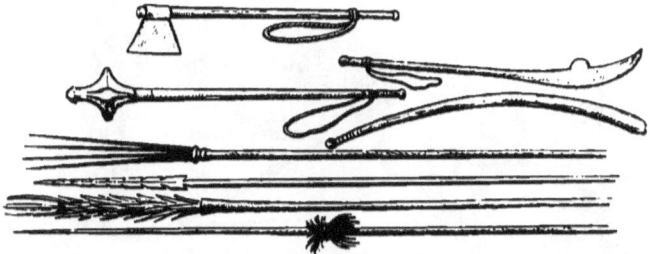

WEAPONS—BLANCHE BAY, NEW BRITAIN.

There are three islets in Blanche Bay: one, mentioned as having been thrown up by an earthquake, which is a bare and sterile mass of rock; Mattupi; and another double islet called the Beehive. These two are covered with habitations, the plantations of the natives being on the mainland.

The inhabitants of these islands are all Papuans. In the mountain villages of New Ireland many of the men attain a height of six feet. Both sexes go entirely naked. They are a fierce, warlike, and treacherous race, and are inveterate cannibals.

I remember, in 1873, asking King Johnny a great chief at Port Hunter, Duke of York I.—what his opinion was as to the relative merits of the flesh of white men and of Papuans. It was on the day after a cannibal feast, when I and others had witnessed the assimilation of an unfortunate "bushman" by King Johnny and his warriors.

"Man-o'-bush very good," said he. "Man-Sydney no good: too much salt."

By "*salt*" I suppose he meant "*rank*." White men eat so much meat that their flesh cannot taste well, I conclude.

Their arms consist of tomahawks, with iron heads, and carved "paddle" handles; clubs—many with stone

HOUSES AND NATIVES—BLANCHE BAY.

heads—spears, and slings. Near Blanche Bay they possess a few muskets, purchased from a German firm which has a station on Mattupi I. They chew betel, that is to say, pounded areca nut, mixed with the pod or leaf of the betel pepper and a little lime. They are also rapidly acquiring a taste for tobacco. Kava they know not. Their dwelling-houses are usually about five feet high, having arched roofs, thatched with palm-leaves.

Their war-canoes are shaped like a whale-boat. They are constructed of planks, "seized" together with twine, and have carved bows and stern-posts. They have no outriggers, and are similar in construction to the war-canoes of the Solomon Islanders. The lighter canoes, used for the transportation of women to the plantations, and for carriage of food thence, are hollowed out of logs. They have plank side-boards, fastened on with twine, and light curved ends. They are fitted with outriggers. These canoes are invariably whitewashed. Their food consists chiefly of bananas, taro, cocoanuts, small yams, sweet potatoes, and fish, together with an occasional "human."

Large wicker fish-traps are in common use. These are about eight feet long, barrel-shaped, with orifices at each end. Weighted with stones, they are lowered by

OUTRIGGER CANOE—NEW BRITAIN.

a rope to a depth of two or three fathoms, being kept in position by a log attached to them, which floats on the surface.

New Britain and New Ireland are lofty and mountainous, some peaks rising over 3,000 feet above sea-level. They are luxuriantly fertile.

Duke of York I. (Neu Lauenburg) lies between them. It is chiefly of raised coral formation, and is thickly wooded. It possesses two good harbours—Port Hunter and Mioko.

At Port Hunter a Wesleyan mission station has been established, where the Revs. Dank and Rickard resided with their wives and children.

Europeans are liable to attacks of fever and ague on the larger islands, but I think that, in Duke of York I., they are exempt from them, probably in consequence of its coral formation. King Johnny once told me that when his people visited New Ireland or New Britain, and stayed there awhile, they often returned sick. I think he called the ailment " mellapun."

At the time of my present visit, a German, named Hernsheim, had a large trading establishment on the north-eastern side of Mattupi I. This comprised some half a dozen dwellings and store-houses, the whole surrounded by a galvanized iron fence or wall. There was a wharf, at which a Hamburgh barquentine—the *Emil Mullenhausen*—was then lying, taking in a cargo of copra for Europe.

Knowing the dislike that traders evince to the visits of labour vessels, as well as that the German would not be likely to influence the natives in my favour, I had some doubts about my probable reception. Nor was I sure of a welcome from the Mattupi people; for there was an old score yet to be rubbed out between them and me.

Ten years before this, the Hamburgh brig *Iserbrook*, Captain Levison, visited New Britain, in order to land John Nash, a trader, there. She lay at anchor while a thatched house was built for him, on the south-western side of Mattupi. Thence she went to Nogai, west of Cape Stephens, at which place I landed, and formed a trading station. The *Iserbrook* then sailed to the Caroline group, whence Captain Levison proposed to return in about three months.

Before the brig left, the natives, with their usual treachery, had formed the intention of murdering us after her departure. The execution of their plot did not altogether succeed, for we escaped. Nevertheless, they got what they most wanted—namely, all our stores, " trade," and some of our firearms.

I remained at Nogai for about four weeks afterwards. During the last week of that period I lived in a state of siege. My garrison consisted of only two men—a Malay, and a native of Rotumah I. One night I got away in a canoe, with my men, from the beach, just as a crowd of savages stormed the station. Early next morning I reached Mattupi.

There, three weeks later, Nash and I, together with two Malays, the Rotumah man, and a woman from the Carolines, had to fight our way out of our burning houses, and take refuge in a small bamboo hut, at a little distance from them. This we held for a time, "rubbing out" eight of the islanders, besides wounding seven more, finally escaping in Nash's boat.

The principal "fighting chief" of the tribe that attacked us—a young man we knew by the name of Torlong—was friendly, taking no part against us. On the contrary, knowing that our oars, mast, and sail had been consumed in the burning store-house, he gave us four paddles. But for him we must have been killed. In consequence of what he had done to aid our escape, Torlong was speared in the thigh by one of his own people. After his recovery from the wound, however, he resumed his position as "fighting chief." At the time of this, my second visit, he had become head chief of the whole tribe.

As soon as the sails had been stowed, Father Lannuzel departed in a canoe for his residence at Nadup, a village on the northern slopes of the Mother Mountain. The G.A. and I then took boat and pulled in to the trading station. Landing on the small boat wharf near the gate of the enclosure, we found some natives awaiting our arrival. After a few questions and answers had been exchanged, I ascertained that Torlong was not only alive, but that he was also now the head chief of Mattupi. His name had been altered to Torlogga.

I noticed another change in a name, too. Formerly

"Mattupi" had been pronounced Mat-*tu*-pi, now it was Mat-tu-*pee*. Probably this was owing to its having been written *Mattupee* by white visitors, then mispronounced by others, whose rendering had been presently imitated by the natives themselves.

Many South Sea Island words—especially names of places—have become corrupted in this way. Early navigators and traders are careless in learning the native names, mispronounce them, and make a greater mess of it when they come to write them down. Other Europeans read their versions, and still further mispronounce them. Lastly, the natives follow the new style, and gradually drop into the corruptions instituted by their white visitors.

In 1870, when I first knew the island of Sandwich, in the New Hebrides group, the missionaries, who are supposed to be great authorities on such matters, wrote its native name, Vate. Since then it was altered to Fate, and now it is written and supposed to be Efate. Niua was once Nieua, now it is Aniwa. Api—and Heaven only knows how it got that name, for it was not its native name in 1870—is now often written Epi. Ambrym, of the charts, is now to be called Ambirr, though in 1870 the natives appeared to me to pronounce it Amberam, or Ambram. Tonga and Tannoa have been confounded, of course.

Again, at Rennell and Bellona Is., though they have been little visited by vessels, and though no white men have yet resided in them, the native names have apparently changed considerably in about a dozen or fifteen years, without any foreign influence. Tom Tamoan pronounced the native names of them Mungava and Mungigi; but during my visits I always heard them called Muava and Muigi.

A present of a stick of tobacco sufficed to send a couple of boys off to summon the chief, Torlogga, whom, for good reasons, I preferred to interview first at the station. Then we paid a visit to Mr. Hernsheim, finding him in his office, his two or three clerks being engaged in weighing and superintending the shipment of copra on board the barquentine at the wharf.

In the course of conversation I recounted my former experiences of New Britain, and of Mattupi I.; and Mr. Hernsheim expressed a strong opinion that it would be absolutely dangerous for me to venture into the native village. This I of course accepted as "bluff," to prevent our becoming so friendly with the natives as to obtain recruits.

Among objects of interest in the office, the G.A. and I particularly noticed a sheet of cardboard, which hung just inside the door. On it was a list of prices, and the equivalent weight of copra to be received from natives for the different articles of trade. The last article mentioned was "one Snider cartridge!"

I called this to mind subsequently, on reading a letter from Hernsheim in the Queensland papers, in which he complained that Queensland labour vessels had been supplying the New Britain natives with firearms in his neighbourhood. A wound I received some three weeks afterwards was caused by half of a Snider bullet.

It is well known that all the Snider rifles—which may be counted by the thousand—now in the hands of natives of the Solomon Is., which are under *British* protection, though of British manufacture, and many of them bearing the "TOWER" mark, have been sold to the natives by *German* traders.

We had been at the station about half an hour, when a boy brought me word that "Torlogga stop." Going down to the gateway—beyond which he did not dare to venture without permission—I found the chief awaiting me, with eight or ten of his principal followers.

Ten years had made a considerable change in Torlogga, but I recognized his face at once. All his party looked upon *me* as a stranger, however.

U

I have no doubt that time, not to say better health also, had changed me considerably since they had first known me. In those days I had been suffering from fever and ague, with a determination of blood to the head, which had affected my eyes to such an extent that I was almost blind. To protect my eyes from the glaring sunlight, I had always appeared out of doors with a white handkerchief tied round my head to serve as a shade. I had also become bald in the interval.

"You savez me?" I asked them, after I had shaken hands with Torlogga.

"No! No savez, Cap!" and they all stared at me without a sign of recognition.

"You savez two white men stop Mattupi, long time ago? He got house other side Mattupi"—pointing across the islet. "Man Mattupi fight alonga him; burn house."

"Yes, me savez."

Then I took out my handkerchief and fastened it round my head, as I used to wear it.

"You savez me now?"

"Cap Wan! Cap Wan!" from the whole crowd, some of those in the rear beginning to sneak off for the cover of the trees close at hand.

Torlogga and two others stood their ground, however; for the chief knew that he had nothing to fear from me. A hand-shake all round sufficed to make peace between us.

By this time the G.A. and the trader had joined me, so bidding good-day to the last, I returned on board, taking Torlogga and two subordinate chiefs with me. The other natives hung back, being evidently doubtful about the treatment they might receive if they ventured to trust me any further. Perhaps they were astonished when the chief returned to them an hour afterwards, possessed of a musket and ammunition, calico, axes, and tobacco—wealth sufficient to constitute him a millionaire in their estimation. For, according to their customs—which I took care to observe—presents are always exchanged between the parties to a treaty of peace.

In return, towards sundown, two canoes came off, bearing Torlogga's presents to me. These consisted of a couple of pigs, and enough yams, sweet potatoes, cocoanuts, and bananas to load the canoes down to the gunwales. Two young women were also sent—part of the gift. However, as they were not intended as recruits for Queensland, they were sent back ashore. Notwithstanding all the talk of our detractors about the immorality on board labour vessels, the regulations on that score are as strictly carried out with us as they are on board the missionary packets.

Friendly relations having now been firmly established, that evening, after dark, the G.A. and I wandered unharmed through the village, where a "sing-sing" was going on. We lost a few sticks of tobacco, certainly, some pipes, and a sheath-knife or so; for these people do not need any instruction in the art of picking pockets. But that was all.

Next morning early, after a bathe on the beach, I rambled over to the other side of the island. There I found a single charred post still standing, a relic of Nash's house, in the midst of a thicket of bushes. Some boys also drew my attention to a cocoanut palm, not far from it, in which there was a hole through the middle of the trunk, at about the height of my head. I was told that this hole had been made by one of our bullets, which had killed a man who was sheltering himself behind the tree.

I lay in Blanche Bay for some three or four days, during which time Father Lannuzel's stock was landed, on the point of the mainland between the two inner bays. The shores were also worked meanwhile for recruits. The barquentine *Hopeful*, of Townsville, Captain Briggs, Mr. Chayter G.A., anchored near the *Fanny* during the day after my arrival. It was here, and in connection with this vessel, that there came under my notice the first case of kidnapping I had seen committed by a Queensland ship since I had been connected with the labour trade.

One afternoon, my G.A. and myself took the boats four or five miles south-eastward. Landing on the mainland we visited the Roman Catholic mission. Father Lannuzel had not accompanied us on this occasion, as he was then engaged at his station at Nadup, a village on the outer side of Mother Mountain.

After spending an hour or so with the Fathers, we were walking along the beach near the mission, to rejoin our boats, when we encountered those of the *Hopeful*. The recruiter of that vessel, McNeil, was in charge of them, the G.A. having remained on board. He had been out all day, and had had no more luck than ourselves; neither ship having obtained any recruits here so far. We left him talking to a party of some half a dozen natives.

A little further on we met a coloured gentleman, clad in a shirt and a "sulu" (waist-cloth), with a book in his hand. He was a Protestant mission teacher, and probably a Samoan, judging from his appearance. He told us his house was some distance away, along the beach, in the direction we were going. Beyond *that* information, however, we could get nothing out of him. He was there to act in opposition to us, and not to give information. As we pulled along the beach, he kept abreast of the boats. Every now and then, when any natives approached the water's edge and tried to communicate with us, he got in the way, and, with a few words, persuaded them to retire.

It was evident that no recruits could be obtained whilst this man was about, so we pulled across the bay, back to the ship. A little before sunset McNeil returned, coming alongside the *Fanny* on his way to the *Hopeful*, which lay inshore of us, to exchange notes with my recruiter.

In his boat there was a New Britain man, who was, he told us, a recruit. After his departure, the truth about this boy came out. McNeil's boatmen had told mine, that, despairing of obtaining any willing recruits, just as they were shoving the boat off from the beach, McNeil had seized this native by his wool and had pulled him into the boat. In point of fact, he had kidnapped him.

That evening, my G.A. and I visited the *Hopeful*. In her cabin I broached the subject of this so-called recruit. Mr. Chayter then explained that, shortly after the arrival of their boats, he had discovered that the New Britain man had been kidnapped. He informed me that on the morrow the man should be relanded. However, as there was no one else on board the *Hopeful* who was able to discharge the duties of a "recruiter," he merely intended to caution McNeil, without depriving him of his billet. My next question was a poser.

"Do you intend to report him to the Government for kidnapping when you get back?"

This Chayter did not like. "It would cause trouble, and do no good. Only 'kick up a row.' McNeil would not do it again. He must have been crazy to try it."

But this was not enough for me.

"If you don't report him," I said, "I will; and you will be home first, so I give you a good chance."

So at last the G.A. promised to report McNeil, and then the subject was dropped.

But he did *not* report him on their return, that I know of. At any rate, I was so informed at the Immigration Office at Brisbane, where I spoke of the matter privately.

McNeil afterwards sailed on two voyages as recruiter of the *Hopeful*, with Captains Voss and Shaw, and with what result will be seen subsequently. Even on this present voyage, immediately after they left Blanche Bay —the *Hopeful* sailed a day before the *Fanny*—McNeil kidnapped another man from Nadup beach. Shortly after that, the *Hopeful* anchored in Port Hunter, Duke of York I., where the natives, visiting the ship, heard of it, and informed the Revs. Dank and Rickards, the missionaries there. Through their instrumentality the man was returned to his home. At least, the *Hopeful's* boats left Port Hunter with him, with the avowed intention of returning him.

This episode occurred previous to an attack on my G.A. and myself at Nadup, which I shall describe presently. It was also the subject of a letter from the Rev. Mr. Dank to a friend in Queensland, which letter was published in a Queensland paper—"The Ipswich Advocate," I think—about the beginning of November, 1883.

Despairing of obtaining recruits on this part of New Britain, where traders and mission teachers combined to frustrate all our endeavours, I sailed over to Duke of York I., and lay at anchor there for a couple of days in Port Hunter, a small but deep bay on the north-east coast.

The mission station there is situated on the north-western "head." The missionary's residence is a neat, substantial wooden building, facing the entrance of the bay, and overlooking the harbour.

Next day, while the G.A. and the recruiter visited the opposite coast of New Ireland in the boats, I was hospitably entertained by the missionaries.

Ten years before, John Nash and I took refuge in this harbour, having been driven away from New Britain. King Johnny was then its ruler. That potentate had been dead some years, having been slaughtered by a neighbouring monarch—his own brother. His wife was still alive, and she was living at the mission as a servant. I barely recognized her when she entered Mrs. Dank's sitting-room, bearing a tray of refreshments. Soap, good food, and a quiet life, "secure from war's alarms," as also from her husband's club, had, together with a neat print dress, made a wonderful difference in her. She now looked younger, instead of ten years older, than when I first knew her.

When the boats returned they brought three recruits, who had been obtained with some difficulty, owing to the opposition of the mission teachers stationed there. Had it not been for them, the boats would have been loaded with recruits. A great number of the younger men were only restrained by force, through the influence the teachers.

Only one of the Port Hunter tribe offered himself. He said nothing to his friends concerning his intention, but quietly rolled up his mats and few clothes and repaired on board the *Fanny*, while I was at the mission. Then some of his friends rushed up to the house with the news, asking Mr. Dank to *order* him to leave the ship. I think they were rather surprised to find that the missionary did not possess absolute control over all white men—myself among them.

The youth was accepted as a recruit and left in the ship. A few days later he was re-landed at Port Hunter; for he soon repented of his temerity, and by then I had plenty on board without him.

I sailed from Port Hunter with a light south-easter, passing over to New Ireland, where I spent three days recruiting. I worked the coast between Cape Givry and Cape Strauch, having the quickest success I have ever experienced.

On the third day, April 28, I engaged seventy-one men by 3 p.m., being even obliged to send back several who came off in the recruiting boats, as my licensed quota was made up. I had now 143 men and one woman on board; and, had I been able to carry them, I might have doubled that number in the course of the next twenty-four hours.

The excitement all along this part of the coast was intense. The boats were sometimes fairly rushed by men eager to get away, who tumbled in without waiting to be asked, and fought and struggled with such of their friends as strove to detain them. Many, who were afraid they might miss the opportunity, paddled off to the ship in small canoes, or on bamboo catamarans. Several even swam off, with the aid of dry logs of wood.

Some of the older men, who disapproved of this wholesale exodus, also took to their canoes and chased the runaways.

A CATAMARAN—NEW IRELAND.

All round the ship at least fifty canoes, carrying over a hundred men, were paddling about, chasing or being chased. There was an uproar of shouting, laughing, very likely swearing also, with prodigious splashing. Every now and then some young fellow, who had been cut off from the ship by his friends, would take a header. Diving down under the other canoes, he would not come up until close alongside, when he would seize a rope left conveniently hanging, and so would speedily clamber on deck.

There was no waiting for "pay," nor yet for any agreement with regard to the term of service in Queensland, or the remuneration at the end of it. All they wanted was to get away, till the *Fanny's* decks began to be crowded.

Suddenly I noticed that a few new arrivals, climbing up on board, were middle-aged men. These were big, muscular fellows, more like stay-at-home warriors than recruits. Then one of the New Britain interpreters rushed aft to me, crying,—

"Look out, Cap! Man, he want to take ship!"

Our merry game was growing dangerous. The ship was now about a mile off shore, lying to, with her head to the land. A pull of the lee braces hauled the yards round; then, as the square canvas filled, she slipped away, clear of the canoes. More than a dozen of the suspected new-comers jumped overboard as the canoes went astern.

A little further in I picked up the boats, coming off with recruits. Well satisfied with the day's work, I then stood off until safe from attack. Next, we took stock of the crowd we had on board, taking down their names and explaining the terms of agreement for service in Queensland. Lastly, we served out blankets, pipes, and tobacco to them. Many had never used tobacco as yet, but they all seemed eager enough to learn how to do so.

My recruit list was now full, without counting the Port Hunter man, whom I landed the second day after. There were four in excess besides, so I made a "board" inshore, putting them off near their village, Kornu. I then worked back southward, knowing it would be dangerous to linger in the neighbourhood. For, many of my recruits must have engaged themselves on the spur of the moment; and, as soon as they began to feel sea-sick, or home-sick, it was too probable some would desert, so long as their home was in sight. I have observed a similar feeling take possession of white emigrants, when going down the English Channel, bound for the colonies.

Luckily, I had filled up my water-tanks on this coast while recruiting; I had also a good stock of firewood on board. So, without anchoring anywhere, I worked away to windward against the south-east wind, fighting the current as well, which, since my arrival, had changed its flow, and was now setting northward.

Off Nadup, I hove to for an hour or so, to put ashore the chief and his men who had acted as our interpreters. I gave them an amount of pay in "trade" that delighted them hugely. At Port Hunter the boy I had brought thence, who had now had enough of the sea, was allowed to land again. I fancy he did not like the companionship of the Kornu men.

Between Point Hunter, New Ireland, and Cape Palliser, New Britain—the narrowest part of St. George's Channel—our progress to windward was very slow; about five miles a day was all we could make against wind and current. The pitching of the vessel made many of the recruits cast sorrowful and repentant looks at the shores of New Ireland.

On the evening of May 7, about 8 o'clock, the G.A. and I were just sitting down to our usual game at cribbage in the deckhouse, when suddenly the boatswain on deck sang out, "Man overboard!"

I had just tacked about, not more than half a mile off the New Ireland coast, some two or three miles south of Point Hunter. I guessed what was up the moment I heard the cry.

"Down with the helm! Hard-a-lee!" I shouted, as I came out of the cabin door; and round came the old craft like a top. So quickly, indeed, did she answer to the helm that she dropped, with her square-sails aback, almost atop of two swimmers. They deemed "prudence the better part of valour," and so climbed up the side again. They were on deck almost as soon as we knew that they had left the ship. But it was not these the boatswain had sighted when he gave the alarm.

Others must be in the water between the ship and the shore, swimming away towards the land. Both boats were quickly lowered and sent away in the direction of the land. They returned in half an hour without having found any of the deserters.

The recruits were now all down below. So, as soon as the boats were secured and the ship on her way again, a rough count was made as they lay in their bunks. They numbered a hundred and thirty, including the woman in the females' compartment. Fourteen men, therefore, had slipped overboard and made for the shore.

Next day the wind fell light and the sky clouded over. Towards evening rain began to fall. During the following night the ship was carried by the current back to Duke of York I., near the northern end of which, a mile or two beyond Port Hunter, I anchored to wait for more favourable weather. That evening the sky cleared again and became fair, with a light breeze still blowing from south-east. My old ship, the *Stanley*, passed me here, going northward in search of recruits, under the command of Captain Harris, Mr. William McMurdo being G.A.

On the following morning, the breeze still being adverse, I weighed anchor and stood over to Nadup to engage interpreters again. My object was to secure fourteen more recruits, to make up the deficiency occasioned by the recent desertions.

The old chief, however, and the men who had accompanied him, were not again forthcoming. They were away at some neighbouring village attending a feast. A subordinate chief, named Tokkolula, and another man whose name I now forget, volunteered to serve as interpreters, and came off to the ship with me.

Tokkolula was not a native of Nadup, but had been adopted by the tribe there. He came originally from Wottam I., which lies about three miles northward of Cape Stephens. Having fled thence in his youth on account of some crime or misdemeanour, he had taken refuge at Nadup, where his fighting abilities had raised him to the dignity of second chief of the tribe.

Tokkolula's advice to me was to go to Wottam, his native island, where, he said, he was certain to obtain for me the required number of recruits.

When I returned on board the *Fanny* with these men, the day was too far advanced to admit of sailing to Wottam I. with hopes of being able to do any work there before dark. So the ship was kept " dodging " about all night off Cape Stephens. Next morning, at sunrise, I found myself becalmed, about a mile from the south-eastern shore of Wottam. The boats visited the island before breakfast, but did not obtain any recruits.

The G.A., feeling hungry, returned to the ship for his breakfast about eight o'clock. He had the second interpreter in his boat, Tokkolula being with the recruiter in the other. The latter officer was too eager after recruits to think about breakfast. He pulled along the shore westward, and, when the G.A. left the ship again to rejoin him, he had gone out of sight round a point of land.

The ship was now becalmed, or I should have kept the boats in sight. For upwards of an hour we saw nothing of either of them. Then suddenly they came into view, pulling hard for the ship. Scanned through the glass, they did not appear to have any extra men in them; on the contrary, there was evidently a hand short in one of them.

So it proved. Poor Tokkolula was lying dead in the bottom of the recruiter's boat, with two spear-wounds through his body and a couple of great gashes from tomahawks—one in his neck, the other in the small of his back.

It appeared that when the G.A. returned to the ship for breakfast, the recruiter had pulled slowly along the shore, stopping here and there while Tokkolula conversed with the natives, a gradually increasing party of these following the boat along the shore. About the time the G.A. was nearing the island, on his return to it, the recruiter was drawing near the western point. The body of natives on shore had then increased to quite two hundred men. They were all armed with spears, clubs, tomahawks, and slings.

With these slings, by the way, they can deliver stones with tremendous force, sufficient to cave a man's skull in at two hundred yards distance. The discharge is accompanied by a sharp "crack" from the sling-cord, nearly as loud as that of a stock-whip.

As Tokkolula evinced no uneasiness, the recruiter, very naturally, did not dream of hostilities; and so he confidently steered his boat in towards a sandy beach, the natives calling out to him to come to them.

After talking awhile with a number clustered round the stern of the boat, Tokkolula, remarking that the sun was too hot for him to remain in the boat, went on shore. He repaired to a large log that was lying near under the shelter of the trees, and sat down upon it.

He had not been sitting on the log a couple of minutes, when down he went under his countrymen's tomahawks, two spears being plunged into his body at the same time.

The boat was attacked simultaneously, but the savages were too eager and crowded each other. For a few seconds there was a scuffle about and in the boat; but, luckily, she was afloat, and a shove of the steering-oar sent her out into deep water. The recruiter got a nasty blow from a sling-stone, and each of the boatmen had some bruises, but none were seriously hurt.

Just then the G.A.'s boat arrived on the scene. With the assistance of his crew a rush was made ashore, and the interpreter's body was brought off. The natives, meanwhile, continued to pelt our people with spears and stones from a little distance.

When the boats came alongside it was dead calm and awfully hot, there being no sign of wind anywhere.

In the afternoon, we deemed it best to bury the dead interpreter at sea, before the body became offensive. The other interpreter was consulted, and he approved of it. So the remains of the unfortunate Tokkolula were decently enshrouded in canvas, with some stones from the ballast at the feet, and quietly put overboard.

About three o'clock, to my surprise, a northerly breeze sprang up. This soon carried the ship back to Nadup, where we hove to. The G.A. and I then went ashore to Father Lannuzel's mission station, taking the other native with us, together with his pay. We also took a quantity of "trade," a present for Tokkolula's friends, in case they should prove disposed to throw any of the blame of the murder on our shoulders.

When we landed a few natives appeared on the beach, as well as the Father, with whom was Buckley, a trader who lived close at hand, being in Hernsheim's employment.

The remaining interpreter's story was soon told to his countrymen—though Heaven only knows what he said to them. He then disappeared with his wages, along with most of the other natives, leaving half a dozen, who remained close to the G.A. and me. Father Lannuzel was much disturbed at the news, and Buckley soon went off to his house, saying he expected there would be trouble. I think very little would have induced the G.A. and me to quit also. For sharp, shrill yells of anger from the men, and long, mournful cries of grief from the women, made our flesh creep. These showed that the feeling in the village, excited by the news of Tokkolula's death, was intense.

But we wished to avert trouble from any future comers, as well as from the whites then living there. So we remained waiting for the chief, who, the natives assured us, would arrive presently.

We waited for about half an hour, and still the chief did not appear. We never suspected that the six savages who remained on the spot, smiling and grinning around us, were only acting as decoys. Their object was to keep us from leaving until warriors could be collected on three sides of us, under cover of the thick forest and underwood. Then they meant to put us two to death.

We had left our rifles in the boat, but we had revolvers in our belts. We were standing close behind Father Lannuzel's house, a structure of thatch and bamboo. We were about five yards apart, with three natives (two spears and one tomahawk) fronting each of us. I was laughing at something, when suddenly my two spearmen thrust their weapons at me. I stooped on the impulse of the moment, so that one spear went over me into the house. The other pierced my right arm below the elbow, struck the bone, and fell to the ground. At the same time, down came the tomahawk. Somehow, the head missed me, though I felt the handle strike my shoulder. The next moment I had a good hold of it, and was struggling for its possession. Meanwhile I kept my foot on the fallen spear, so as to prevent its owner from picking it up and using it again.

The attack had been so sudden, that, for a moment, I was quite bewildered, and only fought instinctively. I was half deafened, at the same time, by shouts and yells, and the explosions of musketry.

I soon got the tomahawk to myself, putting my foe on his back at my feet. It was lucky for him, then, that the weapon and its paddle-shaped handle were almost a novelty to me. Another second and I should have split his head open, when a slug—half of a Snider ball—struck me on the right arm, just above the wrist, crippling the limb.

My adversary now bolted for the bush, as his companions had already done. When I felt for my "bulldog," to send a bullet after him, the holster was empty.

The pistol must have dropped out during the rough-and-tumble, and been lost in the thick layer of dust, sand, and leaves that covered the ground.

Meantime, Fowler, the G.A., with a cut on the shoulder from a tomahawk, had emptied his revolver. So now, with the spear and tomahawk in my hands, we both bolted for the boat, where our boys were making play with their Sniders, firing into the forest, whether they got a glimpse of our enemies or not.

There was a fall of about six feet, from the level ground on which the mission stood, to the sandy beach. Down this we both dropped, and had got as far as the water's edge, when a bullet struck the G.A. on the left arm, shattering the bone. Then I tumbled into a hole, and, before I was up again, a savage had nearly transfixed me with his spear. Luckily, I turned about as the point of the spear entered my left shoulder, causing it to break off short, though six inches of it remained in the flesh.

The next thing I remember was getting hold of the boat's stern, and the stroke oarsman helping me in. Then together we dragged in Father Lannuzel. The G.A. was pulled in forward, and then we cleared off as quickly as we could, amidst a shower of bullets and sling-stones.

My Winchester rifle was lying in the stern locker ready loaded. The natives kept close under cover, however, and I only got a fair shot at one, who showed his head and shoulders. He dropped; but whether he was hit or no, I cannot say. I fired away at the puffs of smoke issuing from the bushes, until the magazine of the rifle was empty. Then I turned to the stroke-oarsman to get his rifle. But my fighting for that day was over. I had the Snider in my hand, and was about to put in a cartridge, when a ball struck the boat near the stern-post, penetrating the planks, and also my left foot. As I felt the bones crunch, a sensation of nausea and faintness overpowered me. Then down I went in the stern-sheets, murmuring, " I'm done, boys ! "

Another bullet struck the boat's stern immediately after, penetrating beneath the planks on which I was lying. This was the last shot that came close to us ; and very soon we were out of range, pulling for the ship, which had drifted off the land to the distance of three miles.

During the skirmish a canoe with four natives in her was alongside the ship. We could have cut her off had we wished ; but we let her go, as the men in her had not been concerned in the attack.

As soon as we arrived alongside, Father Lannuzel climbed on deck. The G.A. and I remained where we were, until the boat had been hoisted up as high as the rail. Then we were helped out on to the deck, and so into the cabin.

Father Lannuzel had got a barked shin, attributable to a bullet. The G.A.s' left arm had been severely wounded by a musket ball and several slugs. He had also a gash from a tomahawk on one shoulder. I had sustained slug and spear wounds in the right arm, a spear wound in the left shoulder, a bullet nearly through the left foot, and, though I did not know it until I arrived at Mackay, a fractured rib, the effect of a sling-stone probably.

The weather being very close and warm, we had our mattresses laid on the main cabin floor. There we both remained until the ship neared the Queensland coast, two solid months of weary, painful existence. The chief mate acted as head nurse, besides having to attend to the navigation of the ship, to look after the recruits, and to keep his watch every alternate four hours.

For several days the *Fanny* lay at anchor in Port Hunter. There we received every possible attention from the missionaries. They cut out the bullet that was in my foot, and furnished us with several medical com-

X

forts that we were in need of, and which, very likely, they could ill spare from their scanty stores. The slug in my arm shifted its position one night, working out from between the bones, and then the mate extracted it.

We were delayed at Duke of York I. for more than a week, owing to light variable winds and calms. The last two or three nights of our stay were spent at Mioko, a snug land-locked harbour on the south of the island. Mr. Farren's head trading station was situated there, and we lay at anchor in company with three other vessels —the *Haabai*, formerly called the *Sea Rip*, the *Niujo*, and the *Falcon*.

At last, one morning, a fresh breeze sprang up from the north, and with the assistance of the captain of the *Haabai*, who piloted us, we once more got to sea. This breeze carried us through the channel and about twenty miles south of New Ireland, when we were again becalmed, and for the next fortnight were fairly in the "doldrums." Gradually, however, though slowly, the *Fanny* crept southward, the wind freshening up as she got further away.

Off the south-western coast of Bougainville I., we spoke the *Carola*, a German corvette. She steamed up to us in answer to our "urgent" signal for medical assistance. A lieutenant boarded us in company with the surgeon, who attended to our hurts. He appeared to think there was little chance that the G.A. would survive till we reached Queensland; for the wounded arm was now in a terrible state.

These Germans did all they could for us. The captain even offered to take the G.A. and me to Batavia in the corvette, so that we could remain under his surgeon's care. This we declined, however, not without many thanks for the offer. We then parted company, the corvette steering northward, whilst we "hammered" away against the freshening south-easter, which blew up into a hard gale off Ronongo I., obliging us to seek shelter under Banquetta Point for a couple of days—an opportunity we used for filling up the water-tanks.

We were now fairly in the "trades" again, and made a dead "beat" as far as the Lihou Reefs. I kept the ship away to windward of these, steering for Flinders' opening in the Great Barrier. After dark, on July 2, the anchor was dropped in Cleveland Bay, off Townsville. The G.A. and I then found quarters in the hospital there, while the *Fanny* went on to Mackay in charge of the mate.

I remained only a few days at Townsville, going on to Mackay in the A.S.M. Co.'s steamer *Elamang*, leaving the G.A. still in the hospital. He eventually recovered his health there, though not the full use of his arm. The elbow-joint remained stiff and useless ever afterwards. As for my own wounds, all, except the spear wound in my left shoulder, had almost healed up by the time we arrived at Townsville. The doctor there said that some foreign body—probably a piece of the spear—was still resting in unpleasant proximity to the shoulder-blade. He was either unable to extract it, or perhaps thought it better to await further developments.

I remained some three weeks at Mackay, and then, as I was suffering agonies from rheumatism in the wounded shoulder, and as there appeared to be little chance of my obtaining relief, I went on to Brisbane in the s.s. *Yaralla*. The passage occupied a week, as the steamer had to call in at several ports on her way. In the meantime, an abscess formed just over the spot where the piece of wood lay embedded.

On our arrival at Brisbane, I was met by a friend, who took me to the hospital. For I was so weak that I now needed assistance when moving about. That same day, August 7, the abscess was opened. The spear point—a piece of wood four inches long—was discovered, lying upon the shoulder-blade. Next day I was put under chloroform, and the thing was extracted ; a third opening having to be made to effect the removal.

For some little time, I believe, my condition was considered rather precarious. Eventually I recovered, and left the hospital, a month after the operation, almost fit for work again. My right hand will never fully recover its strength, and a hit out with the left sometimes causes an unpleasant twinge in the shoulder on that side.

CHAPTER XIX.

FIRST VOYAGE OF THE *LIZZIE*, 1883-84.

I am appointed to the Lizzie—*Fitting out—A bad sailer—The new regulation concerning firearms—Where to go?—I sail from Townsville in December—The Louisiade Archipelago—Teste I.—A sick mission teacher—The* Eileen *and her skipper—Bêche-de-mer collectors—Recruiting at Mewstone I.—Fresh recruits and hard work—Islanders improved by service—Contrast presented in Aneiteum I.—On to the Redlick Is.—Natives alarmed by false reports — Entering the barrier reef—The Calvados Chain—Coral Haven—Report of an affray—Native fishermen—Curious trap-nets—How made—Weapons and houses—Canoes—Character of the people—" Scaly-skin"—A white man infected—Formation of the Louisiades—Mount Rattlesnake—Sam meets his long-lost brother — Native excursionists — Nicholas Minister's stories—Turning homeward—Bad qualities of the* Lizzie—*Arrival in Cleveland Bay—A Royal Commission—Affray at Mackay between colonists and Kanakas—The stirrup-iron as a weapon.*

AFTER leaving the hospital, a few weeks' holiday, together with good feeding, made me, if not "as fit as a fiddle" after the shaking I had experienced, at any rate fit enough to take another command in the labour trade. For this I had not long to wait.

The *Lizzie*—hitherto a barquentine, but now about to be altered into a brigantine—owned by Messrs. Burns, Philp & Co., was lying at Townsville, and was in want of a master. The command of her was offered to me, and I accepted it towards the end of November. A month had to be spent in port, however, before I was ready for sea. During that time, the vessel's mizzenmast was removed. A new mainmast, eight feet longer than the old one, was put in also. A mainboom, more than half the length of the hull, was shipped aft. This stretched a mainsail and gaff topsail, containing nearly as much canvas as all her other sails put together.

The *Lizzie* was the worst old "ballahoe" for sailing that I ever put my foot on board of. I have got eight knots out of her running, but "on a wind" she was nowhere, especially with a strong sea, when she would pitch up into the wind and then tumble off two or three points, enough to drive the helmsman mad!

Owing to a recent proclamation of the Government, forbidding us to supply the islanders with firearms as "trade," when recruiting, my owners and I had grave doubts as to whether natives of the New Hebrides or the Solomon Is. could now be induced to join. Smoothbore muskets, very often even Snider rifles, had become the most common form of present, or "pay," to the friends of intending recruits. It seemed to me pretty certain that I should have to cruise about a long time in my old hunting grounds before the natives became reconciled to the new law. And this more particularly, because, of course, the regulation would not affect the action of French and German vessels. So, for a time, the New Hebrides and the Solomon Is. were likely to yield no recruits to us.

New Britain and New Ireland were also barred. It had been averred that the natives of these islands were an undesirable class of labourers. New Guinea was likewise forbidden as a recruiting ground. Nothing had been said, however, against the group of islands southeast of it, the Louisiade Archipelago, which had been hitherto unvisited by labour vessels. There the natives were not acquainted with the use of firearms, though to some extent accustomed to white men, bêche-de-mer collectors chiefly. So I resolved to go thither.

I sailed from Townsville on December 22. Running northward along the coast, I passed through the Great

Barrier by the Flora Pass, in latitude 17° S., steering thence to Teste, a small island about forty miles from the south-east point of New Guinea, lying within the chain of barrier reefs which encloses nearly all the islands of the Louisiade Archipelago. On the morning of January 1, 1884, we sighted Suckling Reef in this chain, and, passing eastward of it, entered within the barrier and anchored on the northern side of Teste I.

This island, the native name of which is Wari, is about three miles long by half a mile wide. It is lofty, with sharp serrated peaks. On its western shore there is a Protestant mission, where a Polynesian teacher and his wife were living. I engaged four of the natives there as boatmen, two of them to serve as interpreters also. They had a very fair knowledge of English, considering that they had never visited any of the colonies, and that their only instructors had been the bêche-de-mer collectors who have frequented the group for years. Concerning their treatment of the natives, especially towards the south-eastern end of the Archipelago, we heard of atrocities worse than anything related of labour recruiters.

At the time of this visit, the mission teacher at Teste I. was very sick, and seemed to be in a bad way. The G.A. and I did the best we could for him, and supplied him with medicine. Whether he eventually recovered or not, I am unable to say.

The *Eileen*, cutter, came to an anchor off the mission while I was there. She was owned and commanded by an Austrian, Herr Nicholas Minister, and was engaged in the bêche-de-mer trade.

Captain Minister dined with me on board the *Lizzie* the day I met him. During my present voyage he had neither time nor opportunity to do me any harm. When I next visited the Archipelago, however, I found he had assiduously spread false reports among the natives concerning the Queensland labour trade. He had even told them that many would be *eaten* in Queensland, while few, if any, would ever find an opportunity of returning to their homes. He had several fishing stations on the eastern islands, especially in Saint Aignan, Sudest, Renard and Joannet Is. At this time he had probably more influence over these savages than any other European.

I lay at Teste I. one night only, getting under way again next morning. I then steered eastward, with my new interpreters on board, making for the Calvados chain. This is a line of twenty or thirty small islands and islets, lofty and rugged in contour. The chain stretches for fifty miles in length, and lies eighty or ninety miles east of Teste I.

We passed the first night, after leaving Teste, at anchor near the Kossman Is., halfway to the chain; the next near Real I. So dangerous and intricate is the navigation within the barrier reef of the Louisiade, that it was absolutely necessary always to anchor before nightfall.

My first recruits were obtained at Mewstone I. The interpreters I had engaged proved themselves thoroughly competent to make the natives understand what we required, as also what would be expected of such as might be engaged. The first two or three were spoken to in my presence by the interpreters, and I am certain that they thoroughly understood how long they were to remain in Queensland, what kind of work they were to engage in, and, as near as they could be made to comprehend it, what return they would receive for their services. This, I say, in spite of the report to the contrary formulated by a Royal Commission in the year following.

One thing I admit: I do not suppose these men had ever undertaken what we call a hard day's work. They had never had any opportunity of gaining such experience. So, no doubt, they afterwards repented having left their homes, and their easy, slothful life, when they found out what work really meant.

A "Queen-streeter"—a Brisbane politician—to whom I once made a similar statement of this matter, said that, under such circumstances, I had done wrong in bringing these natives away from their islands, morally, if not legally.

Now, I explained to them, through competent interpreters, what they had to expect on their arrival in Queensland. They knew well enough that they had had no experience of the work that would be required of them, but they expressed themselves as being willing to chance that. They engaged themselves, of their own free will, to go to Queensland. So much for my legal right, now for the moral view.

By taking these men away from their island, and from a life of sloth, brutality, and cannibalism, they are improved intellectually, as well as physically, through contact with Europeans. It is said that they pick up the white man's vices. So they may, but a returned island labourer would look with contempt and aversion on the average Aneiteum native, with his thin veneer of Christianity.

As I have before stated, Aneiteum has been under the sway of Presbyterian missionaries for about thirty years. Now, it has not been either war, emigration, or disease that has caused a diminution of numbers there. On the contrary, peace, idleness, and licentious habits have contributed to make the population dwindle away to a mere fraction of what it was.

To change an islander into a decent citizen of the world, he must be forced to work for his living after his dancing and fighting have been stopped. If he is allowed to remain idle, he becomes a very much worse subject—morally and physically, Christian or pagan—than the raw savage.

Passing through the chain, from Mewstone I. we next went to the Redlick Is., which are three in number, lying twelve or thirteen miles further north. On the north-west of the Redlicks, a larger island, called Deboyne, was laid down on the charts in use at that time. But, in reality, Deboyne and the Redlicks are one and the same. About nine miles beyond the Redlicks lies the large mountainous island of Saint Aignan, which I did not visit on this voyage.

The Redlicks lie at the western end of a small atoll or ring reef. I sailed into the lagoon enclosed within this reef, anchoring at first on the northern side of Warri I., and afterwards on its south-western shore. I recruited ten men at the first anchorage; but a scare arose amongst the crowd on shore, which spread to the new recruits, who were frightened by some bogus story about the cannibalistic tastes of white men. Consequently, when we came to our second anchorage, nine men jumped overboard one night, to swim ashore. We recovered five of them.

I left the Redlick atoll by a passage through the northern side of the reef, and stood to the east for about a dozen miles. Coming to Bass' islets, I found a broad passage through the northern barrier of the Archipelago. Standing close in to the outer end of this channel, I could see from aloft that it was not very deep in some places, so I pointed the ship's head out again, northward. The ebb tide, however, was running through southward, at a tremendous rate; and, although the south-westerly breeze was in my favour, and the old tub going five knots through the water, I found myself driving stern first through the channel to windward. So, to make the best of an apparently bad job, I hauled the ship up on the wind, and in a quarter of an hour, got a mile and a half to windward, through the passage and inside the barrier.

I worked the whole length of the chain along its northern side for recruits, with fair success, although these small islands are very thinly populated. I then spent two or three days in Joannet Harbour, a bay on the southern side of Joannet I.

At Grass I., which is close to Joannet, we met some natives who could speak English. Three of them, named Dixon, Sandfly, and Bihia, had been in the employment of the bêche-de-mer collectors, and I believe had visited Cooktown, in Northern Queensland. Sandfly stated that he had been employed for some time on board H.M.S. *Sandfly*, after which vessel he had been named. These men were easily engaged, Dixon and Sandfly serving me as interpreters in the eastern part of the Archipelago.

From Joannet Harbour I went to Coral Haven, on the east of Joannet and the north of Sudest I. There we heard of a three-masted vessel, said to be then lying *outside* the barrier. Her boats had visited Sudest and the smaller islands, and had taken away a good many men. This vessel afterwards turned out to have been the barquentine *Ceara*, Captain Inman, bound for Townsville.

At the same place we heard of a three-masted vessel which had passed through the Archipelago a few days before us, engaging natives for some place unknown. At Grass I. her people had had an affray with the natives. This could not have been a Queensland labour ship; for the *Ceara* and the *Lizzie* were the first two vessels from that colony which visited the Louisiade in search of "recruits." The *Ceara*, which had three masts, was never within the barrier reef of the Archipelago, or we should have seen her.

Nicholas Minister also heard this story, and sent a report of it to Mr. MacFarlane, the missionary. Suspicion fell on the *Ceara*, and inquiry into the matter was instituted in the following July, by Mr. Morey, police magistrate at Townsville.

After leaving Coral Haven, I visited Briarly I. Thence I coasted along the south of Sudest I. as far as a deep bay west of Condé Point, the southern extremity of the island.

On our way, I had an opportunity of seeing a mode

of netting fish that was new to me. Being becalmed one afternoon for a few hours, near Briarly I., we had been obliged to anchor in very deep water. About half a mile from the ship there lay a solitary canoe, with three men and a boy in her engaged in fishing. After about two hours' work, they came alongside, and sold me a hundred and sixty-five fish, averaging three quarters of a pound each. Besides these, they retained about a dozen for their own consumption. I bought at the rate of one stick of twist tobacco (eighteen sticks to the pound) for eleven fish, the whole lot for elevenpence-halfpenny. I also bought two of the three nets they had in the canoe.

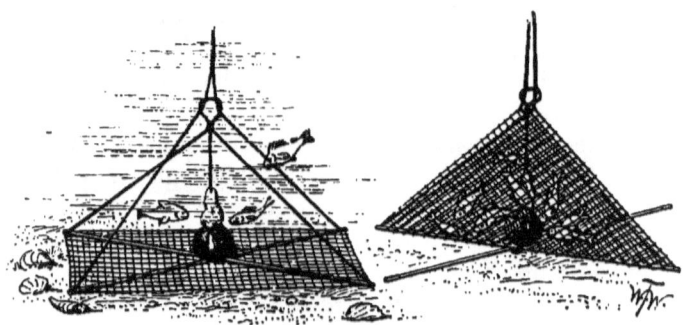

FISHING-NETS—LOUISIADE ARCHIPELAGO.

Each of these was about three feet square, being distended by two diagonal sticks under the net, seized together at right angles to each other. One of the sticks was firmly attached to two opposite corners of the net, but the ends of the other stick could be easily detached from the corners by a sharp jerk of the hauling-line. The two legs of this line were made fast to the respective corners of the net, but not to the cross-stick. It was brought up through a loop in the middle of another short piece of line, the ends of which were fastened to the other stick at the corners.

The bait—usually a piece of squid or cuttle-fish, with

a stone as a sinker—was attached on top to the centre of the net. Possibly the fishermen feel the fish dragging at the bait, but I imagine they have to trust to chance a good deal. A sharp jerk of the hauling-line frees the net from one of the sticks, and running up through the loop, doubles up the net, enclosing in it whatever fish may have been engaged with the bait.

The fish I bought on this occasion had been caught in eighteen fathoms of water. These nets, as also seines I have purchased at different times, are very neatly made of fine twine, spun or twisted from the bark of some tree unknown to me. The seines are twenty or thirty yards in length, and three or four feet deep. They have light wooden floats, and shells as sinkers.

Among the curios I purchased here were many stone-headed axes. These consist of a wedge of "greenstone" lashed on to a wooden crook, with more or less rude carving at the angle. The wedges varied from four to seven inches in length, and are not quite so broad. Such axes, together with spears and rude clubs, were al the offensive weapons I saw in these islands. Apparently the natives possessed neither bows, arrows, nor slings.

The houses in this part of the Louisiade are constructed differently from those on Teste I. and its neighbours. The last are shaped something after European models. They are situated in damp places, often over the water, and are elevated on piles, with the ends of the roofs peaked up. A similar fashion prevails in Strong's I., or Kusaie, the easternmost of the Caroline group. But in the islands of the Calvados chain, and in Sudest I., the houses look like so many gigantic cockroaches. A long narrow floor, about twenty feet by seven, is elevated on piles, four or five feet high. This is covered over with a thatched roof, too low to admit of the inmates standing upright under it.

Their canoes appear to be the most valuable property

the natives possess. They are sufficiently large to carry a score of men, and are often profusely ornamented at the ends with rude carving. They are furnished with the usual outrigger, and are propelled by paddles, or by a long narrow mat sail with rounded ends, which is hoisted diagonally when "on a wind," and horizontally when running before it.

The natives themselves are a poor lot—cowardly, treacherous, and not at all a robust race. Apparently they are of mixed origin, as I noticed several cases of straight hair and Malayan features amongst them.

They are much afflicted with a scrofulous skin disease, commonly called "scaly-skin." I fancy it is a kind of

NATIVE HOUSES—LOUISIADE ARCHIPELAGO.

ringworm. It is an eruption of small, dry, horny scales. These may be removed, to some extent, by rubbing with sand, but they soon appear again. The disease sometimes affects portions of the body, more often the whole of it. Sufferers from it present a most repulsive appearance. The older navigators generally ascribed it to kava-drinking; but, in my experience, it has been most noticeable on islands where the kava plant is unknown, —namely, in the Louisiade, the Marshall, and the Kingsmill groups. From what I have gathered of the social habits of South Sea Islanders, I am disposed to attribute it to inter-breeding.

The disease is slightly contagious. A white man, with whom I was for some time intimate in the Marshall group, had a "scaly" mistress, and he contracted the disease. It left him, however, soon after he discontinued the connection.

The islands are hilly, but of moderate height. The rock formation most noticeable is mica schist, with here and there basalt. In Sudest, Joannet, and Pig Is., there are large quartz reefs. These are generally of the white, "milky" variety, which is least promising for gold. Since I was there, gold has been found in small quantities, however, on Sudest I. The Louisiades compare unfavourably, as regards fertility, with the New Hebrides and Solomon Is., and the rather sparse population depends greatly on fish as a means of subsistence.

In Condé Bay—we gave it that name as it lies close under Condé Point—I managed to get sufficient water to fill up the tanks, though of very poor quality. There is a good watering creek on the north of the island, where a stream runs down from Mt. Rattlesnake, a lofty peak near the centre of the island. I was ignorant of the existence of this stream then.

My principal Teste interpreter, Sam, discovered a long lost relative here, his brother. A canoe, containing about a dozen men, came alongside, soon after I anchored. Sam, looking over the side at it, suddenly ejaculated something in his native language. A youth in the canoe, looking up, answered him, and an earnest conversation ensued. Then the man in the boat climbed up on board. He was Sam's brother, and they had not seen each other for a dozen years or so.

More than twelve years before this, Sam's father had taken him, then about five years old, with a party that had set forth from Teste on a voyage. Heaven knows whither, or for what purpose they went; but I suppose these islanders occasionally feel, like ourselves, a desire to see somewhat of the world beyond their own little

Y

islands. They reached Sudest I., where the men of the party were killed and eaten. The child was spared, and was adopted by the Sudest people who had devoured his father and friends.

The meeting of the brothers was a fortunate occurrence for me. For the younger brother wanted to get away on any terms. So, in five minutes, his name was on my recruit list, and his example produced a large following.

I went no further eastward on this voyage, but turned back, with a light south-easter, and worked slowly along the southern islands of the chain. At Grass I. the natives seemed less friendly than they had been before. Nicholas Minister, or some of his men, had been there since, telling outrageous stories of the bad treatment the natives would receive if they went to Queensland; so all our endeavours to obtain more recruits were of no avail. Here and there canoes came alongside, those in them spinning yarns to the recruits, who evidently did not relish them. There appeared to be a strong probability that some of them would desert, if they got a chance.

One evening, I anchored somewhere near the middle of the Chain, and, from a small island near the ship, I obtained one man, making up a total of a hundred and twenty-six recruits. This was far short of my licensed number; but, so far, I had made a prosperous voyage. So, being rather doubtful of my good luck continuing much longer, next morning I hove up the anchor and steered for Jomard Passage, in the southern barrier, *en route* for Townsville.

When clear of the reefs, I hauled up on the port tack, with a fresh south-easter; and then the old *Lizzie* showed her weatherly qualities in a sea-way. Three knots an hour ahead and three points leeway—now luffing up into the wind and then tumbling off a couple of points—did not look well for getting to windward of the Lihou Reefs.

Luckily, the north-west monsoon was occasionally making itself felt. Every now and again the wind chopped round from south-east to north-west, helping me to make some easting. Anyhow, we blundered along until we just scraped round the eastern end of Lihou Reef, and then, the trade coming steady and strong, I squared away for Flinders Passage in the Great Barrier. After spending one rough, dirty night at anchor, under the lee of one of the reefs, I brought up in Cleveland Bay, off my port, on February 17, 1884. The *Ceara* had arrived a day or two before me.

The whole of my recruits, after being examined by the immigration agent as to the manner of their engagement and the terms of their agreement, were sent to work on Hamleigh Plantation. They remained there only about sixteen months, and were then sent back home in the s.s. *Victoria*. For a Royal Commission was appointed early in 1885, under the Griffith Ministry, to inquire into the circumstances connected with the recruiting. It came to the conclusion that these labourers had all been obtained by "fraud or force." Of this matter more anon.

Shortly after my departure from Townsville on this voyage, an occurrence took place at Mackay, which may be worth mentioning. At the races (December 26) some Kanakas, employed on the neighbouring plantations, were refused drink—according to law—at Dimmock's booth. They retaliated by throwing bottles, and such other missiles as came handy, at the people on the course, from the outside of the surrounding fence. The whites, of whom a great number were mounted, attacked them in turn, and easily drove them away.

The "Anti-Kanakaite" party have never lost an opportunity of accusing their opponents of cruelty to South Sea Islanders. On this occasion, the white belligerents were mostly Anti-Kanakaites, and they abundantly proved what sort of sympathy *they* had for their coloured brethren. The favourite weapon with them that day was a stirrup-iron, swung by its leather —an ugly weapon in the hands of a good rider. Several Kanakas had to be taken to the hospital at the end of the fray. One of them shortly after died from the effects of a "blow from a bottle!" More likely it was a blow from a stirrup-iron!

CHAPTER XX.

SECOND VOYAGE OF THE *LIZZIE*, 1884.

I sail for the Louisiade—The Lizzie *springs a leak—I put into Cairns—Cockroaches—Repairs effected—Reach Teste I.—A mission teacher's wife—No interpreters—By order of the missionary—Active opposition—Kidnapping!—Moresby I.—The recruiter's enemies—Nicholas Minister's stories—Normanby I.—Natives eager to recruit—Back to Townsville—Resignation—The Stanley kidnapping case—German Charley prevents recruiting—Burning of huts—Prosecution of Davis and McMurdo—They are sent to Fiji—Tried and condemned—Released and complimented—Hernsheim "compensated"—Policy of the Government—The new Amendment Act—Painting ships and boats—Deserters not to be recovered—Arrival of the* Lochiel—*Wreck of the* Alfred Vittery—*Rowan and King sentenced for kidnapping—Return of the* Heath—*I take command of her—Proceedings of her G.A.—I appear in court—The* Ceara *case—Report of Mr. Morey, P.M.—No evidence of kidnapping.*

AFTER lying for nearly a month in port, refitting and procuring fresh licences, I put to sea once more on March 14, bound for the Louisiade Archipelago. Passing out through the Great Barrier, as on my last voyage, by the Flora Passage, I cleared the reefs during the evening, and all the following night the old *Lizzie* rolled and tumbled in a heavy cross sea, with a fresh breeze from east-south-east.

About midnight the mate called me up, reporting that the ship was making a great deal of water. In fact, the lee side of the lower deck was all afloat. Both pumps were immediately set going; but the hands had four hours' hard jogging before the weather one "sucked."

In the meantime I searched about for the leak, expecting to find it somewhere between wind and water, but without success. As soon as it was daylight, I steered back westward, repassing the Barrier by a small and tortuous channel a few miles south of Trinity Opening. That evening I anchored off Trinity Inlet, the port of Cairns.

I remained there a week, with the vessel on the "hard," and her rudder unshipped. The leak was discovered in her rudder trunk, and, in smooth water, would have been a few inches above the surface. This helped me to a "wrinkle." The cockroaches that swarmed on board had eaten an oval hole right through the white pine casing of the rudder trunk. I have often heard of rats causing leaks, but never before of cockroaches doing so. In the lazaret there was a water-tank, built of yellow pine. The vermin had paid attention to this, also. Several of its planks were completely hollowed out by them, only a thin shell remaining. The damage to the rudder trunk was soon made good, and the rudder itself also repaired before it was again hung.

I put to sea again from Cairns on April 3. Clearing the Barrier by way of Trinity Opening, I steered as before for Teste I., where I anchored about four days later. There I landed the men who had served me as interpreters during my last voyage, together with their boxes, containing goods they had purchased in Townsville. I also paid a visit to the teacher's wife, who appeared to be the ruling spirit on the island, hoping to engage some more boys to serve as boatmen and interpreters.

The coffee-coloured dame received me with much apparent friendliness. She expressed great pleasure at the safe return of the interpreters, as also in regard to the quantity of "trade" they had been able to purchase with their earnings. I have no doubt she came in for a considerable share of it, for I saw the boxes carefully carried into her own house, and stowed away there for future examination.

In order to propitiate this old lady still more, I made her a considerable present, comprising many fathoms of coloured print calicoes, beads, tobacco, pipes, etc. As soon as these had been safely stowed away, however, she changed her tune, glumly informing me that, by order of the missionary, no boys were to be allowed to leave the island, either as interpreters or as recruits.

This was a knock for me, for I was obliged, by Queensland law, to provide interpreters, not only when engaging men, but also on arrival in the colony. She would not even allow any of the natives to assist in pulling the boat back to the ship. For there was a stiff breeze

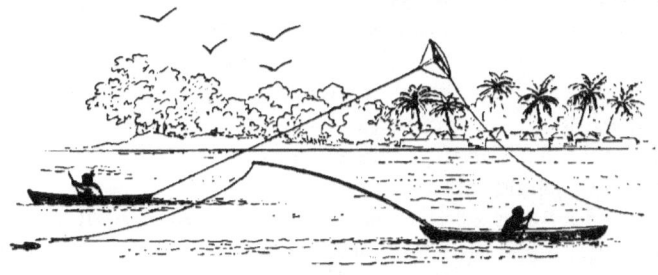

FISHING.

to contend with, and I had only a white man and a New Hebridean with me at the time. I obtained one man, however, in the evening—a runaway.

Next morning, as the chain was being taken in, and sail being made, in order to leave the island, a large canoe, manned by natives belonging to the mission—a fact made apparent by the shirts and calico waist-cloths they sported—passed near us. The design of these people was, evidently, to attend on the ship and prevent me from obtaining recruits. I allowed them to run ahead of me for some little distance, until I saw that I could barely fetch the eastern point of Moresby I. on the port tack. Then I hauled up sharp to northward, and, having the weather-gauge of them by a good mile, came to an anchor in Pitt Bay, Moresby I. I had lain there an hour or more, with my boats working along-shore, before the canoe arrived, its occupants tired out with hard paddling in their heavy craft, dead to windward.

While passing through the channel between Moresby and Kitai—the next island to eastward—I picked up a man who was swimming off to the ship with the aid of a log of wood. As soon as he got on deck, he signified to the man I had engaged at Teste, that he desired to engage as a recruit for Queensland. One would have thought this was fair enough recruiting. Strange to say —that is, strange to the uninitiated—the Royal Commission in Queensland, a year later, declared that this recruit had been obtained by unfair means—that is, that he was kidnapped!!

I spent some three or four days at Moresby I., and picked up a few recruits, notwithstanding the efforts of the mission party. These carefully attended on my boat, watching all her movements. I was sadly hampered for want of efficient boatmen to man both boats, having only a crew for one. However, the day I left Pitt Bay, I fell in with the *Ceara*, bound for Townsville, full of recruits. By offering increased pay, I managed to induce four of her boatmen to leave her and join the *Lizzie*. Captain Inman consented to the arrangement, as he no longer needed their services. Being thus properly manned, I indulged the hope of making as good a voyage as my last one. But in this I was soon to be wofully disappointed.

In the interval that had elapsed since my last visit to the Louisiade, our opponents—the missionaries and the bêche-de-mer collectors—had not been idle. At every mission station at this end of the Archipelago, the native teachers were on the alert, endeavouring to prevent men from leaving. Canoes attended on my boats—generally preceding them—every time they visited the shore. Further eastward, Nicholas Minister, the bêche-de-mer trader, appeared to have visited every island, spreading all sorts of malicious reports as to our treatment of labourers in Queensland, and the extreme improbability that recruits would ever see their homes again, if they ventured to go there. It was even said that we took men away for the purpose of killing and eating them. This would not seem such a very ridiculous story to the natives, who are all rank cannibals.

After working the northern coasts of Moresby, Basilisk, and Hayter Is., I steered for the East Cape of New Guinea. I then crossed over Goschen Strait to Normanby I., a large, mountainous, thickly populated island. There a few more men were obtained—all runaways from their friends. For, notwithstanding the reports that had been so industriously circulated as to our evil intentions, numbers of the younger people were willing to try their luck in Queensland. I feel certain that, if all who wished to leave had been able to get on board, I might have made up my full complement at this island alone.

The Royal Commission of 1885 was of opinion that the few recruits who joined me here, as well as at other islands of the Archipelago, were obtained by unfair means, and, in some cases, were even forcibly kidnapped. If I *had* adopted such practices, I could easily have filled the ship out of the numbers of canoes that flocked around and lay alongside of her.

I then visited Evans and Woodlark Is., next working St. Aignan and the south-eastern portion of the Archipelago, but with very poor success. Nicholas Minister had made the place "too hot" for me. At one time I thought of making for the Solomons or the New Hebrides; but my stores were running short, and the *Lizzie* was such a tub in a sea-way that I deemed it advisable to return to Townsville with the sixty-seven recruits I had already engaged. I arrived there on June 2, and resigned command of the vessel, disgusted with her performances and with my own bad luck. The *Lizzie* was soon after sold to a Sydney firm, and was never again employed in the labour trade.

Some little time before I sailed on the last voyage, and during my absence, the case of the *Stanley* had been before the courts. It attracted the attention of all who were interested in the labour trade. During the last voyage of the *Stanley*, when her career was terminated on Indispensable Reef, in July, 1884, she had visited the Laughlan Is., east of New Guinea, while proceeding to New Ireland. Some men had been engaged there, but were allowed to remain on shore for a night, before the vessel sailed again, to bid farewell to their friends.

There was a German trading station on these islands, belonging to Hernsheim & Co. A man, who was commonly known as German Charley, was the sole resident European at this time. According to native evidence given at the trial, he persuaded the recruits not to keep to their bargain, although their friends had received presents of considerable value from the master of the *Stanley*.

Finding that the recruits did not rejoin the ship at the time appointed, Captain Davis, and Mr. McMurdo, G.A., left the ship with their boats' crews, all armed, as usual. As they approached the shore, a shot was fired at them from the German's hut. None of the recruits turning up when they landed, several native huts were burnt, and with them the thatched huts belonging to the German. Two natives were taken away from the island in the *Stanley*, presumably against their will.

The first notice of this case I had was contained in "The Brisbane Courier" for April 4, 1884. It was therein stated that on the day previous, at the City Police Court, Joseph Griffith Davis, late master of the *Stanley*, and

William A. McMurdo, G.A., were charged on remand, on the information of Chas. Colville Horrocks, acting immigration agent, with having kidnapped two islanders, Sea Whimp and Namee, on April 17, 1883, on the high seas near the Laughlan Is. in the Pacific Ocean. The case was further remanded five times to enable the prosecution to obtain witnesses.

Finally, the prosecution was dropped by the Queensland Government. The prisoners, Davis and McMurdo, were handed over to the Imperial authorities, and on June 18 they were sent on board H.M.S. *Raven* and transferred to Fiji. There they were tried in the Court of the High Commissioner for the Western Pacific—the Governor of Fiji.

By this court, held at Suva, the official capital, on August 6 following, the prisoners were found guilty, and were sentenced to three months' imprisonment, without labour. A week after the trial they were released by order of the High Commissioner, Sir William Des Vœux. McMurdo was even complimented by the High Commissioner for the energy he displayed when the *Stanley* was wrecked. Sir William Des Vœux also headed a subscription that was got up for their benefit with " a respectable amount."

The High Commissioner was apparently of opinion that the treatment of the prisoners by the Queensland Government had been quite sufficient punishment for what little harm they had done. A large indemnity was paid to Hernsheim & Co. by the Queensland Government, to compensate them for the destruction of their thatched huts and the small quantity of copra they had in store.

Messrs. Hernsheim & Co. must have made money by this affair. I have been assured by men who knew the Laughlan Is., and the trading station there, that the whole establishment and stock was not worth a twenty-pound note. When I visited the island in 1884, there was no resident trader there. It was too poor to support one.

I do not remember the amount of the indemnity demanded by the German firm, but I know it was excessive. However, it appears to have been paid without question. The Queensland Ministry of the day were pledged to suppress the trade; so the bigger the indemnity, the worse they could make it for their opponents. The expense they afterwards incurred by chartering the s.s. *Victoria* to take back four hundred and four natives of New Guinea and the Louisiade to their homes was, no doubt, a similar bit of policy.

The Act to amend the Pacific Island Labour Act of 1880, assented to March 10, 1884, was now in full force. It contained many important additions to the original Act; among these was a regulation obliging all vessels engaged in recruiting for Queensland to carry a black ball at the mast-head, and to be painted a dull slate colour, with a black "ribbon." Surely these were the most uninviting colours that could well have been chosen. The "dull slate colour" looked tolerably decent and cool when fresh laid on, but, after a month's cruise, iron-rust and dirt rendered it anything but pleasant to look at. The black band only made it more sombre and repelling. The boats were to be painted red; an old fashion among Queensland vessels. Subsequently, French and German ships cruising in the New Hebrides and the Solomon Is. also took to carrying red-painted boats, with which they could pass themselves off as coming from Queensland.

Masters were mostly troubled, however, by the regulation with regard to deserters. No deserter was to be retaken. An islander might now engage to come to Queensland, get "trade" to the value of a pound or two, give it to his friends, cadge all he could get on board, and then coolly walk or swim ashore. There was one grain of comfort for the master, however. The law did not oblige him to *assist* the "unwilling recruit" in getting ashore.

On March 20, the dismasted labour barquentine, *Lochiel*, arrived at the Burnett River Heads, with the crew of the labour schooner *Alfred Vittery* on board. The last-named vessel had been wrecked in the beginning of February, at Kaan I., near the eastern coast of New Ireland, having drifted ashore during a calm.

After rescuing the crew of the schooner, the *Lochiel* had spoken the *Wilhelmina Frederika*, labour brigantine, at Hardy I. in the same neighbourhood. Mr. Rowe, G.A., and the second mate of the brigantine had both been severely tomahawked in a skirmish with natives. The former was brought home in the *Lochiel*, the G.A. belonging to the wrecked *Alfred Vittery* taking his place. In consequence of his injuries, Mr. Rowe became an inmate of a lunatic asylum.

At the City Police Court, Brisbane, on May 1, Francis Rowan, boatswain, and John McLean, A.B., late of the *Forest King*, were committed for trial, charged with having kidnapped six natives at Fischer I. On June 4 they were found guilty, and were each sentenced to three years' imprisonment, the first year in irons.

Towards the end of May, the barquentine *Heath*, Captain Findlay, Mr. Duffield, G.A., arrived at Mackay. She had sixty-three male recruits and thirty-one females on board. These were all from the smaller islands lying near the eastern coast of New Ireland. Now, whether Captain Findlay had done wrong in taking these people, without their having thoroughly comprehended the agreement they signed, or, rather, put their "marks" to, or whether the G.A. had purposely misled the master, I cannot say.

When I went to Mackay, in the beginning of July, to take command of the *Heath*, I found the recruits all in good health. Though cooped up on board, and not permitted to land, they were "as jolly as sandboys." They seemed quite willing to go to the plantations, while the planters were just as ready to engage them. Yet, as the sub-immigration agent of the port informed me, no competent interpreter could be found to explain the terms of engagement to them. So it had been ordained that all of them should be returned to their homes forthwith.

It appeared to me that the G.A. had led the master to think that he was satisfied with the engagement of these men. But, while allowing him to ship them, he had put off giving Captain Findlay the requisite certificates. On arrival at Mackay, he—Mr. Duffield—had turned round on Findlay, denouncing his recruiting as illegal. It looked to me as if the whole proceeding of the G.A. was nothing else than a deliberate trap for the master. Findlay was debarred employment in the trade, for a while; and Duffield was not again employed by the Government in the capacity of Government agent.

Before I joined the *Heath* as master, I was engaged as a witness on an inquiry held by Mr. Morey, Police Magistrate, at Townsville, in consequence of reports emanating from Nicholas Minister, the bêche-de-mer collector.

I subjoin Mr. Morey's Report as it appeared in "The Brisbane Courier." It will be seen from this that Mr. Morey examined several of the recruits who had been brought by the *Lizzie* and by the *Ceara*, as a result of the first voyages of these vessels to the Louisiade; that the recruits had no complaint to make as to the mode of recruiting, or as to the time they were to serve in Queensland. Mr. Morey was certainly much more competent to cross-question these recruits than were the three members of the "Royal Commission," who, the following year, declared that all these men had been kidnapped, or had been persuaded by falsehoods to leave their homes.

Here is the report :—

The Police Magistrate, Townsville, to the Colonial Secretary.

TOWNSVILLE, 1st July, 1884.

SIR,—I have now the honour to submit a report, as directed, with reference to the operations of the labour vessel *Ceara*, during her cruise for labour in January and part of February last, among the islands of the Louisiade Group, and to furnish the evidence taken before me during the inquiry.

Before commencing any inquiry I carefully read and noted the contents of the respective log-books of the *Lizzie* and *Ceara*, kept by the Government agents during their first visit to that group in January and February last.

And in this connection I may say that the entries in the log-books agree in the main with the answers given to my questions respecting the dates when recruiting began, the number of recruits, the islands from which obtained, and the size and population where known.

If, therefore, the answers given to my questions were untrue, or coloured to make out a good case, then the log-books must have been falsified throughout.

The charge is, that, some short time prior to the 18th March, a large three-masted ship had visited Roussel, Sud-Est, and several smaller islands, and taken away nearly all the males by driving them forcibly, or by enticing them into the boats and carrying them away against their will, the islands being nearly depopulated by the people of this three-masted ship.

It appears from all the evidence I obtained that no Queensland labour vessel had visited and recruited boys from the Louisiade Archipelago prior to the visit of the *Lizzie* on the 4th January, and the *Ceara* on the 14th of January.

The *Lizzie* is a schooner having two masts.

The *Ceara* is a three-masted barquentine.

The charge made can only apply, therefore, to the *Ceara*.

The *Lizzie*, Captain Wawn, began recruiting at Mewstone Island on the 4th January, and continued it at various islands up to the 10th February. While she was at the Redlick Group (between the 4th and 12th January), the *Lizzie got no recruits*, as the natives were scared, and said, "If men go, you make their hands fast."

And on the 13th January, while at Grass Island, natives said that "white man catch-em fish (bêche-de-mer) had fired at them, and taken their women."

Reports of outrages continued to be made to Captain Wawn at various islands, particularly at several points of Sud-Est.

Now, the *Ceara* began her recruiting at Piron Island, close to Sud-Est, on the 14th January. It is plain, therefore, that the outrages reported to Captain Wawn up to that date (14th January) could not be charged against the *Ceara*.

And up to the 18th January, we have evidence that the *Ceara* was obtaining boys by fair means, since a recruit obtained by the *Lizzie* that day told Captain Wawn that the three-masted ship had obtained a lot of boys at Sud-Est, and had given much more "trade" to them than he (Wawn) was giving. Wawn then had to increase his presents, so as to obtain recruits.

Coming now to the two large islands, Roussel and Sud-Est, said to have been nearly depopulated by a three-masted ship (*Ceara ?*), I find that the *Ceara*, between the 15th and 17th January, recruited some twenty-five boys from Sud-Est.

But the *Lizzie* coming after her, namely, between the 18th January and 3rd February, recruited ninety-three boys, mainly from the same island. If, therefore, the *Ceara* had used violence or fraud in obtaining her boys, it is hardly likely the *Lizzie*, coming just after her, could have obtained so many.

I may mention that Sud-Est is a large island—about 140 miles round—is populous and mountainous, and no labour ship could kidnap its people as described in the charge made. Small islands might be outraged in that way, but not populous and large ones.

The story of the three-masted ship (*Ceara ?*) having nearly depopulated Sud-Est is, therefore, not well founded.

At Roussel — the island particularized in the charge — the *Ceara* obtained seventeen recruits; the *Lizzie* did not call there. This island also is a large one, but is reported as not populous.

I can find nothing in the evidence given, especially by the Roussel boys themselves, or in the *Ceara's* log-book, *to raise a doubt as to the fair manner in which the boys were recruited*. I was most careful to ascertain what each boy received in the way of "trade" or bribe to induce him to recruit, and to ascertain what he did with his "trade."

I may here mention that while the *Ceara* was recruiting at Roussel, the natives complained of a brig, Captain Pryer, or Prior, having taken people away against their will.

On the 3rd February, while the *Lizzie* was recruiting at Sud-Est, Captain Wawn was told that a three-masted ship had lately passed through (presumably among the islands), and had several Sud-Est women on board.

On the 25th January the *Ceara* did obtain two recruits from Sud-Est, but the Government agent, the recruiter, and master all say no women were recruited or on board; no women were seen, in fact. If any women were kidnapped and brought aboard they must have been got rid of before the ship arrived at Townsville. I may here mention that Captain Inman's wife accompanied him during that voyage of the *Ceara*.

Another complaint was made against a three-masted ship by the people of Grass Island, on the 8th February, to Captain Wawn. The people told him the "ship had been fighting them."

But on the 14th January the people of the same island told Wawn (on his first visit) that a bèche-de-mer vessel had fired at them.

Now there is no evidence that the *Ceara* was at Grass Island. If, however, outrages between the 14th January and 8th February were committed, and by a three-masted vessel, then the charge points to the *Ceara*, for we have no knowledge of any other three-masted ship being in the neighbourhood.

Coming to the evidence I obtained from fourteen of the recruits from Sud-Est, and from eight Roussel islanders, I may say that their statements entirely bear out the evidence given by the Government agent, the recruiter, and master of the *Ceara* as to *the fair manner in which these people were recruited*. There is a discrepancy as to the names of some of the boys, and name of island from which they came, but I incline to believe that boys belonging to other islands were found at and recruited from Sud-Est, the native name of which is Eaba.

I spent much time in unravelling the confused statements made in reply to my questions, and committed to paper the substance only of what I gathered.

I noticed that when a boy was being questioned as to what "trade" he received, he would correct the interpreter, or rather would inform him if he had received anything out of the usual trade—such as looking-glasses, leggings, and so on.

Although I had to trust to the very imperfect translation of replies to my questions by Pudow, a Kassaway Island native, my own interpreter being useless in the case of all save the Roussel Island boys, yet I feel confident I caught the true intent and meaning of each boy I questioned.

I could not obtain from any of the boys a definite answer as to the remuneration they were to receive. I therefore confined my questions to the main charge—namely, kidnapping.

That outrages of some kind—if not of kidnapping—had been perpetrated on most of the islands visited by the *Lizzie* and *Ceara* there can be no doubt, for both those ships had reports made to them of ill-treatment. In one instance the natives complained of a Captain Pryer, or Prior, master of a bèche-de-mer vessel. This is the same man who took away a woman named Murdie from Eaba (Sud-Est). (See evidence given by Jawille, a native of Eaba.)

There is a Captain Fryer, master of the bèche-de-mer brig *Julia M. Avery*, sailing out of Cooktown.

I learn further that George Rotumah, who took the news of the outrages to the Rev. Mr. Lawes, is connected with one Nicholas Minister, master of the *Eileen*, bèche-de-mer cutter, and is interested in her fishing.

And Captain Wawn says that lying reports of the doings and intentions of Queensland labour ships have been spread by bêche-de-mer people for selfish purposes, and that the alleged outrages by a three-masted ship (*Ceara*) had its origin in that way.

I have thus far commented on the evidence at my command, and now, in conclusion, do myself the honour to report that *there is not the slightest evidence to show the Ceara obtained any labourers on that voyage by kidnapping.*

Nor is there evidence to show she obtained recruits by any unfair means or representations.—I have, etc.,

EDMUND MOREY, Police Magistrate.

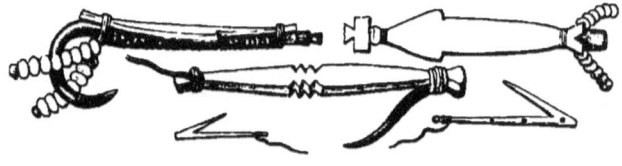

FISH-HOOKS—SOLOMON IS.

CHAPTER XXI.

VOYAGE OF THE *HEATH*, 1884.

I sail from Mackay—Pass the Fanny *at sea—Beating through the Coral Sea—Jomard Passage—My sails—Dead reckoning—Cape St. George—Landing " returns"—Getting their " whack"—Excitement and pillage—Gerrit Denys and Fisher Is.—Back to Coral Haven—Making a new mainsail—Working the Archipelago—Stone-throwing at Normanby I.—A mission teacher joins, plunders me, and deserts—Teste I.— The teacher's wife—Her wrath—No interpreters or recruits—The Barrier Reef—Drifting—Getting within the reef—The Inner Route—I reach port—Bad health — I go to Melbourne—My manuscript—Return of the* Hopeful—*Her ill-doings—False evidence of Kanakas—Material for the Griffithites—Seizure of the* Forest King—*A " Christian" Kanaka's evidence—Trial of Shaw, McNeil, and others—Messiah's evidence—Political dodges—Report of the Minister of Justice—Trial removed to Brisbane—Why—A witness paid by the Government—Kanaka evidence—Sentences—The* Ceara—*Effect of the firearms regulation—Natives incensed —Murders of Booth and Cullen—Of Captain Frier and others—Comparisons of English, French, and German policies in the Western Pacific—General Scratchley's statement—Article in " The Brisbane Courier" — The New Guinea question—Tall talk—Treatment of savages—Cases in point —The Miranda raid— Presbyterian missionaries — Firearms sold to natives by French and Germans—Slavery at Malayta I.*

I SAILED from Mackay in command of the *Heath* on July 19, 1884. Running down the coast, northward, with a fair breeze, I passed through the Great Barrier Reef by Flinders' Passage, and so gained the open sea.

On my way I passed my old ship—the *Fanny*—now

under the command of Captain Lawrence, with whom was Mr. Williams, G.A. She was bound into Mackay, having only a few recruits—eight, I think—on board, after having been out for six months. After this voyage she was sold, and was not again employed in the labour trade. I lost £200 out of my interest in her.

I spent a day at anchor in Whit-Sunday Passage, on the coast. I then filled my water-tanks at Hook I., and sailed through Flinders' Passage, as I have said. Having cleared the Barrier, I hauled up sharp on the starboard tack, hoping by so doing to get more quickly clear of the numerous coral reefs and cays scattered over this part of the Coral Sea. It was fortunate for me that I did so; for, after twenty-four hours' hammering into a head sea, I found myself only a few miles to windward of Flinders' Reefs, and more than thirty miles to leeward of where I thought I was. This was due to the current, which sets to the north-west.

As soon as Flinders' Reefs were well on the lee quarter, I kept the ship away, and, passing to leeward of the Herald Cays, found myself next morning close to two small reefs—one of which had a sandy cay on it—about thirty miles west-north-west of Willis Reefs.

These two reefs were not marked on my chart. I think it probable they may be the two that were seen by Bougainville in 1768, though reported by him to lie further to the north-west.

Though now in clearer waters, I had lost a good deal of my weather-gauge, and found myself unable to round the Louisiade Archipelago. I therefore steered a straight course for Jomard Passage, which I made soon after sunrise one morning, getting through the reefs and islands, and round the lee end of Saint Aignan I., before dark. Next morning I was off the Laughlan Is., whence I had a clear road and a fair wind for New Ireland.

The trade-wind, which had been steady and moderately fresh, then became variable and squally. As the mainsail I had bent was old, and was supposed to be the worst of the two on board, I thought it advisable to bend the other. Unluckily, before we left Mackay, the hands had been required for other work, in consequence of which I had neglected to overhaul the spare sails, relying on the former master's assertion that they were all in good order, and that the mainsail, especially, was a good one. He had said it was nearly new, and that it had been bent only once, and then only for a week or two. When the mate and the hands went below to rouse it out of the sail-locker, however, they found it as rotten as tinder. It would not even bear handling, the canvas giving way as it was hauled on deck.

The locker was perfectly watertight, and I can only surmise that the sail must have been stowed away when damp. Of course it was useless; not even fit for cutting up into parcelling. So, now, I was in a nice fix, having to depend solely on the old rag I had bent, with the prospect before me of a tussle with northerly monsoon weather in the latitude of New Ireland, and, perhaps, of having to beat back home against the "trades." Luckily, I had a good new mizzen, which might have served on a pinch, instead of a reefed mainsail.

The day before we made New Ireland, the weather was cloudy and wet. Being unable to take any observations to determine my exact position, I had to rely solely on dead reckoning. This placed me, at noon, about one hundred and twenty miles south-south-east of Cape St. George—the southernmost point of New Ireland. Relying on this reckoning, I steered to pass about thirty miles east of the Cape. Next morning, about 3 o'clock, the cry of "land, right ahead!" brought me on deck; just after a stiff squall of wind and rain had passed over the ship.

A dome-shaped mass loomed up, black, and unpleasantly near, through the tail end of the squall. One look sufficed to assure me that I was quite thirty miles to leeward of my reckoning, and running straight down upon Cape St. George. To pass it to leeward was to reach perfect safety ; but Heaven only knew whether I could effect this against the wind, and, most probably, a strong current.

Down went the helm. Then, with the wind to starboard, and going a point free, I just managed to scrape clear of the coast. That afternoon I got under the lee of St. John, a rugged and lofty island, where I found an anchorage in twenty fathoms, and landed two or three of my passengers.

I did not avail myself of the anchorage, however, but hove the ship to during the night. The next day I ran under the lee of the largest of the Kaan Is., where nearly half of my passengers were to be landed. As the shore was "bold to," I was able to keep the ship within one or two hundred yards of the landing-place, so that I could watch every detail of the landing through my glass.

Before we sailed from Mackay, the sub-immigration agent of that port had provided the ship with a quantity of "trade," which was to be distributed amongst the "rejected" islanders when they were landed at their homes. Each of them now received his or her "whack" before getting into the boats, consisting of beads, tobacco, pipes, calico of divers hues and patterns, tin pannikins and billies, fish-lines and hooks, tomahawks and knives, etc., etc., etc. Clothing and blankets were provided by the ship.

In the boats they were quiet enough, but, as soon as they got on shore, what an uproar and commotion! They shouted, yelled, screamed, danced, and ran about like a parcel of lunatics. Off came every stitch of clothing, every man and woman stripping as bare as the day they were born. Their countrymen and countrywomen appeared in hundreds, and, no doubt, made a good haul ; for, in all directions, men and boys were continually rushing off to the bush with some article or another—a brightly flashing knife or billy, or a yard or two of red or yellow calico. I expect that the "stay-at homes" got more out of the Queensland Government that day than did those for whom the "trade" had been really intended.

Next morning I arrived off the eastern coast of Gerrit Denys I. Having landed some boys there, I ran down to St. Joseph I. in the afternoon, ten miles further north. There three or four men and a woman were landed. It was after dark, and the boats had considerable difficulty in finding the ship again; for the sky was overcast, and heavy showers fell at intervals. The wind was light and fitful, sometimes easterly, and then again from north-west. We were in the "doldrums," between the south-east trades and the north-west monsoon.

Early next morning the wind came up fresh from north-west, and I had to keep the ship to windward so as to fetch Fisher I. the following day. My old mainsail would not stand much shaking, so I was obliged to "wear ship" instead of tacking, running to leeward every time I went about. Luckily, a strong current set along this coast of New Ireland to north-west. So I lost no ground, and was able next day to discharge the last of my passengers at Fisher I.

I had now an empty hold, and held a licence to recruit another shipful. I was debarred from enlisting natives of New Britain, New Ireland, and their adjuncts; so I stood southward again, and, meeting the trade-wind off the southern shore of New Ireland, I beat up against it back to the Louisiade. Entering the barrier-reef of the Archipelago by Johnson Pass, off the southern coast of Sudest I., on September 5, I anchored off Pig I. in Coral Haven.

My old mainsail was now fairly played out. It reminded one of a chart of the Archipelago, so covered was it with "over-all" patches. Accordingly, the next fortnight was spent lying at anchor, while all hands engaged in making a new mainsail, which required all the spare heavy canvas I had on board. During the progress of this work, the G.A. and I cruised about in the boats. But natives seldom approached either boats or ship, and not a single man was recruited.

As soon as the new sail had been finished and bent on, I left Coral Haven, and, after ineffectually working part of the Calvados Chain, I visited all the islands north and north-east of the Archipelago—St. Aignan, Woodlark, Renard, the Laughlans, Lagrandière, Jouveny, Jurien, Trobriand, and Normanby. I secured very few recruits for all my trouble. The mission teachers and bèche-de-mer gatherers had spread such stories about the ill-treatment of islanders in Queensland, and on board labour ships, that the inhabitants of these islands would rarely even approach us.

On a single occasion violence was offered. This happened on the north-eastern coast of Normanby I. A man was engaged there whose brother disapproved of his going, and threw a huge stone at the recruiter, which narrowly missed its mark. Had it struck his head, it would have certainly dashed his brains out. Others were ready to join in the quarrel; but one of our men in the covering boat promptly fired at the stone-thrower, wounding him slightly in the leg. This had the effect of dispersing the hostile mob—fifty or more of them—who ran off into the bush. As for the wounded man, he fell down under a tree, terribly frightened, though little hurt, whence he presently limped off.

On November 13, I was lying off Moresby I. within sight of the New Guinea coast. There I engaged a man who was supposed to be a mission teacher. He volunteered his services without any solicitation, and I cherished the hope that his example would draw others. But in this I was disappointed. The following night he deserted by swimming, and even persuaded another Moresby man to go with him. He also stole the cook's axe, and as much of the recruits' tobacco as he could lay his hands on.

My provisions were now running short, so, though I had but a score of recruits on board, I thought it best to make for Teste I. The wind failing me, I anchored off the Foolscap Rock, a few miles short of that island.

I had brought three Teste I. interpreters with me from Mackay, whither they had been sent from Townsville, discharged from the *Ceara*. These I now landed at Teste, according to agreement. At the same time I endeavoured to engage one or two others, to accompany me back to Townsville, whither I was now bound.

My old acquaintance, the teacher's wife, opposed all my endeavours. During the absence of the missionary, she seemed to be the ruling power on the island. After waiting for three days in hopes of circumventing her, I was forced to give it up, and to sail again for Queensland. I trusted I might find some man on the plantations there who would be able to act as interpreter for me. Eventually I did so obtain one; but only after much delay and expense.

The principal reason for the old lady's animosity towards me arose from the circumstance that I had put her "in the pepper"—the newspaper—at which she was very wroth. When I returned to Townsville after the second voyage of the *Lizzie*, I had written an account of my voyage, which appeared in one of the local newspapers. In this I had described how her ladyship had accepted all my gifts, and then refused to let interpreters join the ship, although several were ready and willing to go. Of this she had somehow been apprised.

I left Teste I. with a fair wind from about north, and shaped a course for the Flora Passage in the Great Barrier; but as I drew near the Queensland coast, the breeze gradually fell away. I sighted the breakers on the Barrier one afternoon, but too late to admit of getting through by nightfall. I therefore hauled off eastward. That night it fell calm, and a southerly current took hold of the ship. Next day a similar thing happened. Again I sighted the reefs, but too late in the day to get through. Again followed another night of calm and drifting to the southward. Luckily, the weather was clear and fine, so that I was able to take observations, and ascertain the ship's position. I was then in a part of the ocean that had not been surveyed, the outer edge of the Barrier being represented on the charts merely by a dotted line.

Next morning I risked the ship a little more, heading her in towards the reefs before daylight, with a light northerly air. I neared the Barrier about 1 p.m., and fancied I saw a clear passage through just ahead of me. But a topping sea undeceived me, and I had barely time to round the ship to and keep her from running upon the reef. As there was not wind enough to get away again, I let go the anchor in eighteen fathoms, and, when sufficient chain had been paid out, I had the reef, with only one fathom of water on it, not a ship's length astern.

This was about seventy miles south of the Flora Passage. Next it fell dead calm, so we passed the night there. In the morning a fresh breeze sprang up from northward, so I hove short and canted the ship, under sail, with a kedge and warp from abaft the port main rigging. The kedge, with part of the warp, which I had to cut, were abandoned. Then, barely weathering a point of reef astern, I ran through a narrow opening, whence, with the sun astern of me, I conned the ship from aloft, and, for about two hours, meandered through a perfect labyrinth of coral patches and reefs. I reached more open water at last, anchoring at noon in thirty fathoms. For the sky had now become clouded over, and I was unable to see my way clearly.

I was now inside the Barrier, but all the trouble was

by no means over yet. Next morning, the wind, though fair, was light and puffy, the sky being thickly overcast with cloud, making the water and reef all one colour.

However, I conquered that difficulty by sending the boatswain away in one of the boats, with a compass, to steer in towards the land, and signal if he fell in with shallow water. Then, getting under way, I followed him, keeping the ship about a mile behind him, until I reached the surveyed waters of the channel known as " The Inner Route," between the Queensland coast and the reefs of the Great Barrier.

The first land I made was the north end of Hinchinbrook I., right ahead. As soon as I reached surveyed waters, I kept away to the southward for Townsville, where I anchored on November 29.

During the latter part of this voyage I had suffered much from bad health; a determination of blood to the head being, I believe, my principal ailment. This seriously affected my right eye, which had been a " lame duck" since 1859, when it was injured at Bombay.

In consequence of this, I left the *Heath* at Townsville, and repaired to Melbourne. There I put myself under the treatment of an eminent oculist, who operated on the eye, and turned me out again in three weeks fit for service once more.

Service? Yes! But not in the labour trade! My course was run, at any rate for the next three years, as regarded that!

From Melbourne I went to Townsville, and then to Brisbane. I stayed some time at the last-mentioned city, writing up my career in the labour trade to that date. The manuscript, when finished, I sent to my friends in England, whence it was returned to me about a year later. In the beginning of 1890, I sent it to England a second time, with additions. It was shipped on board the unfortunate s.s. *Quetta*, and now lies at the bottom of the sea in seventeen fathoms of water—worse luck!

Two days before I sailed in the *Heath* from Mackay, July 17, the *Hopeful*, barquentine, had arrived at Dungeness, at the mouth of the Herbert River, about fifty miles north-west of Townsville, bringing islanders from the Louisiade Archipelago. Her recruits were examined through interpreters, who were supposed to be thoroughly reliable. Afterwards, they were shown to be great scoundrels. The recruits were landed, and, as no complaints were made either by white men or Kanakas, as to any ill-doings, the voyage was, for a time, supposed to have been conducted in an honest and legal manner. But it had been simply a career of outrage, and even of murder.

The *Hopeful* was commanded by a young man who had never had charge of a ship before. No doubt he had gathered his impressions of the mode of obtaining recruits from outsiders. Her Government agent was an acknowledged drunkard, who acted up to his reputation. He owed his appointment to the Griffiths Ministry, then in power—a ministry pledged to do away with the trade. The recruiter was the same man who was in the ship when I met her at Blanche Bay, New Ireland, and he ought to have been debarred from serving in the trade long before.

In July, 1884, seven Kanakas, brought by the *Ceara* from the Engineer Is., Louisiade Archipelago, were brought before Mr. Wallace, sub-immigration agent at Townsville, charged with desertion from plantation work. During their examination by Mr. Wallace, they each and all said that they had been engaged for three *years*. The following year, when examined before the Royal Commission appointed to inquire into the manner of engagement of the islanders brought from the Archipelago by the *Ceara, Lizzie, Heath, Sibyl*, and *Forest King*, they asserted that they were recruited for much shorter periods of time.

Here is a specimen of the evidence given to Mr. Wallace at this time, before Cago, the rascally interpreter of the *Hopeful*, afterwards relied on by the Royal Commission, had had an opportunity of making them alter their statements.

Veraque said, through an interpreter :—

" He belong Burri-Burrigan; he know he come alonga *Ceara*; he come three *years*, work alonga sugar cane; when he got to Kalamia (plantation), was sent to trash cane; he no like that work; when he stop along his island, no work; when he go alonga sugar cane in Queensland, he too much work; no like him; suppose he work strong fellow, white fellow he no hit him; suppose he lazy, he hit him a little fellow. Sun, he come up, he go work; sun, he go down, he go sleep; no get him plenty ki-ki; plenty boy die; he think he die, too; wants to go alonga home."

Here was easy material to work upon. When the Royal Commission—composed of three ardent Griffithites—came along, how easy for Cago, the interpreter, to persuade the dissatisfied boys to say they were engaged for three *moons*, not for three *years*, knowing that by so lying they would be sent back home at once.

On the eleventh of August, the labour schooner *Forest King* arrived at Brisbane, in charge of Lieut. Bruce, of H.M.S. *Swinger*. This vessel had been recruiting in the Louisiade Archipelago. When lying off Anchor I.— no great distance from Teste I.—she had been boarded by Lieut. Torlesse, of H.M.S. *Swinger*, and seized because the recruits did not thoroughly understand their agreement. The following night, while the two ships were lying at anchor, sixteen of the recruits jumped overboard and deserted, frightened, no doubt, by the proximity of a ship of war.

The *Forest King* case was commenced in the Vice-Admiralty court at Brisbane, on October 8. It resulted in the ship being restored to the owners, with costs.

One of the principal witnesses for the prosecution was a teacher named Jerry, from Teste I. He wofully contradicted himself, and, it came out that this "Christian" darkie did not hesitate to lie through thick and thin, so long as he could stop his people from going to Queensland in the labour vessels. In this respect he had been probably influenced by Nicholas Minister and other bèche-de-mer fishers. These do not like to see the population thinned, because the more natives there are in the islands, the greater is the consumption of tobacco. Consequently, a larger amount of bèche-de-mer is collected by them to exchange for the weed.

Mr. MacFarlane, the missionary, in a letter to "The Brisbane Courier," September 10, 1884, said he preferred that natives should acquire experience under intelligent and gentlemanly planters in Queensland, rather than from bèche-de-mer collectors, and "beachcombers" in New Guinea.

The trial of those concerned in the *Hopeful* case came off in November. Captain Shaw, her master; Mr. McNeil, recruiter; Mr. Scholfield, G.A.; Freeman, mate; Williams, boatswain; Preston and Rogers, A.B.'s, were charged with kidnapping: McNeil and Williams with murder, likewise. The principal witness for the prosecution was Albert Messiah, a negro cook. He had vainly tried to extort blackmail, before the trial, from Shaw and others concerned. Another was Dingwall, carpenter, who had come out of gaol just before joining the *Hopeful*. The remaining witnesses were Kanakas, whose evidence was taken through different interpreters. The chief interpreter was Cago, who had taken part in the alleged misdeeds of the accused, and who was subsequently the chosen tool of the Royal Commission.

The evidence of Messiah and Dingwall was taken on oath. That of the other Kanakas was not. An amendment of the Criminal Law was passed by Parliament— *after* the prisoners had been committed for trial—to admit Kanaka evidence without the oath! The prison records of Messiah and Dingwall were such, that, apparently, the Ministry of that day deemed it necessary to alter the law of evidence in favour of savages, so as to bolster up the case for the prosecution.

Three of the crew, Tulloch, Binns, and Siebert, were not included in the indictment. The law officers of the Crown had taken their evidence, found it favourable to the accused, and—*did not call them before the Court!* Afterwards, in 1890, the then Minister for Justice, reporting on the *Hopeful* case, said :—

> It is a deplorable circumstance, however it may have occurred, that such material evidence then in the possession of the Crown Law Officers, and which was necessary to elucidate the truth, was not disclosed to those upon whom the onerous duty of trying the charges against the prisoners was imposed. In this particular, and in other matters already alluded to, the whole of the circumstances surrounding the cases, and the manner in which the evidence was obtained, were not laid before the court. Verdicts were arrived at upon partial information only, which, in my opinion, could scarcely have been arrived at if the full facts had been brought out.

There was doubtless much hard swearing on both sides; but, from the first, it was evident that the trial was a purely political one. Party feeling ran high at that time, and the Polynesian Labour Trade was the great question between the Government and the Opposition. The former was pledged to abolish the importation of cheap coloured labour. A verdict of "Guilty" against the prisoners in the *Hopeful* case, would help to damn the trade in the eyes of the electors.

Although the recruits had been landed at Townsville, or were employed near it, the offenders arrested there, and the owners of the *Hopeful* were a Townsville firm, the case was removed to Brisbane. The capital was *Anti-Kanaka*, which was sufficient reason for the transfer ; at Townsville, opinions were otherwise. It may also be asked why, since the alleged offences had been committed within the jurisdiction of the High Commissioner for the Western Pacific—the Governor of Fiji—the case was not sent to his court, as that of Kilgour had been. But that, again, might not have suited the political exigencies of the party in power!

Further, it would seem that Messiah was paid for his evidence. Mr. Rollwagen and Mr. Stout, both of Townsville, testified at the trial that Messiah had said that all had gone right on the voyage, but that he had a "down" on McNeil, and would pay him out. On the day before he left Townsville for Brisbane, Messiah said he had "a good thing on." He had got £50, and should get £500; that was better than cooking! Mr. G. E. Cooper, a publican, also stated that Messiah had told him he was getting a pound a day from the Government for his evidence.

What the South Sea Island witnesses' evidence was worth, may be judged from the following—an extract from the Chief Justice's notes of the trials:—

On Tuesday, November 15, 1884, Charley, under examination in the Supreme Court, says:—

"Me go to see Messiah plenty times; Messiah live South Brisbane; me go Messiah's house; Jack go Messiah's house; Harry go Messiah's house; Messiah talk about this plenty time; Messiah tell me to say I see McNeil fire gun; he tell me say I see boy dead."

On Monday, December 1, 1884, Charley, under examination in the Supreme Court, on the second day of the trial, says:—

"I know Messiah, cook; me speak here before; me make a mistake that time; I don't know where he lives; I no been go to his house; it was a mistake when I say last time 'Me, Jack, and Harry go and see Messiah plenty times'; Messiah did not talk to me plenty times about Williams shooting boy; I make mistake that time too; I not go to Messiah house; I tell Messiah live alonga South Brisbane."

The prisoners were all found guilty. McNeil and Williams were sentenced to death; Shaw and Scholfield were sentenced to imprisonment for life, the first three years in irons; Freeman was sentenced to ten years, two in irons; Preston and Rogers to seven years, one in irons. The death-sentence against McNeil and Williams was commuted to imprisonment for life. In 1890, all the prisoners were pardoned and liberated.

Another case was tried at the same time. Captain Louttit, master of the *Ethel*, Christopher Mills, G.A., and G. R. Burton, mate, were found guilty of kidnapping, and were sentenced to imprisonment for different terms. They were likewise pardoned in 1890.

In September, 1884, the *Ceara* took a large number of "returns" back to the New Hebrides. These natives had been engaged under the old regulations, which permitted them to purchase firearms and take them to their homes. The new law, forbidding the purchase and export of firearms, came into force before they left Queensland. They were naturally aggrieved at what must have seemed to them a breach of the agreement under which they had been recruited.

By the time the *Ceara* arrived at Sandwich I., it became evident that the "returns" on board intended to take their revenge out of the ship, as soon as a convenient opportunity presented itself. Fortunately, the *Ceara* fell in with H.M.S. *Miranda*, which convoyed her until all her passengers had been landed. Had it not been for this, it is more than probable that the crew of the *Ceara* would have fallen victims to the anger of the justly incensed islanders.

In October, 1884, Joseph Booth, an old companion of mine, was treacherously murdered by the natives at Port Stanley, Mallicolo I. About the same date, Peter Cullen and another were murdered at Lenurr I. Booth had been in the employment of the *Compagnie des Nouvelles Hebrides*. Consequently, his murderers were promptly punished by a French man-o'-war. I have been at the place since, and I wandered through the village unharmed. This I could never have done if matters had been left to British authorities to arrange.

A German trader was murdered at Tanna I. in the

same month. Shortly after, Captain Frier, of Cooktown, and another, were killed at Basilisk I., in the Louisiade. The brig *Emily*, Captain McQuaker, was fired at by natives of Espiritu Santo. Forty or fifty bullets struck the ship, rendering it a hazardous job to get her under way. More than sixty Snider rifles were in possession of the natives who attacked her, and these had been sold to them by French and German traders.

There was a great difference, at that time, in the treatment accorded to its subjects in the Western Pacific by the British Government, as compared to that which France and Germany dealt out to theirs. This took effect in such matters as the purchase of land from the natives, freedom of trade, protection of life and property, punishment of natives for outrages, and so forth. The attention of the Australian public was too frequently drawn to the subject, provoking such expressions of opinion as the following, which appeared in " The Brisbane Courier," January 6, 1885 :—

General Scratchley's statement as to his duties in connection with the settlement of New Guinea, and the reports we published the other day of doings in the South Sea Islands, furnished by masters of ships just returned from the islands, should open the eyes of Australians to the very unfavourable position in which the difference between the colonial policy of Great Britain, and that of Germany and France, is now placing the Australian people.

The writer went on to speak of the treatment that British subjects receive from their Government, comparing it with the assistance and protection afforded to French and German subjects by their respective Governments. Germany allows her subjects to purchase land from natives freely; Great Britain interposes obstacles. Consequently, Germany cannot recognize the validity of claims made by British subjects; and German ships of war threaten British settlers in the islands, should these raise any objection to Germans taking possession of the lands they have acquired. British subjects are not allowed to sell firearms to natives, even in a British Protectorate; French and German subjects are under no such restrictions. Germany has encouraged and aided the settlement of New Guinea by her subjects; Great Britain has peremptorily excluded hers, *although* Queensland contributes £15,000 to the British New Guinea Government; a sum that can only be used to enforce a blockade against those who have contributed it.

Going farther afield, the writer of this article pointed out that Great Britain is allowing Australia to be surrounded by possibly hostile communities; that the South Sea Island trade has been ruined, so far as Australia is concerned; that' Russia is advancing on India in one direction, while France, in Cochin and Siam, is encroaching on the other; that Germany has now obtained a sure footing in South Africa, on the borders of Cape Colony. From all of which the writer concluded that these steps had been taken by France and Germany in view of the coming dissolution of the British Empire.

Furthermore, the partitioning of New Guinea has taught the colonies two things: first, that Great Britain will neither defend nor allow them to defend what they deem their rights; second, that, through the different policies of Great Britain, France, and Germany in the Western Pacific, the power of the former in that part of the world is rapidly diminishing, and will soon disappear altogether. The article cited wound up with a warning that Australia must be prepared to act for herself. "To trust to England for support will be to lean upon a rotten reed!"

Tall talk, this, no doubt; but Australians know there is only too much truth in it. In the Pacific it is well known that commanders of British ships of war are restrained by their orders, when investigating charges of murder committed by natives upon British subjects, and are enjoined " to avoid bloodshed." Yet how is a murderer to be apprehended, when he has the cover of a thick forest at his back, with his whole tribe, probably his abettors in the crime, to defend him?

Natives of the New Hebrides and Solomon groups now know very well that, for the murder of a white man, or even for the destruction of a ship and all her crew, there is little fear of any punishment being inflicted

RECRUITS.

on them beyond the burning of a few thatched houses, and, possibly, the loss of some canoes and cocoanut trees. For they are sure to receive warning, and be afforded ample time to clear out of danger, before any firing takes place. As instances of this, I may cite the cases of the vessels, *Borealis, Janet Stewart, Young Dick*, and *Savo*; also the murders of Renton, Steadman, and Armstrong, Government agents. Such "magnanimous" treatment only serves to encourage natives to commit more murders;

for they do not understand condonation of an offence, they ascribe it to fear.

The raid of the party from the *Miranda*, across Lepers' or Aoba I., to punish the murderers of Renton and his companions, certainly gave the natives a better opinion of the white man's pluck and energy. However, in that case, the murderers escaped; the shooting of one woman and a few pigs, with the destruction of the village, being all that was effected.

Report even says that, when Captain Belbin's death was avenged, the commander of the *Dart* was reprimanded for what he did.

Some may say that white men have amply avenged themselves on the islanders, citing the case of the *Hopeful*, and some others of a similar sort. But the voyage of the *Hopeful* was an exception, and not the rule. No one execrated the deeds of MacNeil, Williams, and their companions, more than did other labour recruiters, especially such as had been engaged in the trade for any length of time.

Some missionaries also, especially those of the Presbyterian denomination, have cried out against the enormities of what they are pleased to term "the Queensland slave trade." But it must be recollected that many of their charges have been examined into and disproved. Some years ago, when Captain Bridges, of H.M.S. *Espiègle*, investigated charges brought by the Rev. Mr. Paton, of the New Hebrides Presbyterian Mission, the said charges were proved to be entirely without foundation. Yet, still, gentlemen of Mr. Paton's sort have by no means discontinued their unwarrantable outcries.

The stoppage of the sale of firearms to islanders was enforced, I suppose, in order to damage the labour trade of Queensland alone. At any rate, that is all the effect it had. The firearms trade at once passed entirely into the hands of the French and Germans, who are consequently more than able to compete with us in the New Hebrides and the Solomons.

In 1890, I saw two or three dozen Snider rifles, openly exposed for sale to natives, in a French store in Havannah Harbour, Sandwich I., while one of Her Majesty's ships was lying there. In the Solomons, three cases of "buying" boys with firearms also came under my notice.

The German vessel *Maria*, recruiting in 1890 for Samoan planters, at Port Adams, Maramasiki I., engaged seventy-two boys, giving a Snider and ammunition for each : the *Ubea* (German) took forty boys from Tiarro Bay, Guadalcanar I., the same year, the price given for each being a Snider and forty cartridges.

On January 6, 1891, I was off Fokinkava, on the northeast coast of Malayta I. The natives then informed me that a French vessel had left there two days previously, full of boys, for each of whom two Sniders and ammunition had been given. I have good reason to think that, if care is not taken to prevent it, a real slave trade will be established on that coast, for the benefit of the French and Germans. The people of Malayta have always practised slavery, though in a very limited way. The New Hebrideans are hardly advanced enough yet to appreciate "the peculiar institution" more than approximately.

The fact that foreigners are allowed, in a British protectorate, such as the southern portion of the Solomon group, to do what is forbidden to British subjects, while these are not allowed even to trade in foreign protectorates, is but the natural result of that cowardly policy which has caused us, of late years, to bully or make war upon small and weak communities, and to give way before stronger nations, that are better able to cope with us !

MAP V.

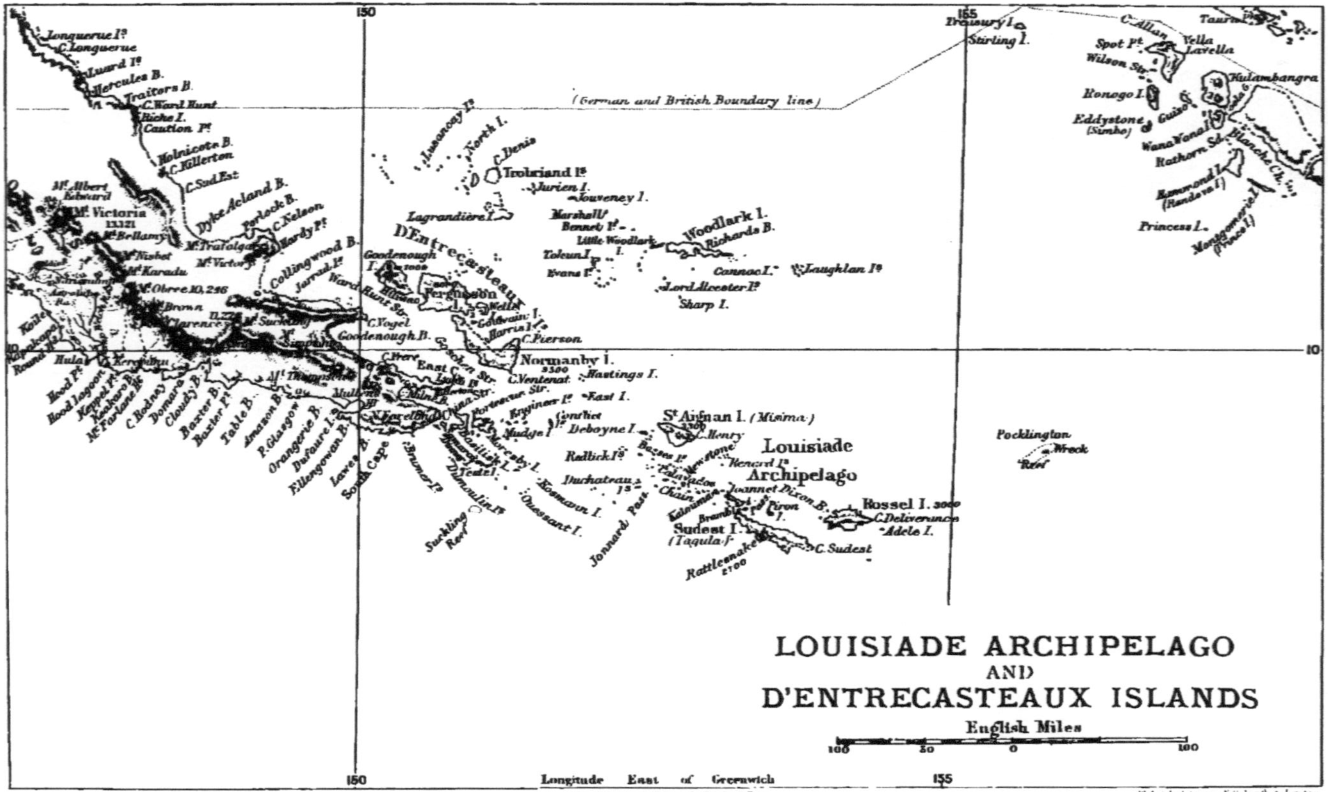

LOUISIADE ARCHIPELAGO
AND
D'ENTRECASTEAUX ISLANDS

CHAPTER XXII.

THE CRUISE OF THE *VICTORIA*, 1885.

The Griffith Ministry and the labour trade—Labourers abscond—A Royal Commission appointed—Its constitution—The interpreters—Mr. Rose's defence of them—Underhand practices—Examination of labourers—Government agents not called—The Report of the Commission—My letter to " The Brisbane Courier"—I court inquiry—And am denied it—I go to Sydney—I am engaged as pilot by the A.S.N. Co.—Fitting out the Victoria—*Mr. Griffith objects to me—The Company stands by me—Appointed, and go to Brisbane—I am served with a writ—Bonds demanded !—The official party—Newspaper reporters—Our fighting strength—Nordenfeldts required !—Mr. Hodgson's offer—My berth not " all skittles and beer"—" After-guard" abuse—I speak up—" Whiskey-skins !"—Some labourers refuse to go home—Mr. Lawes' opinion—How the boys greeted me—Dixon—His report to the Commissioners—He tells me the truth of it—Cago's proceedings—At sea—I visit the islanders' quarters—Dante's Inferno !—Bad management—The doctor's orders—I am placed under restriction—" Land ahead !"—" Where are we ?"—Fisherman I.—In danger—" Pilot, take the ship in !"—A narrow escape—Piloting—It takes a hurricane to put me ashore !*

THE atrocities committed by the crew of the *Hopeful* during that vessel's last voyage, together with the verdict of "guilty" against the offenders, proved a sore blow to the labour trade. Very naturally, the unsophisticated public began to ask if it was possible that the stories told by missionaries and other opponents of the trade, about kidnappings and murders, might not be founded upon facts. It was only necessary for the Griffith Ministry to deal another blow, fairly or otherwise, at the trade, and a soft spot was soon found whereon to inflict it.

The islanders brought from the East Cape of New Guinea, and from the Louisiade Archipelago, had proved almost worthless as labourers. A sudden fall in the price of sugar in January, 1885, made the planters only too glad to get rid of them, even at some loss.

These islanders had all been employed on northern plantations. Nearly every day some of them absconded, took to the bush, and even stole boats, in which to coast northward, in hopes of so reaching their homes. Some succeeded in doing so; many sickened and died. A few who got as far as Cooktown, or Torres Straits, perhaps, were picked up and forwarded to their homes. Some of these, it was said, stated that they had not understood they were to serve so long a time as three years. The truth or falsity of this statement cannot now be ascertained. In consequence of this state of things, three gentlemen, all devoted adherents of the Griffith Ministry, were appointed under a Royal Commission, December 23, 1884, to examine recruits brought from New Guinea and the neighbouring islands, and to report accordingly. These three gentlemen were: Mr. Buckland, member for Bulimba; Mr. Kinnaird Rose, a lawyer fresh from Great Britain; and Mr. Milman, the police magistrate of Cooktown. The last was the only one of the three who had any acquaintance with the character of Polynesians, and his experience was of the slightest. Mr. W. C. Lawrie was appointed secretary. Of him it was subsequently said that he had "resided in New Guinea for about a year, had acquired a fair knowledge of many of the dialects, and become acquainted with much of the southern and south-eastern portions of the island." This was saying a great deal more than was true.

Three interpreters accompanied the party: Cago, who had been on the *Hopeful*; Diene, a mission teacher, and as fit a tool for any dirty work as the first; with another islander, named Toiamina.

After the "Commissioners" had completed their

labours, it was extensively rumoured that, at the different plantations visited, the interpreters, especially Cago, had been amongst the boys previous to their examination, and had schooled them in the replies they were to make to the Commissioners' questions. So instructed, the boys were to say that they had understood, at the time of their several engagements, that they were to remain in Queensland only a few months, not for three years. They were persuaded that, if they admitted they had been engaged for three years, they would have to stay, and work out that term; but if, on the contrary, they said two or three months, they would be sent home at once, with plenty of trade.

It was in consequence of these reports, I suppose, that Mr. Kinnaird Rose addressed a letter to "The Brisbane Courier," which made its appearance in the issue of August 4, 1885. In this he stated :—

> Cago was never permitted to speak to the labourers, except in the presence of the Commission. He accompanied the Commissioners, in the same buggy, to and from Ingham and Hamleigh ; he stayed in the same hotel with the Commissioners at Ingham ; he had no possible opportunity of visiting the plantation alone, without the knowledge of the Commissioners ; he never did so visit the plantation for the purpose described, or for any other purpose. Moreover, Cago was under my own eye for six months. I made a careful study of his character and disposition, and I assert—of course, for what it is worth—not that he was incapable of so acting and lying, but that, as a matter of fact, he did not so act and lie.

Well might Mr. Rose say that his assertion was to be taken "for what it is worth!" Fancy keeping Cago "under his own eye" for six months, while travelling about from one place to another! And where were the other interpreters all the while?

As a matter of fact, several persons connected with the Commission, and one or other of the interpreters—Cago, I was told—*did* visit a number of islanders one evening at the Immigration Depot on Ross I., Townsville, previous to their examination, conversed on that subject, and distributed tobacco among them. Similar things were done at other places, and witnesses could be found, even at the present day, who would prove it.

There can be little doubt that no opportunity was missed of coaching up the islanders beforehand, so that they should say only what was convenient. Whether this was done with the knowledge of the Commissioners, or not, of course I am unable to say.

The Commissioners commenced their work at Townsville, on January 6, 1885. They visited every plantation where natives from New Guinea or its vicinity were employed; on the Johnstone, Herbert, and Pioneer Rivers, and in the delta of the Burdekin. They held thirty meetings, and examined 480 islanders, presumably labourers, among them "two natives of the South Sea Islands, being a portion of the boats' crew of the *Hopeful.*"

Are we to suppose, then, that no other islanders, who had been boatmen in any of the vessels concerned, were examined? Well, I know that some *were* examined; yet their testimony was not included in the Commissioners' Report. Four of the boatmen I had employed in the Louisiade were then working as free labourers on the Herbert River. I met them there myself the following year. These boys gave me a long account of the questions that had been put to them by the Commissioners, together with their answers.

The Commissioners stated in their Report, that "It would have been desirable, the Commission thought, to have examined the Government agents on board the vessels which had recruited the islanders, the subject of inquiry; but it was found that they had either left the colony, or were out of reach."

The three Government agents who had accompanied me on my cruises in the Louisiade *were all in Brisbane,* where they were well known, at the very time the Commissioners made their Report; and they had been there for a good while before.

The Report itself, as submitted to the Governor on April 10, is too long for insertion, but the gist of it is contained in the following extract from a Mackay paper :—

Report of the Polynesian Commission.

The Report of the Polynesian Commission has been published. The report is a lengthy document, and deals fully with the whole subject of recruiting on eight different voyages. The recruiting vessels are dealt with in detail. The conclusions arrived at by the Commission are as follows :—" Regarding the voyage of the *Ceara*, our opinion is that all the recruits brought on this voyage were induced to go on board on false pretences ; that the nature of their agreements was never fully explained to them ; that they had little or no comprehension of the kind of work they had to perform ; and that the period for which they had agreed to come was in no single instance three years. Regarding the voyage of the *Lizzie*, we are of opinion that the nature of their agreement was never clearly explained to or understood by them, and that the method of recruiting was cruelly deceptive, and altogether illegal. Regarding the second voyage of the *Ceara*, the Commission are of opinion that a system of deliberate fraud was practised in engaging all recruits during that voyage. As to the second voyage of the *Lizzie*, on a review of the whole of the evidence as to the recruiting on this voyage, we are of opinion that while some natives were forcibly kidnapped, all were allured on board by false statements ; that the nature of the agreements to which they subsequently attached their marks, was deliberately misrepresented to them, and that they had no clear understanding that they were coming to Queensland to work on sugar plantations for three years." Somewhat similar opinions are expressed with regard to the voyages of the *Sibyl*, the *Forest King*, and the *Heath*. With reference to the notorious voyage of the *Hopeful*, the Report states that the history of this cruise is one long record of deceit, cruel treachery, deliberate kidnapping, and cold-blooded murder. The number of human beings whose lives were sacrificed can never be accurately known, but in addition to the two men killed at Sonorod, for which offence McNeil and Williams were convicted, there is, in the opinion of the Commission, abundant evidence of many other murders."

I was then in Brisbane, and learning from a Maryborough paper that Mr. Griffith, who had perused the Report before it was presented to the Governor, had, in a speech at that place, made some allusion to it in connection with kidnapping, I addressed the following letter to the editor of " The Brisbane Courier," which appeared in the same issue as the full Report of the Royal Commission.

> *To the Editor of "The Brisbane Courier."*
>
> SIR,—Three weeks ago I addressed a letter to you, which appeared in your columns, commenting on some words of Mr. Griffith's at the late Maryborough banquet. He accused me and others of obtaining Polynesian recruits from the vicinity of New Guinea—I took none from the mainland—by fraud or force. His accusation was founded on the lying and interested evidence of Kanakas. Mr. Griffith further stated that the Commissioners' Report would be published shortly. He has been in possession of this Report three weeks, but I have heard nothing of any result. Weeks previous to the Report, I was told at the Immigration Office that I was debarred from going to the islands in the labour trade, until, at any rate, the Report was published, but no specific reasons were assigned.
>
> Twice I applied for an interview with the Premier, but was told it was impossible, through press of public business. I have had employment offered me twice, but was debarred from accepting it. Even here this groundless accusation stands in my way.
>
> I have been ten years in the trade, and have always acted in accordance with both the letter and the spirit of the law to the best of my ability; I court inquiry into all my actions; the only unpleasantness with the Immigration Office having been when I could not agree with drunken or otherwise incompetent Government agents.
>
> If I have done wrong, how is it that I am at liberty and not hunted into gaol alongside of the *Hopeful* and *Ethel* unfortunates? But, if not guilty, why should I be punished by being debarred from engaging in that branch of my profession for which my long experience peculiarly fits me?
>
> It is a Briton's birthright to have a fair trial before punishment; when Mr. Griffith denies me that, he may be acting as a Queensland politician and minister, but not as an impartial judge.
>
> I am, sir, your obedient servant,
> W. T. WAWN,
> Late Master, Polynesian Labour Trade.

What more could I say? I think this letter was a fair challenge to the Government to put me on my trial for kidnapping. For, surely, if there was sufficient evidence to prove that the islanders I had brought had been kidnapped, and that they must be sent back home, and that their employers, who had already spent so much money to introduce them into the Colony, should be deprived of their services, then I, who had brought them, must have been guilty of kidnapping. But "the glorious uncertainty of the law" is often a very puzzling thing to a sailor.

I remained unmolested, as did all the other masters, Government agents, and crews of the five vessels in which those islanders who had been examined before the Royal Commissioners had been brought to the Colony.

The labour trade being now closed to me, I went to Sydney, about the latter end of May, to try and find other employment. At that time, the Geographical Society of New South Wales was preparing to send a party to explore the Fly River, in New Guinea. A ship-master who had had experience amongst savages was required to take the command. I put in an application for the post, along with about forty others, and I stood a very fair chance of obtaining the appointment. Unluckily for me, I was informed that Sir Edward Strickland, the President of the Society, objected to employ any one who had had any connection with the labour trade. So, the evening before the committee made its decision, I withdrew my name.

I think it was in the last week of April, that, one morning, my attention was called to a "personal" in "The Sydney Morning Herald":—

"Captain Wawn call on manager A.S.N. Co."

Away I went, accordingly, to the Company's offices on Circular Quay, wondering what was in the wind. Captain Tronton, the manager, soon enlightened me. The Queensland Government was treating with the A.S.N. Co. for the charter of one of their steamers— the *Victoria*, a roomy but slow vessel of some 900 tons register. She was to carry back to their homes those islanders the late Royal Commission had declared to have been kidnapped. Captain Tronton wished to know if I would give my services as pilot, and what my terms would be. Of course I jumped at the offer. As to terms, since it was impossible to say how long the trip might last, considering that, from what Captain Tronton told me, it seemed that it was to be a sort of "Royal Progress," I asked for a first-class master's monthly wages, which were granted.

As soon as our agreement had been signed, Captain Tronton wired the news to the manager in Brisbane. I went on board the *Victoria*, finding carpenters already busy fitting her "'tween decks" with the usual bunks, constructing hatch-covers, a cooking galley for the islanders, etc.

The intention was to return about four hundred and sixty boys. As soon as I descended to the lower deck of the steamer, however, I was certain that there would not be sufficient accommodation for that number, if the regulations of the Queensland Polynesian Labour Act were adhered to. Subsequent measurements proved that I was right; for the whole space in the "'tween decks" was sufficient for only two hundred and fifty-eight, while some of that was occupied by the machinery of the steam-launch.

For two days I hung about the *Victoria*, with nothing to do but to give a little information about the fittings and the requisite charts, etc. Then "a change came o'er the spirit of my dream." A telegram arrived from the Company's manager in Brisbane, who informed us that Mr. Griffith objected to Captain Wawn accompanying the *Victoria*.

"Never mind," said Captain Tronton, "we'll make that all right. At any rate, they shall not have the ship unless they find me a pilot as experienced as yourself; and, if all is true that is said about you, they won't be able to do that. This is Thursday; give a look in on Monday, say, and I think the matter will be settled then. Meantime, put in your account for two days' pay."

This I did. On Monday the manager showed me another telegram, saying that I was to accompany the *Victoria* as pilot. The Queensland ministry had had to give in. No other pilot was forthcoming, and it was a case of "no pilot, no ship." So there was I, the reputed kidnapper of about half of the islanders to be returned in the *Victoria*, receiving good wages to take them back home again!

Verily, I think that those who stigmatized the cruise of the *Victoria* a ridiculous farce, were not far out in their reckoning.

I left Sydney in the *Victoria* for Brisbane, our first port of call in Queensland, on Tuesday, June 2, 1885, arriving at Brisbane on the following Friday. Of course I was not then doing any pilotage duty, but was simply a passenger. My bargain was to act as responsible pilot in waters I was acquainted with, viz., the Louisiade Archipelago, and to assist the master, Captain Ballistier, whenever we encountered any intricate navigation among reefs and islands, whether I was acquainted with them or not.

We had just steamed up alongside the A.S.N. Co.'s wharf at Brisbane, and the crew were engaged in mooring the ship, when an individual with a long red-sealed envelope in his hand popped his head into Captain Ballistier's cabin on deck—where he and I were then sitting—and asked :—

"Is Captain Wawn on board here?"

I answered in the affirmative, and was promptly served with a writ, or summons, or something of the sort. It came from the Bailiff of the Supreme Court, and was a demand for the payment by me of the sum of £1,500 bond money, £500 for each of my three voyages to the Louisiade Archipelago—two in the *Lizzie* and one in the *Heath* — under the "Pacific Island Labourers' Act" of 1880!!

I felt proud. I had never owed so much in my life

before, and I knew, by this time, that I was tolerably safe from any prosecution for kidnapping. I handed this precious paper to my bondsmen's lawyer in Brisbane, and heard nothing more of it until more than a year after. The bonds were never paid, so my bondsmen—Messrs. Burns, Philp & Co., owners of the *Lizzie* and the *Heath*—informed me. But I was told that some much smaller sum *was* paid to the Queensland Government, to avoid the expense of an action. Burns, Philp & Co. are a commercial firm, and they looked to cash profit before honour.

The *Victoria*, having discharged such passengers and cargo as she had brought from Sydney—notably, a portion of Chiarini's Circus—left Brisbane again on June 8. She now had on board the party of officials who were to superintend the landing of the islanders; with their guard, twelve men of the Naval Brigade, under a non-commissioned officer.

The officials were—Mr. Hugh Romilly, representing the Imperial Government, with his Secretary, Mr. Stanley Harris, and his under-Secretary, Mr. Geo. Harris; Mr. Chester, representing the Queensland Government, whom we may call the G.A. of the party, with *his* Secretary, Mr. Lawrie, lately Secretary to the Royal Commission; Dr. Patrick Smith, a "new-chum" emigrant medico, correspondent of a Glasgow religious paper, who wrote glowing accounts of the missionaries' work in the islands, carefully keeping back such incidents as would not redound to their credit; and Cago, the interpreter.

We had also three newspaper reporters—Messrs. W. B. Livesey, of "The Brisbane Courier," Mr. W. J. Lyne, of "The Sydney Morning Herald," and Mr. Herbert, of "The Townsville Standard," whose presence appeared anything but welcome to the Government party. These did not care to have "a chiel" among them "takin' notes" while they were enjoying what they evidently intended to be a picnic. Last of all came a piano. Abundant "grog" of all descriptions had been shipped early, to make sure that *it* was not left behind.

Mr. A. Musgrave, nephew of the Governor of Queensland, also travelled in the *Victoria* from Brisbane, as a passenger, as far as Port Moresby, New Guinea.

Our fighting strength, in case of any collision with the natives, which the Government party seemed to think was very probable, amounted to ten gentlemen in the cuddy, armed with rifles of the latest fashion, shot guns, and revolvers; twelve men of the Naval Brigade and one non-commissioned officer, with their rifles and bayonets; the ship's company of thirty-seven whites and two Kanakas, for whom Snider rifles and revolvers were provided. Lastly, there was myself, with a "double barrel" and a revolver. This imposing force was strong enough to sweep the whole of the Louisiade! Yet it was not enough, apparently, for it was actually proposed that we should ship two Nordenfeldt guns as well! Possibly this might even have been done, had not somebody growled out that "they had better ship a hundred pounder 'Armstrong' whilst they were about it, and so *prove* themselves to be d——d fools, and not leave people in doubt!"

The Nordenfeldts were *not* shipped!

A friend and old schoolfellow of mine, the late Mr. Samuel Hodgson, merchant and shipowner, told me that he had offered to take the four hundred and odd islanders back to their homes in his vessels, subject to the regulations of the Polynesian Labour Act, for £5 per head. The Griffith Ministry declined his offer, preferring to throw away considerably more of the public money by making a virtuous "anti-slavery" splatter over "the cruise of the *Victoria*."

Leaving Brisbane, the comfortable old *Vic* steamed eight knots an hour to Mackay, off which port we anchored on the 11th, and went on again the same evening. There we received some thirty boys on board—the exact number I cannot remember—and proceeded on to Townsville, where we shipped the rest of the return islanders, making up the total number to four hundred and four.

Shortly after we anchored, a telegram was received by Captain Ballistier from the manager of the A.S.N. Co. in Brisbane, saying that Mr. Griffith desired that the pilot (myself) should not be allowed to land at any place where boys were to be put ashore, for fear of retaliation and consequent bloodshed. I determined that whenever a convenient opportunity should occur I *would* land, in spite of Mr. Griffith, and I subsequently did so. I was serving the A.S.N. Co., not Mr. Griffith, and was, to a certain extent, even independent of the master of the ship.

By this time I had found out that my berth was not "all skittles and beer." If I had, so far, no pilotage work to do, at any rate I had to put up with a good deal of "after-guard" abuse.

Before leaving Sydney, one of the state-rooms in the main cabin was allotted to me by Captain Tronton. I slept in it, and had my meals at the cabin table with the other passengers until we arrived at the Louisiade. After that I generally slept in the chart-room, on the bridge, and often had my meals there; not only in order to keep a better watch over the safety of the ship, but on account of the frequent references to "slavers," "kidnappers," etcetera, which too often greeted my ears when I went aft.

Nevertheless, I kept possession of my state-room throughout the trip, notwithstanding all efforts to dispossess me of it. As for unpleasant allusions, I had been used to them so long in Queensland that I did not pay much heed to the whiskey-begotten epithets I heard on board the *Victoria*—between eight and nine in the evening was the time when they became loudest. When my navigation was impugned, however, I got riled.

One evening, when we were off Cape Pierson, Normanby I., I took the bull by the horns and faced Mr. Chester, who boasted he had served Her Majesty as an officer (E.I.C.) for twenty years—nine months of each year in harbour, I suppose, and the other three getting in and out of it!—and gave him such a talking to as I think he little expected; and then Mr. Romilly chipped in, and, I think, *he* made little by *his* motion either. After that they let me alone, confining themselves to their own troubles; for they had already begun to squabble amongst themselves.

And no mean squabbling either, when one potentate applies the term "whiskey-skin" to another potentate, and that potentate looks as if he would like to "go for" the first potentate, and is only restrained from doing so by the first potentate's big stick! A scene such as I have faintly hinted at occurred one day in the saloon of the *Victoria*, causing me to chuckle—inwardly.

But let us go back to Townsville. Before we sailed, the Admiral of the Australian Squadron had been telegraphed to with a request that one of the war-ships should be sent to attend on the *Victoria*, in case of her getting on a reef! Luckily, all the Admiral's ships were better employed, so we were spared this crowning act of folly.

After all, the whole of the Louisiade and New Guinea boys, then in Queensland, did not return home with us. Notwithstanding all the inducements held out to them, *fifty-eight refused to abandon their employers and break their agreement!* These fifty-eight worked out their three years' in Queensland.

The Rev. Mr. Lawes, a missionary in New Guinea, addressed a letter to "The Brisbane Courier," July 25, 1885. In this he regretted that these fifty-eight boys were not *obliged* by the Government to return home. He considered that the chiefs and their friends would not be satisfied by the assertions of Messrs. Romilly and Chester that the boys did not *want* to return home till they had fulfilled their engagements. Apparently, Mr. Lawes considered that these boys ought not to enjoy any free-will at all in the matter.

Many of the islanders we had shipped at Townsville had been brought to Queensland by me. When they came on board I was on shore. On my return to the ship, I think some of the Government party were rather astonished to see several of these natives meet me at the gangway, shake hands with me, and greet me in a most friendly manner. Even such of them as could not speak more than a word or two of English, gave me a friendly grin, and often a hand-clasp. This was not the sort of welcome one would have expected a kidnapper to receive from his victims!

Among those who greeted me was one named Dixon, a European name given to him by the bêche-de-mer collectors for whom he had worked. Dixon and another, "Sandfly,"—he had served for some time on board H.M.S. *Sandfly*,—had been specially mentioned in the Report of the Royal Commission, and what they had said to the Commissioners had "knocked" me.

In their Report of the first voyage of the *Lizzie*, the Commissioners had said :—

"The first boy presented—at Hamleigh plantation—was Dixon, who had quite a pat story that he had been recruited to 'work sugar in Queensland for three yams' (years)."

Then, a little further on, they say :—

"At the close of our examination of the Hamleigh labourers, which lasted a week, Dixon and Sandfly appeared and withdrew their former statements, which had been made under fear of Mr. Cowley, and said they had been recruited for only three moons."

It was this that had puzzled me—that two islanders should come forward and *voluntarily* admit to the Commissioners themselves that they had told them a lie a week before. Much more likely they would have said to themselves: "A week has passed; the white men have not found out the lie; let it go."

No. There must have been somebody in the background; and very possibly, I thought, Cago had been that somebody.

When I questioned Dixon that day on the deck of the *Victoria* about this recantation of theirs, he said :—

"Cappen, you been take me along three year. Me, Sandfly, both speak, three year. By-and-by, boy belong island; he speak : 'What for you speak three *year*? Very good, you speak three *moon*. Suppose you no speak three moon, altogether, boy, he stop Queensland three year. No good.' Me think all the boy want to kill me; then me, Sandfly, go back and speak we come along three moon."

"Did Cago ever talk to you about what you should say? Did he say you would go back soon if you said 'three moon'?" I asked.

"Yes; Cago, he speak all-a-same plenty time."

Not much time was lost at Townsville, for we steamed out of Cleveland Bay again, going north, about 11 p.m. the same night, June 13. The following afternoon we ran through the Barrier by the Flora Pass, and headed for Port Moresby in New Guinea.

It took us two days to run the distance—420 miles, across to Port Moresby; for the old *Vic* was quite contented with eight knots an hour, and occasionally a little better when she had her square canvas set, and a fresh breeze aft. I think it was during one of these two evenings at sea that the three newspaper reporters paid a visit with me to the islanders' quarters on the lower deck. Of course they were on the look-out for material for their different papers, so I took care to point out to them anything that seemed worth their attention.

It was supposed that the ship had been fitted out in accordance with the regulations of the Polynesian Labour

Act. However, the amount of space allotted for the islanders' accommodation was far less than it should have been. We had 404 islanders on board, and the space between decks was not more than sufficient for 258. I took the trouble to measure it, and make calculations. Out of this, sufficient room for nine or ten men had been allotted to two sick boys alone.

Looking down the fore-hatch, we saw 128 boys scattered, asleep on planks thrown down on the top of the coals in the lower hold. As we peered down the open hatch, and the dim rays of our lantern made visible the figures of the slumbering islanders, sprawling about in all sorts of attitudes on the coals, some ten or twelve feet beneath us, somebody remarked that the sight reminded him of an illustration in Dante's "Inferno."

"Hell asleep, with the fire out!" rejoined another.

The smell arising from 404 "nigs" would not be a pleasant one at any time. When jammed together as these were, on a warm night in the tropics, on board a steamer with furnaces at full blast, the smell of that lower deck was something that no man would revel in. To make matters worse, when the first mate spoke of washing and cleansing the lower deck, the morning after we left Townsville, Mr. Chester and Dr. Smith objected to it, being under the impression that the damp would cause many of the islanders to catch cold.

It seems almost incredible that from June 11, when the first batch was shipped at Mackay, and the 13th, when we took the rest on board at Townsville, notwithstanding that many of the boys, when outside the "Barrier," were sea-sick and unable to get on deck to the latrines, that lower deck in the mainhold was not cleansed, except for a very slight touch with the broom, for nearly three weeks. It is a wonder to me how even the islanders were able to sleep there and keep their health. Surely a good washing could have done them no more harm on board the *Victoria* than on board a "labour" schooner, where the "'tween decks" are washed out thoroughly every morning when the weather suits.

But, of course, "new chum" doctors must know more about islanders than a "slaving skipper."

This was my first and last visit to the lower deck of the *Victoria*. One of the Naval Brigade men, who, in his turn, was "shadowed" by one of the crew, had followed us round the islanders' quarters, and reported every word and action of ours to the authorities.

Next day an order was issued to the sentry at the main-hatch by Mr. Chester, which ran to this effect:—

"The pilot is not to be allowed below in the islanders' quarters, as his presence and conversation tend to make the boys discontented."

On the evening of the 17th, Captain Ballistier reckoned we were about twenty miles from the opening in the New Guinea barrier reef leading to Port Moresby. The wind was then blowing a moderate south-east "trade," with a good deal of sea on, and fine but very hazy weather. The ship was brought to the wind at half-speed, first on one tack and then on the other, and we rolled and tumbled about all night in a most uncomfortable manner. At daylight next morning no land was in sight, the haze preventing us from making out anything beyond five or six miles from the ship. However, we were steaming in what Captain Ballistier thought was the right direction for Port Moresby.

About 10 a.m. there was a cry of "Land ahead!" Looming up through the haze, a small, low, wooded islet of inconsiderable size appeared right ahead.

Fisherman I., near the entrance to Port Moresby, the captain thought. Mr. Chester presently came up on to the bridge with two Port Moresby boys we were taking home. They had been serving as interpreters on board a man-of-war. He was of the same opinion.

This gentleman, by the way, had been to Port Moresby on two former occasions. As an old naval officer, he might have been supposed to have "taken stock" of its surroundings.

The ship was then kept away to pass to leeward of the island, as Mr. Chester and the boys said there was a good passage on that side, although the passage that has been recommended and surveyed is on the south-east.

Now, it happened that the island ahead of us seemed to me to be hardly a quarter the size of Fisherman I., as it was represented on the Admiralty Chart. I ventured to give the captain a hint that perhaps they were mistaken, *although* Mr. Chester had been to Port Moresby, and I had never been near it.

I ran my eye over the chart, getting the coast-line—islets and reefs—for twenty miles on each side of the port well impressed on my mind. Then I went up to the fore-yard, whence I had a good "bird's-eye" view.

The islet was small, and from it a barrier reef, enclosing a lagoon, with the loom of high land beyond it, stretched away south-east for miles, until lost in the haze. To the north-west, on the other side of the islet, there were no breakers. A long, sunken coral spit, showing a bright light green amidst the blue of the deep water, ran out for a mile or more. The ship was then heading straight for this spit at half-speed. I saw immediately where we were.

I was soon down from aloft, and in the chart-room on the bridge.

"Here's where we are, Captain," I said, putting my finger on "Aplin I." on the chart. "That's not Fisherman I.; we are miles to leeward of it."

"That *is* Fisherman I.," asserted a gruff voice outside.

The skipper was puzzled for a moment.

"Do as you think fit, Captain," I continued. "Keep on, and in a quarter of an hour you'll have your ship on that spit ahead. We're close to it now."

Captain Ballistier then saw the danger.

"Pilot, will you take the ship into Port Moresby?

You've had more experience than I have amongst reefs."

" I will," I said.

Then to the man at the wheel :—

" Hard-a-starboard ! " At the same moment I jerked the telegraph handle to " Full speed ahead ! "

We were so close to the reef, with the ship's head lying about north, that there was hardly room to turn her eastward, the shortest way to bring her head to south-east, in which direction we now had to steer, dead in the teeth of wind and sea.

" By Jove ! " I thought to myself ; " if I've made a mistake and a fool of myself, *what* a commencement to my piloting, and won't they grin aft ! "

But I had made no mistake. Three hours' hard steaming brought us up to the real Fisherman I., low and wooded like Aplin I., but six times as long, and thus easily distinguishable from it.

On our way, I had made a rough sketch on paper of the entrance to, and anchorage in, Port Moresby, from the Admiralty plan. With this stowed into the breast-pocket of my grey shirt—white shirts and blue cloth won't do for a fore-yard, with the smoky top of a steamer's funnel near you—I climbed up aloft, and piloted the ship into harbour and safe anchorage.

This mode of piloting may seem *infra dig.* to many masters of ships, but it is absolutely necessary in the un-surveyed waters of coral seas. Even where surveyed, if they have not been beaconed or buoyed, it is impossible to distinguish a sunken patch with, say, ten or twelve feet of water on it, from the bridge or quarter-deck, in time to avoid "knocking it."

I know three or four skippers in the labour trade who would scorn to go above the shear poles. But they have all left their marks, here and there, on coral patches among the New Hebrides and the Solomon groups.

I thank my stars that I have a good eye for colour, so

as to detect shallow water. Also that I have some ability for climbing—first contracted in my apple-stealing days, I suppose—so that I have managed to get through my Pacific experience without damaging any reefs, barring once, in the *Bobtail Nag*, and then it took a whole hurricane to put me ashore.

CHAPTER XXIII.

THE CRUISE OF THE VICTORIA (continued).

Port Moresby—Anabata—Native houses—Our steam-launch and boats — Complaints — Jerry, the interpreter—Prohibitions — Trading not permitted—Planning the route—My duties—First mistake of the officials—Protection Bay—I am forbidden to go ashore—And disobey—Interviewing the natives—Official "funk"—"Savage and warlike!"—Killerton—An imposing ceremony—Mr. Romilly's great speech—"A fair acquaintance with the dialects!"—Backwards and forwards—Kidnapped!—A peace-offering declined—The Samoa—My letters opened—Another ceremony—A "jolly" reception—The Woodlark Is.—Hazy weather—Landing in the dark—The lower deck washed—Hiliwao—Last speech of the voyage—I take a nap—A glass of whiskey—Pumping the pilot!—Direction of the voyage accorded to me—Our list of passengers—Dodging about—Bramble Pass—Difficult navigation—My skirmishes with the skipper—Coral Haven—Sudest I.—The last boy landed—Extract from "The Brisbane Courier"—How the boys were coached up—The doctor's stories—An unpublished incident—Return to Syaney—End of the cruise.

PORT Moresby has been so often described in various books on New Guinea, that I need say but little about it. It is a large bay, about four miles long, on the south-western coast of the south-eastern promontory of New Guinea. Mt. Owen Stanley, supposed to be the highest mountain in the island, towers up 13,000 feet above it, some forty miles inland.

The land surrounding Port Moresby is poor, and fresh water is not plentiful. The principal native village, Anabata, is close to the European settlement, on the south-eastern shore. I rambled through this village during our stay, which only lasted twenty-four hours.

Anabata strongly reminded me of what I have read of the abodes of the ancient lake-dwellers. The houses are all built on piles over the water, just below high-water mark, which obviates any necessity for sewers, apparently. They are generally two-storied, the lower floor being open at the sides and ends. They have high thatched roofs, peaked up at either end. The lower storey usually serves as a depository for fishing gear, provisions, etc., the inmates living on the uppermost. Capital houses are these in case of attack from native enemies, armed with no better weapons than spears and arrows. Nor would a gale of wind hurt them much; for the barrier reef effectually prevents heavy seas from entering the port.

Two English missionaries were settled here: the Revs. Lawes and Chalmers. Our officials were desirous that one of these gentlemen should accompany them on the cruise, but Mr. Chalmers was absent somewhere along the coast, and Mr. Lawes could not leave on that account.

I have already intimated that we carried a steam-launch, the engine of which occupied a portion of the space below, in the islanders' quarters, the boat itself taking up no little room on deck. The ship also carried six ordinary boats, more than sufficient for all the work required. Besides the regular crew, two Polynesian boatmen had been shipped in Sydney, and two or three more were engaged at Port Moresby.

However, neither our own boats nor our boatmen suited the officials. They saw fit to borrow the missionaries' surf-boat, erroneously termed a "whale-boat." When the work of landing commenced, the Kanaka boatmen were rejected in favour of Naval Brigade men. They would have found out the difference had any of the boats been capsized!

Great complaints were made, on our return, that the A.S.N. Co. had not provided the ship with proper boatmen—quite without reason. But, from the very beginning of the voyage, it seemed to be the bounden duty of some of the officials to find all the faults they could, or imagine them, in the ship and her outfit.

Mr. Musgrave left us, landing at Port Moresby on the morning of the eighteenth. We then weighed anchor, and, passing out through the barrier, we steamed along the coast towards South Cape, where it was supposed we had two boys to land. On nearing the cape, however, it was discovered that no natives of that part were on board; so we kept away again for Suckling Reef, on the south-west of the Louisiade. On the eastern side of this is Basilisk Passage, through which Teste I. and the south-eastern capes of New Guinea can be reached.

Shortly after daylight on the twentieth, we cleared Suckling Reef, and steamed northward to Teste I., off which we brought to, allowing the Government party to visit the shore. There they engaged Jerry, a well-known mission teacher. He had been one of the witnesses in the *Forest King* case, and when under cross-examination then had proved himself to be an accomplished successor of Ananias. Jerry's services were now required as an interpreter.

That morning a written notice was displayed on the quarter-deck of the *Victoria*, which occasioned no little sensation and adverse criticism. It informed the gentlemen of the Press that, during the cruise, *only one of them at a time would be allowed to accompany landing parties, and then, only when there was no chance of overcrowding the landing or covering boats.*

What a lot of difference it made, whether one or three of the Press correspondents joined a party comprising from a dozen to twenty Europeans!

Second, the ship's company in general was informed that *trading on shore was prohibited, as tending to create dangerous excitement and confusion!*

The last regulation was more absurd than the first.

Here we had two men, Romilly and Chester, whose names were affixed to the document, and who were *supposed* to have some acquaintance with native character, actually prohibiting what would most please the natives, viz., buying whatever they had to sell!

Before we left Sydney, a quantity of "trade" had been put on board the *Victoria*, for the purpose of enabling the steward to purchase fresh provisions—pigs, fowls, etc. Of this Messrs. Romilly and Chester were well aware, and I think they must have wished to baulk the steward. Pigs and fowls were obtainable in the western islands of the Louisiade, near the mainland of New Guinea; but they would not permit trading until we got to the south-eastern portion of the Archipelago, where neither pigs nor fowls could be had for love or money.

There was a small matter I ought to mention, which occurred either just before, or very shortly after, our visit to Port Moresby.

We were all seated at the cuddy table at dinner one day, when, after a pause in the general conversation, Mr. Romilly observed to Captain Ballistier, that it would be well if he, the captain, Mr. Chester, "and—er—er— the pilot!" were to plan out the route through the islands that the vessel should take for landing the boys.

Now, whether the representative of the Imperial Government thought that I, as an inferior, should have "chipped in" there and then, and given my advice, I cannot say; but I heard nothing more of the matter.

I had nothing to do with the landing of the islanders. My business was to take the ship wherever Captain Ballistier might direct me. If Mr. Romilly or Captain Ballistier had asked my advice as to our route, I would have given it willingly, for the sake of my employers. But this neither of them did, and, consequently, a nice mess they made of it. At last, in the middle of the voyage, after wasting both time and coals, they were obliged to leave the route entirely at my discretion.

They cannot say that, after we left Normanby I. for good, we ever passed twice over the same ground unnecessarily.

From Teste I., by the captain's direction, I took the ship into China Strait, between Hayter I. and the mainland of New Guinea. There, as the day was drawing to a close, I anchored her in Protection Bay.

This was the first mistake made by Messrs. Romilly and Chester. The Engineer Is. should have been previously visited; then Kitai and Moresby Is. Next, we should have gone on to Killerton, thence to Lydia and Normanby Is., passing close to the East Cape of New Guinea, by the channel I had taken the *Lizzie* through.

When we anchored in Protection Bay, there were still two hours of daylight remaining. So the newspaper correspondents asked Captain Ballistier to let them have one of the smaller boats in which to go ashore. For there was no danger to an armed party, at that place, at any rate, so long as they kept within rifle-shot of the ship. The matter was referred to Messrs. Romilly and Chester. The latter at first refused to give his consent, and I believe Mr. Romilly declined to interfere. I was not acquainted with the full details of the ship's charter-party, but I very much doubt if the Queensland G.A. had the power to forbid the sending away of a boat, if the master chose to do so.

At last, after a good deal of growling, leave was granted to the three Press-men to take the dingy—the smallest and also the worst boat in the ship, had there really been any danger in venturing ashore. They were to pull the boat themselves, though, and the whole party was placed in charge of one of the secretaries.

I buckled on my revolver, and, with my double-barrelled gun, set about taking my seat in the boat also.

" Pilot ! " murmured the skipper in my ear, as I stood at the gangway. " Mr. Griffith telegraphed that you were not to be allowed to go ashore anywhere in the islands."

"D——n Mr. Griffith! I'm not *his* servant, and *you* can't stop me!"

Then, in answer to my inquiries, Messrs. Romilly and Chester said that they objected, but had not the power to prevent me. So away I went.

We pulled to the shore, with visions of pigeon shooting. For the creamy and black New Guinea pigeon abounds in these islands. But, before I had gone a dozen yards into the bush, I was called back. They were going to visit a village on the south side of the bay. Here also we landed, but did not go far from the boat.

There were about half a dozen houses in this village, built on piles, about fifty yards from the water. They had the usual low walls, with thatched roofs peaked up at the ends, gable-wise. Not a native was visible when the boat touched the rocks, but presently, when we landed, an ugly old woman, clad in a long loose calico bag—I cannot call it a gown—appeared, and shook hands with us all. Then half a dozen more women, a shade less ugly, turned up, with half a score of children. Lastly, three old men, all unarmed, put in an appearance.

We did a little jabbering in broken English, which lasted a few minutes. Then one of the old men innocently rambled towards the boat.

"Don't let them get between us and the boat!" exclaimed our *pro tem.* guardian, the secretary; and immediately darted into it, calling us all to follow. One of the correspondents and myself exchanged expressive looks, as we obeyed orders; and then we returned to the ship.

I mention this little incident, which was but one of scores like it that occurred later on, to show the amount of "funk" exhibited by some of our officials. Either they were really frightened, or else they wished to make their work appear much more dangerous than it actually was. There was hardly any probability of natives attacking white men in the presence of such a large vessel as the *Victoria*, with sixty Europeans on board of her.

I remember that, later on, when we were anchored in Coral Haven, I was refused permission to take a boat a few hundred yards away from the ship in order to get some mangrove oysters. I was told, though I had already visited that place three times, that the natives were "savage and warlike." That phrase came out of "Findlay's Directory." There would be danger in venturing near them, it was said. At that very time there was a small ketch, with a three-foot free-board, and only three white men in her, lying at anchor half a mile off, trading with natives in canoes alongside.

I never went to the South Sea Islands with such a seemingly timid lot in my life, either before or since!

Next morning we steamed to Killerton, on the south side of the East Cape of New Guinea. This was the "show-place" of the trip.

As soon as we had anchored, steam was got up in the launch, which had been hoisted off the ship's deck and lowered into the water, previous to our arrival. Then the Killerton boys, fifty in number, the largest batch to be landed at any one place, were mustered and told off into two of the ship's boats, their property, in the shape of blankets and "trade," being conveyed in another boat. The launch towed these boats away from the gangway, and then waited for the Port Moresby surf-boat. This was manned by Naval Brigade men, and conveyed the Government officials. The little dingy was allotted to the members of the Press.

To do honour to the occasion, our officials made a grand display of blue cloth, gold lace, and gilt buttons, as well as of clean white linen. Towards the end of the voyage, however, the gold lace and finery were stowed

c c

away in portmanteaux, and the linen had contracted a somewhat discoloured appearance.

A prominent feature of the official's boat was an armchair. Mr. Romilly was lame, and required a seat when interviewing the chiefs and elders. All the boats were towed in a string by the launch to a sandy beach on one of the Killerton islets, where the entire party landed.

The men of the Naval Brigade were drawn up in line; Mr. Romilly placed himself in his chair, with Cago beside him to interpret, and lit a cigar, while a crowd of natives squatted or stood around.

I watched the proceedings from the ship, and was furnished with full details by the newspaper reporters, when they returned on board, an hour or two later.

One of Mr. Romilly's speeches, as reported by the correspondent of "The Courier," was a caution!

Mr. R. to Cago.—" You speak same time as yesterday, you say we bring plenty [boy] along ship; Government of Queensland send him back. Man no savee why he come. Queen Victoria, he send him back home; plenty tomahawk, plenty tobacco, you speak!" Then Cago interpreted.

Mr. R., continuing.—" You speak; man he stop long time Queensland, some man he die, some man he dead." (Cago interprets.) "Queensland Government, every man he die, he send him one fellow all the same them," pointing to the bundles of trade. " Five man he die, he send five all the same." Mr. Chester, pointing, says, " Presents, tomahawk, blanket, knife." Then Cago again interprets.

Mr. R.—" You savee friend along him die, father, mother; he take him that fellow!" (Cago interprets.) " You speak, Queen Victoria, he look out all man stop this place. Ship, he no come. Queen Victoria, he look out no man he come here."

Cago interprets.

" I don't think there's any more to say."

Mr. Chester.—"No."

On subsequent occasions the speeches were shorter, and as we progressed towards the end of the voyage, were dispensed with altogether. Business having been finished at Killerton, the anchor was tripped, and we ran towards East Cape, near which a few other boys were to be landed.

Unluckily, Mr. Chester and his secretary—who "had a fair acquaintance with the dialects!"—were but poor hands at making themselves understood, and equally incapable of comprehending the meaning of the islanders' broken English and signs. Cago and his brethren were not much better.

The landing-place turned out to be on the farther side of the cape. So much time was taken up in reaching it in the boats, and in returning from it, that night had fallen before I could get the steamer back to Protection Bay. I had to keep her under way all night, in Milne Bay;—not a pleasant job in such narrow waters, on a dark night with hazy weather. At sunrise, next morning, I ran back through China Strait, and, coasting eastward along the southern shores of Hayter, Basilisk, and Moresby Is., anchored in Pitt Bay, on the east of the last mentioned.

Off the southern arm of this bay lies the small island of Kitai. Now, when I was running through the deep channel separating Moresby and Kitai, during my second voyage in the *Lizzie*, I picked up a native who swam off to the ship. This man could have had no object in so doing, if it were not to join the ship, which he signified his wish to do directly he got on deck. Yet the Royal Commission reported that he had been kidnapped!

I attempted to converse with this man on several occasions, but his knowledge of English was extremely limited, and he seemed rather indisposed to talk at all, so that I could get no satisfaction out of him. Besides, it was not pleasant that, every time one spoke to an islander, a Naval Brigade man should lounge carelessly up, within hearing, taking stock of all one said. But why particularize each day's doings?

From Moresby I. we went on to the Engineer Is., a few miles east, landing men on each of them. A night was passed at anchor under Slade I.

There, a short time previously, a trader named Reid had been murdered by the natives. They seemed to think that the *Victoria* was a ship of war, which had been sent to punish them. Pigs were presented to Mr. Romilly, as a peace-offering, but were declined with thanks. The women brought heavy loads of native vegetables to the beach, to barter; but no trading was allowed, much to the disgust of the natives, as well as of the steward, who was quite prepared to buy pigs, fowls, or vegetables. However, it is comforting to reflect that the officials had to suffer for it afterwards, when there was nothing but "salt horse" to set before them!

From the Engineer Is. we went on to Lydia I., passing through a deep though narrow channel between Cape Ventenat, on the south-east of Normanby I., and the extensive "Gallows Reef." We became pretty intimate with this channel; for I navigated it no less than four times, before our officials discovered that I was more competent than themselves to determine what route we should pursue, in order to get our coloured passengers landed without waste of time, and without traversing the ground twice over.

From Lydia I. we steamed past Cape Ventenat again, where we spoke the German steamer *Samoa*, bound to the German portion of New Guinea, and thence to Cooktown, Queensland. On board of her was the well-known Dr. Finsch. Messrs. Chester and Lawrie, with the newspaper correspondents, went on board of her. I seized the opportunity, also, to send a letter to my friend, the late Mr. Samuel Hodgson, of Brisbane.

This letter arrived safely, but was delivered to Mr.

Hodgson with the envelope unfastened. It had been opened, and, of course, perused, by order of Mr. Griffith. Several other letters of mine were also opened in the Post Office about this time. I suppose Mr. Griffith was hunting for evidence upon which to prosecute me. If he was, he was sold!

A few boys were landed near Cape Ventenat, and, at one place, there appeared a very great chance of a row.

The officials landed in force at a spot where some five hundred natives were assembled. The Naval Brigade men were quickly surrounded by an excited mob of natives, all armed, whereas not a single rifle of theirs contained a cartridge. Had the natives attacked them, all the whites must have gone down to a man.

My notes, taken from a description of the scene by one of the correspondents, have—" Chester excited, giving away tobacco; Brigade men in line, with empty rifles, surrounded; confusion; no speech heard, shouting and bawling on both sides." The whole party got away safely, however.

Two or three days were spent at Normanby I., and then Welle I. was visited. There, at Sonoroa village, the crew of the *Hopeful* had committed some of their evil deeds. Trouble was consequently expected; so this time the Brigade men landed with loaded arms. But they met with quite "a jolly reception," according to the correspondents. The natives were all in good temper, shouting and laughing. As soon as Mr. Romilly had delivered his speech, however, an l a few pounds of tobacco had been distributed, the visitors got away back to the ship as speedily as possible.

The ship's head was then turned north-east, towards the Woodlark Is. As we had to tow the steam-launch, we were only able to make half-speed, owing to the head wind and the sea. Arrived at the group, no landing was attempted. Several natives, who approached the boats when they were in shallow water, seemed sulky, and as though on their guard. The majority of the inhabitants kept themselves aloof, close to the cover of the forest.

At last, about a dozen or more strolled down towards the boats. The returning islanders were quickly bundled into the shallow water, with their effects, and the boats shoved off again.

So far on our voyage the wind had blown continuously from east-south-east, with remarkably hazy weather. So thick, in fact, was this haze, that it almost amounted to a fog. While we were in China Straits, it was so dense that, at times, objects were barely visible at a distance of two or three miles. Once, I remember, I was hardly able to make out a point not much more than a mile off.

The atmosphere now became bright and clear—a sign of northerly winds. The refraction was so great, that when we were steaming up to the Marshall Bennett Is., quite half of the peak on Goodenough I. (7,000 ft.) was visible from the deck, though we were ninety miles distant from the island.

After calling at the Marshall Bennett group, we visited Jouveney I., and then Jurien I., landing men at each. We then went back to Evans I., a coral atoll we had already passed, while going from Normanby to Woodlark I. We had only one boy to land there. I hove to after dark in the evening, and he was bundled ashore, anyhow —by the light of a policeman's lantern—at the first smooth landing-place that the boat's crew could find; being left to make his way home as best he could.

By this time our officials had discovered that even they, despite the assistance of their precious interpreters, were liable to make a mistake occasionally; also, that it was not such an easy matter, as they had at first imagined, to discover the exact positions of the different native villages the several "returns" belonged to. For instance, after all their questioning of the boys through Cago & Co., Hiliwao village was undiscoverable where they thought to have found it. When its true position was at last ascertained, I had to take the ship between Cape Ventenat and Gallows Reef again, and so on to the south-west of Fergusson I.

It was while we were steaming up to Hiliwao, on July 1, that the after-part of the lower deck was washed down, for the first time since the embarkation of the islanders. The greasy filth that was then expelled from the scuppers sufficed to keep our wake smooth for more than a mile astern, though the fresh trade-wind then blowing covered all the rest of the sea with "white caps." Fortunate it was for us that, so far, we had experienced no bad weather, and only two or three showers of rain, of very short duration. The hatchways had thus been always open, affording thorough ventilation to the islanders' quarters. Otherwise, such an accumulation of filth would infallibly have caused disease, in some form or other.

Heaving to off Hiliwao, rather late in the afternoon, we landed eight men who had been brought thence by the *Hopeful*, with bundles of "trade" for the relatives of eight more who had died in Queensland. Mr. Romilly made the last speech of the voyage there. As soon as it had been delivered, the party returned on board—and not too soon, for night was coming on, the wind was rising, the sky becoming clouded, and there was every prospect of a dirty night in unsurveyed waters. As it was impossible to tow the launch against the wind, and such a sea as was then on, it had to be hoisted on board.

Luckily the night turned out better than I had hoped. The wind died away, and the sky cleared, very soon after we started. Before one o'clock in the morning, we were abreast of the south-western cape of Normanby I. There I slowed down, and headed for the channel I had thrice before travelled, between Gallows Reef and Cape Ventenat. Even a pilot must have a sleep now and then; so I gave orders that I was to be called when the first of the two islets—"Jack" and "Ketch"—on Gallows Reef should be sighted, and laid myself down to get a nap on the settee in the chart-room.

Now, there was only one man of the entire ship's company who had "cottoned" to the Government party. This was the chief mate. Even the hands forward had their squabbles with the "Brigade" men. As for the skipper, as he told me himself, he wished to keep friends with everybody—a very laudable wish, no doubt. Unfortunately, I fancy he fell between two stools. These were—the Queensland Government, as represented by Chester & Co., and the A.S.N. Co. According to the first, everything about the ship was wrong. The outfit, the boatmen, the boats, and the provisions, were all deficient. So was the navigation. All the ship's company, excepting the chief mate, resented the expression of these opinions.

I had just turned down the lamp in the chart-room, and stretched myself on the settee, when "tap, tap," went somebody's knuckles on the door.

"Who's there?" I asked; and the door opened and admitted the chief mate, with a tumbler in his hand.

"Would you like a glass of whiskey, Pilot?" said he.

"Will a duck swim?" rejoined I.

The steward had "turned in" some time before, and I had consequently missed my usual night-cap; so the mate's whiskey was welcome. "But what's in the wind now?" thought I, for the mate and I were at loggerheads, and some hard words had even passed between us already.

"Where are you going to steer for next, Pilot?" he presently asked. Then I felt happy, for this apprised me that the official party were puzzled what to do, and wanted my assistance.

"Don't know," I said; "better ask 'em aft. I go where 'the old man' tells me. Good-night!"

I rolled over on the settee with my face from the light, and the mate took his departure for the quarter-deck, no doubt with the conviction that he had wasted a glass of whiskey. It was not ship's whiskey, either; I perceived that. Most likely it had come out of Mr. Chester's own bottle. What a duffer they must have thought me!

At dawn, the second mate—"Jack Bluff," we called him—roused me up. We were then close to the passage. By six o'clock we had passed through it, heading eastward at half-speed. Then I went aft to ask Captain Ballistier where I was to take the ship next. Five minutes later he was on the bridge with me.

"Pilot," said the skipper, as nearly as I remember. "Mr. Romilly and Mr. Chester will leave the route to you for the future. Take the ship to the boys' homes by the shortest way. They leave it all to you."

For a moment I was inclined to refuse the responsibility, which, after all, did not amount to much. But I remembered that I had promised Captain Tronton that I would shove the ship through as quickly as I could.

They had ignored me at the beginning of the voyage, when planning out their intended route; although Mr. Romilly had mentioned me, in the presence of all, as one of the committee—I suppose I may call it that. Now, after slighting and even insulting me, with their talk about "slavers" and "kidnappers"—one of them called me "a d———d kidnapper" to my face, one day on deck—they wanted my help, and were not men enough to ask me for it themselves.

However, I agreed to what the skipper—as their mouth-piece—asked of me, provided I was furnished with the Immigration Office list of the remaining boys' names, with their respective islands and villages. This of course was forthcoming, and a nice old list it was. Each Government agent had adopted his own peculiar style of orthography, and the whole had been so hashed up and bedevilled by the office clerks, that I had to personally question all the boys on board, so as to ascertain their real names, and where they were to be landed.

I chose my own interpreters, dispensing with the aid of Cago & Co. The inevitable Naval Brigade man also got—and *took*—a broad hint to keep clear of me. After that the work of landing went on as quickly as any one could wish, no ground being passed over twice or time unnecessarily lost.

From Cape Ventenat, I went eastward to the Redlick Is., where two or three boys were landed, miles away from any village. Then I crossed the intervening channel to St. Aignan, along which we coasted. Then the Renard Is. received a few of their lost ones. During the following night the ship was kept "dodging" outside the northern barrier reef, abreast of Piron and Sudest Is.

I might have gone eastward, round the archipelago to its south side, entering the lagoon by Johnston Pass. But the sea was running heavily, and I hoped to save time and coal, by taking the "Bramble" Pass into "Coral Haven." I had never before used this channel, though I had viewed it from the inside. H.M.S. *Bramble*, though only "a little 'un," had gone through it in years long gone by, and given it the name it bears.

Early next morning I steamed in for the "barrier," a little to the north-west of Piron I. Skirting the reef, I soon came to the Pass, and took a good look at it from aloft, "end on." It appeared straight enough, certainly, with a spit from the eastern side overlapping the inner end. But it was very narrow for a vessel the size of the *Victoria*. Her bows, since she had been lightened of passengers and coals, stuck up in the air, and would surely cause her to "pay off," if the trade-wind freshened up while we were in the passage. However, at present it was calm, and I put her to it at full speed, conning her from the foreyard.

The skipper was on the bridge, and as soon as the ship was fairly in the "alley-way," he was "on pins-and-needles," evidently. First he had a look at the reef, a few yards off on one side; then he ran to the other, and found himself as close to danger on that. Next moment his hand was on the engine-room telegraph.

"Don't move that telegraph, Captain!" I roared out; for I was watching him as well as the ship.

"I'm not going to have the ship's bottom torn out!" I expected to hear him reply, for he said as much when we were going into Port Moresby, under similar circumstances.

"If you *don't* let that telegraph alone," I continued, "I'll come down, and you may get her through as you can! The worst is to come yet."

That brought him to his senses, and he let the telegraph alone. We had had two or three little skirmishes on the voyage, and he had learnt by experience that he would be left in the lurch, if he did not give me full control of the navigation.

A few minutes took her through; the rudder, hard-a-port, bringing her head to westward, clear of the overlapping spit. Once past that, we were in the more open water of Coral Haven. We lay there in a secure anchorage, whilst the boats landed the boys belonging to that neighbourhood.

About this time, the officials gave permission to us to trade for food with the natives. But it came too late, for nothing was to be got, either for love or for money. Cabin stores, which had been intended only to supplement supplies obtained at the islands, began to run short. Consequently, there was considerable growling, both forward and aft.

We next coasted Sudest I., calling at Grass (or Garnim) and Briarley (or Duddakai), islands lying on our course. At Condé Point we turned back, and passing along the Calvados Chain, steered westward for Teste I. There we landed the last boy, Bakara. He was a native of Teste, but had been recruited by me at Condé Point,

Sudest I. I think I have mentioned that I released him from a state of slavery, in which he had been held there.

When we were in the neighbourhood of Grass I., one of the reporters, Mr. Livesey, interviewed some of the boys who had been brought to Queensland by me. The result may be gathered from the following extract from his account of the voyage, published in "The Brisbane Courier" : —

> Several of the boys from the neighbourhood of Sudest could speak very fair English, and it was with these I spoke on the eve of their leaving the ship. A native of Grass Island, Sandfly by name, according to the evidence printed by the Commission, made two very conflicting statements when examined at the Hamleigh sugar plantation, on the Herbert River. When first examined, he stated glibly enough that he had been engaged for three yams, and understood he was to remain for three years to work in a sugar plantation. About a week afterwards he came forward with another boy, said he had been frightened by Mr. Cowley, and that he had been told he was only to work for three moons or months, and contradicted his former evidence. Now in Townsville it was openly asserted that boys had been tampered with and instructed what to say before the Commission ; but it must be admitted that proofs of such assertions seem to be entirely lacking. Nevertheless, it seemed a strange thing for a South Sea Islander to voluntarily come forward and make any statement whatsoever, and I thought that I would hear what he had got to say on the subject a third time. Accordingly I found him out one evening, and questioned him. The date was 4th July, and the next morning he was going to be landed with his countrymen at Grass Island. I told him he was close to his island, and he would be landed there in the morning, whether he spoke the truth or told me a lie, for that would make no difference now. He had seen the other boys landed, and had nothing to be afraid of. I asked him if he remembered the labour schooner coming to his place, and he replied that he did. I then asked him how long the captain had told him he would have to stay in Queensland. He replied three years ; and in answer to a further question said he understood how long that meant. On asking him how many moons there were in a year, he said, ' All the same yam,' and held up all his fingers. I next asked how it was, if he had been engaged for three years, he told the Commissioners that he had only been engaged for three months, and he said that Cago, the missionary boy (one of the interpreters), had gone among them on the plantation and told the boys that they were to say three months, and

that then they would all be sent back to their islands with plenty of trade. He also told me, in reply to questions, that the other boys from his island understood well that they were to go for three years, and mentioned especially Cockroach and Dixon, who can both speak English. This boy had a fair knowledge of English before the schooner came to his island, and said he had been engaged in the bêche-de-mer fishery and had been to Cooktown. The above, though divested of its pigeon English and made intelligible, is a true and faithful report of the brief conversation I held with Sandfly, who had no motive to tell me anything that was untrue. I subsequently, in company with another representative of the Press, spoke to two or three other boys, who each had the same tale of missionary boys coming among them and instructing or advising them what to say.

Now, let my reader compare this story about Sandfly having been coached by Cago the interpreter, previous to examination before the Royal Commission, with Mr. Kinnaird Rose's letter in "The Courier," and my remarks thereon, in the last chapter.

We remained only an hour or two at Teste I. to land interpreters. We then steamed away for Port Moresby, passing out into the open ocean about a mile from Suckling Reef, on its north-western side.

That evening I heard the doctor giving an account of some experiences of his in Teste I.

On our first visit there, he had gone ashore in the officials' boat. While on shore he had purchased some small article of native manufacture—a comb, I think—and paid for it. Somehow or other the native vendor managed to retain the article, as well as the "trade" given for it. When the *Victoria* paid her second visit, this native, no doubt thinking it better to deliver up the article than to be punished for theft, met the doctor as he landed, and delivered up his plunder. The doctor said he looked upon this incident as a proof of the good effects of missionary teaching, and that he should send an account of it to some Glasgow paper.

Then he told another story.

An old man and a girl—supposed to be father and

daughter—had met him near the boat, and by words and signs, invited him to visit their house, at the back of the village. He went with them; but, when the old man demanded "plenty tobacco," and the girl—well—made love to him, he fled the scene, at least he said so. I asked him if he would retail this story, also, to his Glasgow paper, as the outcome of missionary teaching!

POLYNESIAN WOMEN IN QUEENSLAND.

But one or two bystanders burst out laughing, and the doctor retired to his berth without giving me a civil answer. I suspect he omitted to mention *that* incident in his correspondence!

At Port Moresby we obtained some supplies from Mr. Goldie's store, and then steamed away for Brisbane, on July 13. A few hours after leaving, it was found that the old *Vic* made such slow progress, with the wind and sea on the port bow, that there was a probability of our eating all our provisions before we arrived at Brisbane. So the ship was kept away for Townsville, where we anchored on the evening of the sixteenth, arriving at Brisbane on the twenty-third. After one night there we went on to Sydney, where we moored at the A.S.N. Co.'s wharf on July 27. Next day I made my report, got my "cheque," and said good-bye to the old *Vic*.

CHAPTER XXIV.

VOYAGE OF THE *ARIEL*, 1888.

I am debarred—The Griffith Ministry—Change of Government —Free once more—The Ariel—*I sail for the New Hebrides —Waisori—White residents—The* Lulu—*The* Windward Ho.—*A woman swims off to recruit—French landmarks— French methods of recruiting—Coasting Espiritu Santo— Making for the Solomons — The chief, Faulanga — Port Adams—An uncertain recruit—Sinnarango—Good fortune of the* Meg Merrilies—*Porpoise teeth—Fortified islets—A wife a purchasable commodity—Billy Fidei—His two wives —The Lord Howe Is.—A coral atoll—James Roberts—His escape from the Carolines—An adventurous voyage—King Wilan—A reception at Court—Native houses—Manners and customs—Royal appetites—The Tasman Is.—Another kingly glutton—A meal for a recruit! — The Floridas — Billy Mahualla—Tavaniakia—Through the Maramasiki Passage —Malaria—A very friendly chief—Big Joe—Hostile tribes— Vessels attacked—Deep Bay—The crew prostrated by malarial fever—Coasting Malayta—Kwaisulia, a Malayta chief—Manoba I.—The G.A. scoffs at danger—A treacherous envoy—The mate's story—How the G.A. landed—A yell!— The mate to the rescue!—Driven back—How Joe jumped out of his trousers—The G.A. killed—Shall we avenge him?— Judge Gorry's words—To sea—Natives put a price on white men's heads—Back at Bundaberg—An inquiry—Published in the papers—Disappearance of my chief witness.*

For three years after my trip in the *Victoria*, I had no connection with the labour trade. In common with other masters, crews, and Government agents, who had brought boys from New Guinea or the neighbouring islands, I was debarred from employment in it, by the Griffith Ministry. This I had been told by various officials, though I had not put it to the proof by making application for a licence.

I was informed at Townsville, in April, 1888, that my name was no longer included in the lists of the proscribed, which were furnished to the immigration officers at the various ports. I wrote, therefore, to the head office in Brisbane, and on my arrival in Sydney received an answer that had been awaiting me there for more than a fortnight. By this I was informed, in a very curt and decisive manner, that I *was* debarred from employment in the labour trade. Still, I cherished great hope of returning to it, and that before long. Election times were drawing nigh! and the Griffith party would have to take a back seat, for a time at least.

At the end of June, the *Pendle Hill*, an intercolonial trader I had been in command of, was sold, and I was thrown out of employment thereby. I then made another application to the Queensland Immigration Department. A new Ministry had just been formed; so the reply I now got was to the effect that my name had been removed from the list of persons debarred from employment in the labour trade. All I had to do, therefore, was to get a ship, and then apply for my licence.

I had not long to wait, and, in the meantime, I went to Brisbane, where I stayed about a week. I was then offered, and accepted, the command of the *Ariel* brigantine, which was lying in the port of Bundaberg. Leaving Brisbane in a little coasting steamer, the *Lady Musgrave*, I went thither and joined my ship on July 19.

The *Ariel* had previously commenced a voyage to the New Hebrides, but, before reaching the islands, she had to return to Queensland, her G.A., Mr. Murray, having committed suicide on board of her, from the effects of drink. Captain Lewis, my predecessor, was debarred from holding a command, in consequence, I believe, of having allowed the G.A. to indulge in his fatal weakness.

The requisite licences for the voyage arrived from Brisbane on July 26. Next day, the *Ariel* was towed down the river Burnett, discharged the pilot at the Heads, and put to sea by 2 p.m. My G.A. was Mr. Armstrong, and I had thirty-five men and one woman on board, return islanders.

After a most unusual course of variable winds and weather, I sighted Aneiteum I. on August 10. Passing it during the night, I hove to, early in the morning, off the south-east coast of Tanna I.

Port Resolution, or Waisori, was the first place I visited. There I hove to close to the mouth of the harbour, sending the boats ashore to engage boatmen for the round trip. If it should prove necessary to take them to Queensland, they were to be discharged on the vessel's return to the island, on her next voyage. Such an arrangement was usual.

During the absence of my boats, I was visited by two copra traders—Larresky, of Port Resolution, and Anderson, a resident on the coast about two miles north of the port. Besides these, there were two other traders on the island—Major W. A. Carter, late of the East Indian service, who lived a short distance from Anderson's station, and Antonio Francisco, at Waisissi. The Rev. Mr. Watts, a missionary, also resided at Gwamera, on the south-eastern coast.

I worked all round Tanna I., shipped the boatmen I required, obtained one recruit, and landed four returns, with their effects. On the fourteenth and fifteenth four recruits were engaged, and two returns landed, at Erromanga I., besides two boatmen from the previous voyage paid off and landed. Then I squared away north-westward.

On the sixteenth I visited Pango Bay, Sandwich I., paying off and landing two boatmen on Mele islet.

The *Lulu*, a French schooner, was now in company with the *Ariel*. This vessel was painted a very light slate colour, though perhaps it may have been *white* once, and had a dark red stripe round her top sides. Her boats were also painted red—a pretty close copy of the Queensland regulation colours.

On the seventeenth the anchor was dropped in Port Sandwich, Mallicolo I., where a French steamer, *Le Caledonien*, was taking in cargo at one of the two trading stations. Next day, she departed, the schooners *Lulu* and *Windward Ho* arriving. The last flew British colours. She was owned by the old New Hebrides trader, Captain MacLeod, but was commanded by a Frenchman. I wonder what the Board of Trade would have said about that?

At dawn, on the morning of the nineteenth, when I turned out to get the vessel under way, I found that a young native woman had swum off during the night from the eastern shore, and was now on board. Of course, Mr. Griffith's "cast-iron" regulations had to be attended to. So, as there was no husband forthcoming, she was landed again, but, at her own urgent request, on the other shore. Very probably she got clubbed, ultimately, for her escapade. Then I got under way, and, towards evening, anchored again off Champion's station, on the south-west coast of Ambrym. This was the place where I had been so nearly shot in 1876, during my third voyage in the *Stanley*.

Next morning, the recruiter obtained seven recruits, apparently run aways from their friends. Weighing anchor in the afternoon, I stood over to the south coast of Mallicolo, dropping anchor next morning in South-West Bay. There I watered ship, and lay for a couple of nights without obtaining recruits. In the lagoon, at the head of the bay, I found part of the wreck of the *Sibyl*, which had been driven ashore during the last hurricane season. Then, coasting northward, we passed two nights at anchor in the west bay of the island.

About this part of Mallicolo, I noticed several of the

stone landmarks of the French New Hebrides Company, by which, during the last few years, all the best land throughout the group—chiefly water frontages—has been bought from the natives. The Company's steamer, *Le Caledonien*, had taken seventeen natives to Noumea, two or three weeks previous to my visit. Snider rifles are the principal pay the natives receive, with a little ammunition. When Sniders are given to the friends of recruits, they themselves receive no pay until the "present" has been worked out. Many of these boys, it is said, are persuaded to go to Sydney from Noumea, and take service there, for which their late French masters receive a money equivalent as high as £10 per head. This information was gleaned from a French recruiter.

From Mallicolo I. we ran down to Cape Lisburne, Espiritu Santo I., and landed a return about a mile north of it. Keeping along that coast, the trade-wind fell light and baffling under the land. Consequently, it was not until the following forenoon that I got to the northern end of the island, and felt the wind again, steady and fresh enough to make my little craft jump in a most lively manner. Soon I had to shorten sail, and it was as much as the *Ariel* could do to hold her own at times. However, by next morning, August 28, I got into smoother water, under the lee of Vanua Lava I., where I anchored off the " Double Waterfall." Here we filled up all the water-tanks and cut a sufficiency of firewood. All the New Hebrides returns had now been landed, those still on board being natives of the Solomon group, where I intended to do most of my recruiting. One day more was spent in ineffectual attempts to obtain recruits, and then I weighed anchor.

The next two days were unpleasant—the wind being variable, with frequent rain and squalls. As we neared the Solomons the weather became better, and by daylight on September 1, I sighted Ulaua, or Contrariete I. Off this island I hove to, and purchased, by barter, a couple of boat-loads of small round yams; but I could obtain no recruits. During the night I remained hove to most of the time, and drifted down towards Cape Zelée, Maramasiki I.

The following morning I picked up Faulanga, a chief, residing in the neighbourhood of Port Adams. He had come off to meet us in his canoe, with half a dozen others. Faulanga was a well-known chief, and, through policy, a friend to the white man. He acted as a "crimp" for recruits in his neighbourhood. He stayed on board for awhile, until I got close into the land at Saa, a few miles north, when he and his men left us and went home.

Between Saa and Port Adams I landed six returns, with their boxes. Then I ran down to Port Adams, where I anchored close under the lee of Elizabeth I., or Tettava. While entering the port between Elizabeth and Mary Is., I passed the schooner *Saucy Lass*, Captain Gibbs, Mr. Potts, G.A., standing out. She was recruiting for Fiji.

I remained there until the seventh, for the weather was boisterous and wet. Then I sailed along the coast northward, with five additional recruits.

The next return to be landed was a man named Nio, who seemed very uncertain as to where he wished to go on shore. First, he said Port Adams, where he had friends. But the temper of these friends had altered in his absence, so he proposed to land at the north end of the channel between Maramasiki and Malayta Is. Then he "bucked" on that, so I sent him ashore at Ulimburi, in Double Bay. There, he said, he found his friends all dead; upon which he returned on board and offered himself as a recruit again. I accepted him, though he would not sign his agreement until we left for the Lord Howe Is.

Nio's business having been settled so far, I stood northward, and, in the afternoon of September 9, entered a large bay south of Cape Arsacides, where I anchored some three miles from Diamond Harbour, or Sinnarango, at which place Mr. Popham, G.A., and some of the crew of the *Young Dick* were murdered. There I sent away the boats, landing a return at Uru, some miles further south, within the bay.

Next morning I was under way again, coasting northward. I landed one return at Manu, and four at Sulabau. I then caught a steady south-easterly breeze, with fine weather, and, by sundown, arrived at the northern end of the island off Sio Bay, finding the *Meg Merrilies* of Fiji, and the *Saucy Lass* at anchor there.

According to the account of Mr. Délamere, mate of the first-mentioned vessel, who boarded us after dark, she had not been out two months, and had eighty-two recruits on board already. Captain Meredith, her master, afterwards told me that he never missed a chance of acquiring porpoise teeth; he was willing to give a pound for a hundred of them. Eighty to a hundred were considered sufficient "pay" or present for one recruit in the Solomons, where porpoise teeth are in great request and serve for money.

That night we lay becalmed, tossing about on the south-easterly swell, now and then deluged with rain, while the ship drifted northward. It was not till the afternoon of the next day that I was again able to get close enough to Sio to send the boats in with two returns. In the evening, the *Meg Merrilies* was close to me, under way. My old acquaintance, Captain Meredith, came on board the *Ariel*, and exchanged experiences with me, as well as certain stores. Next day I landed seven men and one woman at Auki, about twenty miles south-south-east of Cape Astrolabe, Malayta I. It is a small harbour, open to the south-west. There are two "fortified" islets within it.

These fortified islets are, I think, peculiar to Malayta, and are numerous along the northern coasts. They are, originally, sandy reef islets, close to the coast, elevated two or three feet above the level of the highest tides. Round the edges of the coral foundation of the islet, walls have been built up of coral blocks, rising some four feet above the interior surface of the islet. Every here and there are openings in the wall—which at a distance resemble embrasures—and into which canoes can be floated. Once inside, they can be hauled up safely amongst the low thatched houses, which are crowded close together beneath the cocoanut trees, with very narrow footways between them. A low rough wall, or fence of sticks, divides each islet between separate communities—the male and the female. The sexes live apart, although wives are always purchasable, being regarded as the personal property of the men who may have bought them.

About noon, on the twelfth, I anchored in North Alite Bay, some five miles south-east of Auki. This bay is closely connected with the larger Alite Bay by a narrow but deep channel. Both bays are protected to seaward, on west and south, by low, wooded reef islets.

I secured two recruits there. The first, Billy Fidei, was an old hand. He had previously worked out a three years' term in Queensland. His two wives followed him. However, as bigamy is not allowed in Queensland, the eldest one, an ugly dame, gave her more favoured and younger rival a beating with a paddle, in their canoe, before she could climb on board, where I engaged her also as a recruit.

No other recruits offering—the bushmen wanted Sniders for their men—I sailed next day. Currents and wind proving unfavourable, I was unable to get to Coleridge Bay, between Alite and Cape Astrolabe, until the sixteenth. There I took in supplies of water and firewood, landed a return, and obtained one recruit. I had then only three returns left to land, while I had recruited twenty men and one woman—tolerably satisfactory for seven weeks' work, including the passage from Queensland.

I had not heard that any labour vessel had lately visited the Lord Howe Is. on the north. The mate had been told by a copra trader, during his last voyage, too, that there was a probability of men being willing to emigrate from the Tasman Is., which lie some forty miles still further north.

I sailed from Coleridge Bay on the evening of the 19th, and on the 21st, I sighted the low islets on the southern side of the Lord Howe, or Leueneuwa group. This is an immense irregularly shaped atoll, or ring-reef, studded with a great number of low, wooded islets. Three or four of the largest of these are permanently inhabited. The natives are pure Polynesians; big, lusty people in appearance, but not nearly such good workers as the Papuans.

I sailed into the lagoon through a small but deep passage, on the south-western side, and beat up to the eastern end, where I anchored close to the largest island, Leueneuwa. While nearing it, and looking out from aloft for any appearance of an anchorage, I was rather surprised to see a cutter-rigged decked boat sailing towards me, with a white man at her helm, and two or three natives as a crew.

When we had anchored, this boat ranged alongside of us, and her white steersman boarded the *Ariel*. He introduced himself as James Roberts, an Englishman. He informed us that he had left Ascension or Bonape I., one of the Caroline group, in the decked boat alongside, his only companion being his "wife," a native of one of the small Ant Is. close to Bonape. The reason he had left was because he was "wanted" by the Spanish authorities in the Carolines, for selling firearms to the natives. According to his own account, he had been previously employed in the sealing trade, in Behring Strait. How long he had taken to come from the Carolines, I cannot now say; but it seems he had had a rough time of it. Short of provisions and water, and most of the time without his compass, which had been washed overboard, he drifted and sailed to Leueneuwa, where the natives, going out in their canoes, had piloted him safely into the lagoon.

Roberts had been about three weeks in this island, and had promised to give his boat to the head chief, " King " Wilan, whenever he got a chance of a passage to Australia. He was not without means, for, besides his boat, he had some hundreds of dollars in cash, and, so he said, an order on some Australian bank for a larger amount. A bargain was soon struck between us. For £10 Roberts was to have a passage in the *Ariel* to Queensland, messing with the hands forward, and sleeping where he could. As for the woman, she elected, so he said, to remain on the island, and his boat went to King Wilan.

I afterwards heard that Roberts let drop it was his intention to return to Leueneuwa, but he never gave me a hint of it.

After anchoring, the G.A. and I landed and interviewed the king, and also his brother and prime minister, Kabbi. To them we explained the object of our visit. Then about twenty of the ladies favoured us with a dance on an open green space, after which we strolled through the village; and, no doubt, the inhabitants considered us a very inquisitive lot.

Both sexes of the Lord Howe Islanders ornament their persons profusely with tattooing. The national dress of the men consists of a wisp of thin matting round the loins. The women wear a longer mat wrapped round the waist, and hanging down to the knees. The women's heads are shaved close, but the men allow their frizzly locks to grow long at the sides and back of their heads, cutting them short on the top. We saw no weapons of warfare.

It was here that the *James Birnie*, brig, was captured in 1874; her crew, with the exception of one white man and four foreign islanders who escaped, were massacred. The "dressing down" that the natives received for it effectually prevented similar outrages afterwards.

Their houses are stoutly built, generally twenty feet or so in length, with walls five feet high, and lofty peaked roofs, all thatched with palm or pandanus leaves. The

WOMAN—LORD HOWE I.

floors are of hard beaten earth, often having a layer of coral gravel on top. Their canoes do not amount to much. They are rather small, low, and light, and are only fit for lagoon work. They are balanced by outriggers, and the larger ones often spread a triangular mat sail when before the wind. The dead are buried in a piece of ground set apart for that purpose, about half a mile from the village. Each grave is marked by a heap of stones piled on top. Polygamy is practised, the king having seven wives; but the marriage vow is not very binding. Chastity among grown-up girls is unknown. The chief articles of food are fish and cocoanuts, with a little bread-fruit, and very coarse taro. As is the case on all the low coral islands of the Pacific, the earth is far from fertile, being only a thin layer of black vegetable mould.

I engaged four recruits there, and then sailed westward, on the twenty-fourth, to Kala I., on the southwestern side of the atoll. There we lay for a night, but all I obtained was a score of fowls, for each of which I paid three sticks of tobacco, equivalent to three-halfpence per fowl. Next morning, as none of the Kala people were inclined to leave, I ran down north to Palau I., where, immediately after anchoring, I engaged three men.

Kala is under the rule of King Wilan, but Palau boasts of a ruler of its own—King Wailua. The last potentate visited the ship in the evening, and made an awful feed of fowl and yams. In fact, the whole of the inhabitants would have "loafed" on the ship, if they had been encouraged. I think that, now and then, Palau suffers from short commons.

After dark, when the natives had all gone ashore, a stowaway was discovered, and was recruited. He had already been to Queensland for one term of service, during which he was a fellow-labourer of Billy Fidei's.

Next morning the king and his retinue came off—but too late—for another feed. However, he allowed two more lads to recruit. I then got under way for the northern passage, five or six miles westward of Palau. The wind dropped when I was in the passage, and, the tide setting in also, I was obliged to anchor until eleven p.m., when, the breeze freshening up, I ran out in the dark, and steered for the Tasman Is., or Niumango, another atoll, smaller than the Lord Howe group, though of similar formation. These I sighted ahead about 6 a.m. next morning.

My plan of the Tasman atoll, together with some others

I made of Malayta harbours and anchorages, has since been published by the British Hydrographic Department.

This atoll much resembles the shape of a human skull. It extends for about ten miles by seven, with deep water within, and only three coral patches in the lagoon. The entrances, about five in number, are all on the west. I went in by the southernmost of them. Just inside it there is a dangerous coral patch, close to which I anchored, until the sun should bear more favourably for me to see dangers ahead. I afterwards went out by the next passage, in which there are also patches, though not dangerous ones, having five and ten fathoms of water on them respectively. That entrance is a double one, being divided by a small coral reef, awash at low water. Perhaps it should be considered as two separate entrances.

At noon I weighed anchor again, and beat up the lagoon to the eastern and largest island, where the only village on the atoll is situated. The "King," and nearly all his subjects—some two hundred, I think—were temporarily camped on Lotto, a neighbouring islet, to enjoy the fishing, which, about this season, was better there than at Niumango, the capital.

It seemed as though this people, also, were often afflicted with short commons, for they loafed persistently on board the ship all the time we lay there. His majesty never missed coming off at meal-times, though he did not always get what he wanted; for, as he refused to allow his subjects to leave home, he was given to understand that my rule was, "No boys! no grub!"

During the first night we lay there, a boy swam off to the ship during the middle watch. Just before breakfast time his majesty arrived, and demanded the boy back. Luckily, the breakfast table was being prepared in the cabin, and curried fowl, boiled yam, soft bread, and well-sweetened tea, purchased the royal permission. The king got a good square meal. Lord, how he did tuck in! And I gained a recruit.

On the following morning—just before breakfast, of course—the king came off again with another recruit, and got a good meal once more. But he assured me that no more of the islanders would leave home, so I got under way, and beat back westward with a very light wind. This soon dying away, I was obliged to anchor again before I had gone two miles.

The next two days also were spent in the lagoon, for a similar reason. It was not until the morning of October 2 that I was able to get outside the atoll, with a rather light breeze from south. Then I commenced to beat

back to the southern islands of the Solomon group, where, on the 10th, I landed one of my three remaining returns. I then worked back to the Florida Is., where I anchored in the evening in Sandfly Passage, between the northern and the middle islands. Next day I landed the last of my return passengers there—a good riddance!

I worked the Floridas without success until the fourteenth. During the following night I crossed over to Malayta I., where I first visited Alite Bay to replenish my stock of fresh water and firewood. As I had expected, I could get no recruits there; but, luckily, I made the acquaintance of Billy Mahualla, a minor chief of Mgwai-Fau, one of the three fortified islets in the harbour. Billy was a travelled "nig," and had visited Queensland. At some previous period of his life he had committed an offence which had caused him to leave home. Then he became acquainted with the tribes on the southern coast, and all through the narrow channel which divides Malayta from Maramasiki I. he was now commonly called Okarrowa. He offered his services as interpreter for a trip round Malayta, and I accepted the offer. His price was to be a box of tobacco for the trip. He indicated one weighing eighty-four pounds, and earned it well.

I weighed anchor and left Alite on the 18th. As Billy had not much hope of getting men on that side of the island, I worked to windward. The first place visited was Tavaniahia, on the western coast of Maramasiki, since called Ariel Harbour. It is a very small anchorage, suitable only for the smallest decked craft, in fact, but tolerably well sheltered. I was obliged to moor the ship there, close to the entrance, with an anchor ahead, upon the reef nearly, and warps astern to the mainland. By warping further in to the southward, however, I might have got bare room to swing in with a short scope of cable, in seven fathoms.

At this place I engaged two men, one of whom was accompanied by his wife. On the 23rd I unmoored, and, running back five or six miles northward, entered the Maramasiki Passage at its southern end. Billy, my interpreter, assured me that he knew the passage well, and could take the *Ariel* safely through it with the southerly wind then blowing, although it had never yet been navigated by any vessel of her size. He proved a good pilot, and directed me how to get safely through the whole length of the Passage.

For a distance of about twelve miles the Passage is, in many places, not more than half a cable broad. The depth of water varies excessively. Near the southern mouth I got no bottom with the lead at twenty fathoms, towards the other end I found it at two and a half. The banks are thickly lined with mangroves. Here and there occur openings—"arms"—leading to the foot of the hills that fall back from the main channel. The native villages are built well up on these hills, for the air of the Passage is malarious and unhealthy. Of this we had proof, for, shortly after clearing the Passage, several of my crew and recruits suffered for several days from malarial poisoning. The same thing occurred when I afterwards traversed the Passage in the *Borough Belle*.

We spent the four following nights at anchor in the Half-way Reach. There I picked up five recruits, and another after I moved the ship into the estuary, who belonged to the Passage, however.

Sunima, chief of the village of Arlua, seemed unusually friendly. He passed two nights on board, but his followers were sent ashore at sundown. During the daytime I allowed Sunima on the half-poop deck, which was strictly tabooed to the crowd. Two New Hebrideans were placed on guard there, while one of the crew stood under arms forward. All of us wore our revolvers loaded, for there was no telling but what these savages might prove treacherous. If they had been so disposed, and had made a sudden rush, we should have been overwhelmed if not armed. It was dangerous to let them come on board at all, but I was obliged to humour them with a view to getting recruits.

The last day we were there I had a visit from Big Joe, chief of Bullahah, a coast village about a mile south of the Passage. This potentate had travelled. He had been to the colonies, spoke English, and was friendly to white men. He advised me to be very careful in my dealings with the natives along the Passage. He said they would not let slip any opportunity that offered of taking a ship and killing all her people. Sunima's own tribe were not hostile. The Torrosi tribe, under chiefs Kokki and Lahu, inhabiting the Aimaia arm, near our anchorage, had, only three weeks before, attacked the boat of a Fijian ketch, without provocation. Some months previous to that, they had also attacked the boats of another vessel, but were beaten off.

While Big Joe was on board, a messenger arrived in a canoe from Kokki, the Torrosi chief, who wished to present me with a pig and some taro. He probably expected I should visit him; but, following Big Joe's advice, I declined to do so.

Next morning I got under way, and ran through the northern half of the Narrows. Emerging thence into the broader reef and islet-studded waters of the estuary, I anchored on the Flats in two and a half fathoms. There I lay quietly at anchor until the morning of the thirty-first, when, with a light southerly breeze, I stood northward along the Flats as far as Orlu I., a distance of not more than three miles.

The estuary occupied our attention until the morning of November 3. Then, getting under way, I ran northward and anchored again off Takataka, a very convenient watering-place and good anchorage in Deep Bay, off the northern mouth of the Maramasiki Passage.

There the *Ariel* lay from the forenoon of November 3 until the 9th. Two-thirds of the crew, white and coloured, and several recruits, were on the sick-list. Their ailment was a kind of colic, which at first I feared was cholera, and it no doubt resulted from malarial poison contracted in the Passage. My recruit list then numbered fifty, two of whom were women.

I worked on from Deep Bay along the whole of the north-eastern coast of Malayta I. My anchorages were at Unter I., Mannakwoi, Ulimburi, Panchinchi, Sinnarango, Uru, Kwakwaru, Attar, and Uras. The last I reached on December 5, having then on board seventy-three male and two female recruits.

It was at Uras that John Renton was rescued in 1875, as I mentioned in a former chapter. He had lived among the natives for several years, while Kabbau was chief of this part of the coast, his residence being on the small fortified islet named Attargeggei, close to Uras. One of Kabbau's best warriors, Kwaisulia, had succeeded him as head chief, and it was not long before he made his appearance on board with a number of his followers.

Kwaisulia was and is a good specimen of the Malayta people, and has always shown himself friendly towards

AN ATTAR BELLE—MALAYTA I.

white men. He and his men were allowed to roam about the *Ariel* as they pleased. Natives of the neighbouring tribes, living only a couple of miles off on either side of Uras, are not to be trusted, however.

While I was working down this coast from the estuary, the G.A., the mate, who was also recruiter, and I, frequently speculated as to the possibility or otherwise of safely obtaining recruits from Manoba. This is a long low reef island, six or seven miles northward of Uras. It lies about half a mile from the mainland, but is connected with it by a coral reef.

Some experience of the Manoba people had taught me that they were not to be trusted. In truth, they had

E E

always borne a bad reputation. So I told both the G.A. and the mate to be very careful if they went there. The G.A., however, held a contrary opinion to mine. Having landed returns at Manoba on a previous voyage in the *Helena*, he rather pooh-poohed my counsel, being sure that he would be received in a most friendly manner. The sequel proved I was right, unhappily.

Two recruits, the last engaged, were obtained shortly after I anchored. Next day the two boats worked along the coast northward; but I had no idea that they would get as far as Manoba. Shortly before they left in the forenoon, a canoe came alongside. In her was a man, afterwards stated to be Lakkida, once a boatman in the *Fearless*, and an actor in what was to occur. He said that the chief of the village of Warlo had a bad leg, and wanted some "blue water" (blue-stone). None of us then knew that Warlo lay at the south end of Manoba. Accordingly, the G.A. took with him a bottle containing blue-stone in solution. The boats returned about 1 p.m., but without the G.A., and the mate reported as follows.

The two boats—one in charge of the mate, and the other containing the G.A.—pulled along the coast, passing Fulafau islet, and then diverging to Warlo, on the south of Manoba. The G.A.'s boat arrived first, and was backed in upon the beach, where were several men, but no women, to receive them—a most significant sign—before the mate could get within speaking distance. Joe Enau, one of the boatmen, a native of Sio, a few miles west, carried the G.A. ashore on his back over the shallow water. Joe warned him not to venture away from the boat, but the G.A. only laughed at him. Calling on Joe to follow him, he ran up the narrow sandy strip of beach, with the bottle of medicine in his hand. He had his revolver in his belt, but had left his Winchester rifle in the boat. Joe followed reluctantly at a distance.

A minute or two passed, and then the mate—who had

just backed his boat in to the beach, from which all the natives had disappeared—heard a long-drawn, blood-curdling yell coming from the village amongst the trees, about a hundred yards from the boats. Then Joe appeared again, running for the boats, minus two-thirds of his clothing.

Jumping ashore with his rifle, the mate called on his men to follow him to the G.A.'s rescue. Before he had gone twenty yards the natives appeared in force, obliging him to retreat, which he did by wading and pushing the boats off through the shallow water, for the tide was falling fast, while arrows and spears fell thickly around them. Luckily none were hit, and as soon as deeper water was attained, out of reach of bullet or arrow, a council was held, and Joe stated what he had seen.

He had followed the G.A., who was some twenty yards ahead of him, until just within the outskirts of the timber, close to the village. Some half a dozen men were close to the G.A., beside a canoe-house or shed. He saw several men jump out from behind a house in the village, seize the G.A., pinning his arms to his sides, while others struck him with their tomahawks. The G.A. shouted, "Look out!" and then Joe saw him fall. Joe then turned and made for the boats, but the natives near by attacked him also. According to his own account, he fairly jumped out of his trousers, which one of his assailants had got hold of, while making play with his sheath-knife. When he returned, he had certainly left his indispensables behind him!

There could be no doubt that the G.A. was dead. Malayta warriors never make prisoners. Joe had seen the tomahawks cut into the back of his neck. So the boats were pulled back to the ship.

Kwaisulia was on board when the boats came alongside, and the sad news was made known. He immediately proposed to muster his men, and, in conjunction with my crew, attack Manoba, and avenge the death of the G.A. Of course this would not do. I remembered Judge Gorry's words to Captain Kilgour, in consequence of his having defended himself, while removing his employer's boat from the beach of Aoba I. after the murder of Renton :—

"If I had had proof of the death of a single native, I would have hanged you, sir! hanged you!"

The G.A. was dead without a doubt, and the law forbade me to interfere further. All I could do was to leave the matter to the authorities; for I was in a British Protectorate, worse luck!

The *Fearless*, I knew, was on the coast, for I had spoken her and the *Archimedes* at Kwakwaru; but her presence could do no good. So after waiting till evening, to see if anything fresh turned up, I weighed anchor and put to sea. I was unwilling to pass another night at Uras, for half my recruits were from Malayta I., and it was quite on the cards that, fearful of vengeance being wreaked on them, they might swim ashore in the dark.

Coasting along the shore, I ran past Warlo, which appeared lifeless and deserted. Rounding the north end of Malayta the same night, I anchored in Alite Bay on the eighth, where I paid off and discharged Billy Mahualla, and took in wood and water.

After my return to Queensland, I learned that the *Fearless* arrived at Uras the day after my departure. During the night following, according to the natives, a large canoe left Manoba, conveying the head of the murdered man to Sinnarango, there to secure a reward which had been offered by the inhabitants of that place for white men's heads.

For, in the affair with the schooner *Young Dick*, when Mr. Popham, G.A., and several of her crew were treacherously murdered, the vessel itself being nearly captured, a score or more of the assailants were killed. The relatives of these subsequently offered a considerable amount in native shell-money for the heads of Europeans, by way of retaliation. The action of H.M.S. *Diamond*, which vessel carried out the usual farce of cutting down cocoanut trees and destroying houses and canoes, only made matters worse. It served merely to exasperate the savages still more.

I left Alite Bay on December 9, and anchored off the Burnett Heads after dark on the 22nd. The following afternoon I moored the ship in the river at Bundaberg.

When I was consulting with the mate in the cabin of the *Ariel* at Uras, just after he had arrived on board from Manoba, as to which was the best course to take—whether to remain where we were, or to put to sea before half of our recruits deserted—I remember saying to him, "No matter what I do, somebody is sure to find fault with me!" And I was correct in my conjecture.

The sub-immigration agent at Bundaberg was instructed to hold an inquiry into the circumstances attending the death of my late G.A. In accordance therewith, he had interviews at different times with each man of my crew, as well as with me. He had also access to the ship's official log. In this were the reports of the mate and the boatman, Joe Enau, which I had taken down, and which were signed by the two men in the presence of all hands at Uras. These interviews were strictly private, no person being present besides the sub-immigration agent and the man under examination.

Of course this was supposed to be a private inquiry, instituted for the purpose of ascertaining if there was any need of a formal one being held before the police magistrate. However, the sub-immigration agent wofully exceeded his powers. After he had interviewed Joe Enau, and before his report to his superiors in Brisbane had left Bundaberg, he furnished one of the local papers with the whole story, which was published next morning. His opinion was also published. He had arrived at the conclusion that there was no legal proof of the man's death, and that by leaving Uras before I had such proof, I had displayed "an entire disregard for the value of a human life." He also said that Joe Enau denied that he had witnessed the murder.

Immediately after his examination, Joe Enau disappeared, and although hunted for, could not be found. It still remains a mystery to me why and how he disappeared so quickly. In the inquiry held before the police magistrate at Bundaberg in February following, I wanted Joe's evidence most particularly. Had he been there to give it, I hardly think he would have "gone back" on what he told the mate in the boat just after they had retreated from the beach at Warlo, and which he had repeated to me in the cabin of the *Ariel* in the presence of the crew.

However, Joe did turn up eventually at Mackay, where he tried to get engaged as a boatman on board the *Fearless*. He was arrested, but the inquiry was then over, and after a very short detention in the "lock-up," he was released; and so the matter dropped. By then I had gone to Rockhampton, where I was engaged in a mining venture; so I had other things to attend to, or else it is certain I should have made a stir in the matter.

A HEAD-COFFIN.

CHAPTER XXV.

VOYAGE OF THE *BOROUGH BELLE*, 1890-91.

Incidents—Kwaisulia's attack on Manoba—H.M.S. Royalist *there—Captain Brodie at the Lord Howe Is.—Malayta natives attack the* Savo*—Wrecks—Kwaisulia rescues the* Fearless*—The* Maria *threatened—I sail with the* Borough Belle*—Sick returns—A leaky ship—" Hammering" round New Caledonia—Presbyterian converts— Our invalids— Reputation of the* Borough Belle*—An accident—I shoot a man—Trapped at Mboli—A new channel—Going through with the tide—Lying idle—Working out—Waisis Harbour—Reef islands—Wairokai—In the lagoons—Uhu—Secure from the storm—At Waidaia—The* Lochiel*—Murders—Escape of the* Meg Merrilies*—Marau Sound—An unknown wreck—Massacre at San Christoval—I return to Mackay—My last voyage ended—A retrospect—British arms introduced into the islands by French and Germans—Stoppage of the Queensland Polynesian labour traffic—My view of it—Finis.*

AFTER leaving the *Ariel*, at the close of 1888, I was absent from salt water until September, 1890. During this interval there happened several incidents in connection with the labour trade that I will briefly note.

Soon after I left Uras, with the *Ariel*, the chief Kwaisulia mustered his forces and attacked Manoba I. Five of the Manoba warriors were killed, among them being the leader of the party which had murdered Mr. Armstrong, my late G.A. During 1889, H.M.S. *Royalist* was sent to the island. Her commander dispatched the usual warning to the natives to send their women and children away, and then shelled the island. Little damage was done, and no one hurt; the inhabitants enjoying the " fireworks " from a safe distance.

About the same time, Captain Brodie, master of an island trader sailing out of Sydney, visited the Lord

Howe Is., as had been his wont for some years. He was ordered to leave the group, by the new German authorities. Meanwhile, German vessels were trading without stint among the islands under British protection.

During 1889, too, the *Savo*, a little trading schooner, anchored in Waisissi Harbour, Malayta I. Natives were allowed on board to trade, and they made a sudden attack upon the crew. The mate, and Mr. Cooper, a trader from Marau Sound, Guadalcanar I., were cut down by tomahawks. Captain Keating was badly wounded, but, contriving to get into the cabin, opened fire on his assailants from its shelter, and finally drove them out of the ship. Several of the Kanaka crew were killed or wounded, and it was only with the greatest difficulty that Keating and the survivors could get the vessel under way and out to sea again. The perpetrators of this outrage were never punished. Captain Keating subsequently spent eight months in hospital, at Sydney.

The labour schooner, *Northern Belle*, Captain Spence, Mr. McMurdo, G.A., was wrecked about the middle of March, 1889, at Motalava I., in a hurricane. This was probably the same storm which did so much damage to the shipping in the harbour of Apia, Samoa Is., when H.M.S. *Calliope* had such a narrow escape.

Towards the end of the year, or very early in 1890, another labour vessel, the *Gael*, was wrecked on the north-eastern coast of Mallicolo I., a little south of Port Stanley. Not long after, on March 6, another hurricane drove the *Eliza Mary*, schooner, Captain Campbell, Mr. McMurdo, G.A.—the same who was wrecked in the *Northern Belle*—ashore near the remains of the *Gael*.

The *Fearless*, Captain Norman, anchored in Uru Harbour, Malayta I., about the middle of 1890. The natives there conceived the idea of capturing her. Luckily, Kwaisulia, the chief of Uras, thirty miles to the north, knew that the Uru men meant to have a ship if a good opportunity presented itself. So he crowded thirty of his warriors into a war canoe, and arrived alongside the *Fearless* just in time to prevent her capture. He remained with her until she left Uru.

This incident was told me by Mr. Lewis, the mate. During the same voyage the *Fearless* had visited Port Adams, Maramasiki. A short time before, the *Maria*, brigantine, recruiting for Samoa, under German colours, had taken over seventy men from that neighbourhood, giving a Snider and ammunition for each of them. For some unknown reason, the natives all along the northeast coasts of Maramasiki and Malayta Is. as far as Uras, had become incensed against the crew of the *Maria*. A fleet of canoes, coming from various places, assembled to attack her; but her crew were too wary, and no fighting ensued.

Leaving all the gold in Australia to take care of itself, I threw down the pick and shovel I had been wielding, and took command of the *Borough Belle*, in September, 1890. She was a brigantine of 205 tons register, and was then lying at Mackay, and about to be despatched on her last recruiting voyage in the Queensland labour trade. For, by the Act of November 10, 1885, it had been decreed that "*After the thirty-first day of December, one thousand eight hundred and ninety, no licence to introduce islanders shall be granted.*"

From one cause and another, I had to spend more than a month in port, before my papers arrived from Brisbane. It was not until the evening of October 21 that the anchor was tripped, and the ship got under way for the islands.

Besides the G.A., an old friend who had sailed on three voyages with me before in the same capacity, I had on board ninety-seven men, six women, and three children for the New Hebrides, with twelve men for the Solomons, all return islanders. Some half a dozen of these were shipped under sick certificates, and three others were decidedly wrong in the upper storey. Five of the sick men died on board; thus the vessel acquired a bad reputation, which accounted, to a great extent, for the poor success of the voyage.

Another circumstance materially contributed to deter natives from engaging with me. The ship leaked, and, when plunging into a head sea—especially on the port tack—the "deluge" pump had to be kept going pretty frequently. This was not so much to be wondered at, for the vessel's copper sheathing, as well as her caulking, was in a bad state, being nearly five years old. During the voyage, flakes of the copper peeled off here and there, so that the bottom was as ragged as the trunk of an old ti-tree, diminishing her speed considerably—and she never was a clipper.

I left Mackay with the last of the westerly winter winds, which carried me about half-way across to New Caledonia. Then I encountered the trade coming up fresh and squally from south-east. This raised a pretty "jump" of a head-sea, making the old craft pitch bows under, and necessitating constant use of the "deluge" pump. As it was not safe to press the ship, her progress was slow, and after a week's buffeting, my stock of firewood and water got to a very low ebb.

On November 3, I anchored in Port Uarai, on the south-west coast of New Caledonia. I lay there four days, filling up my tanks and wood-locker, while a stiff breeze, almost amounting to a gale, blew outside from south-east. Then came another "hammering" round the southern point of the island, and it was not until November 15 that I landed the first of my returns on the south coast of Tanna I. Thence I passed through the whole length of the New Hebrides group, gradually dropping my passengers at their various homes on the islands, as we passed them going northward.

At Havannah Harbour, Sandwich I., I fell in with H.M.S. *Dart*, Commander Fredericks, and the *Truga-*

nini, a Sydney steamer. She was subsidized by the Presbyterian New Hebrides Mission, for the conveyance of missionaries and their stores to and fro.

The last two of my New Hebridean "returns" were landed at Ureparapara, in the extreme north of the group. Then, after working Vanua Lava and Meralaba Is. for recruits, I took my departure for the Solomons on December 18, with eleven returns and fourteen recruits on board, four of the last being women.

All the recruits, with the exception of one man, who was recruited at Havannah Harbour, were converts of the Presbyterian Mission. For some three months after their engagement, one of them used to officiate as teacher or minister, conducting morning and evening worship, and Sunday services. By the end of that time, however, these religious observances were neglected. A nameless disease had broken out among the congregation, and the teacher seems to have been the one who had introduced it.

Upon our arrival at Mackay, three of these Presbyterian saints—the teacher, another man, and a woman—were pronounced by the medical inspector to be unfit for plantation work. So my owners were put to the expense of doctoring and sending them home again.

Besides the *Dart* and the *Truganini*, I spoke or sighted some half a dozen other vessels, British and French, and one German schooner recruiting in the group. As usual, the French and Germans were trading away Snider rifles to the natives, of British pattern too.

I ran across to the Solomons from Meralaba with a rather light and variable easterly wind. I first visited San Christoval I., then Malayta, again passing through the Maramasiki Passage. Then I called at the Floridas, Savo, and the western coast of Guadalcanar, landing my returns, but not delaying much to seek for recruits. I had found that I must get rid of the former as quickly as possible. Five out of the six men who were ill when shipped at Mackay died on the passage. The remaining invalid, a Florida man, had very little life left in him when he was landed. At every place where we hove to or anchored, the natives shunned us as a "sick" ship. At two different places, natives in their canoes alongside told me that if men went in my ship, " By-and-by he dead!" Travelling canoes spread the news about, and before I left the group the reputation of the *Borough Belle* had been irretrievably ruined.

A most lamentable accident also occurred while we were in the estuary of the Maramasiki Passage, which did not tend to improve matters, nor to lighten our feelings.

I had been overhauling and cleaning my revolver, preparatory to a trip to one of the islets, and, having loaded the chambers, fired them off over the side to make sure the weapon was in thoroughly serviceable order. One of the recruits, a Meralaba man, whose wife was on board, had been watching my proceedings. Just as I pulled the trigger, unaware of his vicinity, he suddenly moved in front of me, and received a ball in his breast.

Even now, it seems incredible to me how such an accident could have occurred—but the fact remains that it did. The evidence of the crew, who witnessed it, shows it was solely due to the man's own movement. The poor fellow died in less than an hour after. His wife attended on him to the last, but seemed to take his death very coolly. She was the woman I have referred to, who had to be returned home on account of her being diseased.

At Mboli, on the north-east of Florida I., I was fairly trapped by the weather. I anchored there in a small bay, the northern mouth of a narrow channel, similar to the Maramasiki Passage, separating the middle from the southern island, on February 1. This bay is open to the north. The day after I anchored, a strong breeze blew right into the harbour, raising such a sea, especially when the tide ran out, that I was kept a prisoner for a week with two anchors down. At the end of that time, seeing no signs of a change of wind, or weather, I hove up my anchors, and, with the assistance of the kedge, to cant the ship, there being very little room, I headed her for the narrow "passage" between the two islands. Where it debouches into the little bay or estuary I had been anchored in, this is divided by a

MBOLI HARBOUR, FLORIDA IS.

reef into two very narrow but deep channels, one on each side of the reef. I steered through the western of these, anchoring as soon as I was clear of the reef. Even there, I had barely room to swing at a single anchor.

Previous to this, as I was told by the natives of the village and mission station near my anchorage, no vessel anything like so large as the *Borough Belle* had passed through this channel, with the exception of the *Southern Cross*, the mission vessel, which was an auxiliary screw steamer, and she had done it under steam.

The wind was now fair for the general direction of the passage, as far as Port Purvis at the other end; and although I had no chart of the place, I judged that, if there was water enough for the steamer, there would be enough for the *Borough Belle*. I trusted a good deal to the tide, also, and eventually owed more to it than to the wind for getting through. Next morning I got under way, and went about a mile with the wind. Then I had to anchor for a few hours, and wait for the afternoon tide.

The breadth of the channel does not exceed two ship lengths in many places, so beating was impossible. We drove through as soon as the tide was at its full strength, going about three knots an hour, with the boats towing ahead to keep her clear of the banks. Only once, a sweep of the current round a sharp bend drove the ship against the mangroves lining the shores; but this delayed us only about an hour, while the kedge was run out and hauled upon.

By sundown, I anchored about a mile from Port Purvis and five from Mboli. Next morning, I reached a safe land-locked anchorage at the head of the port, a spacious well-sheltered harbour on the south-western coast, about three miles long by one mile at its widest part. The western entrance is certainly very narrow, but, with the wind about nor'-nor'-west, was sheltered in part from any heavy sea by reefs and islets outside. I lay there until the 18th, for the weather was too boisterous to allow me to beat out against the sea then rolling in.

The worst of it was that all this time went for nothing. Not a recruit did I obtain, and very little native food— yams or taro—although the natives were most friendly. Even the mission teachers evinced no objection to visit the ship, begging for pipes and tobacco, although they had nothing to give in exchange. I have invariably found, that in the New Hebrides and Solomon groups, the so-called "Christian" natives cultivate the ground less than the unconverted savages do. Consequently, they have less to barter, and are more liable to famine in bad seasons, when there are droughts or hurricanes.

At length, on the 18th, the weather cleared up; a steady north-westerly breeze sprang up, and there was less sea in the entrance to the harbour. I did not like the job of thrashing the *Borough Belle* through such a narrow channel; but by making some dozen short tacks, and by venturing, before going about, much nearer to the reefs on either side than was comfortable, I managed to get her through—as much by good luck as by good management. Once in the open sea, I ran round the south coast, passing the labour schooner *Helena*, from Bundaberg, at anchor off Ghieta. During the ensuing night, I crossed over to Malayta again, where I anchored next day in Waisissi Harbour, a snug and safe refuge from all winds and sea, sufficiently roomy for several vessels of large tonnage, though the entrance is not much wider than a cable-length.

It was here that, a year or so before, the little schooner *Savo* had been nearly taken by the natives, when two of the three whites on board were killed, and Keating, the master, was desperately wounded. But the natives were quiet enough during my stay. I did not allow them on board, besides which we were well armed and on our guard.

Waisis, or Waississi Harbour, like all the harbours on this coast, is enclosed by the mountainous mainland on the north-east, and to seaward by long, low, coral islands. These are elevated only three or four feet above high-water mark, and are thickly covered with lofty trees, of those species that can stand a good drenching of salt water occasionally. In strong westerly gales, such as we were presently to experience, the heavy breakers make a clean breach over the projecting reef into the forest, sending their spray clean up to the tree-tops.

We lay at this place until the 24th, and then put to sea again with six additional recruits. One of these afterwards deserted the ship at Marau Sound, just before my final departure for Queensland.

My next anchorage was in Wairokai Bay, a landlocked harbour some four or five miles south-east of Waisis. This is a roomy bay, but inconveniently deep in the centre, where it is twenty-three fathoms. It is well sheltered from the trade-wind, and there is good anchorage, in moderate weather, off the sandy beach on the main, facing the entrance. This anchorage, however, is open to the southward, and when the wind is in that quarter, the only good shelter is in the south arm, just land-locked, with eleven fathoms, and room for a vessel of 200 tons.

Wairokai is the northern ship entrance to a long chain of five smooth-water, deep lagoons, extending for a distance of some nineteen miles. These lagoons vary from a quarter of a mile to nearly one mile in width. They are enclosed between the mainland and a slightly curved line of long, low, thickly wooded reef islands, averaging a hundred yards in width, and two or three miles in length, and lying parallel with the coast.

These lagoons form magnificent harbours. There are half a dozen deep, though rather narrow entrances. With care, a fair wind, the sun astern, and a good mast-head look-out, a vessel of the size of the *Borough Belle* might be safely navigated from one end to the other. But there are about six different places where the channel is very much contracted by reefs or islets. The deepest and clearest water is almost invariably close to the outer barrier islets.

We lay there for five nights. On March 4 we weighed anchor and stood out of the harbour to the south-east, closely hugging the coast. Three of the narrow entrances to the lagoons were passed, for they trended out so much to the westward that I was afraid, if I took the ship in, I might be entrapped by the wind, as I was at Florida. But for the last few days my barometer had been gradually falling, and the weather had now assumed a threatening aspect. So, deeming it better to be safe—even if in a trap—than outside in a cyclone, I made for the southernmost lagoon entrance, and, about noon, anchored in eleven fathoms in the small but safe harbour of Uhu.

The entrance to Uhu is very narrow, and, for a sailing vessel, anything but good, owing to the lofty trees on either side, which are apt to becalm the sails. In fact, the only way to get out through it, is to take advantage of a land breeze in the morning, about sunrise.

As soon as I had anchored, I almost repented of having come in, land winds on this coast being rare and very light at that season. But, after lying there a day, I became reconciled to the position. For the sky soon became overcast, whilst the wind came up from the west in squalls, accompanied by thick rain, my barometer falling rapidly.

Next day, the squalls and the breeze generally became stronger, backing towards north. The two following days it blew a hard gale from north-west, the barometer falling to 29·46—far below the point usually indicating an ordinary north-westerly gale. Luckily, the ship was well sheltered; but even then she needed both bowers down, assisted by the stream anchor.

This breeze over, the wind shifted to south-east for a few days, with fine weather. Seeing small chance of my getting safely out of the place through the same passage I had entered by, one morning early I weighed anchor, and, with the boats ahead, got through a narrow and tortuous lagoon passage to the next opening on the north —Waidaia. There I lay for a few days longer, vainly striving to obtain recruits. Then the sea went down, outside, and I sailed out of the lagoons again on the 17th.

My stores were now running short, and I had been nearly five months out, and had only secured 27 recruits instead of the 128 I was licensed to carry. I therefore began to think about returning to Queensland. However, I determined to try my luck for another fortnight, although the reputation of the ship as an unhealthy and leaky craft was now well established on every island of the Southern Solomons.

Alite Bay or Harbour was my next anchorage. There I took in wood and water; but even my old acquaintance, Billy Mahualla, to whom a liberal inducement was held out, could persuade none of the natives to engage.

Then, a little further north, I anchored off Fiu, an open anchorage, in company with the barquentine *Lochiel*—Captain Pearn, Mr. Thompson, G.A. She was recruiting for Queensland. Still I had no better luck. At this place, the boatmen of the *Lochiel* found part of a vessel's masthead on the beach. It was of bright (unpainted) pine, and very likely had belonged to some vessel of 100 to 200 tons. Other wreckage was reported further down the coast.

Among other news, Captain Pearn had heard of the murder of Sam Craig, a well-known Sydney trader, by natives at Makira Harbour. Also of the murder of Frank Howard, trader on Ugi I. Pearn had lately met the Samoan schooner *Upolu* at Kwai, on the north-east coast. Through a warning from him the Samoan got under way and left, for the natives meant to attack her on the first opportunity.

Very shortly after the *Upolu* and the *Lochiel* had left Kwai, the *Meg Merrilies* from Fiji anchored there. Some thirty Kwai warriors, pretending friendship, boarded her, but with short-handled tomahawks and clubs concealed in their bags. Every Malayta man carries a betel-nut and chunam bag slung to his neck. Some of them were in the forecastle, and had possession of a sleeping seaman's Snider, when the boats luckily returned, most probably preventing the massacre of all who had been left on board.

The *Lochiel* had lately visited the Lord Howe Is.,

where Captain Pearn purchased a quantity of porpoise teeth—considered to be of great value in Malayta. So, as I saw I had no chance of competing successfully with him, I weighed anchor and stood towards Guadalcanar.

Through light winds and calms it took me three days to get there. I anchored at length in Danäe Bay, in Marau Sound, a snug haven. It has the mainland on the west, and is shut in by numerous reefs and islets. There we found the *Myrtle*, a little trading schooner.

VILLAGE AT MARAU SOUND, GUADALCANAR I.

Shortly after the severe storm we had experienced when lying at Uhu, a large canoe came across from Waisis to Marau. On the way, she passed near the hull of a vessel, bottom up—probably capsized in the gale. This wreck had two masts apparently, and was painted white, or perhaps light slate colour. Such a number of sharks were round her that the natives were afraid to venture near in their frail canoe.

What vessel this was, I cannot say. From the reports

of Captain Pearn, Captain Ericson, of the *Myrtle*, and the natives we met with, I was able to account for all the Queensland vessels that were in the Solomon group during the recent gale, with the exception of the *Archimedes*, and she shortly afterwards turned up in the New Hebrides.

At Marau, I heard that canoes had recently come across from San Christoval I., bringing news that two boats of a French recruiting vessel had been capsized in the surf, eastward of Makira Harbour. The crews, consisting of four white men and eight islanders, were massacred by the natives.

I obtained two recruits at Marau and lost one deserter, who swam ashore during the night. I sailed for Queensland on April 7, with only twenty-five men and four women.

My passage home was uneventful. Light south-easterly winds prevailed at first, with a thunderstorm or two from westward. Afterwards it freshened up, becoming squally as I drew towards the south. I anchored off the mouth of the Pioneer River on April 24, getting up to Mackay next day. On the 27th I paid off my crew, and handed the ship over to the care of a ship-keeper.

So ended my last voyage in the Queensland Polynesian labour trade.

* * * *

As I sit in my room in Glass's Hotel, facing the wharves at Mackay, where the *Borough Belle* has been laid up for sale, I cast a retrospective glance on my experience of sixteen years past. I do not regret one single hour of it.

Notwithstanding all the tales of bloodshed, murder, and kidnapping, in connection with the labour trade, which have been dinned into the ears of the public, for the last few years especially, I conscientiously affirm that it has been, in the main, equally beneficial to the colony and to the islanders themselves.

MRS. ROBINSON'S PUPILS.

What are now the conditions of the sugar industry and of the seaports of Queensland that depended on it? Since the trade has been stopped, will the islanders remain at home? No! Samoa and its German plantations, New Caledonia and its French ones, continue to employ them and reap the benefit of their labour. Has the trading of firearms to the islanders been stopped? No! again. The use of bows and arrows, and even of spears, has gone out of fashion in the New Hebrides and the Solomon Is. Every warrior now owns his British-made Snider and ammunition, sold to him by French or German recruiting vessels. These simply buy their recruits, even in the British Protectorate, from the chiefs and leading men of the tribes.

It may occur to my readers, from my not having made any mention of it, that the South Sea Islander in Queensland has been treated simply as a labouring animal, no attention being paid to his mental or moral education. But such has not been the case.

Private missions have been established in every district with good success, but the only one with which I am personally acquainted is that conducted by Mrs. H. J. Goodwin Robinson, at the Marian Mill, Mackay.

A fine and commodious school-house was erected there, with excellent fittings, prettily decorated walls, and a harmonium. At the time of my visit, Mrs. Robinson was teaching over eighty pupils.

As a further proof of the success of these missions, I quote the following extract from "The Mackay Standard" for June 1, 1891, with reference to the departure of the Anglican clergyman :—

On Saturday evening, a number of Canon Edwards' South Sea Island pupils, to whom he has been in the habit of giving instructions on Saturday evenings for many years past, also waited upon him and presented him with a handsomely bound Bible, on the fly-leaf of which were recorded the signatures of the donors, and this gift the Canon publicly acknowledged in the church on the following day.

In this relation of my experiences in the Labour Trade, and of my voyages to the South Seas, I have confined myself strictly to facts. These have led me to the conclusion that the stoppage of the Polynesian Labour Trade, and, in consequence, the enormous loss of capital and development to the rich tropical land of Northern Queensland, was due to a purely political cry; that the public was grievously misled; that the so-called "Anti-Slavery" party — consisting almost entirely of southern men—know no more about plantation work in tropical Queensland and its labour requirements than an infant in arms!

I trust that the reader who has perused this "log" will be better able to exercise an impartial judgment. At any rate, I have endeavoured to lay before him a plain and truthful statement of my view of the Polynesian Labour Trade.

FINIS

www.ingramcontent.com/pod-product-compliance
Lightning Source LLC
Chambersburg PA
CBHW031955300426
44117CB00008B/775

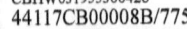